MINUTES OF THE

VIENNA PSYCHOANALYTIC SOCIETY

VOLUME I:

1906 — 1908

MINUTES OF THE
VIENNA PSYCHOANALYTIC SOCIETY

Volume I: 1906–1908

EDITED BY

HERMAN NUNBERG
ERNST FEDERN

Translated by M. Nunberg

New York

INTERNATIONAL UNIVERSITIES PRESS, INC.

CONTENTS

v

*A cumulative Index for all 3 Volumes will appear at the
end of Volume III.*

TRANSLATOR'S NOTE

Every translation presents difficulties, but our task in translating these Minutes was complicated by the fact that the discussions are recorded—to a great extent—in somewhat imprecise colloquial Viennese.

We have consistently followed the principle of staying as close as possible to the original. However, one change was systematically carried out: in recording the discussions, Rank used throughout the subjunctive mode of indirect speech; because the corresponding English construction would result in unnecessarily clumsy sentences, we have substituted the indicative mode of direct speech.

REFERENCES

Key to Abbreviations

C.P.   Sigmund Freud: *Collected Papers*, 5 Volumes. London: Hogarth Press, 1924-1950.

G.S.   Sigmund Freud: *Gesammelte Schriften*, 13 Volumes. Vienna: Internationaler psychoanalytischer Verlag, 1924-1934.

G.W.   Sigmund Freud: *Gesammelte Werke*, 17 Volumes. London: Imago Publishing Company, 1940-1952.

J.   *International Journal of Psycho-Analysis*

Jb.   *Jahrbuch für Psychoanalyse*

S.E.   *The Standard Edition of the Complete Psychological Works of Sigmund Freud*, 24 Volumes. London: Hogarth Press, 1953-

Yb.   *The Yearbook of Psychoanalysis*, 10 Volumes. New York: International Universities Press, 1945-1954.

Z.   *Internationale Zeitschrift für Psychoanalyse*

Zb.   *Zentralblatt für Psychoanalyse*

ACKNOWLEDGMENTS

The editors wish to thank those who have helped in making this publication possible:

Mr. William Rosenwald has granted us a loan for preparatory work.

The families of some participants in the meetings provided us with biographical data; Walter Federn, Ph.D., has contributed to the accuracy of our references by research in libraries and in Paul Federn's personal archives; Leo Kane, M.A., has been a source of information about the literary personalities of the period.

Our special thanks go to Mrs. Lottie M. Newman for her careful editing.

INTRODUCTION

When Freud left Vienna in 1938, he entrusted the *original* manuscripts of the Minutes of the Vienna Psychoanalytic Society to Dr. Paul Federn, who since Freud's illness had been acting president of the Society of which Freud was president. Federn soon followed Freud into exile, taking the Minutes with him. Thus he saved the manuscripts from destruction by the Nazis and preserved them for future publication.

The possession of the Minutes imbued Federn with a great sense of responsibility, toward Freud and toward psychoanalysis. He often talked about them: one gained the impression that he felt it to be his duty to publish them as soon as possible. Ill health, lack of time and funds, however, prevented him from consummating his plans. He was able to publish only one protocol—in *Samiksa,* an Indian psychoanalytic journal. His desire to insure that the Minutes would be presented to the world led him to provide in his last will and testament for their publication after his death. To that end he appointed me to edit the Minutes and to arrange for their publication together with his son Ernst.

The Minutes begin with the year 1906 and continue until 1915. From 1906 to 1915 Otto Rank was the official, salaried secretary of the Society, entrusted with the task of recording its meetings. The Minutes for that period contain records of the scientific portions of the meetings, as well as attendance lists of all meetings.[1] In 1915 Rank had to leave Vienna for military service in the First World War. There are some records of discussions at meetings held between 1915

---

[1] The original manuscript consisted of two parts: (1) the protocols of the scientific meetings which were recorded by hand on large sheets of paper (for examples, see the reproductions on pp. 38-39, 120-121, 229-231); (2) a little black book which contained the attendance lists and communications. The material recorded in the little black book is reproduced here in slightly condensed type (for samples of the original, see the reproductions on pp. 2-5, 228).

and 1918; however, except for one protocol of a meeting in November, 1918, they are so fragmentary as to be virtually unintelligible. We also have Minutes of the meetings which were held from 1918 to the end of 1933; these, however, are of no substantial interest. They consist only of brief records of the business parts of the meetings, attendance lists of members and guests, and abbreviated titles of scientific papers presented. They do not record the scientific discussions that took place.

Although the quality of the discussions was very uneven—sometimes logical and orderly, at other times emotional and confused—Rank carried out his task with deep understanding and great skill. His records were not stenographic; rather than attempting a precise account of all that was said, Rank seems to have taken extensive notes of the discussions and to have edited them later. For the most part, they express with remarkable lucidity what was said in the discussions.

Nevertheless, some of the Minutes are not easy to understand; some papers are rendered in a form that is too abbreviated, while others are mentioned only by their titles. Some speakers discuss one part of an unrecorded paper, others comment on another part. Thus, the Minutes are, at times, difficult to read. After 1910 they became shorter; finally, the contractions and omissions became so numerous that the reader can only surmise a great deal of what was said in the discussions. To some extent we have tried to explicate these unclear sections in our annotations. But we have restricted the annotations to the minimum necessary for comprehension of the text, because we prefer to abstain from influencing the reader's judgment of these Minutes. The careful reader, in spite of the hurdles encountered, will be rewarded by a growing insight into, and understanding of, the problems which at the time occupied the mind of the analyst.

The meetings started in 1902 as Psychological Wednesday Evenings in Freud's own apartment; later they became known as the Wednesday Evening Meetings. The Wednesday was retained as a tradition, as it were, when later on, after the transformation of this loose circle into the Vienna Psychoanalytic Society, its members met regularly each Wednesday evening. There are no records of the Wednesday Evenings for the period from 1902 to 1906. In 1908, when the Vienna Psychoanalytic Society was formed, the meetings became a function of the Society. In 1910, the meetings were moved from Freud's private apartment to the Doktoren Collegium (the College of Physicians). Until 1908, *everyone who attended the meetings was required to participate in the discussions;* from then on, participation was voluntary.[2]

The men who gathered around Freud were interested in psychology in the broadest sense of the word. Dissatisfied with what contemporary psychology had to offer, they looked for new ideas, for new guiding principles, which would help them gain a better understanding of man. Freud's teachings seemed to promise such help.

It is commonly known that from the very beginning Freud's new ideas were not well received by the medical profession; he was severely criticized by his colleagues, hated, and ostracized. Even some of his old friends deserted him.[3] Thus he became a lonesome man. But he was a sociable man as well; he could be a great and faithful friend. (The memoirs of Ludwig Binswanger[4] are a telling testimony to this.) He loved to have people around him with whom he could communicate and exchange ideas. The loneliness into which he was driven—like all men who are ahead of their times—oppressed him; he would often say that the analyst should not be isolated, but that, on the contrary, he should associate with others and exchange ideas and experiences with them. In a letter to his friend Wilhelm Fliess he wrote that Fliess was his "Publicum," his audience.[5] He needed a sounding board. When he realized that Fliess ceased to follow his ideas, he suffered intensely; finally the frienship broke up.

How strong his need for friendship was, and for recognition, is expressed in an address to the B'nai B'rith, a Jewish humanitarian fraternity, on the occasion of his seventieth birthday.[6] He recalled how much the warm reception accorded him and the opportunity for new human contacts offered there had meant to him at a time when he had been deserted by his colleagues and friends on account of his discoveries.

---

2 See Freud's "History of the Psychoanalytic Movement" (1914). *S.E.*, 14:3-66.

3 In later years, he would jokingly say that people used to treat him like a freshly painted wall: nobody dared to touch him. (From a communication by Ludwig Jekels.)

4 *Erinnerungen an Sigmund Freud.* Bern: Francke Verlag, 1956.

5 *The Origins of Psychoanalysis. Letters, Drafts and Notes to Wilhelm Fliess (1887-1902).* New York: Basic Books, 1954.

6 "Address to the Society of B'nai B'rith" (1926). *S.E.*, 20:271-274.

A few years after Freud's relationship with Fliess had ended it was the Wednesday Evening Group which became his sounding board. He attended the meetings regularly and until his illness hardly ever missed a session.

Who were the men who formed the Wednesday Evening Group, and why did they become psychoanalysts?

On the one hand there was a group of men in search of new ideas and of a leader, and on the other hand there was a lonely man who had made important new discoveries and wished to share them with others. So, upon the suggestion of Dr. Wilhelm Stekel who had been successfully treated by Freud, Freud agreed to hold weekly meetings with this group. The aim of these meetings was discussion of psychological problems. Thus, the Wednesday Evening Meetings came into being.

The group was heterogeneous; it consisted of physicians, educators, writers, and others. In short, its members represented a cross-section of the intellectuals at the beginning of the century. Different as they were in their backgrounds and personalities, they were held together by their common discontent with the conditions that prevailed in psychiatry, education, and other fields dealing with the human mind.

During this period a host of ideas were in the process of fermentation in many parts of Europe. It was the time when, in psychiatry, the Nancy School's ideas about hypnotism and the teachings of Charcot were spreading from France all over Europe; when Kraepelin in Germany was trying to bring order into psychiatry, when the Swiss Eugen Bleuler became the leading psychiatrist, and when Wundt exercised his world-wide influence upon contemporary psychology. It was also the time when Darwin's work influenced contemporary scientific thinking, but, as far as psychiatry and psychology are concerned, Freud was, to my knowledge, the only one who applied Darwin's theories.

During the same period the philosophies of Schopenhauer and Nietzsche were making their mark upon the minds of intellectuals in Germany; Dostoevski's novels were widely read; Strindberg had written his *Confessions of a Fool*; Wedekind's *Spring's Awakening* had just appeared; and many other events of importance to the intellectual life of Europe were taking place.

Just as the world in which the Wednesday Evening men lived was torn by conflicts, so were they themselves. We have learned from our analyses that in order to heal inner conflicts it is necessary first to bare their sources and thus to understand them. We have also learned that we often project our own conflicts onto the external world. It seems safe to assume that the urge of these men to understand and to heal their fellow men reflected to a great extent their own need for help. And, indeed, at the meetings of the Society they discussed not only the problems of others, but also their own difficulties; they revealed their inner conflicts, confessed their masturbation, their fantasies and reminiscences concerning their parents, friends, wives and children. It is true that they seem to have been neurotics, but no more so than many others who are not considered ill. I remember the jokes that circulated among us, young psychiatrists, to the effect that psychiatrists are schizophrenics, and that their choice of this profession represents an attempt at self-healing. Actually, some of the first psychoanalysts had undergone psychoanalysis for therapeutic reasons; others undertook a self-analysis if they did not believe themselves sick enough to ask for another's help. Since the publication of Freud's letters to Fliess,[7] it is no longer a secret that he himself had a neurosis which he overcame by self-analysis, a Herculean feat if we consider the circumstances in which this analysis was performed.

Once, when fitness for performing psychoanalytic treatment was under discussion, Freud remarked that, curiously enough, neurotics proved to be good practical psychologists. Parenthetically, it may be noted that a man who is *genuinely* interested in psychology projects his unconscious or preconscious preoccupation with his own psyche onto the psychology of others. However, the blind spots caused by his own conflicts interfere with the ability of such a man fully to understand another. In order to eliminate such weak spots in the analyst's understanding of his patient, Freud—as these Minutes show—suggested at an early time that analysts be analyzed. This clearly demonstrates Freud's realization, soon after he began his work, that not only can the doctor exert an influence over his patient, but that the patient can influence the doctor as well. When the patient's conflicts coincide with those of the doctor, the latter may not see them; he may misunderstand them or identify with the patient. This phenomenon,

[7] *The Origins of Psychoanalysis (loc. cit.).*

which belongs to the sphere of what later was called countertransference, was an early topic of discussion in the Society.[8]

Thus, the Wednesday Evening men, in order to carry out their urge to help their fellow men, above all had to understand themselves. By discussing intimate problems with one another, they hoped to help their patients as well as themselves. This hope, stemming from their belief in analysis, united them in their devotion to Freud; in identifying with him as their leader, they became the first pioneers of analysis.

At the outset they formed an almost harmonious group. Each member showed intense interest in the topic under discussion, whether it was a clinical case, a poet or artist and his work, a teacher, a pupil, or a criminal. Papers were read, books and magazine articles were reviewed, and a variety of problems discussed: biology, animal psychology, psychiatry, sociology, mythology, religion, art and literature, education and criminology, even the association and psychogalvanic experiments. It is worth mentioning that the members borrowed protocols of the meetings, studied and then returned them; this too is faithfully recorded by the secretary.

The reader should keep in mind that the discussions of the first few years were largely based on Freud's early work and that the discussants had not yet acquired wide analytic experience. Consequently we find much guesswork, many premature statements, etc. Moreover, one must not forget that a major part of the discussions was spontaneous, unprepared reaction to papers heard the same evening. Thus not all comments were consistent and logical.

In the discussions the participants stimulated each other and even Freud. For example, Adler very early stressed the importance of aggression in psychic life. Freud accepted this idea and paid more attention to it from then on; however, he integrated the aggressive instinct with his theory of instincts only much later, in the paper "Instincts and Their Vicissitudes" (1915). His theory of instincts took its final shape in *Beyond the Pleasure Principle* (1920).

It was a process of give-and-take which took place in these discussions. Naturally, Freud gave more than the others could take. There

[8] At the Congress in Budapest in 1918, I moved that the future psychoanalyst be required to undergo an analysis himself. The motion was rejected because Rank and Tausk energetically opposed it. It was only in 1926 at the Congress in Bad Homburg that this rule was adopted.

was, of course, a tremendous gap between their understanding of psychoanalysis and his. While they were merely beginners, he had already laid the foundations of his monumental edifice. They came to a rich table, indeed, but not all of them could digest what was offered. Yet, while they still knew very little of psychoanalysis, they were eager to learn. And they learned quickly; they listened with rapt attention whenever Freud talked, they tried to absorb every word he uttered, and they made common cause with him. No doubt, this devotion to Freud and his ideas required great courage at that time, for the psychoanalyst exposed himself to severe criticism and ridicule which frequently drove him into isolation. Some members were reluctant to publish psychoanalytic articles; others published under a pseudonym.

In spite of all the difficulties, those early followers of Freud did not hesitate to consider themselves his pupils and, for a while, worked with him in harmony. But this harmony did not last very long. As in other group formations, here too, ambivalence began to exercise a negative influence. Perhaps this explains the fact that some of these men, in spite of their attraction to depth psychology and their devotion to Freud, still had resistances precisely to what consciously they were attempting to learn; a situation, incidentally, which applies even today to some individual analysts and groups.

Indeed, some members of the Society could not face the Unconscious as revealed by psychoanalysis. As Freud once, after a paper given by Paul Schilder, remarked, they could not breathe in the sticky atmosphere of the dark underground, of the "sewers," as it were, but longed to bask in the bright sunshine on the surface. Of course, all of us would prefer to breathe fresh air, were it possible for the psychoanalyst to indulge in surface psychology. As was to be expected, those who preferred surface psychology soon abandoned psychoanalysis altogether. Within the Society, on the other hand, factions were formed, and rivalries developed, accompanied by quarrels about the priority of ideas and a competitive attitude which manifested itself even toward Freud. There were those who attempted to introduce into the discussions extraneous ideas which clashed with the basic concepts of psychoanalysis. The reasons for the introduction of such elements were many; foremost among them, however, were resistances to psychoanalysis, supported by personal predilections of a philosophical nature and by ambitions. These members tried to impose their own ideas upon the group and, in so doing, impeded the progress of the work of the Society. Finally they had to resign.

Elimination of some members did not weaken the Society. On the contrary, the membership was steadily growing, and the discussions became more substantial and better organized; it was easier to follow the development of certain ideas and to see how they were slowly taking definite shape. Obviously, the resignation of the dissident members made the group more coherent. In this atmosphere of greater harmony some personalities were steadily growing in stature.

As mentioned before, the range of topics dealt with at the meetings was very wide. The discussions, at times, became passionate, confused, and difficult to manage. But Freud never lost control of the group as a whole; he proved a masterful leader. With incomparable superiority he knew how to deal with these intelligent but emotional people. He was always able to bring order into the chaos and to calm the excited spirits. Often, with one observation, one word, he succeeded in showing the essential point of a problem, and in making it crystal clear. While giving everyone full freedom to express his opinions, he did not permit the discussions to run wild. He guided them with admirable skill, always remaining objective. He praised where praise was deserved, he disapproved where criticism was necessary. So he criticized Rank severely for the way in which he presented his material, but praised him for its content; he praised Adler for his contributions to ego psychology, but criticized him by pointing out that Adler's psychology was a psychology of the conscious rather than of the unconscious. There were, it is true, instances in which Freud was a very sharp critic, but on the whole he was mild and forebearing, patient and lenient. He tried to mediate in the conflicts of ideas and personalities. He was extremely tolerant of the convictions and ideas of others. However, his patience and tolerance had certain limits. As long as it was not absolutely clear to him that the divergent ideas threatened his *basic* doctrines, he did not interfere and did not oppose them. Only when it became evident to him that the edifice of *his* analysis was threatened, he was inexorable.

The best example of his patience and tolerance is the case of Alfred Adler. As a member of the group, Adler started, slowly but systematically, to promote his own ideas which, in the end, proved to contradict the basic concepts of Freud. Yet, for a long time, Freud treated Adler with marked distinction: he even appointed Adler president of the Society, a position which he held until the final breach.

On the one hand, Adler overstressed the biological basis of neurosis in maintaining that this illness is the result of an attempt to over-compensate psychically for the inferiority of one organ or another. On the other hand, he overemphasized the significance of the social, that is to say, of the external factor for the causation of neurosis. Being a Social Democrat, he seems to have attempted to reconcile the Marxist doctrine of class struggle with his own ideas about the psychic conflict. He asserts that the *psychic,* the *inner* conflict is an analogy to the *social, external* conflict between the dispossessed and the ruling class. According to him, the inferior, the weak, is the feminine factor, whereas the superior, the strong, is the masculine factor. A neurosis occurs, so he says, when an individual protests against the inferiority of an organ by psychic overcompensation for the malfunction of this organ. The leitmotiv in every neurosis is the idea: "I want to be a man"; this is what Adler terms the masculine protest. Thus, on the one hand, he sexualizes the process of repression by substituting for the psychic conflict the concept of the masculine protest, which implies, of course, that the whole conflict is a struggle between the *homosexual* part of the personality and the *heterosexual* part. On the other hand, he desexualizes the sexual instinct, because he sees in the masculine protest not the intent to help man satisfy the yearning for sexual fulfillment but his yearning for power.

The Adlerian doctrine developed further, with many ramifications, but I cannot give a detailed account of it here. These few words of condensed description, however, should suffice to show that it was incompatible with Freudian psychology. Freud's pupils expected him to take a stand on these questions. Yet, for a long time, Freud remained silent while the majority of the group denounced Adler's innovations. Finally, Adler and his followers resigned. In a later period, when Freud's pupils called his attention to the deviations of Jung and Rank, Freud behaved in a similar way; indeed, it was extremely difficult for him to drop one whom he had once chosen as his friend. The letters to Fliess give us an idea of what the break with Fliess meant to him. The Minutes show how long it was before Freud permitted a rupture to come about between Adler and himself, even though Adler was not nearly so close to him as Fliess had been.

Jung's deviating ideas were not too much discussed at the meetings since he did not belong to the Vienna group and came to Vienna only very rarely. Therefore there is little in the Minutes that would give an indication of Freud's personal reaction to Jung's defection. However, the fact itself that he had chosen Jung his successor, had made him president of the International Psychoanalytic Association, and editor of the *Jahrbuch* would permit us to conclude what he must have felt when Jung deserted him, even if we did not have other sources from which we know how he suffered. Freud had distinctly favored Jung and his Swiss group, and had thus caused jealousy and hurt feelings in the Vienna group. But it is quite incorrect to attribute—as Jones does in his Freud biography[9]—this resentment to the inferiority feelings of the Jew who suspects anti-Semitism everywhere.

The separation from Rank, which occurred long after 1915, was perhaps the most difficult one for Freud, who had been extremely fond of Rank and thought very highly of his capabilities. He had made him editor of *Imago* and the *Internationale Zeitschrift für Psychoanalyse*, and, from the correspondence which Jessie Taft published in her biography of Rank,[10] we learn that Freud had seen in him his successor who would further develop his ideas.

In all these cases, Freud broke off the relations, in spite of his personal attachments, when he became convinced that the basic tenets of psychoanalysis were at stake. It seems that Freud felt it to be his duty to protect psychoanalysis, as a father would his child, and to spread the truth as he saw it.

I have just used the phrase "as he saw it"—that is to say, as he saw what was happening in the human mind. For many years I had the opportunity to watch Freud during discussions in the meetings of the Society. When a speaker's remarks aroused his particular interest or when he was trying to make his own point especially clear, he would lift his head and look intensely, with extreme concentration, at a

[9] *The Life and Work of Sigmund Freud*, 3 Vols. New York: Basic Books, 1953-1957.
[10] Jessie Taft: *Otto Rank*. New York: Julian Press, 1958.

point in space, as if he were seeing something there.[11] This tendency to *see* what he was thinking is reflected in his writings. They contain many pictorial elements, even when dealing with highly theoretical concepts. If his doctrines were considered fantastic speculations by some, we may say that he first looked and then believed, and did not first believe and then see. Only a man with such a vision could discover and see the laws governing the intricate labyrinth of the human mind. I think he greatly underrated his talents when he said in a letter to Fliess that he had a "miserable space-perception."[12]

His adherents could not see all that he saw; they did not have his vision. They could not follow him completely. At the time that these Minutes begin, in 1906, Freud had already written many important articles and most of his basic books, such as *The Studies on Hysteria* (together with Breuer) (1895), *The Interpretation of Dreams* (1900), followed a little later by *The Psychopathology of Everyday Life* (1901), the *Three Contributions to the Theory of Sexuality* (1905), and *Jokes and Their Relation to the Unconscious* (1905). Not all of the discussants, however, were thoroughly familiar with these works. This may account for many misunderstandings. On the other hand, some of the misunderstandings were—as has already been indicated— due to resistances such as we all have against our repressed unconscious. Indeed, psychoanalytic insight could only be assimilated through constant psychic struggle, in the same way as we witness it in our daily work with patients.

As the study of the Minutes discloses, the members of the group saw far more in psychoanalysis than a psychopathology and a method of treating sick people. They knew that man is a social being as well as a biological entity. They recognized that the relations of man with his environment are expressed not only in his behavior but also in works of art and literature, in religion, and in social institutions. Therefore, they found it necessary to concern themselves not only with the sick human being but also with literature, religion, philosophy, anthrolopogy, sociology, and so forth. There were, in fact, many

---

[11] This expression is beautifully caught in the etching by Pollack, in which Freud sits behind his desk surrounded by his collection of antique art objects.

[12] From *The Origins of Psychoanalysis* (*loc. cit.*).

debates about the interaction of biological, social, and historical factors in the development of the individual as well as of mankind.

In those early years it was difficult to obtain suitable case material for psychoanalytic study. But this material was easily available from nonclinical sources. This may explain the striking fact that at the outset, and even later, problems of art, literature, mythology, religion, education, were discussed more than were problems of psychiatry.

Among the numerous discussions there were, of course, also those about psychoanalytic theory. However, the discussants were more concerned, at that time, with the *meaning* of the unconscious than with its theoretical significance. Although Freud, at times, indulged in theoretical speculations, which were, of course, always tested on clinical material, he did not encourage his pupils to do the same. For instance, when I once got into a discussion with Tausk about the nature of attention, Freud interrupted us with the remark that these problems were too *"difficiles."* If we read today his Project (1895) in *The Origins of Psychoanalysis*, where he deals with the same problem, we can well understand his warning to be cautious.

And yet, Freud was criticized at different times and by various critics for indulging in excessive speculation without regard for clinical experience, as he was for overemphasizing sexuality, for paying no attention to the aggressive drives, for ignoring that man has an ego and that it is influenced by sociological factors, in short, for recognizing only biological factors as working on the human mind, and neglecting ideological ones, and so forth.

These Minutes present quite a different picture. Although it is true that in the span of time they cover, analysis *seems* to have been based solely on the libido theory, the attentive reader will find this belief erroneous. For even at that time, not only the sex or life instincts but also the aggressive or death instincts were under discussion. Moreover, Freud repeatedly stressed the contrast between libidinal and ego instincts and emphasized the fact that repression is a function of the ego, as are sublimation and the sense of guilt. As Freud indicated on many occasions, he did not like to be forced to formulate new concepts before they had matured in his mind. The concepts in question were of such a fundamental nature that he had to see them clearly in his own mind before he would convey them *in extenso* to others.

The discussions in the Society disclose, perhaps more clearly than his books and essays, how Freud's mind worked. What we see first is meticulous scientific observation, as is appropriate for a man who for years peered through a microscope in search of facts; observation combined with a soaring fantasy which is restrained by criticism, a need for causality, for systematization and integration. He was not a wishful thinker; he carefully scrutinized the complicated material spread before him by his pupils until he could see the reality behind the façade. He could not compromise once he had seen the truth.

Naturally, in the course of the years, while constantly working on his discoveries, Freud developed and modified his concepts. Because of this he was charged with inconsistency and confusion. These modifications were, however, the legitimate result of growing experience and ever-deepening insight into the workings of the human mind. One can easily discover in these records when it was that Freud made remarks indicating new problems. With very few exceptions, no one grasped their whole significance at the time. These problems gradually became crystallized in the works that he published between 1911 and 1923. To mention only a few of these works: "On Narcissism" (1914), the "Papers on Metapsychology" (1911-1917), *Beyond the Pleasure Principle* (1920), *Group Psychology and the Analysis of the Ego* (1921), *The Ego and the Id* (1923). Discussion of these works took place in the meetings of the Society; but after 1915 there are no records of these discussions.

The Minutes show that the Society underwent repeated changes. From an obscure initial group there developed the well-known and influential Viennese Society and the International Psychoanalytic Association. In the course of these developments, some members resigned, but most remained faithful until the dissolution of the Society in 1938 when Hitler occupied Austria. Of the original Wednesday Evening members, however, only Federn, Hitschmann, and Sadger remained to the very end. They developed steadily and each in his own way contributed his share to the growth of psychoanalysis. Since the death of Federn in 1952 and of Hitschmann in 1957, none of the original pioneers is left.

We do not deem it appropriate to enlarge upon the personalities of the Society. The Minutes speak for themselves; we believe that the reader will develop his own opinion about them. Similar considerations guided us in our task of editing the Minutes. We had the choice of selecting from the material what seemed to us most important, or of publishing all of the material as it is preserved, regardless of the importance or insignificance of some remarks.

It is for the following reasons that we decided to publish *all of the material*.[13] First, we wished to let the reader see for himself how these men influenced each other and how they accepted or rejected what was offered them; and that at times, they were dominated by emotions, prejudices, and influences alien to psychoanalysis. We wanted to spread before the reader those struggles taking place in the Vienna Society which helped its members to overcome their resistances and paved the way to their maturation as psychoanalysts. Secondly, we believe that it is impossible to give a fair account of the relationship between Freud and his pupils without presenting the material in its entirety. Against the background of his disciples, his figure stands out as the embodiment of an unattainable ideal. He leads them through the labyrinth of psychoanalytic theory and technique. They indeed attempt to follow him and identify with him. Yet, this identification was possible only to a certain extent. For he was so far ahead of them that at times it was difficult to follow him.

These Minutes also have a historical significance; they throw light on the way in which psychoanalysis developed and permit us to catch

[13] As mentioned before, Federn published one protocol in the *Samiksa* (1:305-311, 1947), under the title: "Professor Freud: The Beginning of a Case Analysis." In this publication Federn was selective, quoting only some discussants and omitting the remarks of others. His presentation of the protocol is thus incomplete. We are presenting here a complete reproduction of each protocol. The only changes we have made are:

1. We have made the headings "Presentation" uniform, though in the text they differed (for instance, Lecture, Lecture Evenings, etc.).

2. We have uniformly inserted the heading "Communications," though in some instances it did not appear in the original manuscript.

3. We have uniformly introduced the attendance list with the word "Present," though in the original manuscript there were slight variations in the wording.

4. We have not consistently followed the paragraphing of the original manuscript.

5. Whenever we have inserted something which did not appear in the original manuscript, this insertion is clearly indicated in the text by brackets.

6. We have numbered the Minutes consecutively throughout, and not started each year with number 1.

a glimpse of how and when Freud began to emerge from his isolation. They show us how he regained contact with the external world. Thus, we hope that the publication of the protocols will be a contribution to the knowledge of how psychoanalysis came of age, spread, and developed. However, the Minutes are of value for an additional and maybe more important reason: even today, primarily from Freud's remarks, one can learn much from them about the theory and technique of psychoanalysis.

In closing, we cannot think of a better way to illustrate what the meetings meant to the participants than to quote two of them; the first is Lou Andreas-Salomé, Nietzsche's and Rilke's friend, who was a writer and philosopher and became in her mature years a devoted follower of Freud. She was a guest at the meetings of the Vienna Society in the academic year 1912-1913. After the last session she attended, she made an entry in her Diary, from which I quote:

I almost raised my hand and asked for permission to speak because I wanted to say the following: Gentlemen: I never wished to participate in the discussions; I let you do the discussing for me; the thanking, however, the thanking I want to do myself. To thank psychoanalysis, especially for demanding more than solitary work at the desk and thus having brought me here, to a kind of fraternity. Indeed, it is no vague mixture of science and sectarianism which makes psychoanalysis such a living force, but it is the fact that analysis has made of the supreme principle of all scientific endeavor, namely, of honesty, its own vital principle. This it applies continuously and over and again, even within the most individual reality; thus it subjects life to insight—just as, on the other hand, psychoanalysis has bent to life the narrow, withered knowledge of academic psychology, thus laying the foundations of its pre-eminent scientific achievement. This is the very reason why, within this circle and beyond, splits arise and disputes—and it is more difficult to settle these than any others, without endangering the continuity of results and methods. . . . Yet, at the same time, it is beautiful to see men facing one another in honest battle. So much more is it my, the woman's part to thank. To thank all these evenings, even the dull ones, for the sake of the One who chaired them and gave them of his time.[14]

[14] *In der Schule bei Freud. Tagebuch eines Jahres, 1912/1913* [*Studying with Freud. Diary of One Year, 1912/1913*]. Zürich: Max Niehans Verlag, 1958.

The second participant is Max Graf, an esteemed musicologist and professor at the Vienna Academy of Music, who was a permanent member of the Society. In the foreword to his *Richard Wagner im "Fliegenden Holländer": Ein Beitrag zur Psychologie künstlerischen Schaffens* [*Richard Wagner in the "Flying Dutchman." A Contribution to the Psychology of Artistic Creation*],[15] he said the following:

> With this little book, I would like to keep alive the spirit of those discussions of psychological problems within a small society which, during a number of years, met each week in Professor Freud's warm and friendly home. This group of friends undertook the task of testing, in a great many contexts, Freudian ideas and concepts. In this circle, I read a paper about Richard Wagner's *The Flying Dutchman*. The present work grew out of this lecture. The ideas which I develop here are the result of an uninterrupted exchange of thoughts with Professor Freud, and of many suggestions gleaned from discussions in his house, suggestions which slowly ripened over the years. The present article is, then, the fruit of an exchange of thoughts and ideas extending over many years; it would be impossible to separate those which I owe to the guidance of Professor Freud, and those which should be attributed to the criticism of several of my colleagues. Thus, I dedicate this study to the memory of those stimulating and exciting hours spent in mutual intellectual strivings with the circle of friends.

HERMAN NUNBERG

New York
May, 1959

---

[15] *Schriften zur angewandten Seelenkunde*, 9, 1911.

NOTES ON THE MEMBERS OF THE PSYCHOLOGICAL WEDNESDAY EVENING SOCIETY

ALFRED ADLER, M.D. (1870-1937) joined Freud in 1902. He played a prominent role in the Wednesday group, and became chairman of the Vienna Psychoanalytic Society in 1910. The facts about Adler's dissension from Freud are well known today, but the gradual development of the split and its drama can nowhere be observed more clearly and objectively than in these protocols. Here Adler's contributions as well as his shortcomings, his single-mindedness, are forever preserved. Adler was a socialist and a member of the Austrian Social Democratic Party; in later life, his scientific views became greatly influenced by his political beliefs. For a representative selection of Adler's papers, see *The Individual Psychology of Alfred Adler*, edited by Heinz and Rowina Ansbacher. New York: Basic Books, 1956.

DAVID BACH, Ph.D. (1874-1947) was the music critic of the Vienna *Arbeiter Zeitung* [*The Workers' Newspaper*], a Social Democratic daily. He organized the first concerts for workmen in Vienna. Adler introduced him to Freud.

ALFRED BASS, M.D. was a general practitioner in Vienna.

GUIDO BRECHER, M.D., a physician practicing in Meran, South Tyrol (which was a part of Austria at that time and now belongs to Italy), appeared periodically at the meetings, but made no contributions.

ADOLF DEUTSCH, M.D. practiced physiotherapy. He was a close friend of Federn and a prominent member of the Viennese Freemasons. He disappeared during World War II.

PAUL FEDERN, M.D. (1871-1950) was introduced to Freud in 1902 by Hermann Nothnagel, professor of internal medicine at the University of Vienna, one of the few members of the medical faculty who supported Freud. Federn's unswerving loyalty to Freud remained unbroken throughout his life. When Freud fell ill he designated Federn his representative in the Society; in 1924 Federn became vice-president of the Vienna Psychoanalytic Society, a position which he held until the dissolution of the Society by the Nazis in 1938. In addition to his original work on strictly psychoanalytic topics, he applied psychoanalytic insight, in many papers, to medicine, psychiatry, the social sciences, and education. For a selection of his writings, see *Ego Psychology and the Psychoses,* ed. P. Federn & E. Weiss. New York: Basic Books, 1950.

PHILIPP FREY, a schoolteacher, was the author of a book entitled *Der Kampf der Geschlechter* [*The Battle of the Sexes*] which was published by Wiener Verlag, 1904. In 1905 he reviewed Freud's *Jokes and Their Relation to the Unconscious* for the *Austrian Review;* in 1907 he published a paper "Selbstmord und Gewohnheit" ["Suicide and Habit"] in the obscure *Jahrbuch des modernen Menschen* [*Yearbook of Modern Man*], 3:170-177.

MAX GRAF, Ph.D. (1875-1958) was an eminent musicologist and author, a personal friend of Freud's.

ADOLF HÄUTLER was an erudite man, interested in the application of psychoanalysis to philosophic, especially aesthetic problems.

HUGO HELLER (1870-1923), publisher and owner of a bookstore, became the first publisher of the *Imago* and the *Internationale Zeitschrift für Psychoanalyse.* His establishment was a meeting place for the liberal artists and intellectuals of Vienna; he supported many young poets and writers.

EDUARD HITSCHMANN, M.D. (1871-1958) had been engaged in the successful practice of internal medicine; introduced by Federn, he joined the group in 1905. His *Freuds Neurosenlehre* [*Freud's Theory of Neuroses*] (Leipzig & Vienna: Deuticke, 1911) was the first systematic presentation of psychoanalysis. Unfailing in his loyalty to Freud, Hitschmann played an important role in the psychoanalytic movement. In 1923 he became the director of the newly established psychoanalytic clinic in Vienna. He held this position until the Society was dissolved by the Nazis. He immigrated to the United States and settled in Boston, Mass. Hitschmann made many clinical contributions to psychoanalysis, but he also devoted much of his talent to the application of psychoanalysis to the biographical study of prominent men. For a selection of his writings in English, see *Great Men* (New York: International Universities Press, 1957). He was an unusually witty and ingenious man.

EDWIN HOLLERUNG, M.D. was a surgeon in the old Austro-Hungarian Army.

ALBERT JOACHIM, M.D. was director of a sanitarium in Reka-winkel, at the time one of the best private institutions for mental patients near Vienna.

MAX KAHANE, M.D. was as a young physician, one of the four original members of the group. Together with Alfred Adler, Alfred Bass, and Julius Baum, he edited the *Medizinisches Handlexikon für praktische Ärzte* [*Medical Dictionary for the Practicing Physician*] (Vienna: Urban & Schwarzenberg, 1908). He was also the editor of later editions of Freud's translation of Bernheim's book, *Hypnotisme, suggestion, psychothérapie, Études nouvelles* (1892).

ALFRED MEISL, M.D. was a physician practicing general medicine in Gumpendorf, a suburb of Vienna. He published a number of papers expounding Freud's theories.

OTTO RANK (1884-1939) was until his defection Freud's favorite pupil. His disagreement with Freud is not reflected in these protocols because his defection occurred only after the First World War. Some of Rank's contributions, such as *The Myth of the Birth of the Hero* (1909), or *Das Inzestmotiv in Dichtung und Sage; Grundzüge einer Psychologie des dichterischen Schaffens* [*The Incest Motif in Poetry and Saga; Fundamentals of a Psychology of Poetic Creation*] (1912) are classics of psychoanalysis. For a biography of Rank, see Jessie Taft: *Otto Rank* (New York: Julian Press, 1958).

RUDOLF REITLER, M.D. (1865-1917) was a prominent physician in Vienna when he joined Freud in 1902. In the unsigned obituary, probably from Freud's own pen, in the *Internationale Zeitschrift,* he is characterized as one of the first and most important pioneers of psychoanalysis who deserves a place of honor in the history of the psychoanalytic movement. Reitler was a most successful therapist, and also a fine, artistically endowed man who loved to draw and compose songs. At the age of forty-nine he was struck by an illness which led to his death three years later.

ISIDOR SADGER, M.D. belongs to the first and most gifted pioneers of psychoanalysis. Little is known about his personal life. Because of personality difficulties he became more and more isolated in the course of the years and finally disappeared during World War II. His contributions to the understanding of the perversions, particularly of homosexuality, are outstanding. He wrote a considerable number of pathographies.

MAXIMILIAN STEINER, M.D. (1874-1942) was a specialist in venereal and skin diseases. His book, *Die psychischen Störungen der männlichen Potenz* [*The Psychic Disturbances of Male Potency*] (Vienna: Deuticke, 1913), belongs to the very limited number to which Freud wrote an introduction. He practiced and taught psychoanalysis and continued to do so after his immigration to England in 1938.

WILHELM STEKEL, M.D. (1868-1940) was one of the four original members. He had a remarkable gift for the understanding of symbols, a talent which found particular expression in his book on *Sex and Dreams; the Language of Dreams* (1911) (Boston: Badger, 1922). He was a prolific writer and popularizer of psychoanalysis. Freud wrote an introduction to his book *Nervöse Angstzustände und ihre Behandlung* [*Conditions of Nervous Anxiety and Their Treatment*] (1908) (London: Paul, Trench, Trubner, 1923), a rare distinction, as we have mentioned above. He, too, separated from Freud a short time after Adler, but for quite different reasons, as is revealed in the subsequent volumes of these Minutes. Stekel had, and still has, a number of followers although he never really established a new psychoanalytic school of thought of his own. *The Autobiography of Wilhelm Stekel* was published in 1950 (New York: Liveright).

RUDOLF VON URBANTSCHITSCH, M.D. (1879-   ), son of an eminent professor of otolaryngology at the University of Vienna, became himself a physician and owner-director of the fashionable Cottage Sanitarium. He joined the Wednesday Society in 1909. However, the fact that Dr. Urbantschitsch joined Freud and supported him in publications threatened the financial existence of the sanitarium, according to his own account to the editors; therefore he felt compelled to separate officially from the Society. Freud was most understanding and remained on good personal terms with him. Urbantschitsch rejoined the Society at a later time.

FRITZ WITTELS, M.D. (1880-1950), a man of great talent, a prolific, witty, and gifted writer, joined the Wednesday Society in 1907. One of his books, *Die sexuelle Not* [*The Sexual Need*] (Vienna: C. W. Stern, 1907) stirred up much controversy at the time. He wrote also a novel *à clef* involving the well-known essayist and satirist Karl Kraus, which became one of the factors leading to his temporary separation from Freud. He resigned from the Society in 1910. In 1925, in spite of some members' opposition, he was readmitted. Unfortunately he had written a biography of Freud which called forth much justified criticism. Nevertheless, Freud supported him and recommended his readmission. He was fond of Wittels and valued his wealth of ideas.

1

SCIENTIFIC MEETING *on October 10, 1906*

Psychological Wednesday Society, meeting at Prof. Freud's home.
Fifth year: 1906/1907
The first meeting took place on October 3, 1906. First some formal matters were taken care of.
Present number of members: 17

Prof. Dr. Sigmund Freud	IX. Berggasse 19
Dr. Alfred Adler	II. Czerningasse 7
Dr. D. J. Bach	VII. Wimbergergasse 7
	XIII. 5 Hüttelbergstr. 61 [crossed out]
Dr. Alfred Bass	VI. Mariahilferstrasse 105
Dr. Adolf Deutsch	I. Spiegelgasse 4
Dr. Paul Federn	I. Riemergasse 1
Philipp Frey	I. Schottenring 32
Dr. Max Graf	III. 2 Untere Viaduktg. 35 [crossed out]
	IX. 2 Fuchsthallerg. 8
Hugo Heller	I. Bauernmarkt 3
Adolf Häutler	XVIII. Herbeckstrasse 98
	XVIII. Wallriessstr. 43 [crossed out]
Dr. Eduard Hitschmann	I. Gonzagagasse 16
Dr. Edwin Hollerung	VIII. Josefstädterstr. 24
	IV. Favoritenstr. 70

Psychologische
Mittwoch-Gesellschaft bei
Prof. Freud.
Fünftes Jahr: 1906/1907

Die erste Zusammenkunft fand am
3. Oktober 1906 statt.

Es wurden zunächst formelle Angelegenheiten
erledigt.

Gegenwärtiger Stand der Mitglieder: 17.

Prof. Dr. Sigm. Freud,	IX. Berggasse 19.
Dr. Alfred Adler,	II. Czerningasse 7.
Dr. D. J. Bach,	~~III/5. Hütteldorferstr.~~ III. Löwengasse 7.
Dr. Alfred Bass,	VI. Mariahilferstr. 105.
Dr. Adolf Deutsch,	I. Spiegelgasse 4.
Dr. Paul Federn,	I. ~~Wollzeile 28.~~
Philipp Frey,	I. Schottenring 32.
Dr. Max Graf,	~~III/21. Juchkellerg.~~ VII. Lgt. Kaiserstr. 55.
Hugo Heller,	I. Bauernmarkt 3.
Adolf Häutler,	XIV/III. ~~Hollgasse 43.~~
Dr. Eduard Hitschmann,	I. Gonzagagasse 16.
Dr. Edwin Hollerung,	VIII. Josefstädterstr. 24.

IV. Favoritenstr. 70

Dr. Max Kahane,   I. Bauernmarkt 9.

Dr. Alfred Meisl,   VI. Gumpendorferstr. 77.

Otto Rank,   IX. Simondenkg. 8.

Dr. Rudolf Reitler,   I. Dorotheerg. 6.

Dr. Wilhelm Stekel,   V./1 Kastellerg. 2.

21.XI.06. Dr. Isidor Sadger,   IX. Lichtensteinstr. 15.

13.II.07. N. Guido Brecher,

27.II.07. Dr. Adolf Häutler,   XVIII. Hofstattgasse 19.   IX. Garnisongasse 13.

Den Vorsitz führt Prof. Dr. Freud, Als Besol-
deter Sekretär fungiert Otto Rank.

Die Zusammenkünfte finden in der Regel jeden
Mittwoch um 8½ h abend bei Prof. Freud statt;
Beginn der Vorträge ist um 9 h. —

Die Reihenfolge der Redner in der Diskussion
wird durchs Loos bestimmt.

I.

Der erste Vortragsabend fand am 10. Oktober statt.
Anwesend waren die Herren:

Prof. Dr. Freud, Dr. Adler, Dr. Deutsch, Dr. Federn, Frey, Häutler, Dr. Hitschmann, Dr. Kahane, Rank, Dr. Reitler.

Mitteilungen: Prof. Freud bemerkt, seine Vorrede zu der von ihm beabsichtigten Sammlung: Schriften zur angewandten Seelenkunde, wegen Abwesenheit des Herrn Heller, der das Manuskript hat, nicht vorlesen zu können. Er fordert die Anwesenden zur Mitarbeit an dem Unternehmen auf, bemerkt jedoch, dass er den Mitgliedern der Gesellschaft, – abweichend von seinem früheren Entschluss – keinen Einfluss auf die Redaktion der Sammlung, sowie auf die Annahme oder Ablehnung von Arbeiten, einräumen könne.

Dr. Adler stellt den Antrag, es mögen zwei oder drei mit der Litteratur vertraute Herren das ständige Referat über alles Einschlägige übernehmen; der Antrag wird mit der Be-

4

gründung abgelehnt, daß daran eigentlich
jeder verpflichtet sei.

Darauf beginnt der Vortrag:
Rank: Der Inzest - Motiv u. seine Komplikationen.

Dr. Max Kahane   I. Bauernmarkt 9

Dr. Alfred Meisl   VI. Gumpendorferstr. 77

Otto Rank   IX. Simondenkg. 6

[Dr. Maximilian] Steiner   [inserted with pencil]

Dr. Rudolf Reitler   I. Dorotheerg. 6

Dr. Wilhelm Stekel   II. Kastellerg. 2

[Dr. Hugo] Schwerdtner   [inserted with pencil]

11. 21. 1906   Dr. Isidor Sadger, IX. Lichtensteinstr. 15

3. 13. 1907   Dr. Guido Brecher [no address]

3. 27. 1907   Dr. Fritz Wittels, IX. Garnisong. 13

                          XVIII. Hofstattgasse 19 [crossed out]

Prof. Dr. Freud chairs the meetings, Otto Rank acts as salaried secretary. The meetings take place, as a rule, every Wednesday evening at eight thirty o'clock at Prof. Freud's home. The presentation of papers begins at nine o'clock. The order of speakers in the discussion is determined by lot.

The first scientific meeting took place on October, 10.

Present: Prof. Dr. Freud, Dr. Adler, Dr. [Adolf] Deutsch,[1] Dr. Federn, Frey, Dr. Hitschmann, Dr. Kahane, Rank, Reitler.

COMMUNICATIONS

PROF. FREUD regrets that he cannot read at this meeting his foreword to the planned series *Contributions to Applied Psychology,*[2] since Mr. Heller, who has the manuscript, is absent. He invites those present at the meeting to collaborate in this undertaking but states

[1] We have inserted the first name, Adolf, in order to avoid confusion with Dr. Felix Deutsch, who joined the Society at a much later date.

Häutler, whose discussion is recorded below, was omitted from the list of participants.

[2] According to Freud's own presentation in "On the History of the Psychoanalytic Movement" (1914; *S.E.*, 14), the first in this series of monographs, the German title of which was *Schriften zur angewandten Seelenkunde,* was his "Delusions and Dreams in Jensen's 'Gradiva'" (*S.E.*, 9) ["Der Wahn und die Träume in W. Jensen's 'Gradiva'" (Vienna: Heller, 1907)]. Later, Franz Deuticke (Leipzig and Vienna) took over the publication of this series. The foreword to which Freud here refers appeared as an "Announcement" [*Anzeige*] at the end of the first edition of his "Gradiva." It was no longer included in the second edition published by Deuticke, and has not been reprinted either in the *Gesammelte Schriften* (Vienna: Internationaler psychoanalytischer Verlag) or in the *Gesammelte Werke* (London: Imago Publ. Co.). It was published again, for the first time in a translation by Henry A. Bunker, in the *Bull. Amer. Psychoanal. Assn.*, 8:214-215, 1952.

that, contrary to his earlier decision, he cannot grant them any vote in the editing of the series or influence on the acceptance or rejection of contributions.

DR. ADLER moves that two or three of the members who are well versed in the literature be given the permanent assignment of reviewing current publications relevant to our work. The motion is rejected on the grounds that each member really should make himself responsible for such reviews.

The lecture then follows.

PRESENTATION

The Incest Drama and Its Complications (Manuscript)

SPEAKER: OTTO RANK

The paper is not recorded here since it is soon to be published in book form.[3]

DISCUSSION

FREY criticizes the fragmentary and vague character of the paper; Rank has given not a paper but an excerpt from his manuscript; Frey misses the logical outline of the theme. Rank has presented only isolated details.

Frey comments further that the tendency of the paper is to interpret everything according to Freud's method, and that therefore too much has been read into the material and interpreted from it. Some of the occurrences which Rank has interpreted symbolically are, in Frey's opinion, better understood on a purely factual level. For instance, he cannot understand why in Hartmann's poem[4] the shackles which pre-

---

[3] The book was published under the title *Das Inzest-Motiv in Dichtung und Sage; Grundzüge einer Psychologie des dichterischen Schaffens* [*The Incest Motif in Poetry and Saga; Fundamentals of a Psychology of Poetic Creation*]. Vienna: Deuticke, 1912; 2nd ed., enlarged and improved, 1926. Rank mentions in his foreword that he had presented the main substance and the principal points of view of his conception already in 1906 before that intimate circle which later became the Vienna Psychoanalytic Society. He adds that inner inhibitions rather than external difficulties were responsible for the delay of the publication.

[4] Hartmann von der Aue (1170-1210), German poet.

7

vent Gregorius from fleeing are interpreted as a psychic projection of the inhibition due to exhibitionistic tendencies (Freud), or why Oedipus's taking of belt and sword from Laius should be interpreted as a symbol of castration of the father, and of taking possession of the mother, especially since Oedipus did not know that the man from whom he took the sword (whom he castrated) was his father. Rank ought to be satisfied with rendering the probable plausible.[5]

Finally, Frey objects to the incorrect use of the concept of repression; much of what Rank terms "repression" is actually a refinement [*Verfeinerung*], yet not every refinement is a repression.

REITLER comments that the paper was not extensive enough to give a clear idea of its scope. He feels that a closer investigation of the role of penitence in the legends of the saints would have been interesting, since penitence is so closely related to hysteria. The series of gradations postulated by Rank, according to which repression is least operative in the dream, more so in the myth, and most operative in the drama (in art), should be reversed. As an example of paternal hate he mentions that God the Father killed His Son Jesus—indirectly, it is true—His Son Who, together with God the Father is part of the Trinity. Finally, Reitler refers to incestuous allusions in student songs.

[A.] DEUTSCH does not wish to speak as Reitler has anticipated what he wanted to say.

HÄUTLER also comments critically upon the paper. It is his feeling that the essential points have not been sufficiently emphasized; in addition, he misses a unified structure. Though this paper was surely not intended to be a compilation of all cases of incest in literature, Häutler nevertheless has received this impression from it. In his opinion, one can speak of repression only in reference to individuals, not in reference to a nation's psychic life of which we still know very little. Another point with which he cannot agree is the assumption that there always exists a relationship between the personal life of the communicating artist (poets, etc.) and his material; incest is always effective

---

[5] It is interesting to note that some of Freud's first followers utterly failed to grasp the nature of the unconscious, and that they confused conscious and unconscious contents.

material and may gradually have become a merely extrinsic requisite. Finally, he observes that there was too much "interpretation."[6]

HITSCHMANN considers the paper no more than a rather superfluous extension of Freud's discovery of the oedipus complex. Love between relatives does not always have incestuous roots, but may be simply love for the relatives (e.g., parental love). Incest is something pathological; therefore it has such an intense attraction for poets.[7] However, Hitschmann concedes that the unconscious exerts an influence upon the choice of material as well as upon the interest of the audience. In conclusion, he cautions against viewing such broad themes from a far-fetched angle and predicts a sad end for the speaker if he should continue to exclude other points of view.

FEDERN says that first he must object to Hitschmann's argument. He considers the paper an important contribution; he was amazed to learn of the ubiquity of incestuous impulses.[8] He misses a historical (phylogenetic) development of incest, in the primeval and in the individual family. He assumes that the prohibition of incest resulted from the evolution of the individual family unit.[9] He notes that incest between father and daughter was not as strictly forbidden as incest between mother and son; therefore it is a less frequent topic in literature.—The designation of the Eumenides as "paranoic" projections of unconscious impulses should, from a medical point of view, be modified to hallucinations. He objects to the interpretation of black and white as unconscious and conscious.—Castrative desires should not be considered as directed only against the father. In primeval times they were directed against any hated man. Attainment of the supreme

[6] In these early days, the same situation appears again and again: there is complaint that too much is being interpreted, and the oedipus complex has no reality for the discussants. In other words, their resistances are strong. The unreality of the oedipus complex leads on the one hand to Jung's camp, who considered the oedipus complex unreal and only a symbol, and on the other to Adler, who maintained that all conflicts are fictions which screen the masculine protest and all that it involves.

[7] Even Hitschmann shows little understanding of sexuality at that early stage. Besides, apparently he is still influenced by Lombroso's thesis that genius and insanity belong together.

[8] In this discussion (except for Freud), Reitler, Federn, and Adler are the only ones who judge the paper favorably and who apparently take incest and oedipus complex seriously.

[9] At that time—that is, even before the publication of Freud's *Totem and Taboo* (1912-1913)—Federn already saw in the prohibition of incest a precipitate of historical development.

9

power was the main motive of the castration of Chronos by Zeus. He does not concede that the "nose" scene in Auerbach's cellar (*Faust*) represents the repression of an earlier, coarser scene.[10]

FREUD begins by criticizing the speaker's shortcomings: he says that Rank does not know how to stay within the limits of his subject and how to outline his topic clearly; for instance, it was unnecessary to trace back some parts of Hartmann's work to exhibitionistic impulses, since this has no connection with the main theme. Similarly, the Orestes and Clytaemnestra myths might have been omitted, although connections with the main theme have been established quite skillfully.

The second failing of the speaker, Freud continues, is that he is unable to demonstrate his insights and results; he is satisfied when he himself understands the matter in question. He should briefly outline the most important results of his investigations and use several examples to demonstrate them. The scheme Freud has in mind is as follows: Oedipus should be presented as the core and model; then the one tried and tested method of presentation would be on the one hand to group the material around this core, and on the other hand, by developing a series, to follow the theme from this core into its furthest ramifications. It is true that the further you move out from the core, the more uncertain become the interpretations, and it is a matter of personal taste and skill to stop at the right place. Nor can everything be considered from a single viewpoint because other themes also have a bearing upon the subject matter and must be taken into account.

Freud, too, defends the concept of repression against incorrect use; in some instances Rank has termed repression what actually was displacement or mitigation. Freud emphasizes the frequent occurrence of incest among the "Gods," and adds that all that which was later forbidden and finally sanctified was originally [allowed and then] renounced. Hence the double meaning of the word *sacer*.[11]

[10] Goethe: *Faust*, Part 1. At the conclusion of this scene, Mephistopheles casts a magic spell on a group of drinkers. They seize each other by the nose and raise their knives, imagining that they are clutching grape vines.

[11] *Sacer* means both holy and accursed. Several years later, in 1910, Freud developed this theme in greater detail in his paper on "The Antithetical Meaning of Primal Words"—a review of a pamphlet with the same title by Karl Abel—(*S.E.*, 11:153-161), first published in German as "Über den Gegensinn der Urworte" in *Jb.*, 2(1):179-184.

It is too kind, he says, to equate Orestes' recovery with a psychological cure;[12] other factors, such as the introduction of the Apollo cult and the like, surely played a role there.

ADLER begins by saying that the paper's title should be changed. It should indicate that the work concerns itself with the disclosure of a nucleus, and Rank should be satisfied with uncovering this nucleus in his paper and refrain from trying to give detailed interpretations. Adler considers the paper important inasmuch as it confirms experience gained from the psychoneuroses; beginners could learn much from it. He gives some examples from his practice which bear out Rank's findings: in reference to the interpretation of the removal of the belt as a sexual symbol, he mentions the hysterical seizure of a woman patient, during which she unties her belt. The interpretation brought to light the sexual meaning of this act. In reference to the fit of Orestes in which he bites off his finger,[13] and to the sexual interpretation of this symptom, Adler relates an analogy from the hysterias. A female patient, awaking from a dream at night, found that she had bitten her finger till it bled. Analysis led to the interpretation of the finger as a penis (as in the case of Orestes), and the parapraxis suggests a defense against oral perversion. In corroboration of the sexual symbolism of the serpent, Adler cites an example from the psychology of the neuroses. One of his patients declared that a link existed between herself and her father, which was shaped partly like a serpent and partly like a bird. Upon Adler's request she made a drawing of this image, from which it became unmistakably clear that it was a penis. Adler adds that children often call the membrum "serpent," an expression used quite commonly in this sense. (FREUD remarks at this point that in medieval pictures devils are often depicted with a membrum shaped like a serpent.) To Rank's interpretation of skin diseases (leprosy) as a defense against exhibitionistic impulses (Hartmann von der Aue: *Der arme Heinrich*), Adler asserts that eruptions appear frequently in dreams as well as in hysteria. He cites the dream of a female exhibitionist (hysterica) in which a woman friend or cousin of hers strips; the woman has a breast abscess. He then mentions the

12 See Aeschylus's *The Eumenides*.
13 This passage refers to Pausania's *Periegesis*, a description of Greece, quoted by Rank.

symbolic meaning of the nose as a sex organ, in the dream and in the neurosis, adding that this symbolism is not yet quite clear to him. (To Adler's statement about the "eruptions," FREUD comments that eruptions offer a child the best opportunity for denuding himself.) Adler then criticizes the superficial attempt to explain crime: stating that every criminal act has sexual roots explains nothing. The frequent indication in myths and legends, that parents are aware of the child's criminal inclinations, must be attributed to the poet's instincts, who carries his own awareness into the myth. In conclusion, Adler says that the frequent use of incestuous material is proof of its special interest to both the poet and the public.

KAHANE mentions as a case of incest Shakespeare's *Pericles, Prince of Tyre*. In his opinion, the speaker is going too far in some of his interpretations; it is like overextending an elastic band. He refers particularly to parents' affection for their children and calls attention to the sex envy of parents and to their hostility toward their children's sexuality. Certainly, the parental prohibition of masturbation and normal intercourse imposed upon sons and daughters does not originate in moral motives but in sex envy. Only the relationship between mother and son seems important to Kahane. He refers finally to one of Federn's remarks, to the effect that in southern regions mothers lose their youthfulness early and are then no longer desirable to their sons: Kahane feels that this creates the need for poets to make the sons older and the mothers younger.[14]

Following the discussion, FREUD reports a case as an example of the impact of the *sexual trauma:* for a week and a half he has been treating a female hysteric; in her first session, she related an exhibitionistic scene from her fourth year: she undressed in front of her brother who became very indignant. Later, she had an almost incestuous relationship with this brother. From her eleventh year on they used to show their bodies to each other, in this way observing the progress of their development. Between her eleventh and fourteenth year, they had intimate bodily contact, with the exclusion of their hands. They would lie on top of each other, attempting intercourse. All of these are *con-*

[14] That is a considerable misunderstanding: the mother is desirable not because she is young and beautiful *in actuality*; unconsciously, the mother is always beautiful and desirable. The boy desires his unconscious, infantile image of his mother.

12

scious memories of the patient. During a session in which not much progress was being made, she began to talk of everyday occurrences. She related that she was known as an excellent *spot remover*, and that she was a passionate fruit grower, especially interested in growing *apples*. Among other things, she spoke of an experience she had had with her father; he had referred to a certain German lady's breasts as "pious" [*fromm*] and had found fault with her dress which exposed them. She said to her father that he would not have minded seeing the breasts, had they been less pious (pious breasts: *pear*-shaped breasts: *pomme au poire*). KAHANE adds, "Pious because at night they fall on the knees."

2

SCIENTIFIC MEETING on October 17, 1906

Present: Freud, Adler, Bass, [A.] Deutsch, Federn, Heller, Hollerung, Häutler, Meisl, Stekel (who came late), Bach, Graf, Rank.

COMMUNICATIONS

FREUD reports that a detailed review of the *Theory of Sexuality* [*Three Essays on the Theory of Sexuality* (1905)] was published in the *Jahrbuch für sexuelle Zwischenstufen*, Vol. VIII;[1] that [Havelock] Ellis, in the recently published fifth volume of his *Studies in the Psychology of Sex*, expresses views which in many instances are close to our own, especially in respect to symbolism.

Freud informs the members that on November 12, he will give a paper on sexual abstinence at the *Sozialwissenschaftlicher Bildungsverein* [*Society for the Education in the Social Sciences*].

He reads the introduction to his series, *Contributions to Applied Psychology.*[2]

ADLER announces a paper, "Outline of a Theory of the Neuroses," to be given soon.

---

[1] [*Yearbook of Sexual Anomalies*] (lit., . . . *of Sexual Intermediate Stages*), Editor: Dr. Magnus Hirschfeld; published in Wiesbaden.

[2] See footnote 2, Minutes 1.

HÄUTLER announces, for the end of November, a paper on *"The Possessed* by Dostoyevsky." Reports were already scheduled before this by Hitschmann on Bleuler's book, *Affectivity, Suggestibility and Paranoia,*[3] and Hollerung on Semon's *Mneme.*[4]

PRESENTATION

The Incest Drama and Its Complications (Manuscript)

Part II: The Incestuous Relationship Between Siblings

SPEAKER: OTTO RANK

The paper is not recorded here, since it will soon appear in book form.

RANK begins by replying to the discussion of the last meeting. Most of the objections, he says, were directed against the form of the lecture, not against its substance; these shortcomings, however, are inherent in the nature of his work. His main objective was to show the correspondence of certain phenomena in myth and art with phenomena in the psychoneuroses. One must not, however, overwhelm the reader with these new findings; one has to start from a basis which is generally accepted today—in this case the basis is research in the history of literature—and lead the reader from there to the frontiers of psychoanalysis; every step into this domain is risky. Thus this paper is, on the one hand, a compilation of most of the cases of incest found in literature; on the other hand, it includes bold attempts at interpretation. To connect these two extremes was difficult enough in the book, and certainly could not even be attempted in the concentrated form of a paper. This dualism, however, has been the main target of the objections. Then Rank discusses very briefly a few of the objections that were raised: he says that the repeated protests against the mistaken use of the word "repression" were based on a misunderstanding; he did not mean voluntary repression but what, in his *Psychology of Sexuality,* he called "involuntary" repression, which is an essential factor in the normal development of the individual.[5] Rank endeavors to

---

[3] *Affektivität, Suggestibilität und Paranoia.* Halle: Marhold, 1906.

[4] See Minutes 6, Meeting on November 14, 1906.

[5] At that time, Rank did not yet distinguish between repression and suppression. Repression is an unconscious process, whereas suppression is a conscious, or rather, a preconscious one.

refute Federn's objection that the struggle between father and son in myths and stories of royal houses most often concerns only the supreme power, by referring to his own argument that the motif of the struggle for power merely screens the deeper sexual motif.

In response to Adler's remark on crime, Rank adds his explanation of child murder, murder of a spouse, and double suicide.[6]

The second part of his lecture follows.

DISCUSSION

GRAF believes the understanding of the material to be correct as far as he is familiar with it, and feels he cannot form an opinion regarding the material with which he is not acquainted. He mentions his own attempt to trace in Goethe's *Tasso* the poet's veiled love for his sister Cornelia. He based this attempt on the fact that Tasso's beloved sister bore the same name and that Goethe's hero rejected Eleonore as a sex object. Then he speaks of Wagner's love for his younger sister: as a child Wagner had suffered from anxiety dreams; he would suddenly awake at night screaming and call for his sister. Graf could not throw any light upon the mysterious obscurity veiling both the figures of Erda[7] and Kundry,[8] but he assumes that repressed unconscious impulses lay behind the creation of these characters.

ADLER introduces his remarks by expressing his appreciation of the careful manner in which the material was collected and of the logical development of the leading thought so that it shows the infantile and sexual impulses wherever they appear in the material. On the whole, he finds no fault with the paper and cannot consider the reproach justified that Rank has gone too far. Once more he reverts to the subject of crime with the remark that he had gained the impression that the speaker wanted to place crime in any form within the compass of incest; with this, of course, he cannot agree. He then remarks that Rank's findings should encourage the members of the Society to maintain their positions.

The general impression gained from the book leaves him with two thoughts: first, the significance of art for the development (cultural and

6 The explanation is not recorded in the Minutes.
7 In *The Ring of the Nibelungs.*
8 In *Parsifal.*

spiritual) of a people has been overrated until now. Investigations such as those made by Rank do not encourage the development of art; if continued, such investigations could even become dangerous to the mentality of people [*Volksgeist*]. The creativeness of artists would be inhibited if too much were brought to consciousness. The artist would become incapable of creation; this, of course, implies the destruction of art. On the other hand, a loss in this direction might be compensated for by the progress in other fields which might result from expansion of the sphere of consciousness.[9]

The second thought which Adler expresses is an apprehension over the stability of the family. The ethical awareness of people is unsuccessful in protecting children from incestuous impulses; it is a question whether education can succeed in saving the family from disintegration (in the dualism between the parents' conscience and the children's unconscious impulses), so that the family unit may be preserved as a, so to speak, pedagogical cell.

In connection with these ideas, Adler refers to his attempt of many years ago to grasp the psychology of the politician. He had tried to show that the position supported by the politician (especially in questions of reform, and similar matters) is rooted in personal motives. Adler believes, for instance, that the social activists who advocate the dissolution of the family in their program have a vague idea of the incestuous tendencies.[10]

Concluding his remarks, Adler voices regret that he could not follow his favorite idea by showing the organic roots of incestuous impulses; he will confine himself to stating that medical examination of poets has ascertained in every individual examined an abnormal precociousness. Its cause, however, is not immediately clear. As an example, he relates that he has succeeded in proving that Jean Paul[11] was an enuretic.[12]

---

[9] Similar ideas are often expressed in phases of resistance by patients who are creative artists.

[10] Being an active Social Democrat, Adler was interested in the psychology of the politician and the reformer.

[11] Jean Paul, pen name for Jean Paul Friedrich Richter (1763-1825), outstanding German romantic writer and satirist.

[12] Here we see the first forebodings of Adler's theory of organ inferiority, the basis of his Individual Psychology which he developed in later years.

3

SCIENTIFIC MEETING on October 24, 1906

Present: Freud, Bach, [A.] Deutsch, Federn, Graf, Heller, Hitschmann, Häutler, Kahane, Meisl, Rank, Stekel, Adler (only at the beginning, until about 9:15).

COMMUNICATIONS

STEKEL reports that upon the suggestion of Hirschfeld[1] it is
planned to form also in Vienna a scientific-humanitarian committee
for the purpose of fighting the "homosexual" paragraph of the penal
law. Another item reported is an attack on Freud on account of the
Fliess affair[2] in the last issue of the *Waage*.[3]

ADLER remarks that Prévost[4] made a fine psychological observation
in one of his novels, *The Other One:* the physician tells a woman

[1] Dr. Magnus Hirschfeld (1868-1935), a renowned German sexologist and psychologist, fought for the abolition of legal persecution of perverts. (See also Minutes 47 and
48.)

[2] Stekel is referring to the literary feud described by Ernst Kris in his Introduction
to the Freud-Fliess correspondence (see *The Origins of Psychoanalysis.* New York:
Basic Books, 1954, p. 41). See also Jones's *Life and Work of Sigmund Freud,* Vol. 1.
New York: Basic Books, 1953, p. 327.

[3] *Waage* [*Scale*], a monthly magazine published in Vienna.

[4] Marcel Prévost (1862-1941), French author of novels about the middle class.

patient that one can best cure illnesses such as hers by discussing the intimacies of married life with the patient.[5] MEISL announces a paper on the "Significance of Sexual Fantasies," STEKEL one on "The Psychology of Discussion," and GRAF one on "Art and Life."

DISCUSSION

RANK'S PAPER: *The Incest Drama* (second part)

FREUD expresses first his general appreciation and mentions in particular the separate analytic achievements evident throughout the paper. He singles out for special praise the Grillparzer analysis[6] and cites a similar case from practice: Stekel once had an intelligent young man in treatment, a high-school teacher who was possessed by a singular passion for one of his pupils; he was constantly worrying about him, feared to lose him, and so forth. The teacher had a younger brother who died at fourteen years of age; as the parents' favorite he had been in his older brother's way, and the typical brother hatred had developed. With the boy's death a change occurred in the older brother: he transferred his passionate [hostile] feelings for the younger brother onto his young pupil in the guise of a defense. He loved him and, in a way, made up for the love he had denied his brother. Stekel's diagnosis found confirmation in a curious way; as mentioned before, the deceased son had been his mother's favorite; when the young pupil once was visiting with the family the mother remarked: "How strange—he looks so much like my Charles."

Freud mentions then that in his contribution to Löwenfeld's book[7] he himself had already made the distinction between conscious repression and (unconscious) organic repression, a distinction which Rank had represented as a new finding. Freud had termed conscious repression "defense," and the unconscious one, "repression."[8]

---

[5] At that time, it gave great satisfaction to those around Freud when they found corroboration of his ideas in the world outside this circle.

[6] Franz Grillparzer (1791-1872), great Austrian dramatist.

[7] "Meine Ansichten über die Rolle der Sexualität in der Ätiologie der Neurosen." In: *Sexualleben und Nervenleiden*, ed. L. Löwenfeld. Wiesbaden: Bergmann, 4th ed., 1906 [My Views on the Part Played by Sexuality in the Aetiology of the Neuroses. *S.E.*, 7:269-279]. Freud's paper was written, however, already in 1905.

[8] Today we would use the terms "suppression" and "repression" respectively.

19

From the field of literature, Freud mentions C. F. Meyer's short novel *Die Richterin*[9] where the theme is sibling love; at the end of the story it turns out that the two main characters are not really brother and sister, whereupon they marry. This mechanism, which has the purpose of annulling painful conditions in one's own generation, is frequently operative in the family romances of neurotics.[10] Fantasies of the mother's unfaithfulness, for instance, are meant to loosen the tie between brother and sister. In Meyer's life, love for a sister had played an important part and had been the main cause of his marital unhappiness; many of his most beautiful love poems are addressed to his sister.

Freud can corroborate Rank's assertion that jealousy (the paranoid kind) has its roots in childhood enmities. He once had the opportunity to examine a woman suffering from paranoid jealousy; her husband was a hysteric. In the course of the interview, the woman abused herself for her destructive passion; but, she said, that was her character. Even as a child she had had such feelings whenever her father kissed one of her sisters (this marriage ended later in divorce).[11]

In reference to incestuous relationships in the families of the Greek Gods (Uranos, Chronos, and so forth), Freud says that one cannot very well use these illustrious personages as an example, since it is too easy to object that no other [sexual] intercourse would have been possible for them.

In reference to the belief that events may come to pass as a result of a wish (Grillparzer's brother, and so on), Freud recalls a short novel by Alfred Berger,[12] *Dr. Max Gaspari*, in which a man is portrayed who represents, in a manner of speaking, the annulment of the unconscious; a man who understands everything and is incapable of illusions.

[9] Conrad Ferdinand Meyer (1825-1898), famous Swiss poet. *Die Richterin* = *The Woman Judge*.

[10] The word "family romance," mentioned just in passing, appears for the first time in these Minutes. Freud wrote more extensively on this topic in Rank's *Der Mythus von der Geburt des Helden* [*The Myth of the Birth of the Hero*]. Leipzig and Vienna: Deuticke, 1909.

[11] Later, Freud recognized in paranoid jealousy a projection of the subject's homosexuality. See: "Über einige neurotische Mechanismen bei Eifersucht, Paranoia und Homosexualität." *Z.*, 8:249-258, 1922 ["Some Neurotic Mechanisms in Jealousy, Paranoia and Homosexuality." *S.E.*, 18:221-232].

[12] Alfred Freiherr von Berger (1853-1912), Austrian author, at one time director of the Vienna Burgtheater.

Finally, he gets married. One day, his wife makes an excursion to the Rax[13] with his consent, and perishes there. He believes that he has murdered her, because at the very moment that the accident took place, he was thinking of her and of her death. The novel ends with his own journey up the Rax, where he finds the body and throws himself into the abyss. Freud points out that here the obsessional idea is projected upon consciousness, as it were.[14] Concerning the relation between choice of subject matter and the poet's life, Freud points out—as he had already said to Rank in private—that where hate for a brother and love for a sister appear in a poet's work and there is no evidence of similar circumstances in the poet's own life, one should find out whether there had been a child in the family who died at an early age. Suppression [by the future poet of his own feelings concerning the death of a younger sibling] at an early stage in his life might lead to the transformation of his feelings into poetry.

The fight between two brothers for a sister is a theme found also in the stars of the sky. This coincidence opens an interesting perspective for astronomy. The two constellations, "The Twins" and "The Virgin," are side by side in the sky. Their names are of Babylonian origin, but Greek mythology also represented a similar relationship in Castor, Pollux and Helena. Winkler,[15] who took an interest in interpreting the constellations, thinks that they represent a fixation of human relationships (between brothers and sister) in the sky. Winkler speaks in this connection also of the relations among Absalom, Amon, and Thamar.

The comparatively rare occurrence of incest in Shakespeare's plays is, according to Freud, connected with the fact that most of his plays are adaptations of old texts and that the texts are therefore not really his own.

Lastly, Freud cites a case from his practice characteristic of the relationship between brother and sister: he had a young woman in treatment who, as a child, exhibited herself in front of her brother; later

[13] High mountain near Vienna.
[14] Today we would perhaps say that the obsessional idea became conscious in the projection.
[15] Hugo Winkler (1853-1913), German orientalist.

21

they always addressed each other with the formal "*Sie*"[16] and, strangely enough, called one another "Monsieur" and "Madame." When the brother was studying at a foreign university, he mailed letters to his sister to the post office, not to their home. They had started to use the formal *Sie* when their physical relations ended.

HITSCHMANN, having been absent from the previous meeting, asks whether Rank has included in his considerations the cases of incest in Ibsen's dramas. Then, in connection with Adler's remark, he too expresses the fear that the increasing knowledge of psychic processes may inhibit creativity.

Later in the discussion Hitschmann observes that incest as such should not be regarded as so very significant; it should be thought of simply as a component phenomenon of the entirety of sexual needs. The libido tries to find gratification by the way of least resistance: the son, for instance, desires the mother because she represents the vagina within reach, or because she is the first woman whom he has known, or the like; and intercourse with a servant girl occurs just as well, since she fulfills likewise the condition of the vagina which is present. (At this point HELLER asks why it is, then, that incest is considered contrary to the laws of nature.[17])

HÄUTLER begins by expressing his appreciation of Rank's careful work, stating that the application of Freud's theories to other fields is to be encouraged, as is the demonstration of the veins of sexuality in literature and mythology. He must, however, object most emphatically to Rank's pessimism regarding the danger that these incestuous impulses harbor, on the one hand as a source of serious illness, and on the other hand (by reaching consciousness) as an obstacle to intellectual productivity.

Incestuous impulses as initial stages of sexuality are, according to Freud, of great importance in pointing the way to the choice of the sexual object. Incestuous impulses are normal, paradoxical as this

[16] *Sie* is the formal address, in contrast to the familiar *Du*, which has no equivalent in modern English, but is translated by the archaic "thou."

[17] An answer to this question is given by Freud in *Totem and Taboo* (1912-1913). *S.E.*, 13:1-162.

statement might seem. They produce illness only if they become fixated.

Häutler expresses his feeling that at the root of all sublimation lie the incestuous impulses; through these impulses the mechanism of sublimation is acquired, as it were. In support of his view, he mentions that in those nations where children are separated from their parents at an early age (in Sparta, for instance), psychic drives and emotional life are on a far lower level than in other nations. There are many people whose entire ethics is based on the sublimation of their incestuous impulses; he mentions as an example the ethics rooted in the veneration of the parents.[18]

Häutler is strongly opposed to the view that artistic creativity could ever be weakened. So much will never become conscious as to impair a normal individual's power of imagination. Much will always remain obscure in the human mind, hence one of the driving forces of creative writing will never cease to exist; such an end could only come about if all sexual energies were obliterated. Were this to occur, it would bring with it the demise not only of art but of many other human endeavors as well. As long as mankind is capable of passing judgment, there will be poets.

FEDERN names several additional literary works dealing with incestuous themes: a novel by Anzengruber, *Der Schandfleck*,[19] whose subject is love between brother and sister. E. T. A. Hoffmann treats incestuous material in many of his works, e.g., in the *Elixiere des Teufels*.[20] He remembers having found something of this kind also in Körner's work.[21] He speaks then of a story[22] of a mother who has sexual relations with her son in order to protect him against the harmful influences of sexual life. (Several members call attention to a short

[18] See Freud's *Totem and Taboo* which was published at a much later date, in 1912-1913.

[19] Ludwig Anzengruber (1839-1889), Austrian author and dramatist. *Schandfleck* = *Blemish*.

[20] E. T. A. Hoffmann (1776-1822), famous German romanticist. *Elixiere des Teufels* = *The Devil's Elixirs*.

[21] Theodor Körner (1791-1813), German poet.

[22] *Niels Tufverson and His Mother*, by the Danish author Gustav af Geijerstam (1858-1909).

23

novel by Lynkeus[23] and to Bahr's *Mutter*.[24] In J. J. David's novel, *Im Frühschein*,[25] there occurs conscious incest between brother and sister; David himself has termed this novel his best work. From personal conversations with David, Federn has learned that as a very young boy David had erotic feelings for his sister and that he even slept in the same bed with her. He had no desire to get married—probably because of this relationship. Referring to Freud's remark about Uranos, Chronos, and other Gods, Federn adds that the same could be said of Cain and Abel; they could not help but marry their sister.

That the motive for matricide (especially in Greek mythology) is to be found in incestuous impulses, is, in Federn's opinion, an arbitrary assumption of Rank's; he raises the same objection to the derivation of every brother murder from incestuous love for a sister. There are other causes of matricide and fratricide, aside from incestuous impulses. That the Erinyes persecuted only the "incestuous" *murder* and not incest as such, seems to him to show that incest itself was not viewed as *nefas*[26] at the time.

Federn thinks that incest with the mother hardly ever occurs nowadays, and incest with the sister very rarely. Incestuous impulses today are no longer subject to repression, generally speaking, but partly they do not arise at all, partly they have become abortive, as it were.[27] The artistic representation of such inclinations has largely been replaced by the representation of jealousy.

[23] Josef Popper-Lynkeus (1838-1921), a prominent electrical engineer, was an Austrian writer and social philosopher. His most important works are *Phantasien eines Realisten* [*Fantasies of a Realist*] and *Allgemeine Nährpflicht* [the state's obligation to provide nutrition to all the people as a solution of the social problem]. Freud writes in a short article, "Josef Popper-Lynkeus und die Theorie des Traumes" (1923) ["Josef Popper-Lynkeus and the Theory of Dreams"], that Popper-Lynkeus, having had no knowledge of *The Interpretation of Dreams*, had himself discovered the "dream censor." Freud ends his short essay with the following words: "I believe it was my moral courage that enabled me to discover the cause of dream distortion. With Popper, it was the purity, love of truth, and moral clarity of his character" (*G.W.*, 13:359; tr. by the editors).

[24] Hermann Bahr (1863-1934), Austrian journalist, author, and dramatist. *Mutter* = *Mother*.

[25] J. J. David (1859-1906), Austrian poet, author of many short novels. *Im Frühschein* = *At Dawn*.

[26] *Nefas* = crime.

[27] What Federn apparently wishes to express, is that in normal development the incestuous impulses are assimilated by the ego and sublimated.

Federn adds that incest probably was a rare occurrence at the beginning of cultural development, and most likely has appeared only with the beginning of individualism. Incest does not exist in the vegetable world, nor does it occur in the animal world (with the exception of the domestic animals). (This remark calls forth strong contradictions by FREUD, STEKEL, HELLER, and others.) There is no need to fear any damaging effect if these inclinations are made conscious; the artist has enough other unconscious emotions left.

Lastly, Federn objects to Rank's assertion that all virtues are nothing but "repressed" vices; certainly, there exist positive virtues as well.

HELLER voices doubts about the permanence, the "teleologic necessity" (as he expressed himself), of the present-day attitude toward incest. The moral attitude toward sexual matters will, on the whole, become less severe; the idea of "heaven and hell" nowadays connected with sexual matters is unnecessary, and views on the ethics of incest are changeable.

He shares the opinion that through the uncovering of these impulses the poet is deprived of the use of this motif; since tragic guilt is no longer involved, the motif is divested of its tragic character. But the disappearance of one motif does not imply the end of art.

Incest between brothers and sisters is very often encountered, especially in large families who live in close quarters; in mining districts it is a frequent phenomenon.

STEKEL describes the book as a diligent, but schoolboyish work; everything in this book is seen through spectacles colored by Freudian teachings, without going beyond Freud. Furthermore, he has to protest against the manner of the presentation: he found it very trying to listen to the formalistic presentation of an excerpt from a manuscript. He is in favor of a stimulating lecture delivered freely.

In contrast to Federn, he emphasizes the frequency of incest (especially between siblings). He can cite as examples two cases from his practice. The first is that of a man who suffered from "nervous" insomnia; following Freud, Stekel traced it back to ungratified sexual needs. This man had shared an apartment with his sister who kept house for him. He dreamed frequently about his sister. Attempts at

25

intercourse with prostitutes failed.—Stekel advised him to give up the shared apartment.[28]

In the second case, the brother took advantage of his sister's affection for him to gain financial profits. Once he had achieved this goal, he turned his affection to other women, whereupon the sister turned her incestuous feelings back onto her father ("he is just like father"). Stekel considers the "repression" in the neuroses not to be conscious, as Rank does in accordance with Freud, but to be unconscious.[29]

Referring to the Grillparzer analysis, which takes its cue from Brother Straubinger,[30] Stekel remarks that Karl may have wished to reduce his brother, the poet, to the state of a laborer. Stekel relates a dream of his own from his sixteenth or seventeenth year; its content was incest with his mother; this dream had depressed him deeply at the time. He can also recall two dreams with homosexual contents.

KAHANE thinks that the social-economic point of view should not be neglected in the search for the cause of incest. Incest may perhaps have undergone a change in the transition from nomadic life to agriculture. In nomadic life, the desire to keep the herd intact may lead to the intermarriage of brothers and sisters. In agricultural life, on the other hand, this would never bring about an increase of possessions.

MEISL does not agree with Rank's argument, according to which the works of poets seem to corroborate the general occurrence of these infantile sexual impulses.

Rank's assertions rest on a foundation that is altogether too fragile; he eliminates or changes whatever does not serve his purpose. For instance, if a poet in whose work fraternal hate plays a role had no brother, Rank assumes that he created a brother in his fantasy.[31] Or,

---

[28] In this case it is not a question of actual incest but merely of incestuous fantasies.

[29] Freud had always stated that repression in the neuroses is unconscious. Either Stekel's remark was incorrectly recorded, or he misunderstood Freud.

[30] Brother Straubinger is the name used to designate a wandering young craftsman. Grillparzer's brother Karl was a disturbed and asocial man who caused the poet serious concern and trouble. While Grillparzer was living in London (1836), Karl falsely accused himself of murder; this added to the difficulties of Grillparzer, the greatest of the Austrian classics who was constantly in conflict with the reactionary regime of Metternich.

[31] Rank probably had in mind the fact that a typical gratification fantasy appears where the experience of adequate gratification fails to occur. This is a fact which became generally known at a later stage in the development of psychoanalysis.

if someone did not kill his brother, then Rank assumes that repression was successful. These are weaknesses which must be criticized. Meisl sees in a publication of this type (1) a danger for the science of psychology, (2) dangers for Freud's theories. For people would seize upon the opportunity given by the weaknesses in Rank's books to repudiate also Freud's teachings.

Meisl turns also against the "incestuous" interpretation of the sister's "keeping house" for the brother: there are certainly other motives involved. And if a poet in a love poem sings of his beloved as of his mother or sister, he simply wishes to indicate that he desires to concentrate on himself all the love of which she is capable. The interpretation of Schiller's letters to his sister as indicative of incestuous tendencies, Meisl says, is more than audacious.[32]

GRAF advises caution in the interpretation of artistic creations. Only where certain motifs were especially elaborated and were recurrent could one draw conclusions regarding the sexual life. It should be an easy task to interpret Goethe's work, in view of the enormous autobiographical material available. As to Schiller, he has found one motif to be particularly pronounced, that is hate for the father, manifested as hatred of tyrants. In his opinion, Rank's argument, in trying to demonstrate that almost the entire scale of incestuous impulses was present in Schiller, is far too hypothetical.

[A.] DEUTSCH emphasizes the significance of the fact that poets in their early works so often use incestuous material (a fact already stressed by Rank in his paper). It covers the entire range, from the simplest forms of incestuous tendencies to actual incest; we must include among these, for example, the case of a brother spying on his sister while she is undressing. As to the technique of Rank's paper, Deutsch states that he would prefer, instead of a chronological treatment, an effort to crystallize certain formulae and to group the material accordingly.

BACH mentions Grimm's fairy tale *Allerleirauh,* which begins with an incest. Then he speaks of Keller's[33] short novel, *Frau Regel Amrein*

---

[32] Another instance showing the resistances against psychoanalysis in an individual who accepts the psychoanalytic teachings!

[33] Gottfried Keller (1819-1890), famous Swiss author.

und ihr Jüngster,[34] the theme of which is the relation between mother and son. A newspaper clipping has been found which gave Keller the impulse to write this novel when he was a student in Berlin; it was about a fourteen-year-old boy who attacked his mother's lover with an iron rod. Bach sees also in *Der grüne Heinrich*[35] a masked representation of the mother-son relationship; surely, Agnes and Judith were sisters. Love of mother and daughter for the same man is a topic in the dramatic fragment *Therese* by Keller. He believes that only artists who themselves had a definite relationship create this type of literature.[36] Hence one can see that such representations need not be rooted directly in incestuous experiences of the author. Referring in this connection to the fraternal hatred in the *Braut von Messina*,[37] Bach stresses that Schiller had no brother and relates that he had a very peculiar relationship to his wife's sister; there was general amazement when he married his wife.

The question seems even more complex in musicians; in Mozart's *Cosi fan tutte* there occurs an exchange of wives; this is again reminiscent of an episode in *Der grüne Heinrich* which takes place in Munich, where, during a quadrille, the couples change [partners].

RANK explains that he can only reply very briefly to individual remarks. He cannot help but stick to his conviction that art must perish when the unconscious is made conscious. Against Häutler he asserts that artists are the ones who attain the highest degree of consciousness among their contemporaries, and that therefore it is *in them* that such transition takes place. To Federn's remark that incestuous relations are inescapable in the case of Cain and Abel, Rank replies that these myths were indeed a creation of much later cultural periods, onto which the incestuous feelings of these later periods were projected. (It would seem that this consideration also refutes Freud's objection concerning Uranos and Chronos.)

To Hitschmann's remark about the incestuous inclinations, Rank adds that he himself had similar ideas. For just as he had found in

[34] *Mrs. Regel Amrein and Her Youngest Son.*

[35] *Green Henry*, by Gottfried Keller.

[36] This sentence cannot be understood, unless it is assumed that Bach said "no definite relationship . . ." instead of "a definite relationship" [*ausgesprochenes Verhältnis*].

[37] *The Bride of Messina*, by Schiller.

28

his investigations that there is no homosexuality, so there are no "incestuous" impulses either; all of this is to be considered in relation to the subject and not as an objective fact.[38] Often we find that those who attend the children of so-called better families take the parents' place in the neuroses of these children: wet nurse, nurse, housemaid, cook, governess, woman or man teacher, valet, coachman, tutor. It is not true that the child's sexual passions turn to the mother because she is the mother, but because she is the first person associated with the earliest and most powerful "sexual" experiences (sucking, and the like); this is the point from which an investigation of the etiology of incest should start.

Referring to Kahane's "economic" observation, Rank gives examples from legends, where incest between brother and sister occasionally is motivated by the desire to conserve possessions. (This, however, seems to me—as all "economic motives"—a disguising motive designed to mask the sexual root.—Rank.[39])

In answer to Federn's remark that fratricide could have other than incestuous motives, Rank says that in almost all cases the rudiments of incestuous inclinations can be reconstructed.

FREUD, at the end of the meeting, tells of a disguised form of the dream of incest with the mother. The dreamer relates: he and his family, father, brothers, and sisters, are in front of the entrance to a house. The father and the others enter and ascend a narrow passageway. Finally he, too, goes inside. He has the vague recollection of *having been in there once before.*

It is noteworthy that the dreamer enumerates the whole family with the exception of the mother; if one inverts the sentence that all the others go inside to the effect that he alone goes inside, the narration becomes meaningful. It is then the mother's vagina, for this is the place where he has been once before.

---

[38] These are, indeed, bold statements. It is interesting to discover these very early forebodings of Rank's later defection. See Jessie Taft: *Otto Rank—A Biographical Study.* New York: Julian Press, 1958.

[39] Rank seems to have added this observation after the meeting, when going over the protocol.

4

SCIENTIFIC MEETING on October 31, 1906

Present: Freud, Adler, [A.] Deutsch, Federn, Frey, Stekel, Hitschmann, Kahane, Hollerung, Rank.

COMMUNICATIONS

FREUD reports the publication of a treatise by Jung, on hysteria, dreams and associations.[1]

HOLLERUNG mentions a lecture on memory, given by Urbantschitsch at the Philosophical Society.[2] The lecturer reported an experiment in which the high and low tones of a tuning fork had exercised a [differential] influence upon the capacity of experimental subjects to remember (and reproduce).

FREY announces a paper on neurasthenic and idyllic poetry, also a short paper (to be given in addition to another paper) on the megalomania of normal persons.

---

[1] *Assoziation, Traum und hysterisches Symptom* [*Association, Dream and Hysterical Symptom*]. In author's *Diagnostische Assoziationsstudien* [*Diagnostic Studies of Associations*], Vol. II. Leipzig: Barth, 1906.

[2] Dr. Victor Urbantschitsch, Viennese otologist, was the father of Dr. Rudolf Urbantschitsch who became a follower of Freud at an early date. The paper mentioned here is probably identical with the essay, "Über Sinnesempfindungen und Gedächtnisbilder" ["On Sense Perceptions and Mnemonic Pictures"], in *Pflügers Archiv*, 1905.

PRESENTATION

Review of Bleuler's book: Affectivity, Suggestibility and Paranoia[3]

SPEAKER: HITSCHMANN

HITSCHMANN: Bleuler begins by stressing the fact, recognized even by "psychiatry," that the human mind falls ill in typical forms; this leads to the assumption that the structure of the human mind is uncomplicated.

Bleuler endeavors in his book to throw some light on paranoia, which is such a mysterious illness. According to Kraepelin,[4] paranoia develops as a permanent, unshakable delusion; in combinatory paranoia, the illness is based on a mistaken interpretation of incorrect *impressions;* in fantastic paranoia, it is based merely on delusions of the senses. According to Bleuler, however, its basis is a *chronic affect* which had once arisen in response to an actual experience; this affect becomes the starting point for the delusional idea. There are, in addition, the predisposition of which we know nothing as yet, and certain predisposing experiences which Bleuler believes to concern the individual's sexual life; in this he follows Freud.

Bleuler replaces the vague concepts of feelings, sensations, and the like, by the concept of affectivity; he includes in this concept all that which is connected with feelings of pleasure and unpleasure. Bleuler stresses the significance of the affect for mental life: associations are either inhibited or furthered by the affect. In the wish dream and the wish hysteria, he says, it is the emotion, the affect alone, that fulfills the wish. The affect, however, results from the entire psychic constellation of the individual. Bleuler discerns different types of repression, dependent upon the differing reactions of individuals to the affects. Moreover, it is also due to affectivity that we turn our attention only to matters which are of interest to us. In examining the relationship of affects to instincts, Bleuler comes to the conclusion that there is only

[3] Eugen Bleuler (1857-1939), foremost Swiss psychiatrist. The book's original title is *Affektivität, Suggestibilität und Paranoia* (Halle: Marhold, 1906).

[4] Emil Kraepelin (1856-1926), eminent German psychiatrist, professor of psychiatry in Munich, author of a textbook on psychiatry.

31

a single instinct, the sexual one. In the psychoses, the affects are abnormally increased. Affectivity is closer to the processes of willing, that is, to the drives; essentially, affect and drive are one and the same.

In Bleuler's view, suggestibility is one of the manifestations of affectivity. In hypnosis, the affect of submitting-to-being-strongly-impressed plays the chief part.[5] Under certain circumstances, however, there may also exist a primary tendency to reject external influences (stubborn). He considers wishfulfillment dreams to be a result of autosuggestion.

In the chapter on "Paranoia," Bleuler presents several examples, each of which demonstrates the link of the "experienced" affect with a definite complex of ideas. Inherent in each ideational complex is the tendency to assimilate new experiences. Bleuler postulates several complexes, e.g., the *striving to get ahead,* which may turn into a delusion of persecution if there are persons who obstruct its path; *self-reliance* which may lead to megalomania; the *desire to be loved* which may lead to *erotic paranoia;* and several others. However, he is not able to explain the nature of paranoia, nor can he define more closely the [concept] "predisposition."

DISCUSSION

ADLER begins by stressing that Bleuler's book does not serve to give any psychiatrist more understanding. An investigation has to start from the point at which the fixed idea and the hallucinations originate. Freud has taught, through the example of his own work, that psychic occurrences have to be investigated from a psychological point of view and in a psychological way. Bleuler combines physiological with psychological points of view.

FREUD says that he finds himself in agreement with Adler's arguments except on one point. Although it is true that Bleuler's book is not too impressive, still it contains one thought of great originality; namely, the idea that it is an affect that gives rise to the illness; nowhere else in the entire literature on paranoia is this idea to be found. "Affectivity" is indeed a mere term which explains nothing—as Hitsch-

[5] Suggestibility thus seems based on passive, masochistic drives, a craving to submit to authority.

32

mann has already indicated in his review. In general, Bleuler has much too much reverence for words; his way of using the word "complex" is a good example. Freud points to Bleuler's halfhearted acceptance of his [Freud's] ideas; for instance, Bleuler lacks any understanding of sexual matters. True, he lays stress upon the affect of "allowing-one-self-to-be-impressed," but he does not see that this is a "sexual affect," its roots being the sadomasochistic component of the sexual instinct.[6]

In discussing the mechanism of paranoia, Bleuler omitted any mention of repression. The falsifications of memory in paranoia are indeed selective (hence also results of repression). Freud assumes that paranoia is essentially the result of quite definite sexual influences. Furthermore, the source of the affect as well as the delusional idea must be elucidated. As to the overstressed, supervalent idea,[7] Freud emphasizes that it is through repression that such ideas have become overly strong. A repression of this type is, for instance, the repression by means of the opposite entering consciousness.[8] Such reactions characterize the parvenu. These reaction symptoms appear also with many paranoid ideas: this mechanism deserves the name of *mechanism of projection*.[9] The mechanism is frequently employed in normal life and it is from such normal examples that one must proceed.—The mechanism of paranoia is comparatively clear, but the processes leading to paranoia must still be explored.

RANK introduces his remarks by stating that he really has no relationship to Bleuler's work. He, too, has the impression that the affect plays the main part in all psychic processes (whether normal or pathological), whereas the "idea" remains in the background; for the entire human being with all of his past is, so to speak, attached to his affect. In connection with a remark by Bleuler about conversion, Rank raises the question of the nature, conditions, causes, and mechanism of conversion. (FREUD answers this question by referring to Adler

[6] This is an early indication by Freud of the sexual meaning of hypnosis as mirrored in the transference.

[7] The concept of the "supervalent idea" [*überwertige Idee*] originated with the psychiatrist Carl Wernicke (1848-1905).

[8] Today this process would be designated as countercathexis.

[9] The term "mechanism of projection" had been introduced by Freud before this in his "Further Remarks on the Defence Neuro-Psychoses" (1896) (*C.P.*, 1:155-182).

and saying that the preconditions of conversion are to be looked for in sexuality and are connected with the erotogenic zones.)

STEKEL is dissatisfied with the "objective" kind of review Hitschmann has given and misses the personal touch. In the normal person, too, one encounters powerful affects, supervalent ideas, and the like. But, unlike the paranoiac, we can correct, we can balance that. The paranoiac is in the state in which we all are while dreaming; in paranoia, the unconscious spreads itself over the entire waking life of the individual.

Stekel then tries to find short formulae for the various psychoneuroses, on the basis of the "psychic conflict" involved; he thinks that neurasthenia, for instance, could be explained as the result of the conflict between the diseased sexual potency and the powerful sex drive, whereas hysteria originates in the conflict between desires and aversion to sex. In hypochondria, the sexual drive comes into conflict with anxiety, while in paranoia the sexual drive is sublimated to some extent. (In the delusion of being an inventor this sublimation becomes clearly apparent.)

Lastly Stekel expresses his opinion that nothing new or important is to be expected from Bleuler; Bleuler's last book, *Unbewusste Gemeinheiten*,[10] gave him additional reason for this judgment.

Nevertheless, Stekel mentions as an important insight Bleuler's emphasis on the affective aspect of suggestion: it is not the idea, but the affect that is suggested (transferred).

HOLLERUNG finds nothing interesting in Bleuler's arguments. He misses precise definitions of concepts (as, for instance, the concept of will). He asks Freud whether Bleuler's view of psychic censorship as a result of social training is in accordance with his own ideas. (FREUD answers in the negative: the censor is in the first place the result of the organic sexual repression; social rearing is of secondary importance.)

FEDERN says that there can be no thought without affective content either in the child or in primitive man; an infantile component of paranoia might therefore be seen in the regression from intellectuality to affectivity. It would also be of interest to know to what social strata

10 [*Unconscious Meannesses*]. Munich: Reinhardt, 1905.

paranoiacs belong. (FREUD remarks that this particular neurosis affects all strata.)

Finally, Federn stresses that it would be of great interest to ascertain under what circumstances the affect is operative, that is, whether it has to be of a definite intensity, or whether a certain corresponding disposition (with a comparatively normal affect) would suffice to produce paranoia.

HITSCHMANN states, in connection with Federn's remark, that he, too, has the impression that the affect in paranoia is weak, of, so to speak, normal intensity. A sharp delineation of the concept of paranoia seems desirable to him.

FREUD emphasizes in his closing remarks that imbeciles often incline to paranoia, but that, on the other hand, there are also outstanding and highly gifted people who fall ill with paranoia. He calls attention to a certain ophthalmic innervation in paranoid patients (which STEKEL confirms): in this condition the upper segment of the eye is bared.[11]

To demonstrate the dulling effect of affect inhibition, Freud relates that one of his patients on one day was utterly devoid of understanding, whereas on the following day she showed a high degree of intelligence.

To Bleuler's remark that children and hysterics are characterologically similar inasmuch as they are stubborn at one time and accessible to influence at another, Freud adds the explanation that both are accessible to beloved persons and inaccessible to those whom they do not love. Thus, the uneducability of "naughty" children finds its explanation in autoerotism; if the child finds the "love" in himself, he does not need the love of parents and teachers. The accessibility to influence also represents the ultimate source of the capacity to form a judgment: affirmation of the judgment of the cherished person is the source of judgment. Here the derivation of faith from love is apparent. The capacity for independent judgment, however, is acquired only when the human being begins to question parental authority.[12]

[11] "The piercing glance of the paranoiac."

[12] Compare Freud: "The achievement of the function of judgement only becomes feasible, however, after the creation of the symbol of negation has endowed thought with a first degree of independence from the results of repression and at the same time from the sway of the pleasure principle" ("Negation," 1925. C.P., 5:185).

5

SCIENTIFIC MEETING on November 7, 1906

Present: Freud, Adler, Bass, [A.] Deutsch, Federn, Heller, Hitschmann, Hollerung, Häutler, Rank, Reitler, Stekel, Kahane.

PRESENTATION

On the [Organic] Bases of Neuroses

SPEAKER: DR. ALFRED ADLER

In view of the forthcoming publication of Adler's book, we will not record his paper in detail.[1]

ADLER states first that his new paper takes as its starting point the result of his investigations of the "Physiology and Pathology of the Erotogenic Zones," which he communicated last year.

He emphasizes that certain morphological phenomena of deficiency, characteristic of a primary inferiority, can be observed in an inferior organ. On the other hand, an organ's inferiority may be masked in such a way that the organ functions satisfactorily, or even excessively. This

[1] *Studie über die Minderwertigkeit von Organen* [*Studies on the Inferiority of Organs*]. Vienna: Urban & Schwarzenberg, 1907.

increase in efficiency of an (inferior) organ does not, however, occur in the organ itself but rather in the nerve segment responsible for the higher function of the organ. Inferiority of a single organ is a rare finding: in most cases, inferiority is present in two or more organs concurrently. The organ most frequently coupled with another inferior one is the sexual organ. However, this is partially due to heredity. He stresses that he is not talking about phenomena connected with illness, for an individual may be perfectly healthy despite an inferior organ. He adds, however, that it is quite true that the inferiority of an organ can be established with absolute certainty only when it shows an accumulation of morbid symptoms. The so-called "childhood defects" which appear in an organ during the developmental period are also characteristic of the inferior organ. Adler found, for example, severe changes in the structure of the eye connected with color blindness, strabismus, and the like. The intensity of such phenomena may vary in the individual members of a family.

Adler sees a third characteristic of organ inferiority in an anomaly of the reflexes (with heightened sensibility of erotogenic zones). He mentions as an example his observations of the palatolaryngeal reflex; he could demonstrate three different forms of this reflex: a deficient reflex, a hyperactive reflex (before contact, for example), and a normal reflex. Just as "childhood defects" could be traced back through the family tree (that is, were shown to be hereditary), reflex anomalies were also shown to be hereditary.

Adler now comes to his main topic: starting from the organ, there occurs a development of the corresponding areas of the brain and thereby the foundation of the psyche is established ["wie es nämlich vom Organ aus zu einer Ausbildung der dazugehörigen Gehirnpartien und damit zur Grundlegung der Psyche kommt"]. He says that, on the one hand, the higher functional morphological development of an organ is a consequence of the assimilation of external stimuli; on the other hand, it may also be the result of the effort to make an inferior organ capable of performing its function. This is achieved by overcompensation: the inferiority of the organ is counterbalanced by increased cerebral activity. First, the individual's attention is constantly drawn to the inferior organ, which is far more vulnerable than a normal one; such attention is usually provoked by an insignificant

Über die Grundlagen der Neurosen.

Vortragender Dr. Alfred Adler.

Mit Rücksicht auf die von Adler in Aussicht gestellte baldige Publikation seiner Arbeit wird von einer ausführlichen Wiedergabe seines Vortrags abgesehen.

Adler erwähnt zunächst, dass seine neue Arbeit an die von ihm in einigen Jahre mitgeteilten Ergebnisse seiner Untersuchungen über die Physiologie und Pathologie der erogenen Zonen anknüpfe.

Als wichtig hebt er zunächst hervor, dass bei der Minderwertigkeit eines Organs gewisse morphologische Ausfallserscheinungen zu beobachten sind, die die ursprüngliche Minderwertigkeit kennzeichnen. Die Minderwertigkeit eines Organs könne aber auch verdeckt sein, so dass dieses Organ dann genügende oder selbst mehr als genügende (übervertige) Leistungen vollbringe. Die Ueberhebung eines Organs gehe aber nicht von ihm selbst aus, sondern von dem betreffenden Nervenabschnitt, der die höhere Funktion des minderwertigen Organs leistet. Die Minderwertigkeit eines einzelnen Organs komme sehr selten vor; meist komme Minderwertigkeit von zwei oder mehr Organen zugleich vor.

das Organ, das die Minderwertigkeit anderer Organe meist be-
gleitet, ist das Sexualorgan. Es hänge oft um Teil mit
der Heredität zusammen. Es seien jedoch nicht nicht krank-
hafte Erscheinungen gemeint, sondern es sei bei der Minderwertigkeit eines Organs vollkommene Gesundheit des Individuums möglich.
In unzweifelhafter Weise festzustellen sei die Minderwertigkeit eines
Organs allerdings erst dann, wenn sich gehäufte Krankheitser-
scheinungen an diesem Organ zeigten. Ein zweites Charakteristikon

injury to the inferior organ. The organic repression (Freud) which applies to this organ also serves to direct the psyche's interest to it.

There seems to be a direct relationship between this increased activity of the central nervous system in childhood and the development of childhood defects. In neurotics, childhood defects seem to be the rule, and the effort to compensate for these childhood defects marks the entire life of the individuals concerned. The childhood defect is, in reality, nothing but the visible manifestation of the struggle to make an inferior organ capable of cultural adaptation. The persistence of the childhood failing is a consequence of the interest directed toward the organ. The child's entire activity is aimed at gaining pleasure; these sensuous feelings of pleasure link the individual to the external world. In full, normal development, the pursuit of pleasure is gradually relinquished for cultural endeavors; the inferior organ, however, continues to strive for pleasure gain and makes this its habit. Increased external demands also unmask an organ as inferior. The normal organ has a psychic superstructure which corresponds to increased brain activity when the organ is inferior. Harmony between physical and psychic activity—this psychophysical parallelism in the true sense of the word—is characteristic of the development of the normal child. "Overcompensation" often brings about supervalence of the organ, hence also of the psychomotor superstructure. If such an overcompensation cannot be achieved because the inferior organ meets with an inferior brain, then this arrest half along the way could be considered an "unsuccessful repression."

Adler mentions in passing that some childhood defects (such as blinking, vomiting, and so on) are nothing but reflexes which have become manifest.

According to Adler's argument, the chief cause of sexual precocity could be traced to organ inferiority and the presence of childhood defects, since the inferiority of any other organ is accompanied by some inferiority of the sexual organ.

Adler gives only a few indications of the "content" of the psychomotor superstructure: feelings, recollection, and memory are a part of it, as are also criticism, insight into connections, and a certain component of the choice of a profession. As examples of supervalent performances he mentions hallucinations, intuition, and introspection (the ability to see psychic connections). A certain sublimation of the reflex actions represents another group of psychic functions: the affects, for example, stem from the psychic superstructure of the organic reflex (disgust, anxiety, but also the libido and the mental compulsion).

Each organ has its memory, which is a function of the psychomotor superstructure. That kind of memory which derives from an inferior organ will be dominant. In sexual precocity there are two dominant centers. In the course of cultural development, the nonsexual one becomes predominant. The nonsexual superstructure usurps the dominant role; from this point on, a path leads to the unconscious (to sexuality).

Finally, Adler refers to several well-known persons as examples of supervalent performances of inferior organs: Beethoven [who was deaf]; Mozart, who was said to have had misshapen ears; Schumann, who suffered from a psychosis which began with auditory hallucinations. He speaks also of a family which he had occasion to observe, in which an ear disease was hereditary: some members of this family became outstanding musicians; in this same family, there are also cases of neurosis and of precocity.

(FREUD remarks at this point that Lenbach[2] was blind in one eye.)

Furthermore, Adler says, he analyzed a musician whose two auricles were differently shaped. As a child he had suffered a perforation of the tympanic membrane. His first musical recollection stems from his fourth year: [he heard] a schoolteacher playing the violin at a time when he, as a little boy, was in the next room in bed with the schoolteacher's adult daughter. Each further stage of his artistic development coincided with sexual experiences.

Adler has frequently been able to demonstrate [the existence of] speech defects in singers, actors, and orators (Demosthenes, Moses). A profession is chosen upon the demand of the inferior organ; cooks, for example, frequently show abnormal palatal reflexes (however, this is also true of obese people who may be said to have no other occupation beyond eating.)[3]

---

[2] Franz von Lenbach (1863-1904), German painter.

[3] This is the point from which Adlerian psychology proceeds. Subsequently it will become clear how Adler's way parts from Freud's.

DISCUSSION

HITSCHMANN remarks that he himself has always advocated searching for "organic factors" as a background of the neuroses. Both the psyche and the body should be given their just due. In Adler's work he misses statistical data, which are of course indispensable in dealing with such topics. As an argument against Adler's exposition he points out that organic inferiority does not necessarily result in neurosis. He believes, however, that an actual illness of some organ is hidden behind the so-called nervous diseases; this is particularly true of the heart (where, in addition, the neurosis can also lead to secondary organic changes). In his opinion, the investigations of the palatal reflex are of little value in view of recent publications on this subject.[4] Finally, he objects to some of Adler's examples which he does not consider conclusive (for instance, the cases of Schumann, Mozart, and Lenbach; it is not so astonishing, he says, that a musician like Schumann should suffer from auditory hallucinations). There are also many musicians who are blind. He concedes, however, that the struggle of an inferior organ for cultural efficiency [*Kulturfähigkeit*] leads, in some degree, to mental growth.

FREUD first turns against Hitschmann and his "rationalistic" point of view.

He attributes great importance to Adler's work; it has brought his own work a step further. To judge from the immediate impression, much of what Adler said may be correct.[5]

He singled out two leading ideas as significant and fertile: (1) the concept of compensation, according to which an organic inferiority is counterbalanced by a supervalent cerebral activity,[6] and (2) that the repression is accomplished by the formation of a psychic superstructure. A similar formulation had occurred to him.[7]

He can adduce the fact that in persons whose egotism, excessive

---

[4] The reference here is probably to W. Baumann: "On the Palatal Reflex." *Münch. med. Wschr.*, 53, 1906.

[5] With these remarks Freud acknowledges the stimulation he received from these discussions. Over and over again one can see how glad he was to give recognition.

[6] It seems that Freud had in mind what was later characterized as an overcompensation or counterbalance for a narcissistic "injury" although he uses "anatomical" language here.

[7] This may refer to the formulation that repression is accomplished by the ego.

ambition, and the like are prominent, analysis uncovers serious organic defects as the deepest cause. He has found, for example, hypospadia in a young man who was extremely ambitious. A woman of exceptional intellectual capacities had a curvature of the spine. He also knew women who were greatly chagrined by the prominence of the small labia; the entire development of these women was directed toward compensating for this defect.

He considers interesting and significant the fact, pointed out by Adler, that the child's activity is aimed at gaining pleasure freely and that this is given up later on. He should like to offer Adler a formulation which had occurred to him in connection with the investigations of Ehrenfels:[8] the neurosis is to be traced back to the disparity between constitutional Anlage and the demands made on the individual by his culture.[9] The deterioration which is frequently observed in families who move from the country to the city also belongs in this category.

Another idea which he also wishes to single out is that of the derivation of affects from reflexes.

Adler cites examples from German mythology of tales in which the hero's stage of glamour is preceded by a somber youth (childhood). Freud adds the tale of the ugly duckling which becomes a swan.

Lastly, Freud has to voice one main objection. However, this concerns only the formal aspect of the paper: the choice of the term inferiority, which he himself does not like, shows no great originality; it might, perhaps, be better to speak of a certain variability of the organs.

FEDERN says that the work is congenial to him. He would be in favor of analyzing the supervalence or the inferiority of people according to the individual elements of their endowment. Certainly, some part of a neurosis is traceable to organic predisposition. However, this part must be specified.

He opposes Adler's contention that the memory of the inferior organ

[8] Christian Freiherr von Ehrenfels (1895-1936), Austrian philosopher, professor in Prague. His *Sexualethik* [*Sexual Ethics*] was published in 1907. He gave two papers as the guest of the Vienna Society; the protocols of these two meetings will be found in Volume II of these *Minutes*.

[9] Freud may refer here to what was later called "etiological supplementary series," which means that constitution and external experiences supplement each other.

would be the dominant one. In his opinion, the memory of a sound organ would be more likely to be the operative one.

The first indication of organ inferiority may perhaps be seen in the fact that the organ's capacity to distinguish develops slowly. He has known an individual who was color blind during childhood but who later became entirely normal.

Adler's explanation of Beethoven's talent reminds him of Lombroso's theory;[10] the potentiality of illness is much greater in the genius, and, also, his illness is more conspicuous.

He suggests that inferiority of certain parts of the vestibular apparatus may also be of some account in neurotic illness and mentions people who are unable to dance, jump, dive, and the like. An inferior constitution of the musculature combined with a neurotic disposition might lead to abulia. A strong musculature brings a child victorious experiences. He discusses individually the musculature of the pharynx, the intestines, the genital organs (enuresis?), and points particularly to the "cardiac neurosis of puberty." One of the chief causes of all types of inferiority may well be related to vascular anomalies.

In reference to Freud's remark, Federn stresses that it is always an unfavorable factor when a family suddenly changes its standards of living.

REITLER says that he cannot help taking a negative view of Adler's paper. He must state two principal reasons: one contains something new; the other is well known to us, namely, that the child's enjoyment of organic pleasures gradually gives way to cultural activity. The new idea is that an inferior organ can be rendered supervalent by means of compensatory cerebral activity. Adler has supplied no proof for this assertion. Such supervalence might perhaps be a reality for the artist, but even this has not been established. No hysterical symptom can take hold of an organ unless there is already a *locus minoris resistentiae*. However, contrary to Adler's contention, the determining factor is the psyche which takes hold of the *locus minoris resistentiae*.

Lastly, he remarks that it seems to him that Adler attributes far too much importance to heredity.

[10] Cesare Lombroso (1836-1909), Italian psychiatrist and criminologist, tried to prove that genius, insanity, and crime have the same organic roots.

HÄUTLER points out that, in this work, Adler's favorite idea, polarization, again makes its appearance. In considering the development of a higher efficiency in an inferior organ by means of compensation, one must first take into account the point stressed by Freud that any limitation of the individual's capacity to function is of significance in the development of a neurosis. Rather than "inferiority," he would prefer to say "prone to variation." The potentiality for variability might be conceived of in terms of a sum of energies. If an organ endowed with this potential energy is not prone to variation, then it is normal; however, if it is prone to variation, then part of its energy is dissipated in the process of variation.

STEKEL cannot see any progress in this work. In his opinion, it merely paraphrases Freudian ideas in organic terms. Moreover, the lecture has been too tedious. Adler should have introduced his theory by starting from practical cases. Stekel can cite the case of a great pianist: as a child of three he would lie on the floor to listen to piano-playing in the room below; at five, he played the piano; at seven, he composed. In this case, the "overcompensation" would have had to occur at an impossibly early time.

He must completely contradict the contention that in hysteria a predisposing organic component must be present for a symptom to develop.[11] He cites the case of a waiter who was stricken with a hysterical "paralysis" of the hand as "God's punishment" for a "forbidden" handshake.

HOLLERUNG welcomes Adler's paper. He has found one point which he would describe as an incongruence: what is transmitted by heredity comes into conflict, as it were, with social conditions. In the normal person, a leveling of this incongruence is possible. If this leveling cannot be accomplished, development will be abnormal. What is inherited, however, is often atavistic.

RANK says that he is not able to discuss the medical aspects of the paper. He is mainly interested in what Adler has set forth about the artist: Adler's explanation of the "sensualistic" artistic activity seems most plausible and correct to him in so far as it pertains to the painter,

[11] This refers to Freud's assumption that symptoms of conversion hysteria develop only on the basis of an *organic compliance*.

the musician, and the like. However, with the poet, matters are more complicated: here, the psychic superstructure is of paramount importance. Finally, Rank states that, in his book on incest, he came to conclusions similar to Adler's but from a different starting point. In poets, he has found skin afflictions and visual disturbances to be different forms of defense against exhibitionism; in such cases, it becomes quite apparent in what way the psychic superstructure rests upon the organ, for these poets quite easily become the victims of real eye or skin diseases for which they have a predisposition.

HELLER considers Adler's work an impressive intellectual achievement. Its intuitive aspects seem quite plausible to him. He sees in it a continuation of and supplement to Freud's ideas. Among painters of his acquaintance he recalls many afflicted with optic disturbances or visual defects. A Munich physician has diagnosed organic disturbances of vision in 70 per cent of Stuck's students.[12]

BASS begins by thanking the lecturer for the manifold stimulations which the paper has given him, and puts some material at Adler's disposal. He knows a musician who during childhood suffered perforations of both ear drums; he could not stand the sound of brass instruments and had an ejaculation whenever he heard it.

He can also give an example to illustrate the heredity of childhood failings. He himself blinked from his ninth to his tenth year. His child was extremely sensitive to light until his second year. The sudden flash of a match in a dark room would cause him to sneeze. Later on, this sensitivity subsided.

Recently, he examined a patient who was twenty-eight years old, 6 feet 1 inch tall, but who had the genitals of a fourteen-year-old, without hair. He has had no sexual intercourse and is deeply depressed about his genitals. He noticed for some time that his capacity to remember is diminishing. (ADLER remarks that gigantic size is frequently accompanied by small genitalia.)

FREUD remarks that cooks very frequently incline to psychoneurotic disturbances (especially to paranoia) and that good cooks are

[12] Franz von Stuck (1863-1928), painter and sculptor, professor at the Academy in Munich, a leading member of the group of artists who called themselves Secessionists.

always severely abnormal. (He mentions his own cook who invariably cooks particularly well when a period of illness is imminent.)

ADLER concludes by pointing out that he feels that his views have been confirmed by the fact that the same laws are rediscovered throughout the entire realm of pathology.

To the topic of the choice of a profession, he adds that medical men have often suffered from illnesses in their childhood.

6

SCIENTIFIC MEETING on November 14, 1906

Present: Freud, Adler, Federn (late), Graf (late), Hitschmann, Hollerung, Kahane, Meisl, Rank.

COMMUNICATIONS

FREUD proposes Dr. Isidor Sadger for acceptance in the Society and requests a statement on this matter next Wednesday.

PRESENTATION

Review of Semon's book: Mneme as the Preserving Principle in the Changing Processes of Organic Life[1]

SPEAKER: SURGEON-MAJOR-GENERAL HOLLERUNG

In consideration of the difficulties encountered in any attempt to give a brief rendition of Semon's system, perusal of the book itself is recommended.

---

[1] Richard Semon (1859-1918), German zoologist, advocated a new psycho-Lamarckian doctrine purporting that an established stimulus can permanently change an organism, leaving an imprint on it. Inherited and individually acquired imprints together form the *mneme*. The original German title of his book is *Die Mneme als erhaltendes Prinzip im Wechsel des organischen Geschehens* (Leipzig: Engelmann, 1904).

DISCUSSION

HITSCHMANN finds that Semon is merely coining new words for matters which we already know. He cannot see much value in this work.

FEDERN also considers the work on the whole a failure. He points out that Semon contradicts the work of Darwin and Nägeli,[2] denying the hereditary transmission of acquired characteristics. He disagrees with Semon's assertion that engrams can be acquired only through conscious impressions.

ADLER remarks on the unfortunate choice of new terms and takes exception to the useless playing with concepts without a thorough clarification of their meaning. To the question whether acquired characteristics are transmitted by heredity, Semon answers: "Only if they have reached a certain intensity in the chain of ancestors." In Adler's opinion, organic inferiority plays an important part in heredity. The acquisition of a trait is never accidental but is related to the whole constitution of the organ.

MEISL thinks that the group does not appreciate Semon's work adequately because they do not judge it objectively. He himself can supply two examples of the "release [ecphorization] of engrams." Just before he falls asleep, he frequently pictures to himself one of his friends. He can see him very distinctly. Then, with intense concentration, he can also hear him. Each time he feels curious about what the person will say, but afterwards has the feeling that he has heard the words before. This is a case, he says, in which there is an optical engram and an auditory engram releasing each other.

As a second example, he cites Helen Keller who once wrote a fairy tale, "Frost King," without being aware that its model had been read to her some years before. Meisl sees this as analogous to childhood (sexual) memories which initially are unconsciously engraved, and only later emerge as conscious recollections. The poet, too, uses in his works of fantasy his unconscious childhood recollections. He does this without becoming aware that they are connected with his own past experiences.

[2] Karl Wilhelm von Nägeli (1817-1891), Swiss botanist.

FREUD says that he has learned from Semon's book only that the Greek word for memory is *mneme*. The book is characteristic of those pseudo scientists who imitate exactitude merely by operating with numbers and concepts, and then feel that they have accomplished something. Hering's idea,[3] which is Semon's point of departure, is ingenious and subtle, but only the opposite can be said of Semon's work. Only he who has new things to say is entitled to coin new terms.

Freud chooses one example from among many: Semon's dismally miscarried attempt to link periodicity with memory. He does not see any real relationship between Urbantschitsch's experiment,[4] of which Hollerung spoke, and Semon's work. In his experiment, Urbantschitsch had the letters of a word written down in random order. He then asked the subject of the experiment to look at and reproduce the letters. The subject reproduced the letters in the position which they would actually have in the word, although he had not been told the word.

In this connection, Freud gives a most instructive example from his own practice. Among the early recollections of a rather unintelligent patient figured a scene with her brother. All she remembered was that her brother wanted to show her something and dragged her off. A curtain then closed the scene. Freud told her that the essential part of this scene would come to her in a single word. When this was of no avail, he told her (in order to take her censor by surprise) that the word would emerge letter by letter and that, with each pressure of his hand, one letter would emerge.[5] Ten or eleven letters came to her mind in this way. (Of one letter, she was not quite sure.) Under further pressure of his hand she arranged the letters in a certain sequence. First, she gave the vowels a fixed position; then the consonants. The resulting word was *medchnfogl* [*Mädchenvogel* = girl–bird].

In reference to [Helen] Keller, Freud says that Meisl is correct in pointing out a similarity [between her unawareness and] the remaining unconscious of childhood memories. It is difficult for strong im-

[3] Ewald Hering (1834-1918), German physiologist and psychologist. In 1870, he wrote *Über das Gedächtnis als eine allgemeine Funktion der organisierten Materie* [*On Memory as a General Function of Organized Matter*], English translation, 1897.
[4] See Minutes 4, October 31, 1906.
[5] In that stage of the development of psychoanalysis, Freud used the technique of eliciting memories and thoughts from his patients by a pressure of his hand on their forehead.

pressions to remain unconscious. It is easy for memories. Memory has a stronger effect than perception.

HOLLERUNG explains that Semon does in fact accept Darwin's work. The "engram" is nothing but the unconscious. Semon merely avoids this term.

7

SCIENTIFIC MEETING *on November 21, 1906*

Present: Freud, Adler, [A.] Deutsch, Federn, Frey, Hitschmann, Kahane, Rank, Reitler, Stekel.

COMMUNICATIONS

Dr. I. Sadger is admitted to the Society by unanimous vote (notified thereof on November 22, 1906). Häutler's vote is cast by Adler; Bass's by Kahane. Frey enters the name of Mr. Otto Soyka[1] for consideration for membership.

Frey borrows Minutes 1 to 4 inclusive; Deutsch borrows 5; 6 is not requested.

PRESENTATION

On the Megalomania of the Normal Person

SPEAKER: PHILIPP FREY

FREY emphasizes first that there are people who appear quite normal in the social sense but who cannot be considered entirely normal from the psychological point of view. Their souls bear "ugly"

---

[1] Otto Soyka, born 1882, Austrian writer, wrote in 1906 a study in moral philosophy: *Jenseits der Sittlichkeitsgrenzen* [*Beyond the Boundaries of Morality*].

marks, we might say. Freud has drawn attention to these half-normal persons. Indeed, he has shown (in his *Psychopathology of Everyday Life*) that even the "normal" individual is not entirely free of certain manifestations of the unconscious (suppressed). These are the same manifestations which we find, in greater intensity, in pathological individuals. The seeming contradiction in the title is to be understood in this sense. This sort of purely psychic (not sociologic) abnormality in relation to self-assertion is present in many people. In many cases this tendency to megalomania (conceit) turns out to be a compensation for the feeling of one's own inferiority.

Frey mentions Hjalmar (in Ibsen's *Wild Duck*), a man of subnormal will power and desire to work, who indulges in the mystic illusion that he is an inventor destined for great achievement. This illusion gives him strength in his struggle for survival.

Frey points out that it is particularly those people, placed in an intermediate position between real power and subordination, who gradually reach a state of presumptuousness [*Selbstüberhebung*[2]].

He mentions class consciousness and professional conceit and the self-importance of minor officials and similar examples. In instances like these, the individual overvalues his profession as well as his own performance in his profession.

As examples, he cites the head clerk of a Quai firm[3] who deems himself irreplaceable, the beadle inflated by conceit, the sergeant who considers himself more important than the captain, and others. (Later he adds religious presumptuousness.)

Although psychologically abnormal, these people behave normally from the sociological point of view to the extent that they curb their delusional ideas at the right moment and prevent any such expression at times when it would be harmful to themselves. But whenever it does not seem hazardous to give vent to their megalomania (e.g., when they are dealing with subordinates or indulging in fantasies), they give it full play.

This compensatory phenomenon does not appear in people who find real satisfactions in their life and in their work.

[2] *Selbstüberhebung* has been variously translated as presumptuousness, self-importance, etc.

[3] Franz Joseph Quai, formerly a well-known business section in Vienna.

In concluding, he mentions the megalomania encountered in specific professions. A uniform (or special form of attire)[4] seems to arouse a sort of "intoxication" in normal individuals. The megalomania of psychiatrists should be considered in this same category.

At no time have there been as many representatives of such semipathological existences as there are nowadays. They merit more intensive study.

DISCUSSION

KAHANE notes that Frey has entirely omitted to mention the megalomania of poets, actors, and artists. He calls attention also to the megalomania of nations, chauvinism. He mentions also the "chosen people" driven to this compensatory glorification by continuous, fierce outside pressure.

The source of megalomania is in a real feeling of insignificance. In his opinion, megalomania is most likely to develop in people who are faced with the real danger of being undervalued; for example, the actor who is bound to fear that he may lose the favor of his audience or fall into oblivion. The struggle for a position in social life also prepares the ground for megalomania.

In certain primitive tribes, the name for the tribe is identical with the word for human being. This is meant to indicate that people from other tribes are not human beings.

He thinks that the megalomania of poets and artists stems from a lack of true control of their creative work; absolute, incontestable judgment simply does not exist in these fields.

STEKEL says that he is working with the same theme in a play which he is just writing, called *The Insatiable*. He attributes the far more frequent appearance of this phenomenon in our time to decreasing respect for the individual. According to him, the megalomania of the subaltern is an identification with his superior. Certainly megalomania has a sexual root, and "smallness" in the sexual sphere can frequently bring out conceit displayed toward the outside world (henpecked husbands, busybodies in clubs, and the like).

4 Military uniform, for instance, particularly in Austria and Germany.

HITSCHMANN points out that a feeling of magic, of creative power, lifts the poet above all others; in this the poet really is wholly different from the average person. He remarks that some degree of conceit or professional pride often is produced in order to ward off a feeling of shame attached to some occupations. (For instance, the prostitute in Tolstoy's *Resurrection* is not the least ashamed of her profession.) The person in question needs an antitoxin against the feeling of shame, as it were.

Then he refers to the ever-present desire to feel at ease and to eliminate what is disagreeable; the ability to create illusions is related to this human trait.

Whatever increases self-reliance is life-promoting; whatever diminishes self-confidence is inimical to life (asceticism, suicide, world-weariness as in *Werther*,[5] despondency, pessimism and the like).

[A.] DEUTSCH points to one element always present in the etiology of megalomania: an individual who obeys all rules and precepts feels entitled to judge severely those who do not do so; he produces this conceit at the cost of the repressions demanded by strict adherence to the laws.[6]

FREUD remarks that megalomania in women, not mentioned by Frey, is indeed most interesting. Frey has briefly referred to the source of megalomania and Deutsch has amplified his suggestion; the fantasies (daydreams) of *young people* are this source. For later megalomania shows a different character inasmuch as it can so easily be refuted by logic. These persons then procure for themselves in fantasy the fulfillment of their adolescent desires. This is related to the indestructibility of human desires (the dead bridegroom who comes for the bride, etc.): the original wishes return over and over again, only in different forms. This compulsion to satisfy in fantasy the ambitious dreams of puberty (if life has not granted their fulfillment) and the added influence of repressions and renunciations (Deutsch) both combine to produce conceit.

Freud mentions in particular the megalomania of those scholars

[5] Novel by Goethe.
[6] This sentence is unintelligible in the form it has been recorded. Deutsch probably meant to say: ". . . in compensation for the repressions. . . ."

whose attainments have not been equal to their own expectations. They replace their actual shortcomings with exaggerated self-esteem. The megalomania which is a regular attribute of artists has its root in the fact that in the field of art not every capable man is valued and respected as he would be in another profession.

In art, only the very great are honored. Just those artists who have lagged behind are the ones who become presumptuous.

The megalomania of young people, their arrogance, is, one might say, not a permanent, genuine megalomania. In such individuals one discovers that diminished self-reliance, an inner instability, is at the core of the arrogant shell.

Megalomania takes powerful nourishment from that portion of autoerotism which everyone has preserved to a greater or lesser extent.[7] In regard to the concept of "the pathological," Freud comments that not only deviations from the normal belong there but also that which has the character of being useless in life. In a very special sense, however, even neuroses serve a purpose and, *in that respect only*, they are not to be called pathologic. It is this bit of usefulness which harbors the resistance to therapy.

REITLER, in connection with Freud's reference to autoerotism as a source of megalomania, remarks that persons who have succeeded in overcoming the masturbation of puberty by their own will power will show great self-reliance (FREUD, in an interjection, includes childhood masturbation in this context); they have something to be proud of, as it were.

In his opinion, the feeling of potency must play an important part in megalomania. He thinks that eunuchs, for example, would never display traits of megalomania; they just could not be anything but servants.

He mentions Schiller's poem *Männerwürde*[8] as clearly expressing the relationship between sexuality and self-reliance.

In the actor, he says, the sexual component is obvious. Acting is, one might say, a sublimated prostitution (shame of the profession).

[7] In later years Freud would have said that megalomania is nourished by narcissism.
[8] *Männerwürde* = male dignity.

RANK observes that disdain for one's profession is far more frequently encountered than esteem for or overvaluation of the profession; this is the reverse side, as it were. To Frey's remark that one would undermine the power of these people to struggle for existence if one were "to open their eyes," Rank objects that it is just not possible to open their eyes; precisely that is a part of their delusion. As Rank sees it, the reason for the fact that wearing a special attire (uniform, etc.) results in increased self-confidence lies in the awareness of the effect on the opposite sex. In reference to the chauvinism of peoples (Kahane), he remarks that the Greeks and the Romans called all other peoples barbarians.

FEDERN says that the opposite of exaggerated self-confidence, and of megalomania, such as modesty and the delusion of being totally insignificant, is frequently nothing else but disguised megalomania. (Similarly, pessimism conceals in most cases its opposite.)

FREY remarks that the megalomania of artists is caused by the lack of any yardstick or measure for their attainments. He mentions also the conceit of clergymen which hides behind humility and devotion to the Lord, and the megalomania of women which is of a sexual nature.

PROFESSOR FREUD relates the extremely instructive case of an *exquisite paranoia*. The patient was a woman of about thirty-two years. Her own father said that even as a child she was not entirely normal. She came from a wealthy, aristocratic family, but she had made up her mind that she would marry only a poor man. At approximately twenty-eight, in spite of parental objections, she did marry a handsome, well-educated man of thirty. In five years of married life she has had three children; the youngest is ten months old. After the first half of her last pregnancy, she began to change. She became jealous of her husband. This jealousy proved to be pathological since it was entirely unfounded. However, she was convinced of his infidelity. Initially, her suspicion was not aimed at any particular person. First came the idea that he was unfaithful. Then she began to collect individual experiences and let them take root in her mind. The nurse maid was the first person whom she accused.

Freud points out how, in this case, motives which are usually hidden come clearly to light. She gives two "arguments" to substantiate her jealousy: her husband is so handsome that he must be attractive to every woman; and the girl is so pretty and so pleasing to the patient herself that she must be as pleasing to her husband.

From her servants and other persons she now began to hear disparaging rumors about her husband, and around these she evolved a whole delusional system which manifested itself in her speaking in an undertone.[9] For example, while her husband would speak with others in a normal tone of voice, she would hear voices in an undertone: i.e., her own unconscious train of thought.

A physician who was consulted advised a temporary separation of husband and wife. However, during the four weeks of her husband's absence, her condition became aggravated. She began to write letters to young men of her acquaintance, inviting them to her home and indicating that she intended to be very amiable and so forth. In addition, she tried, in questionable ways, to strike up acquaintances in the street. Taken to task by her parents for this behavior, she said, "If my husband is unfaithful to me, I have certainly the right to be unfaithful to him."[10]

Now it is quite evident that she conceals her own suppressed inclination to infidelity behind the supposed unfaithfulness of her husband; that she needs his unfaithfulness as a justification for her own.

Upon his return, the husband very openly gave a full account of his married life. Even before the outbreak of this "mania" he had observed certain peculiarities in his wife; for example, when he took her out during the time of their engagement, she would often (as if accidentally and involuntarily) push against men in the street. In the beginning of their married life, she seemed normal and they lived together very happily. Between the births of the second and the third child, he practiced coitus interruptus which was a great strain on him. Before the outbreak of her jealousy (around the third month of her pregnancy) he had noticed a striking increase in her sexual desires.[11]

[9] The original has ". . . and so evolved a whole delusional system, the technique of which consisted in . . ."

[10] Freud showed later that pathological jealousy is based on projection and is, in fact, a form of paranoia. See "Some Neurotic Mechanisms in Jealousy, Paranoia and Homosexuality" (1922). *S.E.*, 18:221-232.

[11] An increase of libido occurs immediately before the outbreak of schizophrenia.

Freud adds here that this is a case of nymphomania in which the paranoia is secondary; but mania is characterized by the suspension of repressions, and for this reason the entire paranoia is so clear in this case.

The increase in her libidinal desire is expressed in the fact that it is impossible to give her sexual fulfillment although she had previously been capable of normal satisfaction.

Lately, perverse desires have come to the fore: she demands that he masturbate her, look at her from below, and have intercourse per anum. He attributes these desires to her reading which lately has consisted of French novels in which such things occur.

Subsequently, her way of speaking and her behavior became shameless. She has dropped all inhibitions (even in front of the servants); has masturbated in his presence; has made sexual demands upon him at any hour of the day and, when he refused her, reproached him with not being enough for her; she needs other men besides him. Occasionally she has expressed the wish to give birth to a dark child; he has given her only fair children.

She has, in this fashion, acquired the paranoia in order to justify her repressed desires. The main role, however, is played by the nymphomania. She creates the delusional system in order to overcome her psychic inhibitions.

From this case, Freud derives two general points which he has envisaged for some time:

1. It is from the broken-down [*abgetragenen*, demolished] psychic structures that paranoid ideas are formed. The delusional system is fashioned from shame, etc.

2. In paranoia, there occurs a regressive development of sexual life, which is not true of other neuroses.

ADLER says that he has noticed a striking openness in three cases of paranoia which he had occasion to observe; that is to say, the infantile impressions [which are normally repressed] were on the surface.[12] This shows an inferiority of the sexual system;[13] the psychic

12 The German text has: *ein Zutageliegen der infantilen Eindrücke.*

13 Obviously, Adler did not know and could not know at this time that the easy accessibility of infantile material in paranoia is due to the breakdown of the repressions.

formations are compensatory exaggerations [*Kompensationssteigerungen*]. He attempts to fit Freud's case into his own scheme.

REITLER mentions the case of a paranoid woman who accused him of having assaulted her; in a letter to Freud she complained about his pupil (Reitler) and stressed that he was impotent. The woman was a virgin; her husband was incapable of having an erection; she had infantile genital organs (an infantile uterus, etc.). This is a case of an inferior sexual organ combined with neurosis, which seems to speak for Adler's theory.

Reitler observes further that he has always found megalomania to be a primary symptom in paranoia.

FREUD makes the additional comment that his case helps to explain two characteristic traits of paranoia:

1. The incurability of paranoia by psychotherapy.
2. The fact that the pathologic productions become fully conscious and have full reality value in paranoia, whereas in hysteria, for example, they remain unconscious (appearing in fantasies) and enter consciousness only in a disguised form.

ad 1.—In paranoia, as has been mentioned earlier, there is a regressive development of the libido from object love back to autoerotism.

In curing neuroses one takes hold of the floating part of the patient's libido and transfers it to one's own person. The translation of the unconscious material into consciousness is performed with the help of this transference. The cure, therefore, is effected by means of a conscious love. In hysteria and obsessional neurosis, part of the libido is mobile and treatment can start with this part. In paranoia, however, this chance is not available because of the regression to autoerotism. There is no faith in the physician because there is no love. The patient, just like the child, believes only whom he loves.[14]

ad 2.—Freud explains the fact that the products of paranoia become obsessively conscious in the following way: the autoerotic love, which is fully reawakened in the paranoiac, flows into consciousness

---

[14] Later, Freud distinguished between transference neuroses and narcissistic neuroses.

60

and, since we put faith in that which the ego contains (every man believes himself), these ideas become a part of the conscious ego.[15]

Freud surmises that a retrograde development of the libido, similar to that seen in paranoia, occurs also in hypochondria, and sometimes in old age.

In neuroses, constipation is frequently seen to be called forth by fantasies of pregnancy. In such cases, each bowel movement is celebrated as a delivery. Freud mentions he once saw a case of mania: the patient led him to a heap of feces lying in her room and said, "This is my child."

Freud relates two cases in support of the fact that the child associates with words other ideas than does the adult, and also that the child attributes much greater significance to words.

A boy who does not desist from masturbating, in spite of his mother's constant admonitions, is removed from school. At home he *paints* all day long and is enthusiastic about it. Then it is learned that, at school, he used to masturbate with a schoolmate in the following manner: they crossed their membra over one another and rubbed them against the wall until ejaculation occurred: this they called "painting."

The second case is that of a boy who, while breaking himself of the habit of masturbating ("playing"), began to play the piano intensively.

[15] These remarks on paranoia contain the germ of Freud's later conception of mental illnesses, of schizophrenia in particular, and of the narcissistic character types. Nowadays we would add that the obsessive consciousness in the paranoiac is also due to the overpowering of the ego by the id.

8

SCIENTIFIC MEETING on November 28, 1906

Present: Freud, Adler, Bass, Federn, Frey, Kahane, Sadger, Stekel.[1]

COMMUNICATIONS

FREUD reads to the assembly a letter from Jung (in Zürich) sent together with a reply to the essay by Gustav Aschaffenburg.[2]

FREY returns Minutes 1 to 4.

PRESENTATION

Lenau and Sophie Löwenthal[3]

SPEAKER: DR. J. SADGER

The speaker, referring to the latest publication (by Castle[4]) on Lenau and Sophie Löwenthal states that he himself published a

[1] Graf and Rank, whose discussion is recorded below, were omitted from the list of participants.

[2] Gustav Aschaffenburg (1866-1944), professor of psychiatry in Cologne, since 1904 editor of a monthly for criminal psychology and reform of criminal law, published *Crime and the Fight Against It* and other articles. We do not know which article is referred to here.

[3] Sadger's paper appeared as Number 6 of the *Schriften zur angewandten Seelenkunde* [*Contributions to Applied Psychology*] under the title, *Aus dem Liebesleben Nikolaus Lenaus* [*From the Love Life of Nikolaus Lenau*]. Leipzig & Vienna: Deuticke, 1909. Lenau (1802-1850) was one of Austria's greatest lyricists. He died in a mental institution.

[4] Eduard Castle (1875-?), historian of literature, professor at the University of Vienna, published an edition of Lenau's works, the Lenau biography by A. Schurz (see footnote 8), and the book mentioned here, entitled *Lenau und die Familie Löwenthal* [*Lenau and the Family Löwenthal*] in 1906.

pathographic study of Lenau about twelve years ago. The new material confirms his earlier arguments. In part, it suggests a better explanation for some points. The speaker explores Lenau's relationship to Sophie from three points of reference:

1. What was the character of this relationship?
2. How did it affect Lenau's illness and death?
3. What influence did it exert on his characterological and spiritual [*geistig*] development?

ad 1.—The speaker outlines the facts known about their relationship. He mentions that there is evidence that Lenau and Sophie never had sexual intercourse. However, they came close to it. She allowed him to kiss and embrace her. He carried her in his arms and so forth. In his love notes and dreams, Lenau at times took the final step [of consummation]. Therefore Sadger thinks that it was Sophie's sexual anesthesia (for intercourse) which caused the relationship to remain platonic. Lenau should not be blamed for that.

Sophie was hysterical—a characteristic which was evident as early as in her fifteenth year in her relationship with Köchel.[5] She was erotic, it is true, but she had an aversion to intercourse. After her son was born (it was during this pregnancy that the relationship to Lenau became closer) she succeeded in putting an end to the sexual relationship with her husband (she was twenty-six at the time). Sadger believes that this anesthesia also accounts for Löwenthal's conviction of his wife's faithfulness.

ad 2.—It has been established that Lenau died of general paresis, an illness which develops only on the basis of a luetic infection. In all probability, he contracted syphilis before his association with Sophie. His later state of manic confusion leads to the conclusion that Lenau had a severe hereditary taint. However, neither he nor Sophie showed any signs of an anxiety neurosis. In Lenau, obviously, the neurosis due to heredity prevailed; in Sophie, hysteria. The speaker arrives at the conclusion that the association with Sophie did not have much influence on Lenau's death.

ad 3.—The speaker mentions first Lenau's hypochondria; his noc-

[5] Ludwig, Ritter von Köchel (1800-1877), lawyer, naturalist, and musicologist, was as much as engaged to Sophie von Kleyle (later Löwenthal) but broke the engagement suddenly.

turnal brooding (obsessive thoughts). For example, from his twenty-seventh year he was obsessed by the idea that he had forfeited his moral purity. This may perhaps be connected with a girl (Berta) with whom Lenau had a love affair when he was twenty. She deceived him on various occasions, and later Lenau considered her unworthy of himself.

Sadger proceeds to the discussion of Lenau's relationship with his mother. He was her favorite child (which may be partly due to the fact that his was a difficult birth). His mother was downright in love with him. She was a most passionate and somewhat pathologic human being who wanted to die at the time of her husband's death and who also told her son that she would not survive him: if he were to die, she would kill herself (poison). In Lenau's dreams, his mother's death was a recurrent theme. A similar will-to-die-together appeared also in his relationship with Sophie, in whom he found the combination of mistress and mother. (He himself told her so.)

From his sixth year on Lenau was haunted by the fear of death. When Sophie left him he attempted suicide. This death wish, according to Sadger, has some connection with the hope of fulfilling his passionate longing in the next world, a hope which Sophie held out to him. Sadger makes the point that it is generally true and significant that the melancholic knows no other punishment, even for trifling offenses, than death. This seems to him to stem from infantile impressions, that is, from being threatened with dying as a consequence of disobedience and the like. Lenau's insanity first expressed itself in his suspicion that the Reinbecks[6] were intending to denounce him as an assassin. Sophie had once told him that if he should receive a cheerful letter from her, she would soon die. Such a letter actually arrived. He believed that she was dead and that he was the cause of her death—hence, a murderer. On the day after he had received this letter, Lenau had his first seizure of frenzy. He claimed that no further letter arrived after that cheerful letter, which could make her death seem credible but which in no way corresponded to the facts. In Lenau's hallucinations the notion

[6] Georg von Reinbeck (1766-1849), German author, taught German literature in Stuttgart. His home was a center for men of letters, and among them Lenau was the most famous one. He was a regular guest there from 1833 until 1844, when he suffered his first mental breakdown in Reinbeck's home.

recurs that he must kill himself because he has violated the moral laws. In the course of Lenau's insanity, homosexual tendencies also became manifest. He took a liking to the gardener's helper, to stable boys, and the like. Sophie said that he was in love with Anastasius Grün;[7] Schurz[8] reports that he was enamoured of his physician Schelling. Discussing the infantile root of Lenau's homosexual inclination, the speaker mentions the friendship of the fourteen-year-old Lenau with an unmarried cleric who was said to be a great friend of children. Lenau probably owed his violin playing to this man. A memory (from his fifth year) concerning his father may perhaps also belong in this context. The father, who was very ill, jumped out of bed to slap the naughty child. Lenau may on that occasion have seen his father's genitalia.

DISCUSSION

FREUD emphasizes that, according to L. A. Frankl,[9] Lenau was an onanist throughout his life and that this fact must certainly be taken into consideration. Freud approves of Sadger's comment that it is due to other neurotic phenomena that there is no sign of an anxiety neurosis in either Lenau or Sophie. A hysterical woman usually tolerates incomplete intercourse quite well. Anxiety neurosis appears in its clearest form in the normal person.[10]

The term "hereditary neurosis" [Belastungsneurose], which the speaker used, should preferably be avoided, since it does not convey the essential character of any definite symptom complex.

Nor should one speak of a "circular" insanity in Lenau, for the form of the illness has unjustifiably been overrated. The expression "circular" pertains, not to the nature of the illness, but only to its formal character. (Freud gives an example to illustrate his point.) Freud considers it sound to trace the source of Lenau's chaste rela-

7 Graf von Auersperg (1806-1876), Austrian poet.

8 A. Schurz: Lenaus Leben, grösstenteils aus des Dichters eigenen Briefen [Lenau's Life, Predominantly from the Poet's Own Letters], 1855.

9 L. A. Frankl, Ritter von Hochwart (1810-1894), Austrian poet, professor of aesthetics, published a biography of Lenau, Lenaus Tagebuch und Briefe an Sophie Löwenthal [Lenau's Diary and Letters to Sophie Löwenthal], 1891.

10 This statement is consistent with Freud's view of the anxiety neurosis, a view to which he adhered throughout his life.

tionship with Sophie to his relationship with his mother. But one must not imagine this relationship as too crude. In most cases, it takes merely the form of exaggerated tenderness. However, it cannot be stressed too often that the boy learns to love from his mother. In the final analysis, the treatment accorded the child is decisive for his love life. People in love, for example, use for each other the pet names by which they were called during childhood. Man becomes childish when he is in love. All of this will be shown in more detail in a study of man's love life which Freud is planning.[11] This essay will also take up the conditions of love. Love is said to be irrational, but its irrational aspect can be traced back to an infantile source: the compulsion in love is infantile. Such a condition of love found a very beautiful expression in Goethe's *Werther* when young Werther enters the room and immediately falls in love with the maiden. He sees her buttering slices of bread and is reminded of his mother.

Freud cites also two pathological cases: a visitor, who is being shown the family album by a daughter of the house makes a disparaging remark about the picture of her sister and finds her own picture far more beautiful. From this moment, she is in love with him. The condition of love was, for her, to be preferred to her sister.

In another case, a young girl suddenly fell in love with a married man. She had observed this man playing with a little girl, and this had obviously activated memories of playing with her own father.

In connection with Lenau's violin playing, which he carried to a state of ecstasy, Freud refers to an idea which has frequently been used by cartoonists: namely, to represent the violin as a woman and the violin bow as a penis.

Sadger's conjecture that Lenau's homosexual inclination may have been stimulated by the fact that Lenau might have seen his father's genitalia as the latter jumped out of bed seems to Freud to be based on an overestimation of accidental impressions.

STEKEL: Although there is a great deal that speaks for Sadger's interpretation, another explanation is nevertheless conceivable. Lenau was an onanist and probably not very potent. At any rate, it arouses

[11] See "Contributions to the Psychology of Love. I: A Special Type of Choice of Object Made by Men" (1910). "II: On the Universal Tendency to Debasement in the Sphere of Love" (1912). "III: The Taboo of Virginity" (1918). *S.E.*, 11:163-208.

suspicion that he became acquainted, fell in love, became engaged, and then broke off the relationship. He practiced a kind of onanistic activity on women. His pessimistic lyrics are of a masturbatory nature —as are all lyrics. Stekel has experienced this in himself.

The fact that sometimes no anxiety neurosis develops even though there is coitus interruptus can be explained, Stekel believes, by the absence of "psychic conflict" (for instance, the desire of one of the partners for another sexual object).[12]

FEDERN makes the point that Lenau may not really have wanted intercourse at all. Many onanists do not find pleasure in it. The proofs submitted to show the presence of pathological traits in Lenau's mother seem inconclusive to him.

GRAF calls attention to a great similarity between Lenau's relationship with Sophie and that of Richard Wagner with Mathilde Wesendonck.[13]

RANK remarks that Lenau's fear of losing Sophie's esteem, to which the speaker referred, can be interpreted only as a fear of sexual failure (impotence). There is hardly a poet who would not see a connection between love and death (or who would not have incestuous inclinations), so that Lenau's dreams of his mother's death would be dreams disguising their sexual contents. Playing the violin may be an additional characteristic of the onanist, in so far as it is an activity of the fingers.

ADLER: In reference to Sophie's [sexual] anesthesia, Adler says that he knows of similar cases. On the one hand, anesthesia insures virtue; on the other hand, however, it frequently seduces to fickleness. He mentions the anesthesia of prostitutes (Messalines). Lenau's masturbation must have been preceded by early events connected with organ activity (erotogenic zones); he regrets the lack of any information about Lenau's organic constitution. As far as poets are concerned, the absence of anxiety symptoms is explained, he thinks, by the fact that they do not manifest themselves directly but in a transposed form. Many scenes in Lenau's poems are indeed suffused with anxiety.

12 From the very beginning, Stekel opposed Freud's ideas about the causation of the anxiety neurosis.
13 Writer, married to O. Wesendonck, was a close friend of Richard Wagner whose artistic development was influenced by her.

In response to Freud's remarks, Adler emphasizes that, to Lenau, a sexual relationship with Sophie would have meant infidelity to his mother. Fear of death is often found in neurotics. It actually signifies a reproach for their wish for the death of someone else. Lenau may have wished for his father's death.

FREY sees in the mental game that Sophie played with Lenau the substitute for her genuine gratification. That she knew how to captivate him by intellectual interests seems to be demonstrated by their animated correspondence. Frey reads a letter of Lenau's, dated November, 1836, which proves Lenau to have been a discerning "psychoanalyst" of his own moods.

SADGER, in conclusion, replies to the various comments: concerning Lenau's supposed onanism, which was referred to by several discussants, Sadger questions Frankl's reliability. In support of the concept of "hereditary neurosis," he reminds the audience that certain phenomena cannot be explained by psychosexual arguments.

Lenau's daydreams and night dreams do not seem to support the assumption that he was an onanist, because they are about intercourse, and such dreams do not occur in onanists. Besides, onanism is frequently retained as a hysterical symptom (in addition to normal intercourse). It is often used as a means of gaining independence from others, for example, in the case of an individual who feels rejected by his parents. At the end, when Sadger speaks of Lenau's playing with insanity and at the same time fearing it, FREUD calls his attention to the fact that this trait, in particular, is a stigma of masturbation.

9

SCIENTIFIC MEETING on *December 5, 1906*

Present: Freud, Adler, Bach, Federn, Häutler, Hitschmann, Hollerung, Kahane, Meisl, Rank, Reitler, Sadger, Stekel.

COMMUNICATIONS

Freud mentions Bloch's book *Das Sexualleben in unserer Zeit*[1] which has just been published; he characterizes it as a compilation.

PRESENTATION

Review of Stekel's pamphlet: Die Ursachen der Nervosität[2]

SPEAKER: HITSCHMANN

In Hitschmann's opinion Stekel's very definition—that nervousness is a state in which the individual reacts abnormally to external and internal stimuli—is inadequate. In Stekel's assertion that neuroses are

---

[1] Ivan Bloch (1872-1922), German physician. *Das Sexualleben in unserer Zeit* [*The Sexual Life in Our Time*].
[2] *The Causes of Nervousness.* Vienna: Paul Kepler, 1907. The original has "Nervosität" which, in this context, is akin to "neurosis." We have consistently translated it with "nervousness."

69

based solely on psychic conflicts, Hitschmann sees a contradiction of Freud's views.

Stekel believes that the characteristic which distinguishes the healthy from the nervous individual is that the ideational complexes are conscious in the normal, not conscious in the neurotic. In each neurosis, two conditions can be detected: the *psychic conflict* and the unconscious ideational complexes, each determining the other.

The second chapter deals with the nature and the effect of repression, which occurs without the cooperation of consciousness. The energy expended in forgetting an event returns later as illness. Sexual desire and sexual aversion create the conflict lying at the base of the neurosis. At this point, Hitschmann stresses the contradiction in Stekel's paper; that the sexual factor is nowhere acknowledged, yet is especially emphasized as a frequent cause of nervousness.

The following chapter deals with the prevention of nervousness. Joy in any form is the best medicine against nervousness.

In reference to "repression," Hitschmann remarks that perhaps the child learns to "repress" in connection with sexual matters, and later employs the same method in the neurosis. The sexual development of the young psyche may be analogous to later development. A mind of a certain nature proceeds in youth in one direction and in maturity in another.[3]

Summarizing briefly, Hitschmann voices the following objections to Stekel's presentations: it is not clearly stated to what extent the pathological aspect of sexuality is a causative factor in nervousness; furthermore, the conflicts which Stekel holds responsible for the development of neuroses could not possibly be sufficient to cause a neurosis; lastly, predisposition and the constitutional factors have been ignored.

DISCUSSION

FEDERN tries to excuse certain inadequacies of the brochure by pointing out that it was written for the general public. Occasionally, a psychological conflict might be sufficient to create a neurosis. How-

---

[3] The last two sentences must have been recorded incorrectly. Since the sexual development in puberty is a revival of infantile sexuality, the first sentence should be: "Later development may be analogous to the sexual development of the young psyche." The second sentence contradicts the first.

ever, in the majority of cases, the neurosis is based on extremely complex changes. Being suppressed by others can also cause nervousness, just as much as one's own suppression can. Federn assumes that the cause of Grillparzer's nervousness is different from the one Stekel advances. In order to protect himself from nervousness, the normal person must not wish to pursue his thoughts to the end. In normal mental life there is a process by which impressions become abortive (are forgotten). He concludes by quoting Goethe's advice: not to meditate about oneself.

HÄUTLER stresses that not every psychic conflict leads to nervousness. In reference to Adler's arguments, Häutler comments that heredity determines whether the psychic conflict can be tolerated. In every nervous illness, it is a question of summation.

REITLER describes Stekel's brochure as a "neurotic symptom"—a wave of "asexuality" has surged up in the author. Reitler must contest Stekel's assumption of the purely psychic basis of the neurosis. In all of his cases of hysteria, he has found organic changes of the cerebral system; syphilis was particularly frequent in the patients' families. Reitler depreciates Stekel's definition of the nature of nervousness by objecting that the *reactions of neurotics merely seem to be abnormal*. In Stekel's definition of conscience, Reitler misses the emphasis on the emotional sphere to which it certainly belongs. In most of Stekel's examples, Reitler finds analysis and solution inadequate. The title of the brochure should be, "The *Precipitating* Causes of Nervousness."

KAHANE characterizes infantile masturbation as the source of all psychic conflicts. Man's attitude toward masturbation is the sexual component which carries the disposition for neurosis. This is quite apparent in the obsessional neurosis, which is, indeed, the purest psychosis.[4] In respect to "the therapy" of neurosis, Kahane would like to express his opinion in the form of a metaphor: the human being feels a need to react against all inhibitions; to become a pig. The best protection from neurosis is to fall from ethical heights; to become a pig.

FREUD fully agrees with Hitschmann's evaluation of Stekel's brochure. It is true that popularization is enormously difficult and

4 "Psychosis" must be an error of the recorder.

71

that some misrepresentations are probably unavoidable. However, he must raise two main objections to Stekel's pamphlet: (1) to the concept of "cause." There is no cause; that is, not *the* cause. (2) Stekel has arbitrarily confined himself to the popular conception of sexuality. He has completely ignored the broader meaning, namely, infantile sexuality. But infantile sexuality must by all means be taken into account.

Stekel should also have avoided the definitions and referred instead to the phenomena. Concerning the definition of nervousness, Freud relates an observation: anyone who has gained insight into the mechanisms of psychosis can no longer sharply define the borderline between health and illness. Then it seems to us quite natural that the sick individual reacts to certain impressions in a way which appears abnormal to the lay person. (Reitler is quite correct in stating that the nervous person only appears to react in an abnormal manner.)

Freud then gives a brief review of the historical development [of understanding] the etiology of the neurosis and shows that Stekel has remained arrested at the point of view of the *Studies*.[5] His "psychic conflict" is that which is called "repression" in the *Studies*. This, however, is not sufficient either therapeutically or theoretically. In this way one came upon the sexual theme (the second stage, we might say). The sexual factors generate the psychic conflict; the conflict which arises in everyday life [*der gewöhnliche Konflikt*] must combine with the sexual conflict. However, the sexual conflict is also banal, and thus we came upon *infantile* sexuality as a new selective [*auswählend*, determining] force. Finally, one had to go back to the constitution; that is, the sexual constitution of the individual.

We know, for example, that in conflicts between subordinates and their superiors (which Stekel holds responsible for the development of nervous phenomena) it is the homosexual component which plays the main role; that this conflict is actually [caused by] grief over love.

Nor is it true that repression is the cause of neurosis, it is rather the failure of repression. Freud supplements Hitschmann's comment, that the method of repression is learned on sexual matters and transferred

[5] *Studies in Hysteria* (written with Josef Breuer) (1895). *S.E.*, 2.

onto later experiences, by saying that it is particularly in sexual matters that repression basically does not succeed.

As a result of his experiences Freud points out that neurotics transfer their perversions onto seemingly alien material only if this alien matter is converted into something sexual (symbolism). There are two classes of human beings who are comparatively free from neurosis: proletarians and princes.[6]

SADGER cannot confirm the incidence of spyhilis in the family background of neurotics. He mentions the widespread occurrence of nervousness (especially obsessional neurosis and hysteria) among the Polish Jews.

STEKEL admits to having written the brochure in a state of severe psychic depression. He had forced himself to write it, and he himself does not consider it good. The topic really is: when does psychic conflict lead to a neurosis; what kind of people become nervous? In his arguments he meant to refer only to nervous symptoms, not to hysteria, obsessional neurosis, etc. Besides, he does not disavow the role of sexuality as a factor operating in the neurosis.

DR. REITLER:[7] Dr. Stekel's work, under discussion, gives the impression of being a "neurotic symptom." It would be interesting to discover where the "psychic conflict" should be sought in this case. It is likely that an asexual wave has made itself felt in a way disturbing to the author, and it is this disturbance which expressed itself as a "symptom" in the brochure before us.

Passing on to the contents of this work, one takes note, incidentally, that in his introduction (p. 6) Stekel declares himself a dualist. He asserts that there are no organic changes at the root of the functional neuroses; that it never will be possible to show such changes; and, finally, that "illnesses of the mind" can be traced back only to "psychic" causes.

From my mechanistic point of view, I deem it necessary that, in our circle, such a mystic "ignorabimus" conception should not remain

---

[6] This statement can be explained only by the fact that neither proletarians nor princes came at that time to seek psychoanalytic treatment. When, after the First World War, this situation changed, it was soon recognized that neurosis is an illness common to all classes.

[7] This contribution by Reitler was attached to the Minutes as a type-written supplement.

uncontradicted; the more so, since Freud's investigations have absolutely nothing to do with metaphysical problems. But this is only an aside!

Of far greater importance for the reading public is the definition of "nervousness" given in what follows. Dr. Stekel considers nervousness that state in which the individual "reacts in an abnormal way" to external and internal stimuli.

This is entirely wrong.

It is precisely through the insights which we have gained from Freud that we know that the neurotic reacts in an entirely normal way; it is only that the causes for reactions which appear abnormal are not clearly evident. When we have discovered these reasons through psychoanalysis, then we have to admit that all reactions of the neurotic are entirely plausible no matter how queer and grotesque they may appear. Then we can understand quite well why one begins to rage and the other falls into a melancholic stupor. In short, the "abnormal" reactions are really quite "normal."

Therefore, the correct definition would have to be: "We consider nervousness that state in which the individual *seems* to react abnormally to external and internal stimuli."

In the chapter, "Culture and Nervousness," I consider quite valid Stekel's observation that certainly it can be no accident that it is just in America that neurasthenia has become so enormously prevalent. One might add here that the puritanic exaggerations of that way of life are probably to be understood as a consequence of the original criminal instincts of the first immigrants and their descendants. This is, in a sense, the "reversal into the opposite accompanied by a tendency to exaggeration" which we know from psychoanalysis.

The author engages in extensive polemics against the doctrine of "hereditary tainting."

Concerning *one* group of psychoneuroses, hysteria, I, for my part, can state quite decisively that [the presence of] syphilis could be demonstrated in the parents of all the *severe* cases I have observed.[8]

[8] At that time in Vienna there was hardly a middle-class family which was not afflicted with syphilis. Paul Federn, who was family physician to the best Viennese middle-class families (as was Reitler), related once that the sons of one family came to him, one by one, imploring him not to tell their brothers anything about their venereal disease.

Stekel then (p. 19) justly turns against the excessive temperance movement, which may bring about painful psychic conflicts in some persons for whom it is difficult to abstain from a moderate consumption of alcohol. According to Stekel, the closest one could come to a characterization of modern man would be to describe him as "haunted by anxiety." "Due to a superabundance of hygienic restrictions, which are meant to preserve his life, he does not live at all; it is just this anxiety which makes him ill," asserts the author. By no means can one agree with these latter arguments.

Hypochondriac anxiety is certainly not a consequence of exaggerated hygienic precepts. The neurotic does not become ill "out of anxiety." Just the reverse is true: because he is "ill" he becomes subject to feelings of anxiety, which he projects onto the sphere that is closest at hand.

In reality, he is not at all afraid of the consequences of nicotine, of alcohol, of all kinds of infections (of syphilis and gonorrhea specifically). In all these cases psychoanalysis uncovers as the real basis of the anxiety:

(1) that these are persons whose libido is not fully satisfied;

(2) that the feelings of anxiety which they express can be traced back to the fear of the consequences of abnormal sexual activity (masturbation, coitus interruptus, and the like)—a fear which these persons have simply shifted onto an "innocent" hygienic sphere about which they need not reproach themselves in the least.[9]

On page 20 the author, usually such a skillful stylist, has committed a stylistic lapse. He writes: "Freud, *giving new life to an old superstition*, has ascribed to sexuality the main role in the etiology of the neurosis." Most likely, Dr. Stekel did not intend his words to express the idea that the results of Freud's investigations were merely an old "superstition" in new, scientific clothing. This sentence thus may be excused as a stylistic lapse; nevertheless, the author states that "he must deviate somewhat from the road which Freud has built so painstakingly and artfully." Not an abnormal *vita sexualis* but the "psychic conflict" is the decisive factor in the etiology of the neurosis.

"Only when two currents wrestle within us for dominance, only

[9] Both points are polemics against Stekel's view of the actual neurosis, which contradicts Freud's view.

when conscious and unconscious emotions fight each other, only when a major portion of our energies must be expended for the suppression and inhibition of psychic conflicts—only then can a neurosis develop," writes Stekel.

He cites as examples the onanist who resolves to remain chaste and, in this struggle, expends "enormous amounts of energy" and thereby becomes "nervous"; the "white-collar worker" who is forced to sit in an office against his will; and the officer who has to stand silently at attention while being reprimanded by his superior although he would like to "give him a piece of his mind." The choice of these three examples is most unfortunate, for in each instance the "psychic conflict" takes place within the sphere of consciousness, whereas on page 21 Dr. Stekel designates as pathogenic the struggle between "*conscious* and *unconscious* feeling" (he probably means "wishes" or "drives").

In actual fact, a *conscious* conflict can make an individual unhappy, but never ill.

Dr. Stekel says further: "A robust conscience would be the best medicine against nervousness. By 'conscience,' I understand the sum total of all the inhibitions which have inserted themselves between our instincts and our ethical ideas."

No doubt, this definition is incorrect. It is not the "sum of inhibitions" that is of importance but rather the *way in which* the individual uses these inhibitions in relation to his unethical instincts. It is only this *relation* between inhibitions and instincts that produces the feeling which we call "conscience"; it is by no means a *single* factor per se as Dr. Stekel claims for the "sum of inhibitions."

On page 25, Dr. Stekel accuses "repression" of being the "cause of numerous nervous diseases." He claims: "The energy which is used in forgetting certain occurrences and fantasies is not lost; it returns as illness, neurotic anxiety, as obsessional neurosis, or in some other form."

These arguments could almost give rise to the belief that "repression" could be equated with "living force," and "neurosis" with "elastic force."[10] Moreover, this all-too-physical comparison is quite inadmissible for the simple reason that the force which was used for

[10] It is difficult to understand what the author had in mind when he differentiated between "living force" [*lebende Kraft*] and "elastic force" [*Spannkraft*].

the work of repression certainly does not reappear *"in another form"* as neurosis, but appears in precisely the *same form* as before, namely, as the patient's resistance, in the psychoanalytic treatment, against the becoming conscious of the unpleasurably toned and therefore repressed idea.

Finally, it must be emphasized that a "repression" as such, as long as it is carried through *usque ad finem,* never generates any kind of neurosis; it is only the "unsuccessful" repressions that have a pathogenic effect.

There follows next in Stekel's brochure a description of cases whose psychological treatment—in analogy to the well-known "concert painting" where within ten minutes an oil painting is completed—could be termed "concert analyses."

Case 1 concerns a man suffering from agoraphobia which Stekel, probably incorrectly, assigns to the sphere of neurasthenia.

If a person with no experience in psychoanalysis reads the physician's interview with the patient, as Stekel describes it, he must certainly gain the impression that the whole business of psychotherapy is incredibly simple, and that in favorable circumstances it can effect a cure in a single session with fantastic speed.

Unfortunately, however, the simplicity and speed are due entirely to the fact that Dr. Stekel did nothing at all to discover the deeper causes of the illness. For instance, Dr. Stekel suspects, among other things, "that he may be dealing with a case of homosexuality; this, however, is definitely denied by the patient who confesses everything candidly."

And with this Dr. Stekel is satisfied! Indeed, it is entirely clear that even an ideal patient, one who "confesses everything" as candidly as ever possible, cannot answer affirmatively the question whether he has any homosexual relations, simply because the patient himself has no idea of his perversion (unless, of course, he is a manifestly inverted individual). He has, for the most part, repressed his abnormal sexual instinct and has transformed into a "symptom" the part that has evaded repression.

Now, if Stekel believes that this topic has been disposed of by the entirely natural denial of the patient, this is only proof of the fact that in this analysis Stekel has remained altogether on the psychic "surface" and that all deeper determinants have completely escaped him. It could not possibly be otherwise in a single session.

Accordingly, Dr. Stekel discovers as the cause of the patient's agoraphobia (the patient was a cashier) the "repression of the thought of absconding with a large sum of money." Quite consistently, he recommends as therapy the avoidance of the "psychic conflict." He advises the patient, "I can see no other cure for you but to change your position as a cashier for another one which may give you more work but will give less temptation." Having followed this advice, the patient, according to his family's report to Dr. Stekel, has been cured within a half year.

There is no doubt that the psychotherapy taught by Freud accomplishes infinitely more than Dr. Stekel could achieve in a single interview. Psychotherapy, correctly performed, does not heal by removing the patient's "psychic conflicts." In most cases, this would not be possible. Consequently the vast majority of cases would *a priori* be incurable by Stekel's method. Exact psychotherapy achieves its success, quite to the contrary, in spite of existing conflicts by bringing to full consciousness a series of painful ideas whose repression has not been entirely successful. Thus the patient is enabled to form a clearly conscious compromise between his poorly [i.e., unsuccessfully] suppressed instincts and the demands of the external world. But each compromise involves a minor or major renunciation; the patient cured in this way may, perhaps rightfully, feel unhappy—but he will no longer be neurotic.

Lastly, the "definitive cure" in Stekel's case must be seriously questioned.

Dr. Stekel has done nothing more than to uncover the reason why the phobic individual had become subject particularly to *agora*phobia.

The cashier's badly suppressed mistrust of himself, that he might abscond with the money entrusted to him, was the determining factor, as the author found out quite correctly. It was thus very expedient for the patient to direct his anxiety just to the sphere of locomotion because in this way he could protect himself from himself. He made it impossible for himself to run away.

If he received from Dr. Stekel an explanation of this psychic mechanism, if he moreover gave up his position as a cashier, then the anxiety directed to locomotion had lost its meaning for the patient. But surely, he was not cured of his phobia. It is true that he could give up his *agora*phobia, but there is no doubt that his feelings of anxiety must have become attached to another sphere. The symptom was removed; the neurosis remained.

The situation is no better in the second example of psychoanalytic speed-curing.

In this case the patient was a woman who declared that "she could not stay in a room unless there was another person with her. And this person could not be a stranger but must be a close relative of her husband. Lately, she had insisted that her husband stay with her continually."

Dr. Stekel found out that her husband was not especially potent sexually. He suspected, probably quite correctly, that this sexually unsatisfied woman indulged in fantasies of adultery. In order to ward these off, she compulsively desired the constant presence of her husband, or, at least, of a member of his family. In this way she insured her own marital fidelity. As a result of this explanation, supposedly, the condition "was considerably improved; it had almost completely disappeared." And that after a single interview!

Here analysis again has merely scratched the surface and has failed to elucidate the reasons why the obsessional idea centered on the desire not to remain unprotected and alone in the face of sexual fantasies. Here, too, there is merely the explanation of, and perhaps removal of, a neurotic symptom, but by no means the uncovering of the deep roots of the neurosis, let alone its cure.

The same is true of the third case—*mutatis mutandis*—where the pathogenic but quite conscious conflict between "piety" and "sexual sins" is said to have been cured and resolved even by a father confessor.

Case 4 is most interesting.

According to Stekel, an "almost insoluble psychic conflict was present"; and in resignation the author declares. "Needless to say, even a psychotherapist cannot be of much help in such a case."

Most definitely, we cannot agree with this resignation. In spite of the continued existence of external conditions, a genuine, thorough psychotherapy would have had to attain its goal. It is a matter of course that a superficial analysis had to fail.

Luckily for the patient in the fifth and last case, the external circumstances again could be altered: the official obtained a transfer to another office and "soon became a completely healthy man."

Following Professor Freud, we cannot emphasize strongly enough that the commonplace unpleasantnesses of social living only *appear* to be the cause of neurosis. At most, they decide the *form* of the *neurotic symptoms*. But the real roots of illness lie much deeper and invariably have an associative link to the sexual life whose abnormalities have not been adequately repressed in the neurotic.

The fact that Stekel simply ignores these deep-seated links to sexuality, which, after all, must be well known to him; that he even denies them explicitly and wishes to acknowledge as a cause of illness only the conflict hovering on the psychic surface—this fact may indeed justify the opinion expressed at the beginning that the entire work under discussion should be considered only as a neurotic symptom of defense against the author's own sexual instinct.

Taken as a whole, the work could be considered of some merit if all the errors it contains were corrected along with the title. It should not be *The Causes of Nervousness* but, more to the point, *The Causes of Some Neurotic Symptoms.*

10

SCIENTIFIC MEETING *on January 23, 1907*

There is no meeting on December 12, 1906.
There is no meeting on December 19, 1906.
There is no meeting on December 26, 1906.
January 2, 1907: a social get-together.
There is no meeting on January 9, 1907.
There is no meeting on January 16, 1907.

Present: Freud, Adler, [A.] Deutsch, Federn, Hitschmann, Hollerung, Kahane, Meisl, Rank, Reitler, Sadger, Stekel.
Mr. Eitingon from Bleuler's clinic is a guest.[1]

---

[1] Max Eitingon had finished his medical studies but had not yet taken the examination for the doctorate. Therefore he is addressed as "Mister."

His presence at this meeting was of particular importance. In a sense, it signified a new era in the history of the psychoanalytic movement. He was the first man to come to Freud from abroad for the purpose of learning about psychoanalysis at the source. He was sent to Vienna by the famous Bleuler, who was director of Burghölzli, the psychiatric clinic in Zürich, to find out what a psychiatrist could learn from Freud. He brought with him some questions, which were discussed in this and the following meeting. However, it would be incorrect to assume that these questions were broached for the first time only on the occasion of Eitingon's visit. They had been discussed before and they were discussed afterwards; in fact, some of these questions are still being discussed.

COMMUNICATIONS

The following papers [to be presented] have been announced:

FREUD: On Moebius's book, *Die Hoffnungslosigkeit der Psychologie* [*The Hopelessness of Psychology*]

STEKEL: The Psychopathology of the Tramp, and on Jung's *Psychopathology of Dementia Praecox*

ADLER: The Analysis of an Obsessional Idea

GRAF: Wagner's Letters to His Family—Art and Life

MEISL: Hunger and Love (Homosexuality)

HITSCHMANN: *Törläss*[2]

REITLER: *Frühlingserwachen*[3]

BACH: Jean Paul and Schumann

STEKEL: Psychology of Discussion

Minutes borrowed: [A.] Deutsch: 5; Sadger: 8.

PRESENTATION

Hunger and Love

SPEAKER: DR. ALFRED MEISL

This work is related to investigations published previously.[4] In this paper (which so far is just a torso) Meisl tries to draw a parallel between the instincts of nutrition and of propagation and (basing himself on Freud's findings and on the psychophysical doctrines) to gain new vantage points for the understanding of the psychological and physiological processes connected with these two instincts. Since the

---

2 *Die Verwirrungen des Zöglings Törläss* [*The Confusions of the Pupil Törläss*], by R. Musil, 1906.

3 [*Spring's Awakening*], by Frank Wedekind.

4 Meisl published several studies on psychic functioning. Two of them, "Das psychische Trauma" ["The Psychic Trauma"] (*Wien. klin. Rundschau*, 20:225-246, 1906) and "Der Traum" ["The Dream"] (*Wien. klin. Rundschau*, 21:3-6, 1907) are mentioned and summarized by Abraham in *Jb.*, 1:584-585, 1909.

speaker announces that this paper will be published in the near future, we omit recording it in detail.[5]

DISCUSSION

STEKEL criticizes Meisl's reservation concerning the priority of his ideas. He remarks that no one else would want to use Meisl's few novel ideas; everything else, he says, is old and has been known for a long time. Stekel suspects that personal repressions of the speaker lie behind Meisl's postulation of an "asexual[6] component of the instinct of preserving the species." Meisl's "lust connected with sexual appetite" is simply Freud's "forepleasure." Altogether, Meisl should have adhered more closely to the *Theory of Sexuality;* he could have spared himself quite a few hypothetical features of his argument.[7] Accordingly, Stekel misses a reference to the common origin of the two instincts and their common counterpart, disgust (Freud).

In reference to Meisl's racial psychology, Stekel remarks that modern biologists have completely discarded the concept of race. All in all, he wishes to emphasize that he is not in agreement with the speaker's arguments and that, moreover, he has not gained any new knowledge from them. Not even Meisl's differentiation between perverts-in-thought and perverts-in-action is new; every neurotic, indeed, every man, is a pervert-in-thought. And Freud has called neurosis the negative of perversion.

KAHANE cannot join Stekel in his sharp criticism. In his opinion, the work is respectable even though it revives some views which we have already abandoned. Meisl has gone astray in attempting to amalgamate psychology with physiology, and the conceptions he uses are too indefinite. But much of what he says is valid. In general he would characterize this work as "surface psychology"; investigation has to go beyond the facts and look for their causes; matters are not so simple

---

[5] "Hunger und Liebe; analytische Studien über die Elemente der psychischen Funktion" ["Hunger and Love; Analytic Studies of the Elements of Psychic Functioning"]. *Wien. klin. Rundschau,* 21, 1907.

[6] The original has the word *sexuelle* [sexual]; however, the whole context indicates that this is an error and that "asexual" must be substituted for it.

[7] Here we have an example of the very personal turn the discussions occasionally take, as was pointed out in the Introduction. Freud mentions this fact in his "History of the Psychoanalytic Movement" (1914). *S.E.*, 14:3-66.

as Meisl imagines them to be; for example, concerning fetishism, Meisl is still holding on to Binet's point of view which is no longer tenable.[8] Among a hundred people subjected to the same impression, there is only one who becomes a fetishist; hence the reasons must be looked for in the individual himself and not in the accompanying phenomena; he had expected Meisl to take the step that leads away from the dualism of instinctual life to a monism, to the one instinct which is the source of all others. (In his opinion, this is the instinct of self-preservation.) This may be the point where one should have gone back to embryology, which teaches that the sexual organs develop from primary viscera. Meisl thinks he has discovered a way of combining physiological views with Freud's views, but this is a sterile one.

REITLER, on the basis of his experience with prepubertal masturbation, is inclined to conclude that those individuals who masturbate with fantasies about the opposite sex tend to become altruistic in later life, whereas those with purely autoerotic sensations [*Empfindungen*] do not. He, like Kahane, misses a reference to the monism of the instincts. It has evidently escaped Meisl's attention that Freud had already referred to the erotogenic zone of the digestive tract.

SADGER considers the asexual component of the instinct for the preservation of the species to be merely a displaced and modified "sexuality." Concerning the predilection for certain foods, one must not forget that often this has been taken over from parents and siblings, an erotism transferred from the persons onto the food. Psychoanalyses regularly demonstrate that fetishism is caused by sexual ex-

---

[8] Alfred Binet (1857-1911), French experimental psychologist. In his *Three Essays on Sexuality* (1905) Freud says: "Binet (1888) was the first to maintain (what has since been confirmed by a quantity of evidence) that the choice of a fetish is an after-effect of some sexual impression, received as a rule in early childhood." In 1920 he added the following footnote to this remark: "Deeper-going psycho-analytic research has raised a just criticism of Binet's assertion. All the observations dealing with this point have recorded a first meeting with the fetish at which it already aroused sexual interest without there being anything in the accompanying circumstances to explain the fact. Moreover, all of these 'early' sexual impressions relate to a time after the age of five or six, whereas psycho-analysis makes it doubtful whether fresh pathological fixations can occur so late as this. The true explanation is that behind the first recollection of the fetish's appearance there lies a submerged and forgotten phase of sexual development. The fetish, like a 'screen-memory,' represents this phase and is thus a remnant and precipitate of it. The fact that this early infantile phase turns in the direction of fetishism, as well as the choice of the fetish itself, are constitutionally determined" (*S.E.*, 7:154-155).

periences, usually during the period before the fourth year. Concerning the effect of hypnosis (which Meisl mentions also in discussing fetishism), he can only state that it is very insignificant and of short duration. A homosexual who had been in hypnotic treatment with Schrenck-Notzing[9] relapsed after a short period of time; initially, he had fallen in love with Schrenck-Notzing, who has an impressive appearance.

MR. EITINGON (guest from Bleuler's clinic) remarks that the longing for a child is not always the expression of a woman's ungratified sexuality. The "asexual component of the instinct of preserving the species" seems to him to be merely a sublimation of, or an elaboration of, the sexual component.

As far as the Jews are concerned (whom Meisl also discussed), he himself does not believe in the preservation of the purity of races; after all, there are only limited possibilities of selection [*Wahlmöglichkeiten*].

In connection with fetishism, Mr. Eitingon raises the question whether the influence of sexual trauma is of such great importance in all perversions. Then he asks how the frequent assaults by old men on young girls can be explained; is there not also an infantile factor involved?

(MEISL, in elucidation of these questions, refers to his chapter on "Homosexuality" which was not included in tonight's paper. According to him, these acts are perpetrated out of a "hunger for stimuli.")

STEKEL refers to the fact that in demented individuals certain inhibitions are lacking. Besides, every man feels the urge to satisfy not only his own desires but also the woman's; the old man (who does not believe he is capable of gratifying these desires) consequently prefers an object inexperienced in these matters.

FREUD says that in general he can join both the critics and the anticritics. Stekel definitely has gone too far in his criticism. It is gratifying that, on this occasion, Meisl has abstained from his pet theories. It is praiseworthy to concern oneself with the instinct life (the darkest but most important area), and one can expect to gain some insight from a comparison of hunger and love. The comparison,

[9] German physician and parapsychologist (1862-1929).

however, is made difficult by the complications which occur in sexual life. Three such obscuring [*trübende*] circumstances should be especially stressed:

1. In the human being there is the factor of a period of latency in the sexual instinct. There is no comparable factor in relation to hunger. Sexual gratification is delayed until puberty; it is true, however, that we do find precursors at an earlier age. This delayed appearance of sexual gratification, as contrasted with the gratification of hunger, is the reason for our inability to obtain an undistorted picture of the sexual instinct. With animals (where there is no period of latency) the situation is less complicated.

2. We are lacking one important point of comparison; we do not know the organs of sexuality. The seminal glands prepare only the sexual substance, but they do not "prepare," as it were, the instinct.

3. Polarity, which we know in the sexual instinct in the form of bisexuality, does not exist in the nutritional instinct.

Thus the comparison of hunger and love will remain unproductive until we know more about the sexual instinct [and] until we have solved the riddle of the sexual organs, the riddle of bisexuality, and the riddle of the changes to which the instinct is subject during the latency period.

Freud then adds a few remarks to his main points. The differentiation between perverts-of-action and perverts-of-thought has already been introduced by Krafft-Ebing.[10] It is characteristic of persons who indulge in perverse fantasies that they are not only averse to, but actually *incapable* of, carrying them out. The suspension of reality (as in the theater) is in many of these cases a necessary condition for the formation of the fantasy.

One cannot (as Meisl does) equate masturbation with the production of the relative reflex.[11]

Freud does not consider it a fortunate idea to restrict the use of the term libido to pure sexual hunger (whereas Meisl calls the other "sexual appetite"). This separation may be adequate for the hunger scale, but there are actually two scales in libido. In Meisl's scheme,

[10] R. Krafft-Ebing (1840-1903), professor of psychiatry at the University of Vienna, was one of Freud's teachers.

[11] This sentence is incomprehensible without knowledge of Meisl's paper.

the state of being in love (which we might call the normal psychosis) seems to have been ignored.

Meisl sees an important difference in the fact that appetite develops only on the basis of certain experiences, whereas sexual appetite appears before any experience. To this, Freud remarks that there is *one* situation in which even sexual appetite develops only on the basis of experiences: that of the girl brought up in a conventional manner (that is, "well-brought up"); she enters the marital state almost without sexual experiences and acquires sexual appetite only in her married life (which is almost never true of the male). Here it already becomes evident how bisexuality complicates the comparison.

Concerning the asexual component of the instinct of preserving the species, Freud remarks that it is true, it has been an oversight to deny the sexual component of the altruistic drives, but that on the other hand we must ask ourselves whether these drives consist only of this component or whether the sexual component is one among several others.

He has, he says, left one point unclear in the *Theory of Sexuality*. Human love life is divided into two phases: autoerotic and object love. To find the object, however, is, in truth, to rediscover it. At this point the question imposes itself whether the first object is perhaps not an erotic one. It is most probable that the child's love is conditioned by his dependency. Our culture is based on three factors which differentiate us from the animals: the upright posture, the newborn's helplessness, and the latency period of the sexual instinct. These features make us humans. The nutritional instinct introduces the child to his first objects: mother or wet nurse. But the nutritional instinct includes the erotic element [*ist mit dabei*]. The two instincts meet at this point. The asexual component always appears together with the erotic one. We lack the means for solving this question; it transcends the limits of our present experiences and belongs in the realm of "metaphysics."

The sexually satisfied woman does not differ in her longing for a child from the unsatisfied woman. Sexuality has to be understood in its wider compass. The relationship to a child gratifies aspects of the sexual need which the man could never satisfy. In relation with her child the woman is essentially *active* (which she cannot be with the man). In this respect, the "sick man" corresponds to the child. Furthermore, in the woman's childhood there was one powerful wish: to become mother (that is, to become big like father and mother, a desire from which it is likely that megalomania is derived). The fulfillment of this wish is then indispensable for the woman's complete satisfaction.

Freud considers Meisl's explanation of the racial characteristics of Jews to be incorrect. Natural selection [in the choice of the sex object] plays a minor role in humans.

Fetishism: The experiences which psychoanalysis permits us to gather point to the conclusion that that which seems simple is the result of various components (for example, someone's predilection for intercourse with a pregnant woman cannot be traced back simply to the fact that he owes his first sexual excitement to a pregnant woman). Nor can we explain in such a simple way the case of a man who used to attack little girls (Meisl's example); many people have received their first sexual excitement (just as this man claims) as children while playing with their contemporaries of the opposite sex. Why is it that the others permit the girl to grow up with them, whereas this man does not? For him she remains small. We must assume an additional fixating factor.

There are many reasons for the predilection of old men for little girls: Freud wishes to discuss only one at the moment: the libido of every one of us has probably been stimulated by little girls. An analogy to the behavior of a nation can be seen in the behavior of old men: as long as the nation is young, it takes no interest in its genealogic history; the situation is similar in mankind as a whole; the older it grows, the more it progresses in the knowledge of its primeval period. The same is true of the individual: in his old age, he occupies himself intentionally with his conscious childhood memories. To this we can attribute the late emergence of childhood impressions.[12]

FEDERN declares himself to be in general agreement with Meisl's arguments, since for once he has refrained from his mania for blood supply. In his opinion, Meisl's effort is not futile. From his own self-observation he can report that he felt hunger only in the pharynx. Similarly, the sensation of sexual appetite can be transposed to the

[12] In dementia senilis recent experiences are forgotten, whereas experiences of the remote past are revived and dwelt upon.

epidermis. He has observed that his own child of thirteen months has idiosyncrasies against certain foods which correspond to her mother's aversions. From this one must, indeed, infer heredity (the idiosyncrasy of the human being). He supposes that similar factors are at work in sexual choice.

The more affectionately a child is treated, the more altruistic he will be as an adult.[13]

ADLER also feels compelled to start with a criticism. Such a fundamental investigation has value only if it is based on great experience. He must blame Meisl, as he has on previous occasions, for constructing at the desk solutions to problems which can only be settled in practice. The individual cases which Meisl quotes do not give us a clear picture; they are of no value to us.

It is impossible, within the limits of this discussion, to offer a thorough criticism. He wishes to take up only a few points:

Meisl has the world originate through the attentional reflexes and the added association which has been lying in readiness.[14] But, in truth, he would need to renounce all of the association if he goes back to the original excitation.

Disgust cannot be described paraphrasically (as Meisl is doing) as merely the lack of that which does not correspond to the fantasy. Disgust is rather a factor of the unconscious instinct life and appears as a defense against something which was originally desired. He misses altogether some reference to Freud's theory of sexuality (to the erotogenic zones in particular). Here Meisl could find the analogy of the two instincts traced back to a primal instinct for gaining pleasure (just as Adler himself has attempted to do in his work).

Altruism is frequently found in persons who were strongly sadistic in childhood but have repressed their sadism.

HITSCHMANN points out, as a characteristic difference between the two instincts, that it is not possible to live without satisfying the one, whereas this is not absolutely true of the other.

In attempting to trace all instincts back to a single one, we may perhaps discover that the vital power [Lebenskraft] is the sum of all

13 An assumption which, in the course of time, proved to be incorrect.
14 It is impossible, without knowledge of Meisl's paper, to understand this sentence.

instincts. For animate and inanimate matter differ from each other only through the vital force which is inherent in animate matter.

Certainly, the desire to embrace a partner is not present in the nutritional instinct.

That first experiences are retained can perhaps be explained by the fact that satisfaction does not remain constant in an individual; he develops an increasingly more refined taste in the choice of food and of love objects.[15]

HOLLERUNG praises the paper as interesting and stimulating. Altruism quite probably does not stem exclusively from sexual factors. Perhaps one could look to animal psychology for an analogy. The ant workers (and also the bee workers) whose sexual organs are stunted show a sort of "altruism."

RANK refers to his attempt to show the monistic root of hunger and love, which he made in the first part of his sexual psychology.[16] Concerning the asexual component of the instinct for the preservation of the species, he remarks that Meisl may possibly have confused asexual with antisexual. In the examples Meisl chose of the asexual component (*esprit de corps*, friendship, etc.), homosexuality (the aversion to the opposite sex) plays the predominant role. The view that "hunger" drives the prostitute into her trade and the man to the performance of homosexual acts is an entirely superficial one. Today we have gone beyond attributing a decisive role to the social factor in such matters.

MEISL, in his concluding remarks, refers to the sequel to his paper in which some of the misunderstandings will find a sufficient explanation. At this point he will reply at random to only a few of the comments:

Concerning the significance of the oral mucous membrane, he disagrees with Reitler, pointing out that there are two kinds of pleasurable feelings associated with this zone. A considerable portion of the world's people (the Chinese and the inhabitants of Indo-China) do not know our kiss. The mucous membrane of the nose plays this erotogenic role.

He explains the attacks by demented people by saying that these

---

[15] It is difficult to understand what Hitschmann meant.

[16] *Der Künstler; Ansätze zu einer Sexualpsychologie* [*The Artist: The Beginning of a Sexual Psychology*]. Vienna & Leipzig: Heller, 1907.

individuals, having partaken of the entire scale of indulgence, are finally overcome by peculiar desires.

He replies to Freud's remark that we do not know the organs of sexuality, that neither do we know an organ with which we sense hunger: it is true that the sensation of hunger emanates from the inner surface of the stomach but we do not project it there.

Freud's objection that there is no polarity involved in hunger is not of importance: for us, the sexual object is the same as food is to the hungry. In sexual appetite, the concentration on the object lasts longer than that of hunger on food. This situation he has taken into account. A subsequent part of his work deals with the development of the normal sexual appetite. The state of being in love is also discussed there.

It has made him very happy that Freud admits the possibility of an asexual component of the instinct for the preservation of the species. On the other hand, he himself has no doubt that homosexual or sexual components also play a role in this instinct.

11

SCIENTIFIC MEETING on *January 30, 1907*

Present: Freud, Adler, [A.] Deutsch, Federn, Hollerung, Kahane, Reitler, Rank, Sadger, Stekel, Mr. Eitingon as a guest.

[*The Etiology and Therapy of the Neuroses*]

In the course of the last meeting, Mr. Eitingon, from Bleuler's clinic, raised the following questions about the *etiology and therapy of the neuroses:*

1. What other factors have to be at work, in addition to the mechanisms known to us, for a neurosis to develop? (Of what does the disposition to hysteria consist?) Are social components perhaps of some account?[1]

2. What is the essence of therapy? Is it or is it not directed against the *symptom?* Does one substitute something for the symptom (according to Jung's formulation, one complex is replaced by another), or does one only "take away" as Freud expressed it in his simile of sculpture and painting? What is the role of transference?

---

[1] Although this was the first time that the question of the choice of neurosis was raised and formulated by someone who was not a member of the group, it must be pointed out that the same question had been dealt with in one form or another in preceding meetings; however, it had never been so sharply formulated as here.

3. What becomes of hysteria after psychoanalysis?

This evening's discussion is devoted to answering these questions.

DISCUSSION

HOLLERUNG, in response to question 1, offers a modification of the etiological classification which Freud made in "A Reply to Criticisms on the Anxiety-neurosis."[2] Freud proposes the specific, the concurring, and the auxiliary cause; Hollerung would like to substitute "condition" for "cause." What we call cause is, according to him, a certain series of conditions. If a single one of these conditions is not present, the cause cannot appear. The logical conclusions in regard to therapy are self-evident. In connection with a passage in the *Studies [of Hysteria]*, he would like to say that there is no causal therapy but only a prophylactic one; that is true of any therapy.

MR. EITINGON remarks that such generalizations deprive Freud's theses of their specific, most important aspect. Moreover, he cannot concur in this medical pessimism.

RANK says that he cannot answer any of these questions on the basis of experience. He would like to make just one remark which concerns, so to say, the sphere in between these questions. Between the illness and its cure, the symptom and its resolution, there is, one might say, the normal life of the patient; there his social, religious, artistic instincts come to the fore, and it is from here that one can start, even if one has not actually practiced psychotherapy.

FEDERN comments on the disposition to neurosis; there are people who are immune, as it were, to this illness. Frequently all of the conditions [predisposing to neurosis] are present, yet the individual does not become neurotic; on the other hand, a member of a perfectly healthy family may develop a neurosis. Federn assumes that infectious diseases, suffered in childhood, may also be a factor in predisposing the nervous system to neurosis. However, the vicissitudes of the individual's life play an important precipitating role. In addition, a certain cowardice (neurotic running away) and a disposition toward anxiety (which may be of sexual origin) seem to be factors in the

[2] (1895). *C.P.*, 1:107-127.

causation of neurosis. Federn found that the severe neurotic always came from an unhappy marriage; one might even attempt to show a certain similarity of the child's conflicts with those of the parents.[3]

As far as therapy is concerned, in minor cases the results are mostly good. The success depends upon the youth of the patient. Therapy protects the individual from further, severe neuroses.

MR. EITINGON notes that his questions were of a general nature. He had not asked for the specific determinants of each symptom. He wishes to ask whether it is quite necessary to assume a predisposition. Whether one should not perhaps assume a system of stigmata as the basis of neuroses? Whether analysis does not put a stop, one might say, to further neurotic illness? Why it is that women are more prone to neurosis? Whether the frequency of neurosis is greater among Jews? (Most participants answer "yes" to this question. SADGER adds that he had the opportunity of observing numerous obsessional neuroses—impotency, onanism—among the Polish Jews.)

REITLER, referring to Freud's findings, specifies, as a characteristic of hysteria, an increase in perverse libido associated with defense against sexuality. In all hysterics, one can observe that the erotogenic zones outweigh the sexual zone.[4] There is also a special development of the component instincts (a term introduced by Freud). The defense against sexuality (repression) has failed in hysteria. In all of his cases Reitler has been able to demonstrate the presence of syphilis in the family as an etiologic factor. He wishes, also, to refer to the increased tenacity,[5] a factor merely touched upon by Freud (*Theory of Sexuality*). For the hysterics, memories are of greater importance than recent events. Reitler would assume that in hysteria infantile sexuality has remained fixated to such an extent that it is taken along into adult life as a recollection. Again referring to the *Theory of Sexuality*, Reitler sees in the weakness of the genital organ the constitutional Anlage to hysteria. This also explains the predominance of the erotogenic zones. Trivial everyday experiences can never call forth a symptom unless on a deeper level they are associated with sexual factors.

[3] What deep intuitive insight Federn had!
[4] Obviously, Reitler refers to the "genital" not to the "sexual" zone.
[5] [*Haftbarkeit*] of recollections.

As far as therapeutic technique is concerned, Reitler says that one starts from the symptoms; but they disappear only when the entire neurosis is cured. As to the results in hysteria, he must say that usually too much is demanded from therapy; one cannot do away with the unfavorable conditions under which the patient is living. There is no doubt that therapy protects against renewed illness.

MR. EITINGON says that his questions concerning the social components certainly become superfluous if one blames sexuality for everything. He asks whether one might cure a patient by removing the motive for his illness. What, then, would protect him from renewed illness, if a new and powerful motive appears?

(STEKEL answers: insight. REITLER agrees with this answer.)

ADLER: The mechanisms which we see in the neuroses are the same that we see in the normal person. Our question was, indeed, "What additional factors are necessary to produce a neurosis?"

Hysteria, above all, can be viewed from many angles. Adler particularly emphasizes the incongruity[6] of the psychic constellation, and from this point of view one can recognize both a strengthening and a weakening in comparison to the normal psyche: the strengthening consists in the hallucinatory character of the hysteric; to some degree, this characteristic is also found in the normal individual and in the genius; in the hysteric, however, it is increased. The weakening is expressed mainly as a deficiency in introspection.

Therapy consists primarily in strengthening certain psychic fields through a kind of psychic training. The hysteric shows a growth of his psychic qualities during treatment. The patient surprises us by his ideas and a discovery of connections, which sometimes astonishes the physician. During and after the treatment, he masters material which was entirely strange to him before. As he progresses in understanding, the patient gains the peace of mind which he needs so badly. From an unwitting pawn of circumstance, he becomes a conscious antagonist or sufferer of his fate.

In practice, the question of whether therapy is directed toward the symptom is really of no importance. The patient speaks of what is

6 It is not quite clear what Adler means by "incongruity." Incongruity in relation to what?

closest to him. The same driving forces come to the fore in his description of his symptoms and in his other discussions. It is only that the symptom shows us these driving forces clearly and becomes the guiding thread which thus leads us to the core of the neurosis. A number of superficial symptoms may disappear in the course of treatment, whereas a number of symptoms which may have become quite transparent do not disappear until the patient has gained the psychic strength to find different channels for his instinctual drives.

The substitution of one complex for another Adler can envisage only by means of creating another way out for the neurotic development of instinct life (for example, painting, music, or psychology).

The patient's interest in the method can be very promising for therapeutic success. Adler considers transference valuable mainly as a therapeutic tool: it makes the numerous disagreeable things acceptable to the patient.

Concerning pure hysteria, one has to adhere to the conviction that it can be cured. Since Adler believes in an etiology based on the inferiority of an organ, he cannot expect that the patient will be completely normal after treatment.

In reality, limits to a complete cure may be set by the social circumstances of the patient. Discord in the parental home is found over and over again. However, there are already inferiorities in the parents —they differ only in form. Perhaps they are not transformed into neurosis; perhaps, not even into illness. Still there remain peculiarities to which the other parent cannot resign himself and disagreements result.

In the formation of neurotic symptoms, we encounter the participation of organs which in this way are trying to gain pleasure. Not all depends on strength or weakness of the libido, but a great deal depends on how the individual tolerates this libido.

EITINGON says that much of Adler's exposition remains vague and incomprehensible to him. He will wait for Adler's book.

STEKEL first states that the current classification of the neuroses will have to be discarded. The Dubois School[7] knows only nervous

---

[7] Dubois, professor of neurology at the University in Berne, Switzerland, developed a psychotherapy based on persuasion of the patient.

symptoms. Dubois tries to strengthen the ego complex by means of philosophical-ethical complexes. It is the psychic conflict between the instinctual life and the inhibitive ideas that produces neurosis. Going beyond this conflict, one encounters sexuality. The relationship inhibition-instinct regulates the individual's state of health.

In the criminal, instinct life predominates; in the neurotic, inhibition.

Concerning the individual neuroses: neurasthenia is the tragedy of relative impotence; sexual potency comes into conflict with sexual desire. That is why only men become neurasthenics. We do not find such impotence in women. Hysteria is the struggle between sexual desire and sexual aversion. In this illness, instinct life and inhibition oppose one another severely. In the hypochondriac, the sex instinct collides with the instinct for self-preservation (fear of sexuality). He transfers his inhibitions from the sphere of ethics to that of somatics.

In Stekel's opinion, the answer to the question as to what sort of people become neurotic is that neurosis is produced by the amount of inhibitions.

He considers the impediment stemming from the milieu to be the most important factor (not the impediment stemming from the organs). Organic processes have nothing to do with neuroses. Social factors play an important part; the nervousness of the Russian Jews demonstrates this. Hysterical epidemics also prove the absence of organic determinants; plainly, in all, the same repressions are present.

The main task of therapy consists in building up the individual [conflict?] into what is generally human.[8] The patient must be shown the mechanism of repression and must become his own therapist.

SADGER begins with psychotherapy. Therapeutic failures are partly the fault of the physician, partly the fault of the patient. They are the fault of the physician if transference has not been established (transference should appear after the second or third session), or if he neglects to give an interpretation at the opportune moment.

Failure is due to the patient if he has any motive for not wanting to regain his health or if there is an external obstacle in the way of his

---

[8] The original has: "*Die Hauptaufgabe der Therapie sei das Individuelle ins allgemein Menschliche aufzubauen.*" Stekel seems to refer to Freud's idea that psychoanalytic therapy transforms neurotic suffering into common human misery.

recovery. If none of these countermotives are present, then the so-called recovery takes place; but the "nervous" individual is still there.

Sadger now turns to a discussion of his separation of the concepts of degeneration and of hereditary predisposition. In order to gain a comprehensive picture of the symptoms of hereditary predisposition, he has made a study of the pathologic characters among poets. All of the symptoms of hereditary predisposition lead to the ego, to the sphere of bodily sensations, whereas in the degenerative diseases (imbecility) the centers of association have been diseased.

After the cure of hysteria, the picture of hereditary predisposition remains. The "sexual constitution" which Freud found in neurotics also points mainly to the sphere of bodily sensations. So-called normal individuals frequently show hysterical symptoms when they fall severely ill. One cause of "nervousness" is the fact that no fresh blood has been introduced into us since the migration (Nietzsche's blond beast).

Hysteria is the neurosis of love *par excellence*. Neurotic women are the most desired ones. A severe injury in the sexual sphere (most often of a homosexual nature) is the beginning of the neurosis. After analysis, the patient remains well because a neurotic symptom can be produced only unconsciously. This escape has been blocked (unless the patient has withheld something). Therapy is not directed against the individual symptom because all of the chronic symptoms are interconnected. There is only one complex substitution: all symptoms must be transferred onto the physician.

The Jew's disposition to obsessional neurosis may be related to his addiction to rumination. This has been his characteristic for thousands of years (study of the Talmud).

KAHANE prefaces his remarks by saying that the psyche can be comprehended only allegorically: everything psychic is only an allegory. If one looks upon the psyche as an organ, one could compare the neuroses to, say, the diseases of metabolism. They could be called the products of psychic intermediary metabolism.

The psychic Anlage is given once and for all. The psyche lives by means of [energy] charges [*Ladungen*] which it receives. Presumably the first charge is the affect of anxiety engendered in the passage through the birth canal (dyspnea). The first pleasurable charges are probably the first intake of breath and sucking at the mother's breast. The complete assimilation of these charges is the condition for health. If in one form or another residuals remain, they settle where they do not belong, and a neurosis develops. Then the accompanying psychic processes are not adequate to the somatic processes as they would be in the case of a normal person. The hysteric uses psychic residues for somatic cathexis. There are also, one might say, psychic feces, and the neuroses could be compared to obstipation (autointoxication). Some sort of psychic gymnastics is a good remedy for this. From time to time, one needs to shake off the accumulated inhibitions and to fall back to the primitive level of instinct life; this is denied to women.

To continue the metaphor of metabolism, psychotherapy might take the place of a mineral water cure at a spa (as, for instance, with gout). The deposits are washed away with the help of powerful complexes that are introduced.

[A.] DEUTSCH would like to raise again the question of the neurotic disposition. Analyses of healthy persons might shed light on why some fall ill and others do not.

FREUD states that the first question raised by Eitingon also contains the question: which factors have to be at work, in addition to the known mechanisms, to produce at one time a hysteria, at another a compulsive neurosis, etc.? The sexual component of psychic life has more bearing on the causation of the neuroses than all other factors. This assertion can be proven only in so far as any psychological processes can be proven. Mr. Eitingon's question betrays the theoretical disavowal of the sexual etiology of the neurosis, a disavowal which has not always been maintained by the Zurich School. Through sexuality, the intimate relation of psyche to soma is established.[9] Hence the answer to the question must be that the psychosexual constitution is the additional contributing factor in the production of neuroses.

---

[9] Freud's conception that the instinct is a link between psyche and soma was later expressed in the following way: what we perceive as an urge is the psychic representation of an instinct, not the instinct itself. Instinct cannot be defined in psychological terms. It is in the somatic component of the instinct that we would have to see the somatic background of neuroses, especially of hysteria with its tendency to conversion.

Whether this is all, cannot yet be said definitely. It could be that nothing new need be added to the psychosexual constitution and the mechanisms.

One has to look at the problem from the viewpoint of the neurotic. He is not so ill as he appears to us. Part of his suffering stems from the fact that he comes into conflict with us (this is the cause of most temper tantrums). He is ill only to the extent that he suffers. It is here that therapy has its limitations. Therapy can cure the neurotic only in so far as he suffers;[10] where *he* does not suffer, therapy is ineffectual. Such an area of unwillingness, however, is found in most cases.[11]

Perhaps all of us are somewhat neurotic. Under present-day conditions there is even a beneficial hysteria with a corresponding advantage gained from conversion. Practical considerations really determine whether an individual is characterized as ill. The actual difference between mild and severe illness lies only in the localization, the topography of the symptom.[12] As long as the pathological element obtains an outlet in insignificant performances, man is "healthy." But if it attacks functions essential for living, then he is considered ill. Thus illness develops through a quantitative increase. The maintenance of repressions in hysteria requires a certain expenditure of psychic energy. Consequently, the major part of the psychic forces is used for inhibitions. It is the psychological effect of the cure to restore these energies to free disposition.[13] The patient is restored to health by quantitative means.[14]

As to the problem of the choice of neurosis (what are the specific factors determining the development of each form of neurosis?), this is what we know least about. A combination of the psychosexual con-

[10] This causes the great difficulties encountered in analyzing candidates in psychoanalytic training, a difficulty to which I referred in "Character and Neurosis" (Chapter X, *Principles of Psychoanalysis*. New York: International Universities Press, 1955).

[11] The secondary gain of illness seems to be a cause of this situation.

[12] Today we would say: whether the symptom affects the superego or the ego.

[13] Today we would add: to the disposition of the ego.

[14] As early as that time, Freud stated that the quantitative factor plays the main role both in falling ill and in cure. He stressed this fact over and over again. I enlarged upon these problems in my paper "Ego Strength and Ego Weakness" (1939) (*Practice and Theory of Psychoanalysis*. New York: International Universities Press, 2nd ed., 1961) as well as in "Evaluation of the Results of Psychoanalytic Treatment." *J.*, 35:2-7, 1954.

stitution with other constitutions is to be assumed (as, for example, in the artist the specific motor endowments: of language, of sight, of touch).[15]

A second aspect is that of regressive illnesses; since the normal sexual function comes about by way of a certain development, it is to be assumed that in this sphere also there are certain processes of regression (as is the case wherever developmental processes are involved). In hysteria, there is such a regression from the propagative function to its separate components. Obsessional neurosis, in its turn, has a more intimate relationship to the *perverse tendencies*. Obsessional neuroses are found in people of highest moral development (Zola, a fanatic lover of the truth, was an obsessional neurotic). Morality develops at the expense of perversions; it is brought about by their suppression.[16] Jung's assumption that toxic influences are decisive for the choice of a neurosis is premature.[17]

Therapy is powerless as far as the single symptom is concerned. It is the goal of the technique (as Sadger has said) to have the patient develop everything himself. The task of the therapist is always only to remove the resistances.[18]

The nature of therapy could be characterized in various ways: (1) as filling the gaps of memory (which have come about through repression); (2) as removing the resistances; (3) as replacing the unconscious by the conscious. All of this is really the same. There is only one power which can remove the resistances, the transference. The patient is compelled to give up his resistances to *please us*. Our cures are cures of love. There would thus remain for us only the task of removing the *personal* resistances (those against the transference). To the extent that transference exists—to that extent can we bring about cures: the analogy with hypnotic cures is striking. It is only that in

[15] To this day, this problem has not been solved.

[16] In German, this sentence is ambiguous: it may mean "morality develops at the expense of perversions by means of their suppression" as well as "morality develops at the expense of perversions, the suppression of which it achieves in turn." Today we would say: morality develops under the influence of the superego. This does not contradict Freud's formulation in this discussion, because the development of the superego from the ego is in part a reaction to sadism.

[17] *Über die Psychologie der Dementia Praecox* [*On the Psychology of Dementia Praecox*]. Halle: Marhold, 1907.

[18] Even at that time, treatment was not aimed at the symptom as such but at the total personality as well as at the overcoming of resistances.

101

psychoanalysis, the power of the transference is used to produce a *permanent* change in the patient, whereas hypnosis is nothing but a clever trick [*Kunststück*].[19] The vicissitudes of the transference decide the success of treatment. The only thing the method still lacks is authority; the element of suggestion must be added from without. But even so, the need of the unconscious for liberation meets us halfway.[20] The neurotic does not fall ill again because we have made conscious the unconscious infantile contents (the other factor in symptom formation, in addition to the repulsion of repression).[21]

The question whether there is a need for a special psychology of the neuroses has to be answered ambiguously: yes and no. If the generally accepted psychology were correct, there would be no need for a special psychology of the neuroses. Things being as they are, however, it is needed.[22]

[19] See: "Group Psychology and the Analysis of the Ego" (1921). *S.E.*, 18:69-143; and Nunberg, "Transference and Reality," *J.*, 32:1-9, 1951.

[20] Indeed, it is one of the drives of the unconscious to change its state: that is, to become conscious. Therapy seems to rest on this quality of the unconscious instinctual life.

[21] The symptom is formed as a compromise between the repressed (the infantile unconscious) and the repressing forces (the ego or the preconscious). This is not the place to enter into a detailed discussion of this very complex process.

[22] This was one of the most important discussions in the Vienna Society. All of the speakers said some truths, but Freud's contribution contained the core of his later conceptions of the etiology, dynamics, and therapy of the neuroses. The resolution of resistances and the transference, which he compares to hypnosis, play the chief role in the cure, he states. Eitingon's main question, that concerning the choice of neurosis, has remained unanswered to this day. Freud returned to this problem in his paper "The Disposition to Obsessional Neurosis. A Contribution to the Problem of the Choice of Neurosis" (1913; *S.E.*, 12:317-326), in which he shows the specific contribution of the ego to symptom formation.

12

SCIENTIFIC MEETING on *February 6, 1907*

Present: Freud, Adler, [A.] Deutsch, Federn, Frey, Hitschmann, Kahane, Rank, Reitler, Sadger, Stekel.

FREY borrows Minutes 11 and Reitler's supplement to 9, noting that he will pass them on to Hitschmann.

PRESENTATION

STEKEL reviews two books:

On the Psychopathology of the Vagabond:
A Clinical Study by Dr. K. Willmans[1]

and

On the Psychology of Dementia Praecox:
An Attempt by Dr. C. G. Jung[2]

Willmans's book contains forty-one cases of dementia praecox with complete histories. His conclusions are drawn from this material. The

[1] *Zur Psychopathologie des Landstreichers.* Leipzig, 1906.
[2] *Über die Psychologie der Dementia Praecox.* Halle: Marhold, 1907. English translation published by Nervous and Mental Disease Monographs, 1909.

value of the book lies in clearly and emphatically bringing out the sufferings of these people who are subject to the most absurd methods of treatment because the doctors in asylums and prisons have scant understanding of psychiatric problems. On the other hand, the book is lacking in that which would be of most interest to us: that is, psychology. In each case, Stekel misses the deeper psychological explanation, the demonstration of the affect hidden behind the whole picture of illness and of the transition from health to illness.

An attempt in this direction has been made by Jung who demonstrates that the seemingly senseless answers of demented patients are strictly determined (according to Freudian mechanisms).[3] In their "symptoms" the patients compensate themselves for the privations life has imposed upon them.

There are frequent references to an abnormal sex life in Willmans's cases, but they are made in the form of timid hints. Many sexual offenses are reported which had already brought the patients into conflict with the law in their youth.

Stekel believes that he could guess the genesis of one of these cases: it concerns a youth who assaulted his mother; this seems to Stekel to be the negative of the boy's love for his mother. Stekel believes that the drive to run away (desertion from the army; vagabondage) is psychologically more deeply motivated than Willmans assumes.

Jung's presentation also leaves one problem unsolved: why one person becomes hysteric, another demented.[4] Jung finds a way out by assuming a toxin in dementia praecox. Stekel would like to advance another hypothesis: since the human brain continues to grow throughout nearly all of man's life (until the sixtieth year) in proportion to his mental performances, and since, furthermore, repression must also be considered a mental performance, one could assume that a predisposition for such illness (dementia praecox) is created when the brain in its growth is met by an unyielding cranial basis.[5] In persons with

---

[3] Jung is the first to make an effort to discover the hidden meaning in the "nonsense" of schizophrenics. His book represents a turning point in the history of schizophrenia. We need only to remember that in the case histories of that time one would regularly find such observations as: the patient talks nonsense, foolish stuff, etc.

[4] This problem was dealt with in the previous meeting and will be dealt with over and over again.

[5] Stekel's fantasy seems to be limitless.

a peculiar disposition, metopism is often found: that is, the frontal suture has not closed in the course of development (Buschen: *Brain and Culture*[6]). First of all, therefore, cranial measurements of paranoiacs ought to be made and cases of metopism collected.

DISCUSSION

ADLER is amazed that so few general points of view have evolved from the immense material at Willmans's disposal. He regrets that he himself has but little material on which to draw. In regard to the two questions, how the symptom of vagabondage develops and in what way it is connected with wish fulfillment, he wants to call attention to two aspects:

1. In changing his environment, the vagabond creates for himself the same situation that the hysteric does in his flight from the world: the escape from his milieu.

2. The answer to the question, to what part of instinct life vagabondage is to be ascribed, may perhaps be deduced from one of his observations (this is not a tramp in the strict sense of the word although he bears a great resemblance to one; his roving has an instinctive character). The man in question is intelligent, well educated; from time to time he would roam aimlessly through the streets and become calm only after he had done just what he wanted to avoid: that is, to visit a prostitute. He took no money along on these wanderings but would regularly borrow some from one of his acquaintances.

(FEDERN interjects the question whether he had stolen. ADLER replies that had he stolen, the analogy would be equivocal, indeed.)

According to his observations, juvenile delinquents start with vagrancy. Then there is a group of people, the gypsies, who are typical tramps (gypsies very frequently desert from the army). (HITSCH-MANN mentions the nomads in general.)

Concerning the cruelties on the part of physicians and attendants, there are many sadists among them whose cruelty finds an outlet on their defenseless victims.

[6] Georg Buschen, died 1904. *Gehirn und Kultur; Grenzfragen des Nerven- und Seelenlebens* [*Brain and Culture: Borderline Problems of Nervous and Mental Life*]. Wiesbaden: Bergmann, 1906.

A part of Stekel's hypothesis appeals to him: that part which concerns the marks of degeneration of the skull. In his view, also, these certainly play an important role (metopism, stigma of inferiority). He cannot, however, accept all of the causal connections envisaged in this hypothesis.

RANK sees a connection between the flightlike travels of many of our greatest poets and "vagrancy." Kleist's[7] roaming through Germany and France is well known. Schiller's flight from Stuttgart, which must have had deeper (unconscious) motives than those known to the historians of literature, may perhaps also be viewed in the same light. Goethe's flightlike first trip to Italy; Wagner's flight from Dresden; Hebbel's[8] trip to Hamburg (and his later urge to travel); probably also Shakespeare's trip to London. For many poets their poetic vocation begins with a trip (Hebbel, Kleist), as does the neurosis in the vagabond. But we see that in most poets this flight is really an emancipation from their own families (mostly from parents, siblings). For Shakespeare, it was an emancipation not from father, mother, and siblings but from his own family: from his wife and child (this, however, is merely a displacement). The same is true of Wagner. Is it not conceivable that a similar emancipation from the family is the motive of the vagabond's passion? Its neurotic aspect could be formulated in a somewhat rationalistic application of Freud's dictum that the defense is the psychic correlate of flight; thus one could say: in the vagabond, the mechanism reverses itself, as it were, and the psychic defense is again expressed in the form of flight: that is, as a motor defense. This may be what Adler called flight from the milieu.

KAHANE stresses that today's topic belongs mainly in the field of sociology. Vagrancy is no absolute concept but has to be freshly interpreted in the light of conditions in our culture. Transferred to a desert, for instance, the vagabond would immediately lose his criminal

[7] Heinrich von Kleist (1777-1811) was first a professional soldier; he resigned to study philosophy; disappointed, he traveled in France and Switzerland. During his travels he discovered his vocation. He became a great writer of prose and drama. He died in suicide.

[8] Friedrich Hebbel (1813-1863), important German author of prose, poetry, and drama, the initiator of psychological drama. His first drama, *Judith*, plays a role in Wittels's paper, recorded in Minutes 19.

character. He would be doing only what everyone else does. Vagrancy is not always associated with psychosis. In a sense, all of us are "vagranting." Our vacations are nothing but that. Kahane again makes the point that a quick and sudden dropping of cultural inhibitions is a need for us too. In speaking of the gypsies, he raises the question of heredity of vagrancy: perhaps the vagrant is closer to the nomads than we are.

FEDERN first refers to two great "vagrants" among poets: Byron and Béranger.[9] The genuine vagrant is characterized by his lack of a feeling for his home. The neurotic aspect lies in the vagrant's inability to adapt his instinct life to our social conditions. Federn differentiates between symptomatic vagrants (Adler's case) and what we might call essential vagrants. The genuine vagrant is homeless, whereas the symptomatic vagrant could be described as constantly in search of his home. Federn knows a case of such symptomatic vagrancy: a man who, for the flimsiest reasons, incessantly changes his abode.

Federn raises the question of whether infectious diseases do not have some influence on the etiology of dementia praecox. He himself has seen the appearance of dementia praecox after chorea. It may, after all, be a toxic illness.

In view of Stekel's accusations, he wishes to offer some defense for the physicians of insane asylums and prisons; in regard to the impossibility of influencing the patients, he refers to Melschin's *Tagebuchblätter eines sibirischen Sträflings*.[10]

Federn is very skeptical of Stekel's hypothesis. Among other things, he points to the fact that hydrocephalics may also be very gifted people. He mentions Helmholtz and Gauss.

FREUD regards dementia praecox as merely a modern term (Kraepelin). He himself diagnosed as paranoia the subject of Jung's analysis. The symptoms of dementia praecox include neither dementia, nor are they "praecox." This term subsumes what was previously called hebephrenia (the characteristic of which is early imbecility) in addition to a group from the paranoias. Wherever paranoia becomes

[9] Pierre Jean de Béranger (1780-1857), popular French poet.
[10] L. Melschin (P. F. Jakubowitsch) (1860-1911). [*Pages from the Diary of a Siberian Convict*]. Leipzig: Insel Verlag, 1904.

manifest, even if only to some extent, one would do better to call the illness paranoia.[11]

The topic of the vagrant is primarily a sociological one. The nonsensical treatment of these people in prisons (in so far as they are demented) is only a part of the general neglect of duty in the field of the care of the poor. If there existed a therapy for such conditions (dementia praecox and the like), then their treatment in jail would be a crime.

A layman, R. M. Meyner, once asserted (in the Viennese weekly *Die Zeit*) that it was impossible for a normal person to utter complete nonsense. Through displacements and substitutions, one can discover the true meaning hidden in such utterances. This is what Jung did. He found the meaning hidden behind the nonsensical talk of his patients. The major share of the change [distortion] is due to the mechanisms of wish [fulfillment] and of repression. The paranoiac escapes from life into illness. A repression of that which is real [*des Realen*] takes place as it does in all neuroses and psychoses.

It is often impossible to make a correct diagnosis at the onset of an illness. The clinical picture is the same in many cases. Freud mentions a woman whom he treated (with scant success) as a hysteric. Sometime after the treatment had been broken off, she began to hallucinate spirits and the like; she had a clear-cut spiritualistic paranoia. Obviously, the paranoia had been latently present before but could not be recognized at an early stage.

Freud does not consider Stekel's hypothesis to be the nearest answer. Between an answer that can be substantiated by our present knowledge, and Stekel's suppositions, there must lie, he thinks, a whole series of links.

Rank touched the core of the problem when he attempted to apply the common factor in the flight of poets to an elucidation of the flight of vagabonds.

Freud again reminds us of his division of love life into object love and autoerotism, and furthermore of the retrogression mentioned before (regression of the libido) which also has a bearing on paranoia.

---

[11] Bleuler subsumed all of these groups in the term "the schizophrenias." This is an unfortunate term, for, as Freud pointed out, the ego of neurotics is also split, although to a lesser degree than the ego of schizophrenics.

The vagabond who runs away has a similar motive: *to flee* from his *instincts;* from *object love.*

Hysteria, on the other hand, is distinguished from paranoia by an overemphasis on the object. Hysteria is an excessive being in love. When we remove the patient from his home as a therapeutic measure, we do for him what the vagabond does for himself. The hysteric (in contrast to the paranoiac) is tied to home and to person; he becomes anxious when he moves a little farther from home than usual. The hysteric exaggerates object love and thereby becomes incapable of moving; he fixates himself. The vagabond, on the other hand, tears himself away from his object.

(ADLER, in connection with somnambulism, suggests that *running* is the autoerotic activity of the vagabond.)

Freud is inclined to explain the tendency to see "malingering" [in everything] in terms of the general psychology of the public official. Since the public official is strongly tempted to dissimulate (he gets paid a set salary even when his performance is substandard), he is overly ready to consider everyone else a malingerer.

The fact that there are no violent characters (murderers) among the vagabonds (demented) speaks for a deficiency in object love (they do not hate their fellow man because they cannot love him either).

SADGER considers dementia praecox a "fashionable" psychosis to which much is ascribed that really belongs to hereditary weakness. In vagrancy, the urge to wander, symptoms of heredity are also present. The aversion to associations[12] is a case in point; such an individual cannot bear a permanent tie, his own self is unwilling. Sadger relates the kind of flight that is often seen in hysterical women to infantile tendencies to alarm [frighten the environment], to attract attention, and the like. Such a woman usually does not travel far, so that she can be brought back easily and be pacified by caresses—just like a child.

He can accept neither Jung's toxin hypothesis nor Stekel's cranial theory.

In the practice of nursing, in addition to sadism, homosexuality also plays an important role. Being a male nurse is almost a typically

---

12 [*Assoziationswiderwille*]. Compare with Minutes 22.

109

homosexual vocation. Neurotics also often yearn for an institution out of homosexual desires.

HITSCHMANN first calls attention to a book: *Denkwürdigkeiten eines Arbeiters*[13] in which the author presents a picture of the typical vagabond (without dementia praecox). The book contains nothing erotic, yet reading it one gains the impression that this man is masturbating.

Traveling always means to us a journey of conquest. But one becomes a hero only after he has mastered his love for mother. The home is often also an erotic inhibition. In the vagabond one must also take into consideration the complexity of forces which may not permit him to leave his milieu once he has become enmeshed in it. The choice of vagrancy, moreover, betrays a deep lack of culture which must be based on serious defects.

For the distinction of paranoia and dementia praecox, Hitschmann missed references to the age of the patients in the individual cases.

The discontent with the environment is, in his opinion, mostly a dissatisfaction with the self: a sort of hypochondriacal state.

(FREUD observes here: if it is true that anxiety neurosis is the somatic equivalent of hysteria, there must also exist a somatic condition that has an analogous relationship to paranoia—and that is hypochondria. In this state, a return of the libido to the subject's ego also takes place and is always accompanied by corresponding changes to unpleasurable sensations.[14])

[A.] DEUTSCH mentions the (homosexual) friendship between the poets Rimbaud and Verlaine. One day both disappeared from home. They wandered about together for years. Suddenly they fled from each other, only to reunite later on.

STEKEL speaks of a case of dementia praecox following rheumatism with chorea.

The most important factor in vagrancy is the friend who drives the vagrant into flight. Finally, he calls attention to the similarity of the anxiety neurosis to morbus Basedow.

[13] Karl Fischer: *Denkwürdigkeiten und Erinnerungen eines Arbeiters* [*Memoirs and Recollections of a Worker*], 3 Vols. Leipzig, 1904-1905.
[14] This thought is more clearly crystallized in later works of Freud.

13

SCIENTIFIC MEETING on *February 13, 1907*

Present: Freud, Adler, Federn, Heller, Hitschmann, Kahane, Reitler, Rank, Sadger.

Hitschmann returns Minutes 11 and Reitler's supplement to 9.

PRESENTATION

Spring's Awakening, by Wedekind[1]

SPEAKER: DR. REITLER

Reitler begins with a characterization of the three main figures: Moritz Stiefel, who remains arrested at the stage of infantile sexuality

---

[1] Frank Wedekind (1864-1918) called his play *Frühlingserwachen, Eine Kinder-tragödie* [*A Children's Tragedy*], and he was indeed less concerned with individuals than with the minor and major tragedies of young people awakening to sex without knowledge and without guidance, misunderstood and derided by parents and teachers. The plot is simple: the student Melchior and fourteen-year-old Wendla find answers to their questions in a hayloft. Wendla becomes pregnant; before she dies during an abortion, she asks her helpless mother, "Why did you not tell me these things?"

Melchior's friend Moritz commits suicide because of bad marks in school. His distraught father, searching through Moritz's room, finds an obscene treatise on coitus in a strange handwriting which is discovered to be that of Melchior. Melchior is expelled from school and, fleeing from his parents who want to send him to a reform school, he comes to the cemetery. While reading the inscription on Wendla's tombstone, he suddenly sees Moritz, who has stepped out of his grave, come toward him with his head in his arms. Moritz attempts to lure his living friend into his realm but then the *"Vermummte Herr"* ["The Masked Gentleman"] appears to chase the phantom back into his grave and to take Melchior with him. It is life itself which is personified by the "Masked Gentleman." It is "To the Masked Gentleman" that the play is dedicated by the author.

(autoerotism); his friend Melchior Gabor, who develops beyond infantile sexuality to normal sexuality (intercourse with Wendla); and Wendla who has marked masochistic tendencies. In the very first scene, Wendla betrays her fear of awakening sexuality (thoughts of death, and the like).

Reitler then goes through the drama, scene by scene, giving his interpretations as he goes along. He shows, for instance, how Wedekind connects the incipient atheism and the simultaneous loss of parental authority with the knowledge of parental sexual activity. He mentions the writing of a diary as a sort of psychic discharge.

Reitler understands the story of the headless queen (Maria) and the king with two heads, who gives one to the queen, as a symbolic representation of bisexuality.

In the last scene, Reitler interprets the ghost of Moritz as a representation of the wish to return to infantile sexuality, whereas the Masked Gentleman represents the sexuality of the adult. Both figures are merely projections of the struggle which is going on in Melchior's soul.

From the standpoint of the theory of sexuality, no fault can be found with Wedekind. One might possibly consider it an omission that he does not sufficiently emphasize the importance of the erotogenic zones in presexual life [for later development].

In commenting on the process involved in Wedekind's creativity, Reitler refers to Professor Freud's observation that Jensen in his *Gradiva* gives a correct clinical description of the development of a delusional idea. Replying to an inquiry, Jensen stated that he came upon this intuitively, without any knowledge of the clinical picture, let alone of the mechanisms of delusional ideas. Wedekind cannot be considered equally uninformed.

DISCUSSION

FREUD characterizes Wedekind's book as meritorious but not a great work of art. It has lasting value as a document relating to the history of civilization. We must assume that Wedekind has a deep understanding of sexuality. This is shown by the mere presence of constant sexual undertones in the manifest dialogues. However, to assume a conscious intention in the creation of all of this is no more justified than in the case of Jensen. One can produce the most beautiful symptomatic act without having any knowledge of the concept or nature of symptoms. Freud mentions a slip of the tongue in *Wallensteins Lager*[2] which Schiller certainly could not have explained. After the discourse between Questenberg and Octavio (and Max), Octavio says "Let us go." When Questenberg asks "Whither?" Octavio answers, "To her," but immediately corrects himself to, "To him." During Questenberg's speech it occurred to him that Max's trip with the princess had been arranged only for the purpose of making him fall in love with her, thus tying him to Wallenstein's party. That is why he says "To her" when he is about to go to the general. (He is thinking of the intrigue with the princess.) This motivation of the slip of the tongue is then expressed in the scene between father and son.

The sexual theories of children constitute a theme well worth an independent study: namely, how children discover normal sexuality. In all of their misconceptions, there lies a core of truth.

In considering the dream in which the boy sees legs, clad in tights, stepping over the pulpit, one must not forget that, to the boy, school is partly a means of keeping him away from sexuality. Behind the school tyrant he sees the woman.

Diaries can with equal justification be called a means of repression [just as well as expression]. Freud has at present a patient who used to write zealously in his diary. Now that the diaries can be examined in the light of psychoanalysis, we discover that the essential, the unconscious of early periods, is consistently omitted from the entries.

Concerning atheism, faith in God regularly coincides with faith in the father. Freud mentions a woman patient who lost her faith in God when she lost her trust in her father.

The ill treatment of children in the sack reminds him of the punishment customary for masturbation.

[2] The passage mentioned here appears in the drama *Piccolomini* (Act I, Scene 5) and not in *Wallensteins Lager*. Max Piccolomini, colonel and son of the leader of Wallenstein's enemies at the Austrian imperial court, has just accompanied Wallenstein's daughter on a trip. In a conversation with his father he extolls enthusiastically the blessings of peace. This seems suspicious to the Count Piccolomini since his son was an ardent soldier. Schiller, here, makes use of the fact that the imperial court accused Wallenstein of peace negotiations with the enemy and therefore planned his murder. Freud quotes this example in his *Psychopathology of Everyday Life* (1901). *S.E.*, 6:96-97.

He considers it a fine bit of observation that Wedekind depicts the longing for object love without object choice in Melchior and Wendla who are not at all in love with each other. The fact that Wendla, the masochist, is not beaten by her parents also demonstrates that Wedekind has not followed the usual cliché: otherwise he would have had her beaten in childhood. On the contrary, Wendla complains that she has not been beaten enough. Children who have been severely beaten do not become masochists.

Freud believes that Reitler's interpretation of the fantasy of the headless queen is incorrect. He wants to mention only a few elements: the poetic source [of the fantasy] points to Moritz's later fate; Moritz himself later appears as a "headless" person.[3] With his suicide he follows an old fantasy (what Adler once claimed to be true of all suicides). The organic source of the fantasy is the anonymity of the fantasied woman; he is still too timid, one might say, to love a specific woman. Women frequently indulge in fantasies about headless men (masks). The fantasy of the two-headed king is reminiscent of Plato's sexual fantasies.[4] Lastly, a "headless" individual cannot learn and Moritz is tortured precisely by his incapacity to learn.

The last scene acquires its grimly humorous character with full poetic necessity. The humor of the last scene means only: all of this is basically childish nonsense. The two characters should certainly be understood as two currents in the boy's soul: as the temptation to suicide and as the temptation to live. But it is also true that suicide is the climax of negative autoerotism. In this respect, Reitler's interpretation is correct. The negative of self-gratification is suicide.

The inquisition to which the Masked Gentleman is subjected is not simple humor. Deeper thoughts are behind it. The demon of life is, at the same time, the devil (the unconscious). Life is being subjected to examination as it were. This questioning is a regular characteristic

---

[3] The German text has: ". . . die poetische Quelle ist der Hinweis auf sein späteres Schicksal; Moriz selbst trete ja dann als 'kopflose' Person auf." The literal translation is: "The poetic source is the allusion to his later fate; indeed, Moritz himself appears later on as a 'headless' person."

The meaning seems to be: the fantasy of the headless queen has two sources, a poetic source in the poet's anticipation of Moritz's later fate, and an organic source in the anonymity of the fantasied woman.

[4] Plato's belief in the bisexuality of man is expressed in the form of a legend in his *Symposion.*

114

of the anxiety state. For example, in an anxiety attack, an individual begins to examine himself, allegedly to find out whether he is still in his right senses. Oedipus's examination is also linked with anxiety. Behind the Sphinx lurks anxiety (Sphinx means the strangler.)[5] The question at the base of all these examinations is probably the question raised by the sexual curiosity of the child: where is it that children come from? The Sphinx puts the question in reverse: what is it that comes?[6] Answer: the human being. Quite a few neuroses begin with this question.

Freud reads to the members a letter, written by an eleven-year-old girl to her aunt. The little girl asks her aunt to enlighten her about the origin of children. When she was twenty-three years old, this girl became ill with a severe obsessional neurosis.

RANK maintains that Wedekind is a striking example of Adler's inferiority-overcompensation theory. Wedekind surely had an inferior genital system. It suffices to refer to his undoubted enuresis, which can be proven "symptomatically": the arsonist in one of the earliest short novels by Wedekind (*The Fire in Egliswyl*) is already highly suspicious, but the *pisser-au-lit* scene in one of his last dramas (*Pandora's Box*) is definite proof. He feels certain that other such passages could be found. From Reitler we have already heard about masturbation (solitary and mutual) as well as about emissions and wet dreams (*Spring's Awakening*). He also mentioned the homosexual relationship between the two boys, beginning in the vineyard. There is a wet dream also in *Rabbi Esra*. Later (genuine) homosexuality is quite clear in many of his poems. Proof of the genital inferiority by means of circumstantial evidence: enuresis, emissions, masturbation (solitary and mutual), homosexuality has thus been produced. A second inferior organ is the mouth: Wedekind is known as a hard drinker (enuresis), is cleanly shaven,[7] and expression of a marked oral per-

[5] According to Robert Graves (*The Greek Myths*, 2 Vols. Baltimore: Penguin Books, 1955), the question of the Sphinx is: What creature with a single voice has sometimes two feet, sometimes three, sometimes four, and is weakest when it has the most feet? Oedipus answers: Man, for he crawls on all four as a baby, stands erect on two feet as a youth, and supports himself on his cane as an old man.

[6] In the unconscious, causality can be represented only by a sequence. The development of man is expressed by a series of people beginning with the infant and ending with the old man: each engenders the next.

[7] In those days men on the Continent used to wear beards.

version is found in his works (in *Fire in Egliswyl* and in many of his poems).

The supervalence of the mouth is manifested by the fact that Wedekind became an orator (actor) and singer.

Rank considers Wedekind's sexual symbolism to be for the most part unconscious.

KAHANE emphasizes that one has to defend society against the analytic criticism directed against it. And Wedekind's book is, in essence, a critique of society. All civilization is indeed based on sexual repression as Freud has shown. Education necessarily has to follow this path even though some may perish in the process. This is, we might say, the touchstone held out to the individual by society. Furthermore, one must not seek only the poet himself in his work as Rank is doing. It seems to him that Wedekind did not work consciously. His work turned out too well.

In connection with the headless queen, he wishes to remark that the head symbolizes the penis and that the boy's penis is, so to speak, still a headless penis. Perhaps this implies also that one could not look in the face of the person with whom one has had sexual intercourse. Moreover, the head (reason) is the impeder of sexuality (inhibition).

Examination: onanists who think that their memory is becoming weak examine themselves frequently. And Oedipus too may personify the individual who has not been depleted by autoerotism to the extent that he can no longer answer the question.

SADGER regards Wendla's white garment (last scene) also as a shroud (dying: unfulfilled sexual longing). He calls attention to the change brought about in children by sexual enlightenment: if the enlightenment comes from the parents, admiration for them increases, especially for the mother who "must have suffered and been tormented." However, if enlightenment is given by someone else (servant girl and others), the child thinks: what a good time she must have had.

It should also be emphasized that Wendla has no father. She has known only the homosexual love for the mother and envies her friend who is beaten by her father. Her yearning for a beating is therefore

116

a yearning for heterosexuality.[8] The switch is a symbol for the penis (pointed and flexible). Thus, she is longing for a caress from a father. Etiology of masochism: first caressing.

The headlessness refers to the penis (head means also the behind). The headless queen is the "repressed" mother ("Queen of Hearts"). Lastly, Sadger points out the characteristic trait shown by Moritz's father who after Moritz's suicide claims that Moritz was not his son. In this way, he fends off the disagreeable. (FREUD: That is his solace.)

HELLER, too, is of the opinion that Wedekind did not set out to create with conscious intentions, as Reitler claims. Then he disagrees with Kahane's assertion that sexual struggle is a means of social selection. Indeed, there are quite a few gradations between perishing through something and the mastery of it. There is scarcely a person who emerges from this period without some scar, and it is not always the worst ones who perish.

FEDERN stresses that, of all the great psychologists among modern writers (Dostoyevsky, Musset, Jacobsen, and others), only Wedekind has recognized the importance of infantile sexuality. Perhaps it is a sign of the time; [it] may have become ready for it. Wedekind's work plays some part in curing mankind from the torments of sexuality. On the other hand, our kind of education (through its forceful moral precepts) fulfills a good purpose in so far as it shields the child from sexuality and its torments for a long time. In addition, the powerful tendencies toward cruelty which are inherent in mankind are bridled by our Judaeo-Christian upbringing. In spite of this, it is true that our moral education has to be changed.

ADLER says that he has never regarded Wedekind as a poet but rather as an extremely ingenious person. At the time he wrote *Spring's Awakening,* he was living in Zürich, in licentious company, and was considered a depraved individual. When he was asked what he was doing, he would reply, "I am perishing." It was in this frame of mind that he reached a solution of these problems. In him it is not repressed material that finds poetic expression: he *knows* everything.

[8] Beating as proof of love. See Freud's "A Child Is Being Beaten" (1919). *S.E.,* 17:175-204.

For example, he portrays the masochist Wendla also as a sadist who gratifies her cruel impulses in doing charitable work.

Wendla's speech about short or long dresses betrays her desire to be denuded.

In the headless queen, there lies the germ of a paranoid idea. Contrary to Rank's idea, Wedekind is not a typical example of Adler's theory.

HITSCHMANN points out that Wedekind himself experienced most of what he portrayed. He did not, by a long shot, put in as much morality and "purpose" as one likes to read into it.

Headless: the woman acquires a "head" only through the man. The analogy with the sack is very striking: here too the child's head and body are separated. The pretense of being ignorant in *sexualibus* [sexual matters] is a sign of hysteria: the pleasure in hearing of such things is hidden behind it. It seems doubtful that the child would feel the sadistic tendencies of his parents. (ADLER: Wedekind just *knows* this).

It is a fine characterization that Melchior makes fun of Wendla's charitable activities. In the seduction [of a woman] it is important that the man fight the moral attitudes of the woman. Recalling his own school days Hitschmann points out that a boy with normal sexuality would be expelled (as in Wedekind). During intercourse, Melchior says that he does not love Wendla; nor does she love him: sex and erotism are separated here. Finally, Hitschmann raises the question of where the onanist's *Weltschmerz* comes from.

REITLER adheres to his original interpretation of the final scene (autoerotism—normal sexuality), whereupon

FREUD remarks, concerning the concept of autoerotism, that Havelock Ellis uses this term when only *one* person is involved (thus, for instance, also in relation to hysterical symptoms), whereas Freud uses it when there is no object; for example, those who masturbate with images [*Bilderonanisten*] would not be considered autoerotic.

14

SCIENTIFIC MEETING *on February 20, 1907*

Present: Freud, Adler, Bach, [A.] Deutsch, Federn, Heller, Häutler, Hitschmann, Hollerung, Kahane, Meisl, Rank, Reitler, Sadger, Stekel.

PRESENTATION

PROFESSOR FREUD speaks about
The Hopelessness of All Psychology, by Moebius[1]

The pessimism of the title seems to be psychologically related to the circumstance that the book was written shortly before Moebius's death. It is an important book, of special interest to us because Moebius, taking a different path, comes to conclusions which have been familiar to us for a long time. However, the reviewer cannot agree with all of the author's conclusions. It is an insoluble psychological riddle to him how Moebius could, throughout his life, ignore the Freudian doctrines, especially since they were known to him (as is shown in a passage in the foreword to the translation of Sancti's dream book);[2] and then, in his last work, he advocates views which are in

---

[1] *Die Hoffnungslosigkeit aller Psychologie.* Halle: Marhold, 1906. Paul Moebius (1853-1907), German neurologist and psychiatrist.

[2] Sante de Sancti (1862-1935), Italian physician and dream explorer.

1

Professor Freud
    spricht über __Möbius__ Buch:
„Die Hoffnungslosigkeit aller Psychologie."

(Marhold, Halle 1906).

Der Pessimismus des Titels scheine psychologisch damit zusammenzuhängen, dass die Schrift kurz vor dem Ableben Möbius verfasst sei. Das Buch sei bedeut- und für uns darum von besonderem Interesse, weil Möbius auf einem andern Weg zu Ergebnissen komme, die uns eben lange geläufig sind. Mit allen Resultaten jedoch könne sich Ref. nicht einverstanden erklären. Ein für ihn unlösbares psychologisches Rätsel sei es, dass Möbius sich Zeit seines Lebens über die freudschen Lehren hinwegsetzen konnte, besonders da er sie (nach einer Stelle in .... en Übersetzung von .... Breuerbuch) gekannt habe und in seinen letzten Arbeit vielfach die gleichen Anschauungen vertritt. Das Buch sei übrigens eine Gegenschrift auf Bleuler's ; Assoziations- tätigkeit und Baumstein. —

Ref. bringt nun einzelne Stellen aus Möbius Schrift zur Verlesung, die für uns besondres Interesse haben und knüpft daran einige Bemerkungen. —

120

So sagt Liebius, dass unsere Sinnesorgane nur zur Wahrnehmung
der Aussenwelt eingerichtet seien und nicht zur Selbstbe-
obachtung, wozu Prof. Freud bemerkt, es sei ganz richtig,
dass die Funktion, mit der das Bewusstsein verbunden sei,
nur auf die oberflächlichen Wahrnehmungen eingestellt sei;
während von den inneren Kraftvorgängen nichts wahrge-
nommen werde. Erst jetzt lernen wir durch einen Kunst-
griff die Aufmerksamkeit auf gewisse innere Vorgänge

many respects the same. Besides, the book is a reply to E. Bleuler's "Assoziationstätigkeit und Bewusstsein" ["Associative Activity and Consciousness"].[3]

The reviewer reads aloud a few passages from Moebius's book which are of special interest to us, and adds several comments.

Moebius says, for instance, that our sense organs are equipped only for the perception of the external world and not for self-observation. It is quite correct, Freud remarks, that the function with which consciousness is connected[4] is adjusted only to surface perceptions, whereas nothing is perceived of the internal thought processes. It is only late and by means of a trick [Kunstgriff], as it were, that we learn to direct our attention to certain inner processes. These enter our consciousness by associating themselves with verbal representations. The perception of our thought processes occurs only with the help of words. Moebius also states that whatever we possess of psychology is deposited in language. There is a need now for an entirely new psychology based on self-perception and the use of language.

Moebius starts from the simplest: from animal psychology. As he observes animal life, two points of view force themselves on his mind: that the animal's psychic life is based on *instinct;* and that, for the most part, it takes its course *unconsciously.* Professor Freud remarks that proceeding from the most complex psychic phenomena, the pathological ones, he has reached the same conclusions.

Moebius then compares animal psychology with human psychology and finds that the logical performances of the human being have been overrated to the detriment of the unconscious ones. Most of the psychic processes are unconscious. At this point, Freud remarks that this fact did not require discovery; it is common knowledge gained through experience that most of the psychic processes are unconscious.

Moebius says further that one could, in fact, assume as many instincts as there are aims or capabilities. However, one has been satisfied

---

[3] The correct title is: "Bewusstsein und Assoziationen" ["Consciousness and Associations"]. In: *Diagnostische Assoziationsstudien,* ed. C. G. Jung. Leipzig: Barth, 1906.

[4] It is not likely that Freud actually used the formulation "function with which consciousness is connected. . . ." The ideas he expressed here had already been presented very clearly in the theoretical chapter of *The Interpretation of Dreams* (1900) where he states that the function of the system Cs. is perception (*S.E.,* 5).

to assume two basic instincts in the human being: the instinct of nutrition or self-preservation and the sexual instinct. Anxiety (fear) is the most important manifestation of the life instinct. Translated into rational language, fear means, "I do not want to die." Professor Freud would supplement this certainly correct viewpoint with the following suggestion: the nonneurotic anxiety (fear) which is a manifestation of the life instinct should be contrasted with neurotic anxiety which is an expression of disturbance of and threat to the sexual instinct.[5]

Moebius distinguishes sharply between emotions and instinctual drives, but does not quite know how to classify the emotions. At any rate, it is certain that they emanate from conscious ideas.[6]

He designates as "character" the proportionate strength of the instincts. Freud remarks to this that perhaps the localization of instincts should also be taken into account.[7]

Moebius reaches the conclusion that the core of our being must remain hidden from us. Freud contradicts this, pointing to the general as well as the individual process of development; the adult knows more of his inner life than does the child; there is a process going on within us which aims at disclosing our inner psychic life to us. (This is what we do in miniature in psychotherapy.) This process might be called the conquest of the unconscious.[8]

Moebius goes on to discuss the concept of the unconscious which he defines exactly as we have been accustomed to until now. Then he takes one aspect of psychic activity after another and demonstrates how little of it is conscious. (He also points out that the goblins of fairy tales symbolize the work of the unconscious.) Moebius then distinguishes between a relative unconscious (which can temporarily

[5] This remark permits us to conclude that already at that time Freud thought—though in a vague form—that anxiety is a reaction to an instinctual demand which cannot or must not be fulfilled immediately. This concept was later clearly formulated in *Inhibition, Symptoms and Anxiety* (1926). *S.E.*, 20:77-174.

[6] This sentence cannot have been correctly recorded by Rank, since emotions and affects are, according to Freud, sensations and changes in innervation which are perceived by consciousness.

[7] This formulation, as recorded, is not quite clear. It does not state to what the proportionate strength of the instinct refers; whether the relation of instinct strength to ego is meant or something else. Is it possible that in speaking of the localization of the instincts, Freud already saw character in terms of "psychic structure"?

[8] Using the terminology of *The Ego and the Id* which was published at a much later date (1923), one could say that, in treatment, the id is conquered by the ego. Freud said, "Where id was, there shall be ego."

become conscious) and an absolute unconscious (to which he assigns the instincts, for instance). At this point Freud mentions his own differentiation of the preconscious.

It is evident then that in his cheerless title Moebius refers only to empirical psychology which comes to a halt before the unconscious.

At the end Moebius raises the entirely unjustified and superfluous question: how unconscious processes are possible (a question which could, indeed, just as well be asked in regard to conscious processes).

Finally, Moebius goes so far off as to put down this sentence: Since the unconscious processes do not fall into our consciousness, they must fall either into no or into a strange consciousness. Moebius decides that they fall into a strange consciousness. Professor Freud finds Moebius's question unintelligible and entirely dependent on his use of the uncommon phrase, "to fall into a consciousness." The psychic processes are essentially unconscious; becoming conscious, or being conscious, is not a necessary characteristic of psychic life.[9] But behind Moebius's question, there is the assumption that psychic life is conscious—an assumption from which he was not able to free himself. But with this hypothesis his whole reasoning collapses.

Finally, Moebius espouses a kind of "idealistic monism" in representing psychic life as the truly imperishable and essential. Professor Freud regards this point of view as insufficient and finds its explanation in Moebius's personal feelings: just as the presentiment of death betrays itself in the "hopelessness" of the title, so the hope for an eternal continuation of life manifests itself in the end.

Such personal factors, however, can never be entirely excluded. One would have to be completely normal to provide an entirely objective picture; otherwise it is always distorted.

DISCUSSION

KAHANE, without knowledge of Moebius's book, has an idea which forced itself upon him: namely, that the psyche must be a continuation of something that is there, has been set down [is given] spatially, outside of and temporally before each individual. In the psyche there are far more inherited elements than acquired ones. Consciousness (the

---

[9] This formulation is almost identical with one given in Freud's last work, *An Outline of Psychoanalysis* (1938). New York: Norton, 1949.

degree, the acuity of consciousness) is the result of the individual's own independent work, accomplished with the inherited material. One has to go back to conception and the embryonic development and— peculiar as this may sound—decide on a "psychology of the embryo." The unconscious processes of life are already prepared at this time. The unconscious has been inherited from countless developmental series. The complete Anlage of the mature man is already given in the infant. (One might say that already in his cradle, Goethe was completely "Goethe.") Moebius was right in starting with animal psychology; but one should really go down to the lowest forms of animal life. The very simplest psyche is so dependent on external "charges" that it functions only so long as it receives charges from the outside; the more complicated psyche is less dependent on these charges. The incomplete working up of the charges is the source of abstract thinking, which is also connected with the dulling of our sense organs. A being with acute sense organs will not have a higher psychic life. One has to conclude, in view of the intelligence of some higher animals (dogs), that they are capable of complex psychic performances.

A stratification of the unconscious must be assumed: an unconscious capable of becoming conscious, which is the motor of the psychic processes; and behind it an "eternal unconscious."

Kahane solves the question of why Moebius took no notice of Freud's doctrines by asserting that Moebius simply ignored them: this is the defense of one who finds his own results already discovered by a predecessor. There are only two possibilities in relation to Freud's doctrines: adhering to them or ignoring them.

STEKEL remarks that in an unpublished review of Moebius's book, he has contested the hopelessness of *all* psychology and accepted this cheerless prospect only for academic psychology. There is much else in the book that provokes opposition, as, for instance, the definition of character, the essence of which Stekel sees in the relation between inhibitory ideas and the instincts. With the inclusion of the animal series in the discussion, the old question arises again: at what stage does consciousness begin. Perhaps one has to allow each cell a certain form of consciousness (as Haeckel does).[10] The mistake, however, is

[10] Ernst Haeckel (1834-1919), German biologist and follower of Darwin.

that we must think anthropomorphically. The dog has a verbal image. He thinks in the words he has learned from man.

HOLLERUNG mentions that Moebius, in his first paper "On the Three Ways of Thinking" (at the beginning of the '90s), completely shared Fechner's[11] pantheistic point of view. He may have been the first who, as a *physician*, started from a psychological viewpoint. He took language into special consideration.

In the final, philosophical part of his last work, Moebius professes a sort of monism. Then, however, one must also conceive of psyche and soma as a unity which, seen from different points of view, the introspective and the objective, only seems to show different aspects.

HITSCHMANN regrets that so little, almost nothing, is known about Moebius as a person. However, from his writings, one could learn some things about the man. Apparently he belonged to the species of "women repressers" [*Weiber-Verdränger*]. He wrote about the physiological imbecility of woman.[12] He remained unmarried, was a dog lover, etc. In many respects Moebius resembled Schopenhauer, whom he revered. He has an equally pessimistic outlook which expresses itself also in his opinion that all men are "degenerate." The "hopelessness" stems partly from here, but is in addition connected with his sufferings. He gives the impression (in his criticisms, for example) of a man torn by his affects. But he is incapable of seeing through himself. He would never have known that his pamphlet against women stemmed from an unconscious affect. His ignoring of Freud's doctrines seems not to have been a conscious act but rather the result of an instinctive distaste (repression).

He believes that Moebius took a step forward when he enlarged the content of the unconscious and did not—as we do—see in it only the sexual.[13]

It is not admissible, without making reservations, to draw conclusions about the human being from the observation of animals.

Kahane's arguments are, in part, not new. It would be worth while

---

[11] Gustav Fechner (1801-1887), German experimental psychologist.
[12] This book was widely read and discussed at the time.
[13] This was never Freud's conception of the unconscious.

to explore the verbal ideas and the thinking of deaf-mutes. This should be very instructive from a psychological point of view.

Finally, there is the question of where the expansion of consciousness will lead. Whether one will have to expect it to bring about a complete change in poetry? The drama is, after all, dependent on the concept of [personal] responsibility—a concept which would have to be relinquished. In Ibsen, this concept is already beginning to be doubted.[14]

[14] This is incorrect. See Freud's analysis of Rosmersholm in "Some Character-Types Met with in Psycho-analytic Work" (1916). *S.E.*, 14:324-331.

15

SCIENTIFIC MEETING *on February 27, 1907*

Present: Freud, Adler, [A.] Deutsch, Federn, Häutler, Kahane, Sadger, Stekel [Rank].

COMMUNICATIONS

PROFESSOR FREUD reports that Dr. Guido Brecher, physician in Bad Gastein[1] (an internist), is applying for acceptance; expression of opinion is expected at the next meeting.

Professor Freud relates further that chief physician Bresler, the editor of *Psychiatrisch-neurologische Wochenschrift* has invited him to be co-editor of a new journal dedicated to theological-psychiatric border problems. He has accepted and has sent in a contribution for the first issue.[2]

CONTINUATION OF LAST MEETING'S DISCUSSION

(Moebius: *The Hopelessness of All Psychology*)

Before the discussion begins, PROFESSOR FREUD relates an unusually clear solution of a hysterical attack. The patient is an intel-

---

[1] Bad Gastein is a spa in Austria. Dr. Brecher moved later to Merano.

[2] "Zwangshandlungen und Religionsübung" ["Obsessive Actions and Religious Practices" (1907). *S.E.*, 9:115-127]. *Religionspsychologie*, 1:4-12, 1907. The journal was edited by Bresler and Verbrodt.

ligent girl who suffers from severe hysteria ("absences"). The attack which is coupled with slight convulsions usually begins with her becoming anxious and exclaiming, "Oh! What a terrible tightness in my chest!" Since she frequently has had an attack while riding in a trolley car and would then speak to some strange man in an affable manner, it is natural to think of a prostitution fantasy. She is a visual type: when nothing comes to her mind during the psychotherapeutic session, she looks at the wallpaper and sees pictures and figures there: thus she saw a *man* who squeezed two small children to death. At the time this could not be interpreted. Later, the memory of a childhood experience came to her mind: when she and her siblings were small children, her mother would often ask, "Who wants to be squeezed to death?" When one of them stepped forward the mother would lift the child up and press the child tightly to herself. The patient did not enjoy this type of caress. She was about five years of age when this occurred for the last time. Once when the governess asked her mother why she did that, what good she derived from it, the mother laughed. The patient thought that this must have been a sensual excitement for her mother, brought about by the children's feet pressing against the mother's genitals. It is more likely that the child herself felt a pressure on her genitals during these embraces and was thus stimulated. (She had been masturbating by pressing the thighs together.) Finally, she was very much afraid of these embraces and that is why she lost her breath. This was what she repeated in her seizures. Losing her breath is, of course, the "repression." (It is only when the woman is not excited during sexual intercourse that she complains of the pressure, the weight of the man.) In its origins, therefore, this childhood experience is based on love for the mother.[3]

Later on, the prostitution fantasy also found an explanation: she said that the clarification of the seizure had pleased her very much; then she added that her brother used to be very eager for these embraces, whereas she was afraid of them. However, since the mother promised the children a penny each time, she, too, submitted to them. Thus she was even at that time one who provides sexual pleasure for

[3] See "Some General Remarks on Hysterical Attacks" (1909). *S.E.*, 9:227-234.

money. Prostitution[4] can here be reduced to its very basic expression.[5]

The image on the wallpaper proved likewise to stem from this childhood experience; but the woman (mother) was transformed into a man (rendered unrecognizable; change of sex).[6] Shortly before these embraces were given up she had begun to exhibit herself.

DISCUSSION (continued)

STEKEL repeats that, in his opinion, Moebius's disregard[7] of Freud is improper. Moebius was a thrower of sensational bombshells ("On the Pathological in Goethe"; *On the Physiological Imbecility of Women*),[8] and with the book under discussion he has just thrown his last bomb into this world. What he says about the instincts as *primum movens* is of value. But Stekel misses the reference to the pairs of instincts (Adler) such as hunger-disgust. In the discussion of memory he misses a reference to Freud. According to Moebius, the young boy is indifferent to the opposite sex—an assertion which shows clearly that, as far as sexual development is concerned, Moebius shares the academic viewpoint which lets sexual life begin only at puberty.

Moebius is unable to explain the instinct: indeed, it is simply a reminiscence [*Erinnerung*] of the unconscious.[9]

Stekel summarizes his opinion: there are magnificent passages in the book; the title is misleading; it refers only to academic psychology. Besides, this book is not an honest piece of work: to some extent Moebius is a follower of Freud—a fact which he passes over in silence. There is a compromise of psychic currents in his heart.

[4] The original has: "*Der Vorwurf der Prostitution . . .*"; literally: the blame, reproach for; accusation of; or, possibly, the shame attached to prostitution.

[5] This is an excellent example of the overdetermination of a symptom.

[6] In the symptom, the traumatic experience is repeated in a distorted form. See *Studies on Hysteria* (1895; *S.E.*, 2) and "Hysterical Phantasies and Their Relation to Bisexuality" (1908; *S.E.*, 9:157-166), especially the following sentence: "(1) Hysterical symptoms are mnemic symbols of certain operative (traumatic) impressions and experiences" (p. 163).

[7] "*Vorbeireden*"—literally, bypass in speaking; looking the other way.

[8] Original German titles: "Über das Pathologische bei Goethe" and *Über den physiologischen Schwachsinn des Weibes.*

[9] In this form, the sentence is unintelligible. Perhaps it should read, "a reflection of the unconscious."

ADLER has read only part of the book. He regrets that fate did not allow Moebius to develop further along the lines indicated in this book. His "throwing of bombs" might some day have been the occasion of a revolutionary deed in the realm of psychiatry. Several passages in his book seem to indicate that he was familiar with Freud's writings. As a philosopher, he deserves credit for attaching so little importance to association psychology. The phenomena of psychology take a course parallel to that of instinct life. They are the external forms of manifestation adapted to our sense organs. The next step for Moebius would have been to go back from the instinct to the organ—a step which Adler has taken. In regard to "emotions," Moebius has not struggled through to a conception as deep as his conception of instincts. Adler calls the emotions that facet of our instinct life which is adapted to our perceptual faculty. Moebius distinguishes too sharply between instinct and feeling.

On several points, especially concerning philosophy (categorical imperative), one cannot help but agree fully with Moebius. It is absurd to argue whether the animal has a soul or not. If everything is merely a perceptible expression of instinct life, then it applies to the animal as well as to man. It is the sphere of the instincts which needs further exploration.

[A.] DEUTSCH first quotes a passage from the book where Moebius says that the concept of an unconscious as such is meaningless to him. Deutsch himself has had the same experience; consequently he has come to assume stratifications (Kahane). He cannot consistently find confirmation of Moebius's statement that the unconscious is always "rescuing."[10]

He wonders whether the anthropomorphism, this constant source of error, could not be corrected by a new set of definitions of concepts. Moebius is wrong in assuming that split-off [parts] or derivatives of primary instincts are independent instincts.

SADGER believes this book to be the most important of Moebius's works. He was a clear thinker who pursued his thoughts to the end. He possessed great linguistic skill and was one of the very few neurologists who are also psychologists.

[10] Unintelligible without knowledge of Moebius's book.

Sadger then mentions five reviews by Moebius of Freud's papers (none, however, of the *Dream* book or of the *Theory of Sexuality*), published in the *Schmidtsche Jahrbücher*. The reviews are not enthusiastic, it is true, but they show understanding.[11]

The Speaker remarks here that perhaps we may be inclined to overestimate the significance of the Freudian teachings for psychology; that is to say, the importance of the sexual factor for psychology, for the unconscious.[12] There exists also a nonsexual unconscious, as is demonstrated by the psychology of everyday life, into which we therefore cannot penetrate very deeply. There are a great number of "unconscious" states which the present results of psychoanalysis cannot elucidate.[13] Moebius tries to fill this gap by viewing the instinctual drives independent from the sexual drive. For we can ferret out the unconscious only when it is linked with the sexual and only to the extent that it is linked with the sexual.

What a perception is; how thinking comes about; how will transforms itself into action—these things we cannot fathom, and in them Moebius seems to see the hopelessness of all psychology. His merit, therefore, is merely a negative, critical one. It is no mean feat to have stated for the first time something which is self-evident.

Concerning the quotation from the Odyssey about the blood-drinking shadows, Moebius may very well have taken it independently out of Homer.

HÄUTLER sees the panpsychism, so prominent at the end of the book, foreshadowed in some of the earlier passages: Moebius's entire way of thinking is impregnated with it, as it were. Moebius's polemics against Darwin, for example, in which he argues against the fruitfulness of chance, are essentially a result of his intelligence-blueprint of the world [*Intelligenzweltplan*]. In his conception of character a similar view is foreshadowed.

---

[11] Actually Moebius had also reviewed Freud's *Interpretation of Dreams*, in *Schmidts Jahrbuch*, 269(3) : 271, 1901; as well as Freud's *Psychopathology of Everyday Life*, in *Schmidts Jahrbuch*, 282(1) : 104, 1904. (Cf. Alexander Grinstein: *The Index of Psychoanalytic Writings*, 3:1393. New York: International Universities Press, 1958.)

[12] It is evident here how beset by doubts Freud's pupils were at that time and how incapable they still were of fully grasping Freudian ideas.

[13] At that time, Freud had already postulated the three states of psychic life: conscious, preconscious, and unconscious. Evidently Sadger did not understand this.

His viewing the world as cosmos and each living being as related to the great cosmos has led him to his "hopelessness": in each human being, there is so much which can never become conscious and which nevertheless greatly influences the continuous development, which he sees in each individual, that he must necessarily think of psychology as hopeless. Psychology is concerned only with manifestations in the individual, but not with the cosmic. For our intelligence can recognize only that which is of the same kind (homogeneous). Moebius should have said, "There is too much of the past in us for us ever to be able to understand this past with our intelligence, especially since it is the younger and heterogeneous factor."[14]

Concerning the question of which comes first, idea or matter, Moebius's decision in favor of the idea follows the demand of a logic which attempts to envisage a totality.[15]

Moebius misunderstood Kant's Categorical Imperative as did so many others: Kant did not postulate a moral law for the individual but merely stated the fact that man feels within himself a "Thou shalt" when he acts.

We cannot escape anthropomorphism ([A.] DEUTSCH): we cannot divest ourselves of our psyche.

RANK finds a certain (in part contrasting) harmony between his book written two years ago (*The Artist: The Beginnings of a Sexual Psychology*) and the book by Moebius. In a certain sense, his work can be viewed as the exact opposite [*Gegenschrift*] of Moebius's book; where Moebius sees hopelessness, he sees hopefulness.

The harmony refers only to fundamentals: like Moebius, he too has made the animal his point of departure; but, as Kahane demanded, he started from the lowest organism. Like Moebius, he realized that he first had to study instinct life.[16] But in contrast to Moebius, he endeavored to develop a monism of instinct life. He found the first to be the instinct to avoid displeasure (life instinct); the instinct to gain pleasure (sexual instinct) is its consequence. There are various "life instincts," dependent upon external conditions. However, every life

[14] This is difficult to understand, probably because of too much condensation in the recording.

[15] Unintelligible.

[16] The original, literally translated, would read: ". . . he too first came upon, encountered instinct life [. . . *sei auch er zuerst auf das Triebleben gekommen*]."

instinct can become a sexual instinct (in the Freudian sense) as can be seen in the excremental perversions. The apparent variety and multiplicity of the instincts is attributable to this mutability of the few basic instincts. With this [concept of] transformation, the development of the "psychic and the cultural" from the instincts becomes evident.

In any case, instinct life is not so inaccessible as Moebius thought. In his work, he has referred particularly to the conquest of the unconscious, of which Professor Freud spoke last time, and to the end which threatens poetry in the course of this development. Had Moebius lived longer, he would probably have become a follower of Freud.

FEDERN sees no change of views in Moebius's last work that might have been caused by a premonition of death. Moebius took the same stand in his earliest writings. As far as the unconscious and his ignoring of Freud is concerned, Moebius was not in the least interested in discovering the unconscious. To him, it is merely one more proof of the need for a metaphysical point of view. The conclusion of his work was determined beforehand, and the new work serves only to support his old views. This book belongs to the type of books which always appear in the wake of a newly discovered principle, presuming to explain everything by this one principle; this is its greatest shortcoming.

Moebius assumes special instincts for individual endowments: in this context one could also ask whether in the course of development new drives do not arise (love of beauty, search for truth).

Another consideration would be whether something in the order of an inner perception exists. The idea is the sensory experience of an inner process. Our consciousness is not exclusively dependent on language. The emotions are something well defined. We know as much about them as we do about red or white.

PROFESSOR FREUD replies to each discussant in turn.

He cannot sympathize with Stekel's harsh treatment of Moebius. In his opinion, Stekel overrates his (Freud's) merits—a point to which Sadger's comment is relevant; for example, the topic of memory is far from being exhausted by the few remarks which he has made about it. The whole problem of remembering and forgetting has not yet been dealt with, neither by himself nor by anyone else.

134

The fact that Moebius ignored his teachings, Freud does not consider a willful attempt to conceal his knowledge of the work, but he sees in it a sign that Moebius has failed to take any stand regarding the psychoanalytic movement as a whole.

Adler's objection to Moebius's sharp distinction between emotions and instincts is not justified. Moebius's attempt to construct a new elementary psychology within the confines of so small a pamphlet was of course bound to fail. However, if one wanted to create such a new elementary psychology (a metapsychology which ignores the difference between conscious and unconscious),[17] one would need to make a sharp distinction between instincts and emotions. First, one would have to establish: instinct is a concept, a term for the dynamic or disturbing influence which organic (structural) needs exercise on psychic processes. The instinct bridges over from the organic to the psychic. Emotion, however, belongs entirely to the psychic realm. Consciousness (the inner sense organ) is attuned to two end points of a broad arc of processes: that is, geared to perceptions and emotions. Everything else is not subsumed under the concept of consciousness. The schematic representation of such a psychic apparatus would look like this:

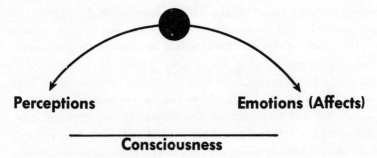

Perceptions   **Emotions (Affects)**

Consciousness

(Instinct means the dependency of this scheme on the organic structure.[18])

---

17 From this remark on metapsychology, we may deduce that Freud, even then, considered the psychic apparatus from several viewpoints, a fact which becomes ever clearer in his later writings.

18 The dynamic conception of instinct is very clear in this passage. The instinct is of organic origin and, as such, unconscious. Sensations and perceptions are conscious, but they are dependent on the organic structure, as is the instinct. In Freud's later work this conception becomes increasingly clear.

The psyche is roused by external stimuli, and [the changes called forth in consciousness by] these excitations are [what we call] perceptions.[19] One has to substitute the affects for the movements (of the motor end) at the other end of the arc; the affects are motoric in nature; they are internal discharges. External stimuli evoke feelings in us (this is a secretory, centrifugal process—*Interpretation of Dreams*): this is all that the psychic world encompasses (an Indian penitent would fit this scheme).

The nervous system acts as an intermediary between ourselves and the outside world: perceptions call forth emotions; these emotions are inner actions. These internal processes then serve as a new sensory apparatus for generating motor functions. These actions [directed] onto the outer world occur automatically. We do not perceive them. It is only the change in the outside world which we then perceive again.—Something positive must be inserted to fill this gap which Moebius left.[20]

The answer to Deutsch's question concerning anthropomorphism is that it is not at all necessary to outgrow it. Our understanding reaches as far as our anthropomorphism. As to the question concerning the nature of the unconscious, one must above all not presuppose that psychic processes are conscious. The unconscious is the psyche (which is not identical with the conscious processes). One can try to comprehend the nature of the unconscious only in terms of its processes.[21]

Sadger's comment, that the results gained from psychoanalysis ought not to be overrated as to their usefulness for psychology because these results always deal only with sexuality, becomes immaterial when it is pointed out that through psychoanalysis we discover not the pathological but rather the normal characteristics of the psyche. It is true, however, that drawing the necessary conclusions does require a certain amount of practice and reflection. The sexual material is merely the content. The mechanisms are quite independent of it. Psycho-

[19] The original has: ". . . *und diese Anregungen sind die Wahrnehmungen*" (". . . and these excitations are the perceptions").

[20] This "positive" is obviously found in the unconscious as Freud has very clearly shown in his *Outline of Psychoanalysis* (1938). New York: Norton, 1949. See also the "Project for a Scientific Psychology" (1895), in *The Origins of Psychoanalysis*. New York: Basic Books, 1954.

[21] The unconscious is not accessible to direct observation; it can only be inferred as Freud has stressed on many occasions.

analysis is the main source of knowledge about *normal* psychic processes.

Federn has, indeed, grasped the core of the book when he says that Moebius used the unconscious merely as a prop for his *Weltanschauung*.

To Häutler: if the categorical imperative were nothing but the observed fact that man has a conscience, the value of Kant's achievement would amount to nothing.

To Rank: the "drive" to gain pleasure is certainly not a primary instinct. Originally, the instincts have no intention. It is only in the psyche that "pleasure," the intention, is added.[22]

Moebius's viewpoint regarding the singularity or plurality of the instincts is, in his opinion, quite correct, since Moebius complies with linguistic usage. (Plural of instinct.) [Moebius speaks of instinct*s* rather than instinct.]

The obsessional neurosis is particularly suited to throw light on the nature of intellectual performances and processes. From the analysis of obsessional neurosis one learns how the psychic apparatus is structured in its higher strata.[23]

[22] The instinct is organic; pleasure, intention, desire are psychic.
[23] Here Freud evidently refers to reaction formations, protective measures (precautions), doubts, speculations, to the manifestations of conscience, and the like.

16

SCIENTIFIC MEETING on *March 6, 1907*

Present: Freud, Adler, [A.] Deutsch, Federn, Graf, Häutler, Heller, Hollerung, Kahane, Sadger, Stekel, Rank.
Drs. Jung and Binswanger from Zurich as guests.[1]
Dr. Sadger borrows Minutes 15, returned on March 20.

PRESENTATION

A Psychoanalysis

SPEAKER: ADLER

The patient is a young man, a Russian student, from a wealthy family. He introduced himself as a stutterer. From his sixth year, he had undergone various treatments for nervousness.

In his childhood he suffered from headaches, pavor nocturnus, and insomnia, and after puberty he suffered from melancholia, fear of physical contact, and attacks of palpitation of the heart. He remembers that he was told in his fourth year that, as a newborn baby, he was at his mother's breast for only a few days and then was weaned to the

---

[1] Present for the first time in the Vienna Society.

bottle. For a long period, he suffered from intestinal catarrh. All in all, the patient seems to be a man with an inferior alimentary tract. He was a thumb sucker and was excessively fond of sweets. Between his seventh and his tenth year he became frugal in regard to his own needs; he was miserly and developed an aversion to eating. To others he was generous. He had the reputation of being a naughty, malicious boy. He was the "speaker" of the family ([prone to] lectures, etc.). In connection with eating and regularly with sexual recollections, disgust would appear. Rumbling of the bowels, bad teeth (their position), and hemorrhoids were further indications of an inferior alimentary tract.

Analysis disclosed strongly suppressed[2] sadism and exhibitionism. The exhibitionism [was] a family trait. He frequently slept in his father's bed, and on these occasions his father would tell him about his own unfaithfulness to the mother (mental exhibitionism).

There was rivalry with his younger brother. He had a recollection from his third (or fourth) year: when the brothers were in bed they played with their genitals. The patient made comparisons and found his brother's penis to be larger than his own.

In his recollections his father stands out as a giant who could conquer all difficulties. Asked whether he had not compared his own penis to his father's, he said, "Father—oh, he had such an enormous one" (he means that altogether no comparison could be made). It also bothered him that the growth of his pubic hair lagged behind that of his brother.

[There also had been] games of undressing with other children; he put his hand under his governess's skirt; scenes of dressing up when he would disguise himself as a girl (also dreams of this kind); traces of enuresis, the recollection of which emerged when he was talking of a bathing establishment which his father owned. He asked about the external differences between the sexes when he saw a certain picture in a museum.

Adler then presents the analysis of this patient's compulsion, which is connected with bathing.

The compulsion: When he took a bath he *had* to submerge and *had*

[2] At that time "suppressed" and "repressed" were not yet sharply distinguished.

139

to remain submerged under water until he had counted either to 3 or to 7 or to 49 (or all three numbers together). He was often near suffocating. He explained this action by saying that he had grown up under difficult circumstances. (As a Jew, he had studied in an anti-Semitic gymnasium; altogether, his *"Jewish complex"* was very much in the foreground.) If he could stand this water procedure, he would also be able to surmount the difficulties of life.

Associations: 3 is the sacred number; one counts 1, 2, 3, when taking a run for jumping; 7 is the Jewish holy number; $7 \times 7 = 49$; this is the Jewish Jubilee year.

Bath associations: when submerged in the water, he may have his usual palpitations of the heart; he also had them when he was riding a bicycle in Berlin in front of others. Explanation: because one's pants can easily fall down when one is riding a bicycle. The patient has an inclination to keep his pants on. Even during "intercourse" with girls he frequently keeps his pants on. At times he even leaves them buttoned. In Russia, he continued, one bathes without pants. There are people who, in this situation, hold their hand in front of their genitals; he has also done that. Why? "Perhaps because I am a Jew."

He submerged [himself] in order not to see. If one looks at the matter as a whole, the patient says, then it looks like a baptism.

Adler refers only briefly to the fact that this compulsive act has the character of a compromise. He predicts that the patient will also lose the stammering when he is freed of his psychic burdens.

DISCUSSION

FEDERN, in connection with the childhood defects, raises the question of whether man could not be spared further unfavorable development if a change were effected in the causative factors. It would be interesting to observe to what extent such symptoms of illness might disappear spontaneously. One can certainly not infer the inferiority of an organ from intestinal catarrh.

The obsessional need to remain dressed could be connected with a fear of soiling the pants. (He knows of such a case.)

Isn't the excessive taste for sweets [a sign of] a repressed sexual factor? The mania for lecturing is connected with exhibitionism.

HELLER asks to what extent the obsessional need to remain dressed is connected with exhibitionism.

HÄUTLER believes that the meaning of the numbers and their determination is not sufficiently explained. The submerging may also be traced back to a childhood game: timid children, while bathing, are often forced to stay under water by their playmates. Voluntary submersion would then be a reaction to this.

GRAF points to the coexistence of stinginess and lavishness in the patient. Childhood game: competitive diving: counting to see who can stand it longer. Fondness for eating sweets may be traced back to a strong emphasis on the oral zone and is analogous to smoking.

SADGER does not consider any of the symptoms adequately explained. In addition, it seems to him that the organ inferiority has been overemphasized. It is much simpler to explain the patient's disgust as stemming from an identification with his mother (who suffered from hysterical vomiting) than to attribute it to organ inferiority. His passion for disguising himself as well as sleeping with his father is in accord with an identification with his mother.

As to eating delicacies on the sly, the objects are usually substitute sexual symbols. This is particularly true of fruit (kleptomania).

One of his patients remembers having been weaned from his mother's breast at six months and having reacted with vomiting.

Exhibitionism goes back to infancy: caresses during swaddling and unswaddling. Masochistic ideas can, likewise, often be traced back to the helplessness of the infant.

Anti-Semitism: one of his patients, whose father was anti-Semitic, had anti-Semitic ideas about him (Sadger); in this, he imitated his father. The patient was once homosexually in love with a Jew (without success). Now he wants his Jewish physician to be the Jew who loves him homosexually. At the same time, he transfers from the father onto the physician.

STEKEL considers the choice of this analysis unfortunate. In addition, Adler has overlooked several points: for instance, in Stekel's opinion, the patient submerged [himself] primarily in order not to be seen. The number 3 may perhaps be determined by the patient's having begun to play with his genitals at the age of three years.

141

He regards stammering as a hysterical symptom (when a stammerer is alone, he does not stammer).

Two cases: A Jewish preacher suddenly could not continue to preach at a certain point. He is a "saintly" man. However, his fantasy life is extremely voluptuous. When he was a boy, he became intrigued with a passage in a Talmudic book belonging to his father, where the letters of the name Jehova were interpreted as sexual symbols. He had repressed this recollection; it emerged later. He broke down in his speech at the point where this name was to be pronounced. When he was cured, he offered Stekel a gift—a chest containing games[3] (a homosexual gesture).

The second case is that of a boy who believed that one could detect his masturbation from the blue circles under his eyes. Assurance to the contrary freed him from his stammering.

RANK thinks that the numbers 7 and 49—the small and the big Jubilee year—represent the small and the big penis. The repugnance against eating food (which his mother ordered him to eat) is a revenge on his mother who did not suckle him.

FREUD, commenting on these remarks, says that 3 may perhaps represent the Christian penis; 7 the small, and 49 the large Jewish penis. The smaller Jewish penis is represented in the compulsion by the larger number. Of course, this does not exhaust the determinations. It is just as in number dreams where everything is determined to the minutest detail and nothing is accidental. In proof of this exactness of psychic determination, he relates several compulsive actions of a woman patient. (In view of the forthcoming publication of these compulsive actions, we refrain from entering them in the Minutes.[4]) In this case, the physician had only the task of removing resistances over and over again. Then the meaning of the actions suddenly became clear to her.

As far as Adler's inferiority doctrine is concerned, certainly it has added something to our knowledge of the organic basis of the neurosis. However, the patient's development is not in accord with Adler's conception: the patient was first an "orator" and only later did he begin

---

[3] The original has: ". . . *sämtliche Spiele* . . ." (". . . all of the games"—those which he had spoken of?)

[4] See the essay "Obsessive Actions and Religious Practices" (1907), mentioned in Minutes 15 (n. 2).

to stammer. Speaking belongs to exhibitionism and stammering is a symptom of suppression. It is the characteristic feature of the obsessional neurosis that the symptom originates in the impulse which is destined for suppression.[5]

Sadger's remark on exhibitionism should be welcomed as an enrichment. However, one should not give credence to a recollection from the sixth month: reliable recollection begins only at a year and a half or a year and three quarters. Anyway, we do not really have true recollections from early childhood. All of them are constructed later.[6] For this, the individual takes up his own childhood recollections and weaves into them material gained from the observation of small children.[7] Whenever we are dealing with a fantasy of infancy, we are always faced with the question at which time the fantasy was formed.

Stinginess and lavishness are a contrasting pair; both of these opposites are always found together, but in different areas. Hence, this patient's lavishness is not a form of repression of his stinginess.

[A.] DEUTSCH does not consider the analysis incomplete. Adler has presented the main features. He asks whether the patient did not have a feeling of triumph with the number 49. The words used by the teacher who yelled at the boy might have been significant for the stammering, which appeared again after this scene. (ADLER: the teacher was an anti-Semite.) The swaddling of infants apparently exercises no influence on masochistic development (Sadger) because English children, who are never swaddled, frequently do become masochists.

KAHANE defines the obsessional idea as the façade of a coherent psychic complex which protrudes into consciousness. Rooted deep in the unconscious, it is a complex to which religion and sexuality contribute the material. The patient's submerging should perhaps be interpreted symbolically: as a return into water: he wishes to begin a new life. Here, too, one might find a root of the stammering: just as life once started, so the word once uttered, cannot be undone.

HOLLERUNG asks about the patient's sexual activity.

[5] This is later termed "reaction formation" in the obsessional neurosis.
[6] Obviously Freud means: unadulterated early childhood recollections do not exist.
[7] See the Wolf Man, in "From the History of an Infantile Neurosis" (1918). *S.E.*, 17:3-122.

DR. BINSWANGER asks whether the patient did not experience sensual pleasure (sadomasochistic) during the submersion.

DR. JUNG remarks that he is unable to make any extensive criticisms because he is just beginning to familiarize himself[8] with Freudian ideas. He is still viewing things in a different way. Freud sees from within. He sees from without. Considering the selection of numbers, while granting that a great influence is exercised by the emotional constellations, one should also remember the frequency value of certain numbers. During his association experiments, he has learned to observe how often frequency numbers are selected (i.e., number of children, of members of the family, etc.).

The inclination to dressing up is a mystery to him.

The criticism directed at the doctrine of organ inferiority seemed too harsh to him. In his opinion, it is a brilliant idea which we are not justified in criticizing because we lack sufficient experience.

ADLER deals briefly with a few details: the exhibitionism is to be traced back to scoptophilia.

Concerning the further derivation of the stinginess, he relates the following: the patient suffered from intestinal catarrhs and was not permitted to eat certain foods. This is the origin of the deprivations which he later imposed on himself. He also suffered from involuntary bowel movements. When he was sexually excited he could not retain his feces (e.g., while talking to a favored girl). His fear of examinations (fear of involuntary evacuations) is also connected with this.[9]

He must reject Stekel's interpretation of the stammering.

The patient's sexual activity: during his seventeenth year, he occasionally had intercourse with prostitutes after drinking bouts (ejaculatio praecox). He was impotent with his fiancée, a circumstance to which both his repressed exhibitionism and his stinginess (the girl was poor) contributed. Now, after he has been given the explanation, he is able to perform normal coition.

[8] The original has ". . . *an den Freudschen Ideen heraufzuklettern*"; literally: ". . . to climb to the peak (mountain) [ascend the ladder]," which is also in German an unusual way of putting it.

[9] It seems that it was not yet recognized that the obsessional neurotic goes through a regression to the anal-sadistic phase of libido development and that stuttering is based on a fixation of anality.

The frequency numbers are preferred because they have a double meaning.

The interpretation of the small and the larger penis is absolutely correct. In a numerical dream of the patient, there appears the constellation 27.03. Associations: 7^2 (instead of 27): 7 squared equals 49 and, written mathematically, $7 > 3$; 7 is greater than 3.

That childhood recollections are really constructions is borne out by the fact that we see ourselves in them.

The patient refrains from generous actions when he is hungry: from this it follows that his tendency toward lavishness is fed by suppressed stinginess. One can assume that the "water craze" [*Brunnenkoller*], the nervous states during reducing cures, is based on similar connections. (He knows a patient who rages against his father-in-law whenever he is hungry because his father-in-law had cheated him in the dowry.)

The sensual feelings during the submersions are explained by the enuretic constitution which also explains to us the choice of place for the compulsive action. The dressing up is connected with the marked homosexual component.

FREE DISCUSSION

PROFESSOR FREUD points out the connection of stinginess and lavishness with the stress on the anal zone. Such people are distinguished in later life by special characteristics: they are orderly, clean and conscientious, stubborn and peculiar in money matters.[10]

Finally it should be pointed out that the contents of the symptoms have the nature of a compromise: It is as if the patient said, "I want to be baptized[11]—but the Jewish penis is still larger. (Thus I remain a Jew.)"

---

[10] See "Character and Anal Erotism" (1908). *S.E.*, 9:167-175.

[11] To be "baptized" equals to be submerged in water and to come up again—which is also a symbolic expression for rebirth. It has, in addition, the meaning of cleansing, which would be characteristic of the rejection of anality in obsessional neurosis.

17

SCIENTIFIC MEETING on *March 20, 1907*[1]

Present: Freud, Adler, Federn, Häutler, Hitschmann, Kahane, Rank, Stekel (part of the evening), Sadger, Brecher.

COMMUNICATIONS

DR. SADGER proposes his nephew, Dr. Fritz Wittels, for acceptance as a member. Dr. Brecher resigns.

Hitschmann borrows Minutes 16.

PRESENTATION

Mysticism and Comprehension of Nature

SPEAKER: HÄUTLER

Comprehending nature goes back to mystic roots. The mystic drive and the drive to understand nature are often found together, frequently even in the same individual (as in some romantics). Primarily, however, they are found together in three great epochs of civilization: in

---

[1] No meeting was held on March 13, because Professor Freud was indisposed. [Note in original manuscript.]

the Greek civilization of the sixth or seventh century; in the Renaissance; and in the epoch of the Romantics (Schelling in particular[2]). This simultaneous appearance permits the inference of an intimate connection between the two drives. The most essential aspects of mysticism are the following:

1. The tendency toward achieving a unity [*Vereinheitlichung*] (man's feeling of being one with God, of God being one with nature, of man being one with nature). This unification of all of life, such a repression of the impression of manifold and varied reality, is possible only with a pathologically intensified emotional life (which resembles a Bacchusian state). Unification is accomplished, as in the dream and in neurosis, by means of visual representation. This *feeling* of unity is then projected onto nature and transformed into the understanding of nature. Already Thales,[3] the first natural philosopher, tries to unify everything: he says, "All is One." From that time on, this principle has never been abandoned in European science; but like the following principles, it was not discovered empirically and cannot be demonstrated by logical means. Rather, determined by internal experience, it was projected onto nature.

2. The feeling of contrast. When the mystic awakes from his blissful mood and returns to sober reality, he feels impelled to establish a connection between these opposites. This induces him to construct a world on the basis of two contrasting sensations as Anaximander[4] has already done. According to his theory, the world originated from "warm" and "cold." From then on this principle of contrasts has not disappeared from science. It can be traced even to positive and negative electricity. This principle, too, is projected from emotional life onto nature. The same is true of

3. The concept of the infinite, first introduced by Heraclitus.[5] This concept, which became so important for science in later times, stems also from emotional life; from the exalted religious feeling in which God is that which has no boundaries.

These three principles of the comprehension of nature have thus

[2] Friedrich Wilhelm Schelling (1775-1854), German philosopher.
[3] Thales of Milet (640-546 B.C.).
[4] Greek natural philosopher (611-547 B.C.).
[5] Greek philosopher (554-475 B.C.).

been taken over from the sphere of human emotions into science and have been transposed into comprehension. With the rise of mysticism, therefore, there is a parallel extension of consciousness; and since mysticism originates only in an abnormally intensified emotional life, the development of the intellect must be viewed as a pathological symptom.

According to Häutler, causality, a concept of the greatest importance for the understanding of natural phenomena, has been learned from religious compulsions: the religious ceremony is the academy for the concept of causality: there man learns that each offence is followed by a consequence. Thus, this principle, too, is no empirical discovery but has been found through analogy and then has been applied to nature.

Lastly, the concept of harmony, which resolves all contrasts, was introduced by Pythagoras[6]—also from Orphic regions.

Also the Greeks' predilection for *logos*, the word, has even today devastating effects on science. By means of the word, the Greek anthropomorphizes nature. It is characteristic of this adulation of the word that Greek natural philosophy developed after the knowledge of writing had spread, and the mysticism of the Renaissance after the invention of the art of printing.

DISCUSSION

HITSCHMANN comments that the theme is too specialized to suit him. Besides, the newer natural philosophies are closer to his way of thinking; frequently one can observe that great scientists devote themselves to one or the other mystical philosophy, in contrast, as it were, to their constant preoccupation with the material world. Swedenborg,[7] who was schooled in technical science, became one of the greatest mystics. Mach[8] relates somewhere that the idea of his monism came to him while he was taking a walk on a beautiful Sunday morning. This derivation of his image of the world from a purely emotional state has always seemed to Hitschmann reason for the most serious objection to such an image of the world.

6 Philosopher (about 510 B.C.).
7 Swedish scientist, philosopher and theologian (1688-1772).
8 Ernst Mach (1836-1916), Austrian physicist and psychologist.

The feeling of being one with the world is also induced by the first love. Music, too, can produce a similar reality-detached mood.

ADLER points out that [one's] *Weltanschauung* is permeated by the most personal feelings. However, he does not agree with Häutler's opinion that there is always a state of excitation involved. Rather, in the development of philosophical comprehension of the world, a process similar to that in the choice of a profession takes place: the permeation of the world by one's most intimate wishes and desires. Other, deeper determinants must play an additional role, for other people have also been in the situation described by Häutler. It would be rewarding to investigate for what sort of people numbers play such a prominent role (people whose rhythmical sense is especially developed).

Great importance should be attributed to the view of intellectual development as a pathological symptom.

The development of intellect in certain apes must have been enormously influenced by the use of the hind limbs as feet.

FREUD remarks that in metaphysics, we are dealing with a projection of so-called endopsychic perceptions. The explorer of nature, on the other hand, may, through practice, have sharpened his powers of observation to such an extent that he can apply them to the outside world. But the segment of the outside world which he can understand still remains relatively small. The rest, he "thinks," will be as I am; that is, he becomes anthropomorphic in relation to the rest; the remainder, therefore, he replaces with the dim perception of his own psychic processes. In exploring the problem of the psychological origin of philosophical concepts, we must first turn to the old philosophers where the concepts are still fresh. But even there, the problem is still too elusive. Therefore one has to study it in relation to smaller, more tangible subjects closer at hand, and the deliria are such subjects. They, likewise, are combined performances of a systematic nature. With these formations patients mask their symptoms. According to the patients' thinking, the symptoms proceed directly from the deliria. These deliria, of which there are several kinds, may be considered analogous to the great [philosophical] systems. In addition to the deliria, familiar to psychiatry, which are called "confused de-

149

liria" and must first be translated [into ordinary language], two kinds of deliria can be distinguished: (1) *anxiety deliria,* and (2) *obsessional deliria.*

[1.] The first are conscious systems of thought by which the patients try to justify [or rationalize] their anxiety and to understand it. These deliria represent merely projections. They are translations of a number of psychic drives from the unknown, unconscious, to a known, conscious sphere, where the symptoms become manifest. In a case of locomotor anxiety, for example, the patient justifies his inability to walk alone according to a logical system of conditions. This delirium is a means of transporting [*Transportmittel*] the motives and impulses from the sexual sphere to that of locomotion. An example of such a system in science is Wernicke's[9] delirious psychology, as one might say. He transferred his brain anatomy directly into the realm of psychology.

2. These deliria become, by way of a complex psychic activity, a true reflection of the processes taking place in the unconscious. The mental life of the child is important for the psychological understanding of philosophical concepts. One should observe during what years the child lays the foundations of a moral law and when he begins to apply this to the outside world (e.g., justice, causality, etc.). In the course of the observations, one would find that these things happen in connection with commonplace situations of everyday life. When we take the infantile factor into account, however, we must leave aside the idea, more humorous than provable, that Thales, who let everything originate from water, was an enuretic, and that Heraclitus, on account of his auditory hallucinations and his sense of orderliness, was an analerotic.

The high valuation of the word seems to contain the meaning that perceptions can become conscious only by being given a name.[10]

FEDERN suspects that states of ecstasy are not unknown to the speaker himself. Consequently, Federn does not find it hard to under-

[9] Karl Wernicke (1848-1905), professor of psychiatry in Breslau and Halle, Germany. He was one of the first contributors to the theory of aphasia. He introduced the concept of the "supervalent idea," i.e., of the overemphasized idea which underlies mental disorders (hallucinations, delusions).

[10] These ideas were already formulated in the theoretical part of the *Interpretation of Dreams* (1900). They appear again in Freud's metapsychological papers.

stand the opposition of those who are not ecstatic. The speaker has reminded us again that knowledge, which seems so self-evident to us today, was once gained laboriously.

Ecstasy seems to be the condition in which the great discoveries were made. The narrowing of the ideational field, combined with the feeling of pleasure induced by ecstasy, causes the ecstatic individual to experience a totally different ego; hence his feeling of oneness with God.[11]

RANK remarks that someday one will perhaps be able to establish the specific etiology of mental activities, just as Professor Freud has established the specific etiology of "mental illnesses" (hysteria, obsessional neurosis, etc.). One cannot avoid the impression that the philosopher, for instance, is the typical onanist (in analogy to the obsessional neurotic whose neurosis likewise goes back to infantile masturbation). Philosophizing is of a decidedly autoerotic character. The creative writer, on the other hand (the dramatist in particular), exactly corresponds to the hysteric; both are very close to object love. The mystic's position, then, would be midway between the two, though much closer to neurosis. Faust's mystic drive is in fact refined [*veredelt:* ennobled] autoerotism; he is cured as soon as he gets a woman.

BRECHER raises only the question how metapsychology is related to the psychology commonly practiced by the philosophers. He asks, for instance, whether the need for causality issues *exclusively* from unconscious factors.

HÄUTLER repeats that the scientific law of causality was taken over from religious life, which links guilt and punishment.

FREUD: Religion would then correspond to the obsessional neurosis, and the philosophical system to a delirium.[12]

SADGER assumes that philosophizing has its deepest roots in the child's question about the nature of the genitals of the opposite sex; that is, of mother or father respectively.

[11] See also Helene Deutsch: "On Contentment, Happiness and Ecstasy" (1927), *Psa. Rev.*, 15:90, 1928; and Federn's papers on the ego feeling in *Ego Psychology and the Psychoses*, ed. P. Federn & E. Weiss. New York: Basic Books, 1952.

[12] See Freud: "Obsessive Actions and Religious Practices" (1907), *S.E.*, 9:115-127, and *Totem and Taboo* (1913), *S.E.*, 13:1-162.

(PROFESSOR FREUD interjects that the question is limited to the origin of children since the child does not yet know anything about different genitalia; the child assumes that everyone has genitals like his own.)

SADGER believes that he has discovered this in his own analyses. Furthermore, the idea of the world's unity springs from the wish to put oneself in father's place.

The ecstatic state can be likened, he says, to the emotional state during coition (see the ecstasies of monks or nuns; genitals of Jesus and Mary[13]). The feeling of contrast stems from the disproportion between excessive sexuality [*Übermass*] and real life.

Religious laws are, in the last analysis, precepts given by the father. Principle of causality: to the child, one individual is the cause of everything and everybody, and that is the father.

The feeling of "harmony" appears when the child has taken on the father's role.

KAHANE thinks that the material sensations from the sexual sphere may have constituted points of departure for certain philosophical concepts. For example, the concept of order might stem from the phenomenon of menstruation, the enlargement of the ego from erection, and the like. The fact that only men have been given the faculty to fathom the world may perhaps be accounted for by the circumstance that ecstasy is a psychic companion to the physical processes of sexuality only in men.

The psychic phenomena appearing in prepuberty might be decisive in this respect. Prepuberty is the philosophical period of every human being, and one might see an analogy in this period and that of Greek natural philosophy.[14] Each individual may, in his psychic development, have to go through all the developmental stages of the entire series.

---

[13] This reference is obscure.
[14] A. Gesell, in his *The Child from Five to Ten* (New York: Harper & Brothers, 1946), also remarks on the philosophical tendencies of the prepuberty child.

18

SCIENTIFIC MEETING on *March 27, 1907*

Present: Freud, Adler, [A.] Deutsch, Federn, Hitschmann, Reitler, Sadger, Stekel, Rank [Kahane].

COMMUNICATIONS

PROFESSOR FREUD announces that the second, enlarged edition of *The Psychopathology of Everyday Life*[1] is going to be published in the fall. Furthermore, that Rank's *The Artist: Beginnings of a Psychology of Sex* has been published.[2]

DR. WITTELS is unanimously voted a member of the Society.

DR. KAHANE announces that he will not be able to attend regularly on Wednesday evening during the summer semester since he is editing the "Encyclopedia" [*Medical Dictionary*]. The question of assessment of a financial contribution is settled with agreement that at the first meeting in May an account will be rendered.

DR. STEKEL announces a paper on "Anxiety Neurosis" for April 17.

[A.] Deutsch borrows Minutes 17.

[1] *Zur Psychopathologie des Alltagslebens* (1901). Berlin: Karger, 2nd ed., 1907.
[2] *Der Künstler: Ansätze zu einer Sexualpsychologie.* Vienna & Leipzig: Hugo Heller, 1907.

PRESENTATION

Somnambulism

SPEAKER: DR. SADGER

SADGER first mentions the superstition that a person walking in his sleep is moon-struck. In the scientific literature, there is almost no explanation of this phenomenon. In *Belles Lettres,* the only somnambulists known to him are: Lady Macbeth, the Prince von Homburg,[3] Maria (by Otto Ludwig[4]), and Lene Tarn in *Jörn Uhl.*[5]

Then, using two psychoanalyses as his basis, the speaker goes on to discuss the close kinship between somnambulism and dream life. He emphasizes that what is always involved is wish fulfillment, that is, for the most part, fulfillment of sexual desires (exhibitionistic acts, homosexual relations with parents or teachers, and the like). The concrete actions which one performs in sleep stem only from sexual wishes.

In one of the two analyses, it became clear that the little girl pretended to be sleeping in order to commit a number of otherwise forbidden sexual acts. (The worship of Mary is similarly based on the desire to enjoy pleasure without guilt.) The girl would also speak in her sleep, but without betraying any sexual secrets. This girl was homosexually in love with her mother; for a long time she had slept in her parents' bed. Her somnambulism expressed her desire to climb into her parents' bed after them.

A prominent part in the state of being moon-struck is played by the source of strong light (moon: natural light). The patient says, "The light calls me to my mother while I am unconscious." The patient is enuretic. Another important factor is the habit of some parents to turn a light on the sleeping child (especially when he is ill) to ascertain whether he is resting well.

The second case concerns a young man, an obsessional neurotic, who is in love with his father. In his childhood his mother had played sexual games with him. In his neurosis, the nocturnal satisfaction of

[3] *Der Prinz von Homburg,* by Heinrich von Kleist.
[4] German author (1813-1865).
[5] By Gustav Frenssen (1863-1945), German writer.

excretory needs also plays some role, as does the homosexual affection (just as in the first case).

At the same time, the patient satisfies his exhibitionistic inclinations by approaching his father in his nightgown. In this case, also, the somnambulistic episodes prove to be manifestations of the wish to climb into bed with his father (with his parents). He identifies the moon with his father, for his mother had told him that the moon is the father, looking down to see whether the child is sleeping as he should. When the moon shines into the room, the child thinks that his father is coming with a light to see whether he is sleeping and he pretends to sleep.

Otto Ludwig's portrayal of Maria leaves no doubt that the girl's sleepwalking expresses her unfulfilled yearning for love. The "White Woman" represents the virgin in her nightgown. The girl's somnambulism originates in the desire to enjoy sexual pleasure without guilt. A similar motif is the theme of Kleist's *Marquise von O.* (it is a frequent fantasy of hysterical women that the physician has abused them sexually during a fainting spell). In the case of Lady Macbeth, the clinical picture is distorted in deference to dramatic requirements.

DISCUSSION

HITSCHMANN, having listened to Sadger's arguments, still finds the phenomenon of somnambulism unexplained.

FEDERN refers not only to the significance of the moon as a source of light for the sleepwalker, but also to the influence it generally has on sexual processes: the copulation of fish occurs during full moon; protozoa also copulate at this time.

KAHANE remarks that sleepwalking is a transitory stage, as it were, between motor dreams, that is, actions felt in sleep, and the real actions of waking life.

RANK doubts that one can draw general conclusions from the analyses of two individual cases. He points to the similarity of moon-struck behavior and symptomatic actions.

FREUD comments that the speaker has scarcely touched upon the core of the problem. The fulfillment of sexual wishes is characteristic not only of somnambulism but of all neurotic manifestations. Sadger is right in seeing a connection between somnambulism and dreams; but the puzzling question is: how is it that the paralysis of motility, which is characteristic of the dream, can be undone in sleepwalking while dream life nevertheless continues?

Somnambulism frequently appears in childhood and ceases in later years. One must caution against accepting the statements of patients as fully valid scientific material (as in the first analysis). On the contrary, they must be critically scrutinized since they present a falsified picture, compounded of fantasy and reality. Fantasy fills in memory gaps in a plausible, often very clever way. Normal people, too, project their fantasies onto the past: e.g., we find this in lovers who cannot tolerate the thought that their present state is a new one and who are soon convinced that they have known each other long ago. The hysteric, too, in the etiology of whose illness seduction, for instance, has played no role and who has had an autoerotic childhood, does the same thing when he transforms the autoerotism of his childhood into object love by means of fantasies corresponding to his present thinking. The historian proceeds similarly when he projects the views of his own time onto the past.[6]

Otto Ludwig has hit the core of the problem and has given the only valid explanation of somnambulism in his story *Maria*. The girl, sleepwalking, enters an alcove and lies down on a bed which stands precisely in the spot where her crib used to be. This, Freud says, is the essential factor in somnambulism: the desire to go to sleep where one has slept in childhood.

In the first analysis, the patient's moon-struck mother cannot find the bed (and the pot) because she is under the suggestive influence of her old memory. Her conduct can be understood if the location is taken into account. The wish to be taken into the parents' bed is only a secondary cause; the core of the phenomenon is—going to bed.

The case of Lady Macbeth is not one of ordinary somnambulism but something more like a nocturnal delirium. Case 1 is characteristic

---

[6] Freud expresses similar thoughts on fantasy in his later work, e.g., in *A General Introduction to Psychoanalysis* [(1916-1917). Garden City, N.Y.: Garden City Publishing Co., 1943], in the Wolf Man ("From the History of an Infantile Neurosis" [1918]. *S.E.*, 17:3-123), and in other papers.

in that people who talk in their sleep never give away their secret on that occasion; what they say is only a substitute for what they are hiding (people who talk much have a secret). Yet Lady Macbeth, strangely enough, betrays the secret; but then, it is not her own secret, not that of the Lady; for she plays everything in the role of her husband. She betrays only something which has some connection with her own secret.

STEKEL stresses how much stimulation the speaker has given. He mentions a book (Lagerlöf[7]) in which lovers find each other in a somnambulistic state. Toward an explanation of the phenomenon, he remarks that sleep changes into an autohypnotic state as somnambulism sets in. The desire becomes so powerful that it may induce a kind of hypnosis.

He has found that in female patients, the moon occasionally symbolizes the testicles.

Moreover, the biological significance of the moon for man should not be underrated (lunar periods).

REITLER thinks that a generally valid explanation of this phenomenon can hardly yet be given.

Climbing into bed with the parents is not identical with the simple wish to sleep, but with the wish to experience something.

Several years ago, he had the opportunity to observe an eight- or nine-year-old girl who was enuretic. Without waking at night, she would go on the chamber pot. She would go from her room into that of her brothers or her parents in order to use her brothers' or her father's pot. She would suffer from a compulsion: she had to wash her anus and the back of her thighs until they bled in order to cleanse these parts from a possible contamination by the "male" pots.

The case of a five-year-old girl—which, it is true, was only casually observed—contradicts Professor Freud's explanation since no change of location can be found in her childhood history.

ADLER shares Kahane's opinion that somnambulism belongs with the motor dreams.[8] From here, the way to psychoanalysis is to be

---

[7] *The Saga of the Manor House* by Selma Lagerlöf (1858-1940), famous Swedish author.

[8] Literally: belongs in the same series as dreamed-of motor sensations.

found. One should not overlook the possibility that the somnambulism of children and adults may differ. It is possible that sleepwalking cannot always be traced back to childhood. The inhibition of motility is not completely removed in sleepwalking. With children, the primary, pleasurable sensation in the organs of movement is at the root of sleepwalking.

Persons who dream of daring motor performances have actually accomplished such feats in childhood. These are people with originally stronger [than average] motor impulses. The fact that the somnambulist not only lies down but also gets up, argues against Freud's explanation.

SUPPLEMENTS

HITSCHMANN observes that this state is not a real sleep; it resembles rather the hypnotic or the hysteric state (perhaps double consciousness[9]).

STEKEL: The somnambulist is in search of the sexual object.

---

[9] The original has the French *double conscience*.

19

SCIENTIFIC MEETING on April 10, 1907[1]

Present: Freud, Adler, Bach, [A.] Deutsch, Federn, Graf, Heller, Hollerung, Hitschmann, Rank, Reitler, Sadger, Stekel, Wittels.

COMMUNICATIONS

PROFESSOR FREUD reports on a curious essay by a Dr. Bezzola in Zurich.[2] Further, he mentions a review of Rank's *Artist* in the *Tag*.[3]

ADLER calls attention to an essay on obsessional ideas by Friedmann[4] (in one of the latest issues of *Monatsschrift für Psychiatrie und Neurologie* [21, 1907].

STEKEL mentions an article in *Zeitschrift für fortschrittliche Ärzte*.[5]

Hitschmann returns Minutes 14; [A.] Deutsch returns Minutes 5, 6, and 17.

---

[1] There was no meeting on April 3, because of the holidays. [Note in the original manuscript.]

[2] "Zur Analyse psychotraumatischer Symptome" ["Contribution to the Analysis of Psychotraumatic Symptoms"]. *Journal für Psychiatrie und Neurologie,* 1907.

[3] Vienna newspaper.

[4] "Über die Abgrenzung und die Grundlagen der Zwangsvorstellungen" ["On the Demarcation and the Bases of Obsessional Ideas"].

[5] *Journal for Progressive Physicians.*

PRESENTATION
Tatjana Leontiev[6]

SPEAKER: DR. WITTELS

The speaker undertakes to set forth the deeper motivations for Tatjana Leontiev's deed. For the psychologist, there is no such thing as a "heroine." Unfortunately a psychoanalysis is not possible; but a comparison of Leontiev with other female assassins of history and fiction may disclose some typical traits.

In the book of Judges, Chapter 4, it is recounted how Jael kills the commander Sissera. She invites the fugitive into her hut and covers him with a cloak, but he sends her outside to keep intruders away. She then kills him by driving a nail into his temple [while he is asleep]. She had obviously expected him to make sexual overtures and then took vengeance for her repudiated love. The nail is a penis symbol.

The case of Judith is similar. She beheads Holofernes with a sword. The sword is a less appropriate symbol than the nail. It is said that Judith's father, a commander, slew the heathens because they uncovered women's nakedness. Probably, Judith was not spared either. Judith, most likely, had the idea—like all women in besieged places in earlier times—that she would be raped sooner or later (Holofernes, moreover, had clearly announced this). It was therefore quite natural for her to anticipate this and in satisfying the cry of the flesh to accomplish also a praiseworthy deed. What has been liberated from repression invariably seeks gratification under the cloak of an idealistic motive. Judith, too, is rejected by Holofernes and is resentful. Hebbel[7] does not follow the traditional account at this point; in his drama, Judith succumbs to Holofernes before she kills him. Moreover, Hebbel has the widow be a virgin, which is explained in a peculiar way: Judith was married to Manasseh, but on the wedding night he proved incapable of performing intercourse (Nestroy: impotence).[8] The speaker

---

[6] A Russian revolutionary who attempted to assassinate a high official of the Czarist government, named Durnovo. He was allegedly in Switzerland at the time.

[7] Wittels refers here to Hebbel's drama *Judith*.

[8] Johann Nepomuk Nestroy (1801-1862), the outstanding Viennese satirist, wrote a travesty of Hebbel's drama under the title *Judith and Holofernes*. In both plays Judith describes how her husband on their wedding night suddenly became incapable of moving. In Hebbel's drama, Judith says Manasseh was insane; Nestroy, in his play, alludes to impotence.

is inclined to apply to Judith herself what she says of Manasseh. She may also be a virgin because blood must flow during the deed which she plans to commit. When her father was leading her to her wedding, she looked up to him and said, "Surely, Manasseh looks quite different." Here, for the first time, the importance of the father is indicated. We can readily assume that in all these cases the girl's first sexual affection for her father plays its role; for this love is indeed always rejected.

Jeanne d'Arc should also be mentioned in this connection. Though not an assassin, she is still a heroine. She heard voices, liked to wear men's clothing, and slept with other girls in one bed.

Finally, Charlotte Corday belongs here, too. She was in love with a young man who had to go to war. She killed Marat. After her deed, it was said that she would have done better to kill Robespierre. She had a beautiful gown made for herself (otherwise she would not have been admitted); Leontiev, likewise, put on a beautiful new dress before committing the deed; and Judith prayed to God to make her beautiful.

The repression has become more intense in the course of time, but the symbolism is more transparent. In the Bible, it is still a nail; with Corday it is an ebony knife that fits into a sheath; with Leontiev it is a Browning revolver. The revolver is a well-known symbol of the male genitalia. Corday, in her trial, pushed the knife away in disgust. Leontiev, questioned whether *this* revolver had been her weapon, answered, "Yes, if it has not been exchanged." Psychologically, it was indeed a different one at the time of the deed.

Leontiev's father was living in Warsaw. She had been, for a long time, in Switzerland with her mother. Mother and daughter had little love for each other (jealousy for the father).

Durnovo and Müller[9] did not look in the least alike. When Leontiev was confronted with this fact and particularly when her attention was called to the differences in the style of hair and beard, she said that hair and beard can be changed. This idea is frequently encountered in paranoiacs. Müller, whom she killed, was any man, one might say. She imagined also that Durnovo had taken rooms in the hotel under the assumed name of Müller. The scenes she made while she was un-

---

[9] Müller was an innocent person whom she killed instead of Durnovo.

dressed[10] and photographed (she is said to have spat in the face of the examining judge) may perhaps be explained by her wish to present herself as a virgin.

Lastly, the speaker expresses his personal dislike of Leontiev and of all hysterics.

DISCUSSION

STEKEL remarks that, by this attitude, the speaker has projected the unpleasant self-knowledge of his own insignificant hysteria onto a quite harmless class of people. It must be stressed that great deeds are performed only under the pressure of a great psychic compulsion which is capable of effecting such a narrowing of the field of consciousness. The speaker has, with good reason, pointed to the great importance of symbolism (which is typical of dreams). There is also no doubt concerning the part played by the love for the father.

BACH thinks that everything can be explained far more simply. Leontiev's mental illness was a defensive maneuver. Her behavior before the examining judge was intended to provoke "abuse of the prisoner." This belongs to the martyr's role of the Russian revolutionary.

It is usually daughters of generals who commit such pseudo-revolutionary deeds. The discussion should have focused on the genuine Russian revolutionists who express the pathology of the atmosphere of an entire period and social class, and not [just] that of individuals who are of course tied to the ethical and sexual conditions of this class.

The Bible story of Judith was invented at a later period, and naturally represents Judith as a pure, immaculate heroine.

ADLER finds the arguments ingenious but not applicable to the case of Leontiev. A person really familiar with the circumstances could not be misled into drawing such conclusions. Nor can one follow Wittels in his opinion that, in a real event, the ideology can be totally divorced from what we call emotional life or milieu. It is true that ideology does not explain anything; but ideology itself can be explained.

[10] Before the trial, she was subject to bodily examination in the search for hidden weapons.

The symbolism of the revolver as such is correct, but it plays no role in the case of Leontiev. The revolver is simply the most modern, most dependable weapon. Not only Leontiev but the entire Russian colony believed Müller to be Durnovo. Her attire is explained by the scene of the action, which was in a fashionable hotel. Alienation from the mother frequently occurs in Russian women, etc.

Above all, one must note the ascetic attitude toward life which most revolutionaries (men as well as women) have. Leontiev belonged to a sect which despised and suppressed all free sexual activity. In Russia the suppression from above has led to a release of sadism. As a rule, all revolutionaries are benevolent, charitable, and unassuming; but from time to time their sadism breaks through. In the final analysis, this release is basically provoked by the sexual repression.

HOLLERUNG finds the conclusions drawn by the speaker rather far-fetched. His investigation has had no results. For the rest, he agrees with Adler's "sadistic" arguments.

HITSCHMANN disapproves of the superficiality of the arguments, the overestimation of symbolism, and the determination in terms of compulsion. He expected to receive an explanation of heroic deeds in general, an answer to the question about the roots of heroism in the individual. The revolutionary's act is a kind of suicide. Certainly, abstinence and asceticism are contributing factors.

SADGER endorses Wittels's view of the importance and significance of symbolism. He mentions the analysis of a Russian woman student who also "regretted" that she had not been raped (she expected the sexual act).

Manasseh is deterred from sexual intercourse by a fantasy about his mother.

The material is insufficient to provide a psychological explanation of Leontiev's deed.

GRAF, too, refers to the scantiness of the material. In most cases, one cannot help admiring the precision with which such murderous attacks are executed. Leontiev, however, is, so to speak, an "untalented" assassin; her action is the outcome of a compulsion to imitate, but without talent. The frequent assassination attempts by women

163

have a counterpart in the mass epidemic of women's suicides. The theory of asceticism does not always apply.

HELLER comes to Wittels's defense against Bach's objection to the revolver symbolism. The speaker, he says, has explained the deed by direct means, not by sublimation.

FREUD emphasizes that the speaker in an ingenious manner (and with personal complexes) has said something very serious. He has exposed the psychology of the assassin quite correctly: in his opinion, it is the suppressed erotism which puts the weapon in the hand of these women. Every act of hate issues from erotic tendencies. Repudiated love, in particular, renders this transformation possible.[11] It takes hold especially of the sadistic component (Adler). It is usually the father who is the object of these emotions. Bach's observation that the women in question are most often the daughters of generals corroborates this.

It is the practical conclusions that constitute the questionable part of the paper. One must not condemn the assassins so harshly and unmask them because of unconscious motives. The harshness of such a judgment would be repulsive. Rather a certain tolerance is required toward these hidden emotions. The unconscious motive deserves forebearance.

Wittels's conception of symbolism is entirely correct and his opponents' objections are not sound. For we generally look for the unconscious motivations of actions, which also do not lack their conscious motivations. In one case, the symbolism is evident; in the other, it must be ferreted out. It is perhaps not accidental that the life-giving and the death-bringing tools have the same shape.

Both extremes are present in the character of the hysteric. Here, there is a defusion of opposites which, in the normal person, are fused in appropriate proportions.[12]

In regard to the happenings between Judith and Holofernes, Hebbel has merely restored the original situation which had been mitigated in the Biblical tradition (Bach). For the sake of the strongest effect of

[11] Freud speaks here of the *transformation* of love into hate. Later, he repudiates this idea and separates the two instincts, love and hate; these instincts cannot change one into the other.

[12] Could this "defusion of the opposites" contain the core of the concept of the "defusion of the instincts" which was formulated much later?

164

contrast, he places the motif of repudiated love elsewhere: that is, with Manasseh. Sadger must have brought up a mother fantasy in Manasseh only because of the theory of psychic impotence.

FEDERN comments that to the slips of the tongue and the hand, we now must add slips of shooting. He criticizes the superficiality of the diagnosis which cannot be substantiated. Here, too, he sees the error of those who, totally imbued with the Freudian way of thinking, ignore all other points of view.

RANK considers the relation to the father to be the most important factor. Indirectly, this can also be demonstrated in the case of Leontiev, for she tries to induce the two daughters of a Russian general to murder their father.

There is something similar in Schiller's *Tell* where the hatred of the father, which is behind Gessler's assassination, breaks through in an entirely different place, namely, in the parricide scene. Also the beheading (Judith) points to the father whose anonymity (defense) is effected in this way. (Compare the headless queen in Wedekind's *Spring's Awakening*.)

WITTELS reiterates in conclusion that woman's sexuality permeates whatever she does or feels. Hence, this deed, too, cannot be explained by ideological motives. We must not overrate our small bit of consciousness.

20

SCIENTIFIC MEETING on *April 17, 1907*

Present: Freud, Adler, Bach, Federn, Hitschmann, Rank, Sadger, Stekel, Wittels.

COMMUNICATIONS

RIKLIN has offered, for publication in the *Contributions* [*to Applied Psychology*] a paper on fairy tales.[1]

A report on modern theories of hysteria is to be given at the Congress of Psychology and Psychotherapy in Amsterdam in September, 1907. Freud has declined. Jung and Aschaffenburg[2] will give the report.

The resolution has been adopted to request the membership dues in writing.

[1] Dr. Franz Riklin, Swiss psychiatrist, at that time Bleuler's assistant. This paper was published in 1908 under the title *Wunscherfüllung und Symbolik im Märchen.* Vienna & Leipzig: Heller. [*Wishfulfillment and Symbolism in Fairy Tales.* New York: Nervous & Mental Disease Publishing Co., 1915.]

[2] German psychiatrist.

PRESENTATION

Jean Paul[3]

SPEAKER: DR. BACH

Dr. Bach refers to Moebius's essay on Schumann[4] in which the composer is shown to have suffered from dementia praecox. The statement is also made that Schumann's music was as "nervous" as the composer himself. In the speaker's opinion, this is not so. Schumann's music is the sleepy, typical, German home music.

All in all, it is difficult and very risky to draw conclusions about a composer from his music. One moves on somewhat firmer ground when there is a text [written by the composer for his music], as in Wagner's case. The literary tastes of the composer might also give us some clues to his personality. There exists a letter from Schumann's student days which escaped Moebius's attention. From this letter it is apparent that Schumann was eagerly studying the works of Jean Paul. He writes that he fears he will lose his mind over this preoccupation.

Jean Paul's work had, and still has, a powerful effect on musicians in general. He himself was a musical person. His full heart made him yearn for tunes. Perhaps this should be attributed to his endeavor to hide as much as possible of his innermost self and to his fear of giving away too much of it.

The bombastic, exaggeratedly exuberant, and peculiar form of his writing should be considered in this context. He always tells tales about himself, lest someone attempt to divine some of his secrets. He displays the garrulity of those who have something to hide. Bach leaves undecided the question of whether this secretiveness and fear are connected with Jean Paul's enuretic constitution (Adler).

In his short, humorous writings, however, he dares to say openly some things for which he seeks spiritualistic disguises in his more serious works. Apparently he does not consider these small human frailties

---

[3] Johann Paul Friedrich Richter, called Jean Paul (1763-1825), was a famous German writer. His father was a schoolteacher, organist, and later Protestant minister. Jean Paul's very original and peculiar work had a great influence on the contemporary literary and artistic world.

[4] Robert Schumann (1810-1856).

shameful in lower-class people, of whom he writes mainly in his short stories (Katzenberger's repulsive actions and his disgust which is based on imagination only[5]).

His heroes die from "superlove." They are entirely incapable of enjoying a real love relationship. He says, "The first kiss is love's grave." His women are neuropathic; they take poison, etc. Graves play an important part in his novels. He frequently describes the bliss after death, mostly in direct relation to and in the context of erotic scenes.

He always had four or five amorous relationships at the same time. Many ladies of high aristocracy (he called them Titanides) worshiped him. Among them were Charlotte von Kalb[6] and Frau von Stein.[7] He finally married a girl by the name of Rosinette. The marriage was happy only in the beginning. Later, he separated from his wife because, he claimed, she made excessive demands on him. When she was fourteen years old, his wife had attempted suicide because of her love for an actress.

He was averse to all speculation. Philosophizing was to him a loathsome preoccupation with oneself. From him comes the phrase, "Onanism of pure and impure reason."[8]

Biographical data: his mother, Rosina, was not a remarkable person. He treated her with disdain. She was one of those women whose life, according to Jean Paul, was "frittered away in washing, cooking, and sewing." His father, a minister, believed in spirits, and brought up his children to believe in spirits and ghosts. Jean Paul was his father's favorite and slept alone in the same room with him. The boy had often to wait a long time until his father came home at night. Alone in the dark room, he would be tormented by dreams and fears.

Later, he formed passionate [schwärmerische] friendships, and friends determined his fate. His youngest brother died early, a suicide. His brother Samuel became depraved (he stole, ran away, etc.); his brother Adam suffered from an urge to roam [Wandertrieb] (he became a barber and soldier). Jean Paul himself had a decided liking

[5] Dr. Katzenbergers Badereise [Dr. Katzenberger's Trip to a Watering Place].
[6] A friend of Schiller.
[7] Goethe's famous friend.
[8] An allusion to Kant's "pure reason."

for traveling on foot. For this reason he once ran away from Berlepsch when he was making a trip with her.[9]

His first love was a pock-marked dairymaid, much older than he. All of the women he loved were considerably older than he was.

He was an [excessive] beer drinker and is said to have been stingy. His son devoted himself to mysticism and died a young man.

Jean Paul himself reached the age of sixty-two. His illness began with intestinal indispositions. These were followed by intermittent fever, skin eruptions, and finally dropsy. He also became blind.

His dreams became famous.

DISCUSSION

FREUD emphasizes that the speaker has offered an abundance of stimulating ideas. Jean Paul is of a complex nature, a peculiar saint. He seems to be one of those who remained arrested at the point of psychic onanism. This is of great importance for understanding the artist. It expresses itself in the physical disappointment which artists usually cause their women. In *Siebenkäs*,[10] the only work which he himself knows, an aversion to wives is quite evident. Friendship between men is valued higher than matrimony. It would be interesting to investigate the relationship between his works and the age at which he wrote them.

HITSCHMANN, being himself interested in pathographies,[11] welcomes Bach's undertaking but thinks that only a physician has enough insight into human nature to solve such a problem in a satisfactory way.

The physical disappointment which the poet causes women (while at the same time giving them intellectual satisfaction) is perhaps represented symbolically in *Dr. Katzenbergers Badereise* in which the girl, although full of enthusiasm for the poet, marries the soldier.

WITTELS has never been able to finish reading any of Jean Paul's works.

[9] Emilie von Berlepsch (1757-1831), author, divorced her husband in order to marry Jean Paul, but at the last moment he deserted her.

[10] *Tod und Hochzeit des Armenadvokaten Siebenkäs* [*The Death and the Wedding of Siebenkäs, Lawyer of the Poor*].

[11] The term "pathography" was created by Moebius. It designates a biography written from a medical point of view with particular attention to psychic anomalies.

The ideal woman which men (especially Germans) have created for themselves becomes a source of suffering for them since they cannot find her in reality. It is quite understandable that this ideological image lasts only until the first kiss and that the man becomes speechless when confronted with a real woman.

With older women, such as Jean Paul preferred, this respectful attitude makes some sense in view of their motherliness.

Alcoholic intoxication should be considered a substitute for and surrogate of sexual intoxication.

FEDERN stresses that in order to understand Jean Paul's character one must enter completely into the spirit of the age. The unnaturalness [*Unnatur*] can be explained by the incomplete integration of an enormous amount of intellectual stimulation. Women's high degree of sexual repression (that is, their deficient sexual development) may possibly have contributed to their "idealized image." Horrid desires, similar to those related by Bach from Katzenberger's journey, are seen in some patients.

STEKEL remarks that he has gained the impression, from reading a description of Jean Paul's youth, that the poet was sexually precocious. His personality can be understood only from the standpoint of neurosis. He slept in the same room with his parents, and that is where one should look for the source of his later anxiousness [*Angstmeierei*]. His playing with ideas of death and graves also goes back to his anxiety. He was not capable of tying himself to one woman, and so he finally married the first woman who came along (as did Goethe). Like every neurotic, he is bisexual; hence the obviousness of the homosexual component. To infer ejaculatio praecox (which Bach suspected in contrast to Freud's assumption of psychic onanism) is risky.

SADGER misses the exposure of deeper connections. Some traits can be recognized as hereditary symptoms: e.g., the urge to roam [*Wandertrieb*] (Kleist, Grillparzer's brother Karl, etc.), and the alcoholism.

His strong homosexual tendencies probably go back to his sleeping with his father; and his disdain for his mother also has its roots in homosexuality. The white ghost, or the spirit, may be mother, father, or sister in a nightgown.

170

RANK knows, aside from *Schmelzle*[12] (Adler), only one other line by Jean Paul which would speak for an enuretic constitution. "The light has an exciting effect on the genitalia." Perhaps, the disdain for the mother may have developed, as it did in Byron, as a reaction to a primary love for her. In Catullus's[13] *Poems ad Mentulam* we find a symbolic designation similar to the one Jean Paul gave to his estate which he named *Mittelspitz* [Middle Point].

ADLER comments that the conclusions are valid only for us. From our standpoint most of the conclusions are correct. Love for an older woman appears mostly where love for the mother has been repressed. Mother love, as Rank has said before, sometimes assumes peculiar forms: the child longs for simply *a* mother, perhaps because of ill-treatment or for some other reason.

Adler is inclined to infer an inherited nephritis in Jean Paul.[14]

Loss of sight is a professional disease of musical people: the blind musician is, indeed, a type.

BACH, replying to some of the objections, emphasizes that he was not concerned with looking for further interpretations.[15] He was interested in the attempt to explain the form of Jean Paul's works from his psychic make-up.

FREE DISCUSSION

To Sadger's contention that those who are heavily burdened with a hereditary disposition display an abnormal need for stimulants, FEDERN replies that degenerates do many things which are harmful to themselves, whereas normal people avoid such actions.

FREUD confirms Sadger's interpretation that the psychosexual root of the belief in ghosts is given by the appearance of the nocturnal visitor who comes to look at the child (masturbating, enuresis, etc.).

In dealing with pathographies one must guard against classifying the material under the types of the psychology of neuroses; there are also other types which are, one might say, better equipped for sur-

---

12 *The Army Chaplain Schmelzle's Journey to Flätz.*
13 Greatest Roman lyricist (84-54 B.C.).
14 Again a reference to organ inferiority!
15 The original has "*Andeutungen*," literally "intimations."

vival. The psychology of neuroses can be used only to illuminate the pathographic material. Each case must be dealt with individually. Our presentation begins to be conclusive only with the intimate detail.[16]

The mother-etiology can be inferred with certainty only in those individuals (1) who have already begun in puberty to make a peculiar separation of sex objects. On the one hand, they put the woman in such an exalted position that they dare not think of her in connection with sexual enjoyment. On the other hand, they open what we might call a separate account for the common wench: they look to her for sexual gratification. If these two attitudes finally meet, various conflicts can arise: either they sublimate the harlot or they suffer disappointment with the lofty object and then become misogynists.[17]

(2) who show a strange mixture of faithfulness and unfaithfulness. They are always in search of the deliveress, the redeemer (Wagner), and put all kinds of women to the test.

(3) who are interested only in women who belong to other men. The unattached woman does not attract them.

Only those who have all three characteristics can with certainty be considered as cases of mother-etiology. Wagner is an exquisite case [in point]. Not one of these conditions is present in the case of Jean Paul.

Rank's explanation does not seem valid either. Every psychic effect, as we all know, can have originated in two entirely different ways: either directly or as a reaction. How it originated we cannot guess by merely looking at it and therefore one must be very cautious in drawing conclusions.

It is doubtful whether enuresis is due to an inferiority of the kidneys (Adler). It seems to be the result of early sexual stimulations and hence is a sexual inferiority.

Professor Freud finally relates the case of a seventeen-year-old boy whom he recently saw in Görlitz. Since his twelfth year he has been

[16] The thought that the individual artist, rather than artists in general, should be the subject of investigation if one wishes to learn something about the creative process was carried through in more detail in Freud's later writings.

[17] Later, in 1912, Freud discussed this idea more extensively in his "Über die allgemeinste Erniedrigung des Liebeslebens" ["The Most Prevalent Form of Degradation in Erotic Life"]. *C.P.*, 4:203-216.

separated from his parents and placed in institutions because of his horrible screaming. This case was diagnosed as dementia praecox.

As a child, the patient was unmanageable and, by screaming, tried to force the fulfillment of his wishes. He was always fed, nursed, cared for, and brought up by his mother. He treated his father with disdain. Between his tenth and eleventh year, he obtained sexual information from his schoolmates. From that time dates his utter hostility toward his parents: he had discovered his mother's unfaithfulness, as it were, and even in the institution he did not want to have anything to do with her. When his father visited him, the boy told his father that if he were in his place he would be ashamed to do such a thing and would rather have cut "it" off himself.

The patient gives the impression of superior intelligence. He hears voices (allegedly that of his grandmother whom he saw only once when he was one and a half years of age; she died soon afterward—the impact of the first experience with death!).

In his fit, he yells and screams, spits, and passes two fingers up and down the groove of the door panel, counting in the process: in this way he represents a series of sexual acts (the counting) in which the spitting imitates ejaculation. At the same time he hallucinates. This is clearly a hysterical attack. As early as his ninth year, the patient began to restrain his unruliness—[at that time] by means of compulsions. The hysteria then grafted itself on this obsessional neurosis[18] for the following reason: in response to the explanation of his attack he replies that he does not care about *that* in the least; it does not matter to him at all. He is a very proud person. He himself says that his genitalia are underdeveloped and he actually has infantile genitalia. His pride does not permit him to become depressed on account of this discovery, but, he says, he is completely indifferent to the entire matter. However, this is possible only if he places the suppressed affect elsewhere. In order to be able to feign this indifference in front of the physician, he must first rid himself of the affect in the attack. That is why he had an attack at the time for which Professor Freud's second

[18] Several times Freud stressed in his writings that one type of neurosis can graft itself upon another type; that one can regressively take the place of the other; and that, inversely, even a psychosis can heal by changing into a neurosis, most frequently into an obsessive neurosis.

visit had been announced. After the attack he was able to continue playing the farce of his indifference with Freud.

The fantasy of intercourse goes back to the parents in whose bedroom he slept until his tenth year. The representation of intercourse is also influenced by the fact that, according to his story, the boys in school "pantomimed" coitus.

21

SCIENTIFIC MEETING on *April 24, 1907*

Present: Freud, Adler, [A.] Deutsch, Federn, Frey, Hitschmann, Rank, Reitler, Sadger, Stekel, Wittels, Graf, Heller.

PRESENTATION

Psychology and Pathology of the Anxiety Neurosis

SPEAKER: DR. STEKEL

The speaker takes as his starting point the dream of a female patient in which there is a clear fusion of death and sexuality; a man appears in it who is Eros and Thanatos in one person. The thesis is advanced that all anxiety is fear of death (minor forms of transition to normalcy are: stage fright, dizziness, fear of speaking, and the like). Freud has traced anxiety neurosis back to coitus interruptus: he sees the origin of anxiety in the deflection of the somatic sexual excitement from the psychic sphere. Stekel stresses that, in contrast to this opinion, he must adhere to the conviction that also in anxiety neurosis—as in any other neurosis—the psychic conflict is essential. In this case, the conflict is between sexual excitement and rejection of sexuality. The weaker wish

175

turns into anxiety. In view of the fact that anxiety may occur in some toxic conditions, one must take into consideration the possibility that some toxins may help to precipitate anxiety states. Stekel refers to morbus Basedowi [hyperthyroidism] which actually corresponds to an intensified anxiety neurosis. Accordingly, one must assume a more intimate connection between anxiety neurosis and the thyroid gland (popular belief: to test a girl's virginity by touching her neck— Catullus). Fliess[1] interprets anxiety entirely as sexual feeling; in his opinion, it is that part of the libido which pertains to the opposite sex.

In order to demonstrate the great importance of psychic conflict in the formation of anxiety neurosis, Stekel discusses several cases in detail:

In the first case, three components of the neurosis could be established:

coitus interruptus

psychic conflict (bad conscience)

thoughts about the death of a beloved person.

This projection of thoughts about death onto the spouse or onto the children is especially frequent.

Similar aspects are brought out in the second case. Dream interpretation revealed: thoughts of adultery, a wish for the husband's death, etc.

In the third case, it is a matter of the relative impotence of the husband (wife is difficult to stimulate).

In the fourth case, the fear that her unfaithfulness will be discovered is the most important component. Otherwise, the familiar factors again appear: coitus interruptus, psychic conflict, thoughts of death; in addition, the image of a gigantic penis, which also plays a role in other cases, and which goes back to a fantasy of an infantile scene.

Sex symbolism from the dreams: the man as a wet nurse; small child and big child: soft and erect penis; the little girl = vagina, the little boy = penis; policeman: with married couples, one spouse watching the other (unfaithfulness).

[1] Wilhelm Fliess (1858-1918), the German physician, nose and throat specialist, who was the author of the theory of periodicity and was, for many years, a close friend of Freud. See: *The Origins of Psychoanalysis.* New York: Basic Books, 1954.

In all of these cases, anxiety always proves to be a neurotic symptom, originating in painful (sexual) ideas.

Anxiety as such must be considered from the standpoint of instinct life. There are no isolated instincts. The sexual instinct, for example, always appears accompanied by two instincts: the life instinct and the death instinct. Life instinct and sex instinct are often considered identical (*sich ausleben*[2]). The stronger the life instinct, the more developed is the feeling of anxiety.[3] Coition is indeed, as Swoboda[4] has argued, a partial death. Anxiety neurosis is the interplay of the life and death instincts. Stekel summarizes: anxiety neurosis cannot be traced back to coitus interruptus alone, but [in its etiology] the psychic conflict must also be taken into account.

DISCUSSION

REITLER says that he cannot agree with the purely somatic view of the anxiety neurosis. Stekel's cases, however, are not conclusive since they are not cases of simple neurosis, especially not typical anxiety neuroses, but rather cases of hysteria with anxiety. Perhaps, hysteria without anxiety does not even exist. Compulsion and anxiety also belong together. The mechanisms in hysteria, compulsive neurosis, and anxiety neurosis are identical up to a certain point: if the detached affect is not converted into somatic expressions, then it becomes either anxiety or compulsion. Anxiety can be shown to lie behind every compulsive act. Because anxiety seeks an object, it generates the compulsive idea or act. Anxiety is something decidedly psychic. It is not a deflection *from* the psychic (Freud) but *into* the psychic realm. Moreover, the gratification of man's sexual instinct is not at all a matter of the emptying of the spermatocysts, as Freud says.

[2] *Sich ausleben* means to live according to one's desires, to lead a life of pleasure; the literal translation would be to "live oneself out," to "spend oneself in living," to exhaust one's vital powers.

[3] We note that already at that time one spoke of life and death instincts, although in a vague sense. This theory of the instincts was crystallized much later by Freud in *Beyond the Pleasure Principle* (1920). *S.E.*, 18:3-64.

[4] Hermann Swoboda, a Viennese philosopher and biologist, published in 1904 a pamphlet: *Die Perioden des menschlichen Organismus in ihrer psychologischen und biologischen Bedeutung* [*The Periods of the Human Organism in Their Psychological and Biological Significance*]. See the Introduction by Ernst Kris to *The Origins of Psychoanalysis*. New York: Basic Books, 1954, pp. 41-42.

Reitler doubts that the idea of the death of a beloved person always plays a role.

From a manuscript, Reitler then communicates a case of a supposed slip of the hand,[5] combined with feelings of anxiety, which he plans to publish.

FEDERN at certain points (especially in relation to the interpretation of sexual symbolism) misses the evidence. In the way in which it is formulated the idea is probably not tenable that every phobia is based on a repressed sexual idea. Nor is Freud's explanation that unsatisfied sexuality is converted into anxiety understandable. It seems to him that women re-experience anxiety before every sexual act (not only before the first one); this anxiety remains when the sexual act is abnormal, whereas it disappears with normal intercourse.

The death instinct is not primary; it is much rather a flight from anxiety; the wish for death is really a consequence of the fear of death.

HITSCHMANN characterizes the end result of Stekel's presentation as a total confusion of all he knew before. Freud has described the anxiety neurosis as an almost purely physical state which is combined with anxiety without specific content.

He cannot understand the death instinct. In general he criticizes a few superficialities. Anxiety neurosis seems to him to be based on complex causes. A vulnerable heart, for example, plays a prominent part. For those suffering from heart ailments it is very important to attain full and complete sexual gratification.

FREY, on the whole, agrees with Hitschmann. He himself has a cardiac defect and anxiety sets in whenever he suppresses an emission in the state of erection.

Stekel tried to elucidate the psychic aspect of anxiety neurosis; but, in his thesis, the mental link[6] between psyche and soma is missing. The objections raised against the "death instinct" are most likely due only to the unfortunate choice of words. The concept itself is not without merit (for instance, passionate gambling in order to escape anxiety attacks). But it [the death instinct] is nothing primary and

[5] The original has "*ein Fall von vermeintlichem Vergreifen*," which means, literally, "misgrasping," "mistouching."

[6] The original has: "*das geistige* [spiritual] *Band*."

arises only on a pathological basis. Stekel's examples are cases of hysteria.

ADLER welcomes Stekel's work as an effort to take more extensive notice of the organic factors in the neuroses. At present it is probably not yet possible to find a purely organic basis for anxiety neurosis. The brilliant summary of his dream interpretations is worthy of praise. Stekel has gone too far in some of his conclusions, since the means of proving them are not yet at our disposal. Anxiety neurosis is found in all conditions which show physical impairments, most frequently in cardiac changes, affection of the genitals, and in gastrointestinal ailments. Completely normal people cannot really acquire an anxiety neurosis.

One need not venture so far as Freud, who sees anxiety in the process of birth; but anxiety can be traced back into childhood. The absence of anxiety in the child can perhaps be guaranteed only through the satisfaction of a certain amount of the child's need for love.

WITTELS remarks that he has almost nothing to say about anxiety neurosis from his own experience. That the death instinct appears in association with love is as old as the world. He is not sure that anxiety is always fear of death. Anxiety does not relate to something specific; rather, anxiety is a primal feeling. Anxiety has probably also given birth to the first philosopher.

The anxiety of children may well be connected with what Adler has called the orientation in the milieu. This, however, coincides with finding one's ego [*Ichfindung*]. A great deal of infantile anxiety can be explained philosophically.

SADGER first objects to the confusion of concepts which Stekel endeavored to create. In cases of pure anxiety neurosis, the anxiety can be removed, without psychoanalysis, through normal intercourse.

Anxiety is always a late repetition from the child's earliest years of life. In many cases, the child's first anxiety stems from overhearing parental intercourse. The child believes that the parents are fighting (the mother is being killed): this engenders anxiety. Moreover, ill-considered educational practices also frequently contribute to the development of neurotic anxiety; e.g., the parental threat to send a child away (that is to say, withdraw their love from him).

179

Incidentally, the most severe hysterical-compulsive symptoms erupt because of homosexual reasons.

Adler's remark that a normal individual cannot acquire an anxiety neurosis must be contradicted. Usually, such people are conspicuously healthy. As a rule, the hysteric is not damaged by coitus interruptus, because the larger neurosis cancels out the lesser one.

In his opinion, the most valuable part of Stekel's presentation is the application of Jung's ideas to psychoanalysis.

(*Supplement to lecture:* When the patient shows great resistance to interpretations and does not want to talk, Stekel gives him a stimulus word—preferably chosen from the patient's dream—and has the patient quickly recite all the words which come to his mind as a reaction. He then analyzes these words individually by means of the associations the patient advances for each word. In this way, a seemingly meaningless series of words acquires meaning.[7])

FREUD considers the dream analyses correct and finds the technical innovations useful. He himself has changed his own technique to the extent that when the patient does not want to talk, he leaves the material aside and first attempts to remove the resistances.

Patients are silent in two situations: when they do not want to accept sexual symbolism, or when the transference presents an obstacle.[8]

He, too, must agree with the opinion of those who have diagnosed Stekel's cases as hysterias in which anxiety plays a major role.

He must also agree with Sadger that, as a rule, persons who do not arouse any suspicion of neurosis[9] (especially men) show the most beautiful anxiety neuroses.

In view of the fact that these cases should be diagnosed as hysteria,

---

[7] See C. G. Jung: *Studies in Word-Association: Experiments in the Diagnosis of Psychopathological Conditions.* London: Heinemann, 1918. Carried Out at the Psychiatric Clinic of the University of Zurich under the direction of C. G. Jung. (First published in German under the title: *Diagnostische Assoziationsstudien; Beiträge zur experimentellen Pathologie.* Leipzig: Barth, 1906.) Much experience proved that the technique of psychoanalysis did not gain from the application of Jung's association experiment.

[8] These remarks show how early Freud analyzed resistances. Here he formulates ideas already expressed in his earlier writings (for instance, in the "Project" contained in his letters to Fliess).

[9] "*. . . neurotisch ganz unverdächtige Personen . . .*"

the psychology of "anxiety neurosis" which Stekel wished to present becomes untenable. At most, the issue is the psychology of anxiety in hysteria. The problem of anxiety is the most delicate, central problem in the theory of neurosis. Neurotic anxiety arises, as a counterpart to life anxiety, from the threat to the sexual instinct, just as ordinary anxiety has its origin in a threat to the life instinct.[10] The assumption of a purely somatic anxiety could be justified. Anxiety is a phenomenon composed of physiological manifestations plus psychic sensations, but one cannot determine its origins by looking at it. Thus, it is not valid to maintain that all anxiety must be derived from the psyche; with the separation of ordinary (life) anxiety from neurotic anxiety, it becomes just as untenable to maintain that every anxiety is fear of death.

Fliess's point of view diverges from his own. Fliess maintains, for example, that man's anxiety is his repressed female libido. His own opinion is to be found, in part, in his theory of sexuality; namely, that the libido is masculine; we must supplement: anxiety is feminine.

It is probably true that there is some relationship to Basedow's disease, but Stekel's assumptions do not elucidate it. The chemical theory, in particular, which, incidentally, does not deserve a high regard, should be left for the remote future.

The question is why there are hysterias with a great deal of anxiety and hysterias without any anxiety. The difference between pure conversion hysteria and other forms of hysteria may perhaps be found to be determined by whether or not the anxiety generated can be psychically bound. If anxiety is utilized in physical innervation, then a hysteria without anxiety develops; on the other hand, anxiety which is bound psychically results in hysteria with phobias.[11]

Reitler is right in saying that there is anxiety behind the compulsion. Here, too, the anxiety is bound psychically; that is, it is inhibited by a certain psychic constellation, namely, the reaction formation.[12] If this [reaction] formation is lacking and if the anxiety is connected with a specific idea, hysteria with anxiety results. Hysterical anxiety is tied

[10] At that time, and even earlier, Freud had already assumed two causes of anxiety: the sexual instincts and the instinct of self-preservation.

[11] See: "Fragment of an Analysis of a Case of Hysteria [Dora]" (1905). *S.E.*, 7:3-122; and "Analysis of a Phobia in a Five-year-old Boy" (1909). *S.E.*, 10:3-149.

[12] See Freud's "Notes upon a Case of Obsessional Neurosis" (1909). *S.E.*, 10:153-318.

to certain ideas in the unconscious and is then, in consciousness, transposed to other ideas.[13]

Finally, it may also happen that anxiety cannot be bound at all by psychic elements. There are also mixed cases in which a part of the anxiety is bound, another part is not. Fear of death predominates so frequently because the anxiety attached to sexual complexes is in consciousness replaced by fear of death, which stems from the life instinct.

Childhood anxiety, which is almost universal, is enhanced by the circumstance that in the child the two sources of anxiety coincide: for the child loves only the object that satisfies his instinct of self-preservation (in this way he finds the object). Thus, if he is threatened with loss of this object (a popular educational measure), both sources of anxiety are opened up.

RANK, in view of the late hour, limits himself to protesting against the manner of presentation. The paper, particularly the first part, was read off much too hurriedly.

STEKEL, in his closing words, rejects the objection that his are mixed cases by stating that precisely those cases which at first were considered to be cases of pure anxiety proved, on closer investigation, to be psychically determined. Pure cases of anxiety neurosis do not exist.

[13] This process is closely connected with repression. See Freud's metapsychological essays and his *Inhibitions, Symptoms and Anxiety* (1926). *S.E.*, 20:77-174.

22

SCIENTIFIC MEETING on May 1, 1907

Present: Freud, Adler, Federn, Frey, Heller, Rank, Reitler, Sadger, Stekel, Wittels.

COMMUNICATIONS

RANK renders an account of expenses. Contributions toward the expenses for initial supplies are still outstanding from five gentlemen— Bass, Frey, Hollerung, Meisl, and Reitler (Frey and Reitler pay their debt immediately). The expenses for mail up to May 1, 1907 amount to *Kronen* 7.30. According to the resolution, each gentleman pays *Kr.* .50 which adds up to the sum of *Kr.* 10.00. The surplus of *Kr.* 2.70 is to be credited as an advance to next year's budget. All those present pay the amount of *Kr.* .50; i.e., 9 times .50 equals *Kr.* 4.50.[1]

FREY borrows Minutes 13 through 20.

WITTELS announces a paper on "The Great Courtesan."

PRESENTATION

Discussion on Degeneration

Opened by DR. SADGER

SADGER first wishes—if merely in consideration of the purely literal meaning of the terms—to distinguish between the concepts of

[1] Four *Kronen* were, at that time, worth one dollar.

hereditary weakness[2] and degeneracy,[3] reserving the latter for morons and imbeciles. In the neuroses, however, we frequently see certain symptoms which cannot be elucidated by means of analysis and which must be attributed to some "hereditary taint" (especially severe phobias and obsessive ideas must have developed in the soil of a strong hereditary predisposition).

The physical symptoms of "hereditary deficiency" have been adequately described in the literature; this is not the case with the psychic symptoms; these symptoms have often been regarded as character defects. In a study of several poets with severe hereditary taints, Sadger has found the following symptoms to be typical of hereditary deficiency:

1. A severe depression, out of proportion to the actual circumstances; deep melancholia alternating with exuberant cheerfulness, occasionally seen even in childhood, but most frequently appearing in puberty; a yearning to die which may become intensified to the point of suicide.

2. An aversion to associations [*Assoziationswiderwillen*], that is, a disinclination to any permanent connection with one's own self.

a. Oscillation between one science and another, between one profession and another (dread of holding office and of regular occupation); various aimless pursuits; unbounded thirst for liberty, which leads to

b. pathological urge to travel (*Wandertrieb*); they are the born gypsies, travelers to America, etc. Schubart,[4] e. g., had a pathological urge to travel.

Some occupations meet the aversion to association halfway: acting, circumnavigation of the globe, etc. Connected with the aversion to associations are: an ever-increasing tendency to avoid people, hurried speech (stumbling over one's own words), incapacity to remain faithful to one passion (those with a severe hereditary taint are often poor husbands; they cannot love one person permanently); absence of a sense of orderliness (for instance, in money matters and the like).

[2] *Belastung*, literally: burden, encumbrance. It has been variously translated here as hereditary taint, deficiency, weakness.

[3] *Entartung.*

[4] Christian Friedrich Daniel Schubart (1739-1791), German poet and freedom fighter.

3. An abnormal carelessness and intensity; the hereditarily tainted lives almost always in extremes; vanity, pride, self-assertion are pronounced, as is hypersensitivity.

4. Excessive emotionality and impressionability; in the physiological sphere: growing pale, blushing, etc.; an abnormal desire for certain stimulants (alcohol, tobacco, coffee) or intolerance to them; abnormal reactions of the central nervous system to normal physiological stimuli. This is usually combined with hereditary deficiency in the sexual sphere (what Freud calls the sexual constitution).

Concerning the anatomical basis, we can say that hereditary deficiency involves an abnormality in the sphere of bodily sensation, while imbecility is an abnormality of the association centers.

Lastly, Sadger wishes to propose two new concepts: hereditary neurosis [*Belastungsneurose*] and hereditary psychosis. Much that is called dementia praecox would be more correctly diagnosed as hereditary psychosis.

DISCUSSION

REITLER does not see any necessity—even in respect to the literal meaning of the terms in German and in French (*dégénérer*)—to distinguish between the two concepts. What Sadger terms hereditary deficiency may very well be included by others under the term degeneracy.

According to Moebius, we should not call everyone who differs from the average type of the mass of people a degenerate, but only those who show certain disharmonies in their psychic behavior. In his *Theory of Sexuality*, Freud postulated two main factors as determining degeneration: a considerable number of severe deviations from the norm, and disturbances in social behavior.

We may perhaps yet have to assume that abnormality is hereditary. Poets are not dependable material because one cannot get to know anything about their *vita sexualis*.[5] Many symptoms of "hereditary deficiency" could probably be illuminated by psychoanalysis (flight, change of residence may perhaps represent search for an adequate love object, etc.).

[5] In spite of this, Sadger made extensive use of biographies of poets to gain insight into psychic life. At that time, there was so little clinical material available that biographic, literary, or artistic material was used to supplement the few clinical cases.

FREUD: Before discussing Sadger's arguments, Freud precisely defines his own position. He does not distinguish between degeneration or deterioration and hereditary deficiency.

Three sources can be shown to have been used in the observation [of patients] to determine the concept of degeneration:

1. The morbidity of parents shows up also in their children; hereditary degeneration.

2. The deviations from what is considered normal and which are found in most people.

3. Certain injurious deviations which are found in some people.

ad 1. There is no objection to limiting the concept of degeneration to a family, but there is [objection] to the extensions and generalizations.

ad 2 and 3. This is unfortunate and harmful and deprives the concept of its value. But the concept has to be completely discarded in respect to the historic meaning which it contains: that there once actually existed a perfect generation whose descendants have gradually degenerated. This is untrue. Such men never existed and we are no more degenerate than our ancestors of a hundred years ago or of a thousand years ago.

The stigmata of degeneration are not symptoms but character disorders and we have no right to subsume them under a clinical picture. We have no idea whatsoever about the formation of a character. Symptoms develop as a result of the repressed, but character is determined by the repressing forces.[6] We do not know the psychic material that must be taken into consideration in the problem of the significance of degeneration.

Sadger's ingenious and independent stand in general deserves appreciation even though there are some doubts concerning specific points. It is a happy thought to emphasize dejection and the aversion to association. However, some other points (strong stimulants, etc.) certainly do not deserve special emphasis. The peculiarities of those with a "hereditary taint" may be traceable perhaps not to individual experiences but to the psychosexual constitution, in any case. As to the "soil"

---

[6] Nowadays this would be expressed in the following way: symptoms develop as a result of a failure of repression and are a compromise formation, whereas character is a product of successful repression and of the ego's assimilation of the repressed.

of hereditary deficiency which Sadger postulates for the obsessional neuroses, phobias, etc., one can only say that the *inclination* to these phenomena characterizes the degenerate. Besides, it is worth noting that the obsessional neurotics show in many respects behavior opposite to that of degenerates. One must guard against Sadger's attempt to see the anatomical basis in an abnormality of the sphere of bodily sensation or of the sphere of association, respectively. This is superfluous and of no value for the theoretical understanding of the neurosis. By the same token, the new concepts of hereditary neurosis and hereditary psychosis should be rejected.

STEKEL states that Sadger has mistaken cause for effect. We are dealing with neuroses, and the concept of hereditary deficiency has been construed [in an effort to find] a cause of the neuroses. The only deficiency that one can accept as valid is the one postulated by Freud, namely, that of the milieu. (Two cases in which two brothers and two sisters have similar symptoms stemming from the same sexual traumata.)

The aversion to associations applies only to permanent associations; for the individual in question continually seeks new associations.

Dejection is frequently found in onanists (self-reproach, etc.). The flight from the self corresponds to a search for a sexual ideal. A psychoanalysis on the basis of the biographies of poets is impossible; on the basis of their works it is very fruitful.

FREY emphasizes that he, on the other hand, has frequently found *fear* of changing places [in such cases]. He would describe the positive value of Sadger's work in the following way: from the negation of the psychophysical constitutional characteristics which Sadger ascribes to the hereditarily tainted, the philistine could be construed.

The normal human being exists only as an ideal (Rousseau's natural man).

WITTELS, from the artistic point of view, calls the concepts of hereditary deficiency and degeneration hostile to art and to life. It is not a mere coincidence that it was Freud who succeeded in annihilating also the alleged truth of degeneration.

ADLER misses a precise definition of the concept of hereditary deficiency and thinks that Sadger has merely put together the symp-

187

tomatology of those who are called deranged. Leaving aside the somewhat arbitrary compilation, he has found nothing but well-known
"symptoms." Dejection, for instance, is one of the most common
symptoms in all kinds of psychoses and neuroses. The only original
contribution is the concept of aversion to association; this aversion,
however, is from the first accessible to psychoanalysis and proves to
have several determinants.

The degenerative phenomena are not characteristic of the individual
as a whole but pertain to single organs and are apparently—as Sadger
also assumes—connected with an illness in the sphere of somatic
sensations.

HELLER, from his own personal experience, can state that the
contrasting phenomena mentioned by several discussants (the urge to
keep changing one's place of residence, and the fear of changing it
at other times) are often found in one individual side by side.

RANK suspects that the artists dissected by Sadger may have been
done an injustice by the diagnosis "degeneration or hereditary deficiency," and that many other people who are not known to have
"symptoms or to commit symptomatic acts" would, on close examination, probably prove to be equally hereditarily deficient.

FEDERN stresses the importance of the whole question and, in
contrast to Freud, considers it very necessary to deal with this problem
now, in spite of our deficient knowledge in this field.

The question arises which illnesses are already present in the germ
cell and which illnesses appear only in the course of its development.
Adler was the first to attempt a solution of this problem.

The minor stigmata of degeneration are perhaps more likely to be
found in the somatic sphere. With regard to degeneration, one must
go back to atavism, for the majority of the somatic symptoms are
atavistic. This point of view, however, is not valid for the psychic
sphere. Inferiority might best be characterized by the formula: too
weak inhibitions against strong (normal) impulses.

He would accept the concept of hereditary neurosis.

SADGER had expected more objections. The last phenomena mentioned by him, so well known to some of the members, were taken
from general psychiatry. He has chosen poets because they are extreme

cases in whom even the layman can recognize pathological character-istics.

There is hereditary deficiency without degeneration, but there is no degeneration without hereditary deficiency. Sadger doubts the psycho-sexual explanation of symptoms of hereditary deficiency. Those with severe hereditary deficiency show almost no symptoms, especially no chronic symptoms; for other impressions do not affect the individual with a severe hereditary taint, and neurotic disturbances which may nevertheless develop are in the category of the hereditary neuroses. (Lenau, for example, did not develop an anxiety neurosis in spite of continuously frustrated excitation).

The families of those with a severe hereditary deficiency become extinct in the third or fourth generation, at the latest; it seems that the genius has only the task of bringing about cultural progress, while the species is regenerated by the multitude.

It is not merely a question of peculiarities of character, but of a high-grade development [*hochgradige Abwicklung*] of a type best described as normal or seminormal.[7]

The *works* of creative writers cannot be used for psychological investigation because the degree and kind of idealization (distortion) is not known.

---

[7] Unintelligible.

23

SCIENTIFIC MEETING *on May 8, 1907*

Present: Freud, Adler, [A.] Deutsch, Federn, Hitschmann, Rank, Sadger, Wittels, Stekel (part of evening).

PRESENTATION

Walter Calé[1]

SPEAKER: DR. [ADOLF] DEUTSCH

DR. DEUTSCH speaks about the young poet, Walter Calé, who recently died by suicide. His case is worth noting because in him one can demonstrate the sexual problem and its influence on life. The short biography which prefaces the collection of his posthumous writings (Berlin: S. Fischer, 1907) does not refer to this material. Frequently, statements of the biographer even contradict what the poet has said about himself.

Deutsch then gives a short account of the external circumstances of Calé's life (gymnasium, study of law) which ended in his twenty-third year. Aside from external conflicts, the poet must have been beset

[1] 1881-1904.

by deep inner doubts. From this point of view, Deutsch now tries to reconstruct the course of Calé's life. The shy aloofness, so frequently reported in Calé, is characteristic of all brooding young autoerotics. The same is true of his "nervousness" and melancholia. Between his fourteenth and fifteenth year, he began to write. At seventeen, he wrote the Artus drama, *Klingsor*, which is characteristic of him because of its subject matter: Klingsor castrates himself in order to acquire power.— Calé repeatedly stresses his "being a child" and his feeling childlike. He also reveals, repeatedly and unmistakably, the persistence of his infantile impressions.

Calé's works speak for themselves: they create the atmosphere of anxiety dreams. Almost all of his poems are addressed to his sister and betray deep love for her. (Deutsch quotes passages from the poems and from the diaries.) Whether this incestuous love remained in the psychic sphere or was actually consummated cannot be ascertained. Some lines, however, in which he speaks of guilt and atonement, might lead one to suspect that incest was carried out.

Repeatedly he expresses the fear that his sister might turn to another man. One cannot tell from the material whether he himself ever turned to another woman, though he must have wanted to escape to another one. In his search for some way out, the idea of a homosexual relationship may have vaguely entered his mind (*Franciscus*). His sexual development, then, could be summarized approximately in this way: the love of this child, so precocious and in need of love, was probably first directed to his mother and then transferred to his sister. It is uncertain, but not improbable, that the incestuous act was committed. He did not find a way out of the conflict inherent in this love. He could neither escape to another woman nor find salvation in a homosexual love. Thus he chose suicide.

DISCUSSION

ADLER does not think this case worthy of serious consideration. All we see here is the fact that Calé conspicuously underscores his love for his sister, a trait which can be found in many young poets. To infer an incestuous act is hardly admissible. Had such an act occurred, these emotions would probably not have found poetic

191

expression. In these cases we are dealing rather with incestuous thoughts and fantasies which always strive for an appropriate form of expression.

SADGER stresses that the picture of Calé shows some symptoms of hereditary deficiency, which he has also found in other poets: avoidance of other people, fear of publicity, melancholia alternating with exuberance, aversion to associations, and many more. It is questionable whether suicide is an indication of hereditary deficiency. Be that as it may, the tendency to suicide does belong in the chapter of severe hereditary deficiency (Kleist's double suicide). The act of burning their papers, which Calé and other poets are reported to have carried out, is also attributable to hereditary deficiency in so far as it is an expression of the aversion to associations.

Concerning the sexual problem in Calé, it is striking that he speaks so openly of his love for his sister. There is probably something else and something deeper hidden behind it: presumably, the love for his mother. We find something similar in Goethe, in whose case love for the mother (= Frau von Stein) is likewise hidden behind love for the sister. Viewed from this aspect, Calé's homosexual leanings go back to the father. Invariably one comes upon the parents as the first love objects.

HITSCHMANN remarks it is obvious that Calé was an unusual and one-sided individual. But one should not overextend these characteristics for the purpose of demonstrating the pathological aspect of his personality. In the end, one must be content with some assumptions. Hitschmann would stress only the important role of abstinence, which must certainly have played a role also in Calé's life. (He cites a passage dealing with the struggle against the sexual world which is considered to be evil.) Deutsch has not elucidated the suicide.

FEDERN advises caution in regard to "cases of incest." Calé shows that such a relationship can render a person incapable of living even if there is no hereditary inferiority. Our experience, however, is not yet extensive enough to permit us to infer such relationships from the works (Rank).

In regard to suicide Sadger is mistaken. There were times when it was not abnormal to end one's life by suicide (Sophocles), and individuals who kill themselves in grief caused by love are by no means degenerate.

FREUD begins farther back with a correction: concepts of degeneration, superiority, and inferiority are not anatomical but intellectual distinctions. Among the propositions advanced by Sadger last time, only the concept of aversion to association is new. The diagnosis of hereditary deficiency is altogether of no value, and in the case of Calé it is also quite arbitrary.

He can confirm the influence of the mother in the case of Goethe, to which Sadger referred; it is expressed most clearly in his later love relationships. Werther falls in love with Lotte at first glance when he sees her spreading butter on bread—a picture which brings to his mind the image of his mother distributing food to the children. (The proverb, "The way to a man's heart is through his stomach," goes back to the fact that the mother is both the provider of food and the beloved.) Such conditions of love are found in everybody; all of them go back to infantile life. The path of love—that is, of the normal psychosis—is chosen in order to avoid other paths which would otherwise lead to more serious neuroses. The histories of marriage are extremely interesting: many marry to punish themselves, etc., etc.

Concerning the case of Calé, most of the objections raised are justified. Most likely *infantile* love relationships are involved here, as Federn has already intimated, and these were later sublimated into the yearning for love. As far as love for the mother hiding behind the obvious love for the sister is concerned, the poet's present, actual fantasy certainly refers exclusively to the sister. In other cases, one may succeed in uncovering the mother in such fantasies. Calé, who is delirious about these emotions, shows in his mental state a reflection of the dissociation of the sexual components.[2]

Calé's suicide reminds Freud of a young man who shot himself because he could not bear his sister's pregnancy (that she was not pregnant by him!). In this case the presence of the sister complex is confirmed by a detail (the pregnancy). Deutsch has submitted no proof of this kind of connection in the case of Calé.

[2] Rank must have made some mistake in recording this sentence. It cannot be understood.

193

RANK thinks the assumption of actual incest can with certainty be discarded. As Freud has stated occasionally, these emotions (especially in poets) are usually of an extraordinarily subtle nature. The poetic treatment of this theme by the only poet who is said to have been involved in actual incest (Byron) is altogether different from that of other poets (*Manfred, Cain*). *Manfred* presents directly the neurosis with repression and seizure [*Anfall*]. (In *Cain*, FREUD points to the interesting selection of the only situation in which incest is permitted and is no crime, and shows how the entire incest complex recedes as the complex of brother murder and death is put in the foreground.)

Rank concludes by saying that suicide, in most cases where young people are concerned, should be considered a miscarried search for the sexual object.

[A.] DEUTSCH stresses in conclusion that he was aware of being on uncertain ground with his suggestions; but the material at his disposal is actually too scanty.

24

SCIENTIFIC MEETING on May 15, 1907[1]

Present: Freud, Adler, Graf, Hitschmann, Rank, Reitler, Wittels [Federn].

COMMUNICATIONS

FREUD reads Wilhelm Jensen's reply to "Delusions and Dreams in Jensen's 'Gradiva' " which Freud had sent to him.[2]

REITLER borrows the *Journal* [*für Psychologie und Neurologie*].

DISCUSSION OF WITTELS'S ESSAY

Female Physicians[3]

FEDERN comments that Wittels has not discussed the essential question of woman's wish to study.

---

[1] There is no protocol preserved of the following meeting on May 29, 1907, the last scientific meeting of the season. Only the attendance record and the title of Wittels's paper were found.

"*Present:* Freud, Adler, Federn, Frey, Häutler, Heller, Hitschmann, Kahane, Rank, Stekel, Wittels.

"FREY returned Minutes 13-20."

On May 29, Wittels gave a paper entitled "The Great Courtesan," which was evidently meant to be a sequel to his paper "Female Physicians." For some progressives at that time, the courtesan [*Hetäre*] represented an ideal, the quintessence of womanhood. The topic was thus relevant to the fight for woman's sexual equality. The idealization of the courtesan was probably based on a misconception of her status in ancient Greece. Be that as it may, it had its counterpart in the protest of young middle-class girls against marriage for the sake of financial security only. Social reformers and feminists regarded such marriages as legalized prostitution. As long as prostitution existed, they argued, it should take the form of courtesanship and not marriage.

[2] Cf. Minutes 1, note 2.

Jensen's letters to Freud were published in *Psa. Bewegung*, 1:207-211, 1929. For a description of Jensen's reaction to Freud's essay, see Strachey's note to the English translation of Freud's essay in *S.E.*, 9:4.

[3] Wittels's essay appeared in the periodical *Die Fackel* [*The Torch*], Vol. 9, No. 225, May 3, 1907, under the pseudonym of Avicenna, which was the name of the great

195

He is quite mistaken if he believes that sexuality is the only drive of the human being. The importance of work and the concept of giving a meaning to life through work have to be taken into account in evaluating women's wish to study. The need to work is not rooted solely in social conditions, but is one of those instincts of man which have developed at a late period.

To balance Wittels's onesidedness, Federn calls attention to the lascivious perversity of numerous male physicians and to their sexual exploitation of many women. It is not admissible to single out women for the reproach that, in studying medicine, they give vent to their

---

Arabic physician and philosopher (979-1037). The editor of *Die Fackel* was Karl Kraus (1874-1936), one of the most distinguished satirists of his time. He crusaded against the hypocrisy of the middle-class society of that period. Women were looked upon either as slaves exploited by middle-class society and by its male members, or as bourgeoisie's dangerous representatives. Frank Wedekind's demonic women and Peter Altenberg's glorifications of prostitutes are examples of these contrasting conceptions. Peter Altenberg (1859-1919) was a distinguished moralist and writer.

To facilitate a better understanding of the ensuing discussion, we append a brief summary of Wittels's essay, "Female Physicians."

Wittels distinguishes between those professions which society forces upon women, such as teaching, and the profession of physician which is chosen voluntarily. The former are, according to Wittels, a consequence of social conditions which prevent a woman from following her true profession—which is to attract men. The latter must be attributed to her own wish.

A woman studies medicine in order to surpass other women. The more hysterical she is, the better a student she will be, since the hysteric can deflect her sexual drive from the sexual aim. She may be as immoral as she likes without having to be ashamed. Men who call themselves feminists but who are actually masochists might approve of the woman medical student; but the average, half-way normal student regards his female colleague as nothing but a prostitute.

As long as a woman is still a medical student, she is harming no one except herself. As soon as she becomes a physician, however, she becomes a danger for others. Women patients can have no confidence in her; nurses will not like her, and a sick man will never be able to surrender himself to be examined by a woman without at the same time having sexual thoughts.

Wittels cites two extreme examples to demonstrate the absurdity of woman as physician: (1) the female psychiatrist: being a woman, she can never understand man's psychological secrets; (2) the woman doctor in the public health service—a position which might in the future be open to her. Never should she be allowed to become the superior of male colleagues: she would always abuse the power of her office. Flattery would easily sway her to grant unwarranted favors; and she would be inclined to treat female patients as rivals.

Nowhere does Wittels envisage the possibility that a female physician could be married and have a normal family life.

Wittels summarizes by saying that hysteria is the basis for a woman's desire to study medicine, just as it is the basis of woman's struggle for equal rights. The suppression of "basic femininity" has obliterated the "true woman" known in ancient Greece.

sexuality. This is a prudish point of view. However, one can agree with Wittels that it is not permissible to have women publicly handle men's genitals.

Lastly, Federn mentions a number of details which characterize Wittels's warped point of view.

GRAF, without going into details, stresses the intense affect accompanying Wittels's discussion of this sociopsychological topic. In his opinion, this disproportionate affect stems from Wittels's anger that women wish to study rather than to have sexual intercourse. As a matter of fact, man's achievements also spring from sensuous sources. The question can only be whether studying is harmful for women. In Graf's opinion, it is.

Concerning the medical profession in particular, he thinks that woman will never make contributions of importance equal to those of man since she lacks the great personal influence, the suggestive power, which, in addition to knowledge, is indispensable for the competent physician. Even the present-day physician cannot yet dispense with this bit of priesthood (the first physicians were priests); and the physician's authority, which is in a way a continuation of the parental authority, plays an important part in treatment and cure. The female physician, who lacks this authority, is better qualified to substitute for the mother, i.e., as a nurse.

REITLER is inclined to agree with most of Wittels's arguments in so far as they concern psychological understanding.

But he would reject some of the details, such as the unjustified hatred of hysteria or the assertion that all these women are just out to capture a man. Women who study medicine without some compelling necessity have, for the most part, renounced men (because they have recognized their own physical defects).

HITSCHMANN points out that we do not really know the "female physician" but only the female student. We know those who are the vanguard. We have not yet found the proper forms of social intercourse with them, but they rather deserve considerate treatment precisely because of their exposed position.

If Wittels reproaches them with hysteria, he extends this concept

197

quite incorrectly beyond its limits. The ample enlightenment they receive is actually rather a prophylaxis against hysteria.

In addition to hysteria, they are reproached with physical defects. This aesthetic judgment should not be used as a reproach—though we must admit that most female students are ugly and are true amazons (bosomless).

But in addition to their rejection of sex, Wittels accuses them also of sexual aggression (enticing the man). This is a blunder in logic.

Besides, the sexual repression which Wittels dislikes so much in women is a general characteristic of "well-brought-up" girls. As a father, Wittels would certainly approve of it in his own daughters. Woman's rejection of sexuality stems from the difficult conditions of her sex life: after all she belongs to the tribe of those Asra who become pregnant when they love.[4]

It must be conceded, however, that erotic experiences are a part of the development of a full personality. On the other hand, one must not overvalue sexuality as enormously as Wittels does, or look at the world from the *"Vögelperspektive"*[5] and encompass it all in the formula: *coito ergo sum.*

It is the female principle to have children; but this is the principle of the species. Not everything is necessarily *actu;* some things are merely *potentia.*

The danger of being caught by one of these "monsters," which Wittels sees as a threat to some male students, is not so grave as all that, and such a young man's fate is still better than that of quite a few others who squander their youth on prostitutes. Even the relatively free behavior of female students (they are said to be promiscuous) is still preferable to the hypocrisy of many a *virgo tacta* (Gersuny[6]).

At the end of Wittels's article it becomes clear that his views are based on the ideal of the Greek woman, the courtesan, an ideal which has become alien to us. This is more "Greek Alley" [*Griechengasse*]

---

[4] An allusion to Heinrich Heine's famous poem, *Der Asra*, which ends with the lines: *Und mein Stamm sind jene Asra, welche sterben, wenn sie lieben* [And those Asra are my tribe who must perish when they love].

[5] *Vögelperspektive* is a pun which cannot readily be translated. *Vögeln*, in Viennese slang, means to have sexual intercourse; but *Vögel* is also the plural of *Vogel* (bird). *Vögelperspektive* means both "bird's-eye view" and from the "perspective of sexual intercourse."

[6] Well-known Viennese pediatrician.

than Greece. Wittels is enthused with a presyphilitic era, and now he wants to breed *"das Übermensch."*[7]

FREUD first expresses appreciation for an original, high-spirited, ingenious essay. On the other hand, he sees in it certain half-truths and quarter-truths.

First of all, one must reproach Wittels with a lack of courtesy in the higher sense. Woman, whom culture has burdened with the heavier load (especially in propagation) ought to be judged with tolerance and forbearance in areas where she has lagged behind man.

Furthermore, a sense of jutice is missing in this article since its attitude is skeptical only toward the new, whereas it leaves unchallenged what is old but also reprehensible. Indeed, improprieties have not been introduced by women into the medical profession but have existed for a very long time.

Wittels is quite correct in pointing to sexuality as the driving force of the wish to study; except that he neglects to differentiate between sublimated and crude sexuality, which, to him, are equivalent. But the displacement of sexuality onto the thirst for knowledge is at the root of every investigative endeavor.

Wittels represents a juvenile point of view: that of a young man who at first greatly adores women and does not dare to ascribe such human emotions to girls. Only gradually does he learn to recognize that woman is by no means averse to sexuality; but whenever he "finds out" the woman, he reproaches her for it. Very soon there follows hatred of women. He despises woman (as he has unconsciously despised his mother). This article also tries to expose a once-admired object.[8]

In Freud's opinion, it is true that woman gains nothing by studying, and that on the whole woman's lot will not improve thereby. More-

---

[7] Hitschmann, who was known for his biting wit, evidently could not refrain from making one pun after another. The *Griechengasse* in Vienna was a well-known red-light district.

In German, the term for human being is *der Mensch* (with the article of the male gender, *der*). If the neuter article, *das*, is used (*das Mensch*), it becomes a derogatory Austrian slang expression meaning a woman who does not amount to much, or a prostitute. *Das Übermensch*, therefore, connotes a "superprostitute," whereas *der Übermensch* [the superman] is the well-known term which Nietzsche introduced.

[8] See Freud's essay, "On the Universal Tendency to Debasement in the Sphere of Love" (1912). *S.E.*, 11:177-190.

over, women cannot equal man's achievement in the sublimation of sexuality.

The ideal of the courtesan [*Hetäre*] has no place in our culture. We endeavor to uncover sexuality; but once sexuality is demonstrated, we demand that the entire repression of sexuality become conscious and that the individual learn to subordinate it to cultural requirements. We replace repression by healthy suppression.[9] The sexual problem cannot be settled without regard for the social problem; and if one prefers abstinence to the wretched sexual conditions, one is abstinent under protest.

The sense of having sinned which opposes sexuality is very widespread, and even the sexually free feel that they are grave sinners.

A woman who, like the courtesan, is not trustworthy in sexuality is altogether worthless. She is simply a *Haderlump*.[10]

RANK, setting aside Wittels's essay, points to one of the infantile sources of the study of medicine. Here, too, the question of where children come from (Freud) plays the chief role. The medical student settles this question in reality. He is, one might say, the least neurotic. The philosopher solves it by way of defense (obsessional neurosis) in broadening the question: from where does man come; from where the world? The theologian answers it by saying, "They come from God"; and so on.

In referring to Freud's comments on the hatred of women, he characterizes Wittels's opinion that whatever woman does is sexual (see especially Leontiev[11]) as only a reactive manifestation of an earlier developmental stage in which he regarded woman as asexual.

ADLER finds that Wittels says nothing but familiar things, but says them by misapplying a less familiar terminology. It is a well-known fact that there are limitations for women who study medicine. An inquiry which was circulated brought the suggestion that special courses be arranged for women students to present the diseases of the genitals.

[9] Repression means to forget the ideas but to retain the affect, which is sometimes attached to another, substitute, idea. Suppression means to retain the idea but to control or discipline the affect.

[10] Viennese slang for "scamp," "ragamuffin," "cad."

[11] See Minutes 19.

The impression which he gained from Wittels's articles could be rendered in the following way: Wittels lifts the skirts of female students and says, "They have female genitals." But that is characteristic not only of the female student.

Wittels has given away part of our secret: that medical art works with sexual energies. There is a danger that the masses will misunderstand this just as Wittels has a wrong idea of it.

Just recently, Freud stressed that the unconscious components [of mental life] deserve a certain amount of consideration and tolerance.[12]

WITTELS feels so shaken by a word of Freud's (the courtesan is a *Haderlump*) that at the moment he cannot answer the objections in detail.

His aim was to present a *Weltanschauung* which would do justice to the basic difference between men and women which is not yet fully understood.

Proceeding from the great courtesan who gives full play to her sexuality in all its aspects, he has come to have a low opinion of her counterpart, the female student who has crippled all sexual instincts. He finds it impossible to esteem more highly the woman who does not heed the call of the period.[13]

---

[12] See Minutes 19.

[13] The Minutes of this meeting mark the close of the record of the work year 1906-1907.

As stated above, there was a scientific meeting on May 29, 1907 for which the protocol was not preserved. Only the following notations were preserved:

"There was a social evening on June 19, 1907 which was attended by: Freud, Adler, [A.] Deutsch, Federn, Frey, Heller, Hitschmann, Rank, Stekel, and Wittels.

"Another social meeting and final session was held on July 3, 1907. The following were present: Freud, [A.] Deutsch, Federn, Bass, Häutler, Hitschmann, Stekel, Wittels.

"*Communications:* Hitschmann makes the suggestion that, in the coming year, special evenings devoted to reviews be instituted. Rank announces Meisl's resignation.

"Freud announces the dissolution of the Society, planned for the fall, and the constitution of a new society to follow immediately thereafter [see Freud's letter, drafted in Rome on September 22, 1907, in Minutes 25].

"Federn borrows Minutes 1-5.

"*Accounting:* The membership dues for the second semester of 1907 have not yet been paid by Dr. Hollerung. Contributions for supplies in the amount of Kr. 1.36 from Meisl, Hollerung, and Bass. A contribution of Kr. .50 from Bach, Brecher, Häutler, Kahane. Kr. .86 are returned to Graf (a mistake had been made). Expenses for mail from May 11, to the end were Kr. 2.70, which is balanced by a credit of Kr. 2.70.

"*Carried over:* Federn, Minutes. Reitler: *Das illustrierte französische Witzblatt* [*The Illustrated French Comic Journal*]. Sadger: Minutes 8."

25

SCIENTIFIC MEETING on *October 9, 1907*[1]

Present: Freud, Adler, [A.] Deutsch, Federn, Graf, Heller, Hitschmann, Hollerung, Rank, Reitler, Steiner, Sadger, Schwerdtner, Stekel, Wittels.

COMMUNICATIONS

Dr. Federn proposes Dr. Hans Abels (pediatrician) for acceptance as a member.

Professor Freud, Dr. Schwerdtner, and Dr. Steiner pay membership dues.

Sadger borrows Minutes 24 (returned October 16).

Papers announced:

Adler: *Fragment from the Analysis of a Case of Paranoia*
Stekel: [No title]
Freud: *The Beginning of a Case History*
Sadger: (For January) *K. F. Meyer*

APPENDIX[2]

Rome, September 22, 1907

Dear Colleague:

I wish to inform you that I propose at the beginning of this new working year to dissolve the little Society which has been ac-

---

[1] First meeting of the new working year.

[2] The following letter was found appended to Minutes 25. The translation is quoted from Ernest Jones: *The Life and Work of Sigmund Freud*, 2:9-10. New York: Basic Books, 1955.

customed to meet every Wednesday at my home, and immediately afterwards to call it into life again. A short note sent before October 1st to our secretary, Otto Rank, will suffice to insure a renewal of your membership; if we hear nothing by that date we shall assume that you do not wish to renew it. I need hardly emphasize how very pleased I should be at your re-entry.

Allow me to give the reason for this action which may well seem to you to be superfluous. We are only taking into account the natural changes in human relationships if we assume that to one or another member in our group membership no longer signifies what it did years earlier—whether because his interest in the subject is exhausted, or his leisure time and mode of life are no longer compatible with attendance, or that personal associations threaten to keep him away. Presumably he would still remain a member, fearing lest his resignation be regarded as an unfriendly action. For all these cases the dissolving and reorganizing of the Society has the purpose of re-establishing the personal freedom of each individual and of making it possible for him to stay apart from the Society without in any way disturbing his relations with the rest of us. We have further to bear in mind that in the course of years we have undertaken (financial) obligations, such as appointing a secretary, of which there was no question at the beginning.

If you agree after this explanation with the expediency of reconstituting the Society in this way you will probably approve of its being repeated at regular intervals—say every three years.

> I remain, with best compliments
> and cordial regards,
> Yours,
>
> [signed] Dr. Freud

Membership List 1907/1908

Prof. Dr. Sigm. Freud
Dr. Alfred Adler
Dr. D. I. Bach
Dr. Alfred Bass
Dr. Adolf Deutsch
Dr. Paul Federn

203

Dr. Max Graf
Hugo Heller
Adolf Häutler
Dr. Eduard Hitschmann
Dr. Edwin Hollerung
Otto Rank
Dr. Rudolf Reitler
Dr. Maxim Steiner
Dr. Isidor Sadger
Dr. Hugo Schwerdtner
Dr. Wilhelm Stekel
Dr. Fritz Wittels
Dr. Rudolf Ubantschitsch (beginning 1.15.1908)
Dr. Hans Abels[3]
Dr. Albert Joachim (beginning 2.12.1908)

PRESENTATION

The Somatic Equivalents of Anxiety and
Their Differential Diagnosis

SPEAKER: DR. STEKEL

STEKEL refers to the work of Hecker[4] who was the first to call attention to the equivalents of anxiety, though he did not assign any psychological motivation to anxiety. After Hecker, Freud in his work on anxiety neuroses emphatically stressed the importance of [anxiety] equivalents.[5] Later, Fliess[6] showed in numerical terms the relation between anxiety and its equivalents.

[3] This name is crossed out in the manuscript.

[4] Ewald Hecker, German psychiatrist.

[5] See Freud's "The Justification for Detaching from Neurasthenia a Particular Syndrome: The Anxiety-Neurosis" (1894). *C.P.*, 1:107-127. In the latter essay, Freud mentions Hecker's paper on "Masked and Abortive Anxiety States in Neurasthenia" ["Über lavierte und abortive Angstzustände bei Neurasthenie." *Zbl. Nervenheilkunde*, Dec., 1893] and says: "I found, as E. Hecker had done before me, that the neurotic symptoms in question could all be united under the head of 'pertaining to the expression of anxiety'" (p. 107).

[6] Dr. Wilhelm Fliess is the friend to whom the letters were addressed which were published by Bonaparte, A. Freud, and E. Kris under the title, *The Origins of Psychoanalysis [Aus den Anfängen der Psychoanalyse]*. Stekel refers here to two books by Fliess: *The Course of Life* and *The Structure of Life [Der Ablauf des Lebens* and *Der Aufbau des Lebens]* published in 1906.

According to Stekel the most frequent anxiety equivalents are:

heart symptoms (palpitation, etc.)

respiratory symptoms (nervous, i.e., sexual asthma)

stomach symptoms (singultus, vomiting, pains, nervous diarrhea, tenesmus, spasms of the pharynx, etc.)

bladder symptoms (enuresis)

skin symptoms (only in a few cases)

muscular symptoms (spasms)

peripheral nerve symptoms (paresthesias and neuralgias).

Stekel then presents a number of his own cases which are supposed to show, among other things, that *equivalents can, under certain conditions, take hold of an erotogenic zone.*

Case 1: A man who has been sexually abstinent for some time because of psychic impotence, has a violent burning and boring sensation around his eyes. From information gathered from an encyclopedia, he believes that he has *holes around his eyes.* He prefers to have intercourse with older women (incestuous thoughts: root of the psychic impotence). One morning, his housekeeper kissed him on the forehead while he was in bed. He had intercourse with her, and has been well ever since. When asked about this, he explained that she kissed him as his mother used to kiss him.

Case 2 (not a pure equivalent): A lady wakes up in the morning with violent pains in her neck, dizziness, and feelings of anxiety. The pains do not subside in spite of all kinds of treatment; morphine injections in the evening are followed by a sleepless night; her nose was itching (the old saying: when the nose itches, there will be a fight). She has a weak husband (coitus interruptus); besides she has had an affair with a smart young man who had first kissed her on the neck and then bitten her in the same place during intercourse. The husband called this young man when her pain did not subside and he promised to come again if she did not improve. Shortly before this attack, he had broken off the relationship with her (fighting).

Case 3: A man has severe stomach pains after his mid-day meal. The pains subside only after he has put his finger in his throat and vomited. Previously he had attacks of anxiety. In the evening, when he eats at home, he has no pains. His wife is, as he says, a whore. He does not have intercourse with her since she is openly unfaithful to him.

205

However, at night, supposedly when he is half asleep, he does have intercourse with her. Formerly he would also have intercourse with her in the middle of the day (presumably fellatio: finger in mouth). It seems also that the particular attachment in such cases (of the partner's unfaithfulness) is due to perverse gratification.

Stekel next mentions a case of spasm of the pharynx, one of nervous diarrhea, and another of paralysis of the hand. In connection with these cases he expresses some basic ideas on the development of anxiety and its equivalents. The entire anxiety attack may be an equivalent of coition (Fliess). Overhearing parental intercourse often engenders in the child feelings of anxiety which come from the unconscious. *Anxiety is the contribution of the unconscious to sexual excitement.* Every sexual excitement in which libido is repressed becomes anxiety. The equivalents originate partly by way of conversion and partly as a consequence of the suppressed libido diverted from its aim.

DISCUSSION

GRAF mentions only that Goethe's sister developed a facial rash whenever she wanted to attend a ball.

[A.] DEUTSCH relates the case of a girl who had a platonic affair and whose considerable artistic talents in several fields (singing, playing the piano, painting) failed after a short time. It seems that in this way she was saying, "My life is worthless since I cannot fulfill its only purpose."

He further asks: what did the diarrhea mean for this traveling salesman (at home, with his wife, he had diarrhea; on the road, where he could have intercourse with other women, he had none)? STEKEL: It was a coitus substitute.

REITLER suspects that Stekel views the symptoms that accompany anxiety as its equivalents; he does not believe this to be a valid characterization. It should be possible to reverse an equivalent ($a = b$; $b = a$).

HITSCHMANN states that he has not learned anything new from the paper. Stekel gave some interesting examples, not all of which are to the point. In Case 1, he does not see any "anxiety." The itching of the nose in Case 2 might have been produced by the morphine injection. Organic affections cannot altogether be excluded in these cases (for instance, the pain in the neck). Affections of the heart, in particular, must not be overlooked.

STEINER contributes a personal recollection. At a time when he was abstinent, he met the wife of a friend who was impotent due to a severe illness. At first, he did not approach the woman because he feared he would not succeed. He then suffered from insomnia, physical discomfort (particularly in the intestinal tract), and spasms of the stomach. As soon as he had begun an intimate relationship with her, he became well. Whenever this woman went away on a trip, his ailments reappeared.

In Case 1, the kiss on the forehead is obviously a childhood recollection. Mothers often do "kiss the pain away."

ADLER stresses that this paper shows all of the advantages and drawbacks of Stekel's manner of working. Advantages: he brings many data and much evidence and organizes them around a central point. Drawbacks: he permits himself digressions which do not seem acceptable to everyone, and is satisfied with a few hunches which are often far from exhausting the material.

Case 1 is an obsessional idea. This, however, makes no difference in Stekel's conception, for the obsessional idea is also an equivalent of anxiety. It is of no importance whether we rediscover the source of anxiety in anxiety itself or in its equivalent. The localization of the equivalents has not yet been proven. Its choice is determined not only by events but rather by the entire constitution and development. Most equivalents concentrate themselves in an inferior organ [literally: look for, seek an inferior organ].

The symptom of the paralyzed hand requires further discussion; he has frequently encountered it in elderly *spinsters* (not, as Stekel has, in ungratified wives) in whom it showed the closest connection with masturbation.

FEDERN notes the discrepancy between title and content of Stekel's paper. The title ought to be: a resolution of symptoms of repressed sexuality. The paper touches on the basic problem of the etiology of neurosis. But Stekel has not shown any new connections. What he brings are equivalents of sexual gratification which has not been

207

achieved. An exact investigation should determine whether *in the place of anxiety* there can appear disgust without anxiety, pain without anxiety, feelings of unpleasure without anxiety, and sensation of hunger without anxiety.

In reference to Stekel's definition of anxiety, he must state that the other sexual functions are no more and no less unconscious than is anxiety. Anxiety is merely a topical sensation of the heart. Perhaps, the anxiety component during intercourse also is nothing but a sensation of the heart.

There are also chronic anxiety equivalents of a neurotic nature which are the consequences of anxiety affects from childhood (for example, bent posture).

SCHWERDTNER relates the case of a singer who has always been in good form but recently has had anxiety states (hoarseness, etc.). Previously he had many affairs, but since his marriage he has been faithful to his wife. Now she is pregnant, and he does not find gratification with her.

RANK says that he too did not have the impression of an anxiety equivalent in Case 1. He considers it simply a neurotic symptom. He cannot decide whether the obsessional idea should be considered an anxiety equivalent as Adler suggests. The attachment to a perverse partner has far deeper roots than mere fear of the difficulties of finding a new partner. The two partners are linked, among other things, by a sense of gratitude of such depth and intensity as are not found in any other relationship. The sense of gratitude is probably connected with the feelings of happiness which gratification of his perversion brings to the pervert. (FREUD: Happiness is the uninhibited gratification of the perversion.)

WITTELS disapproves of the confusing element inherent in the theory of anxiety equivalents. It takes us back to the earlier viewpoint when everything was regarded as neurasthenia. Now one says: anxiety equivalents, instead of dividing, as Freud has done, the actual neuroses into those with anxiety and those without anxiety, and tracing them back to the individual sexual trauma.

Stekel has not demonstrated that these equivalents are connected with anxiety.

208

SADGER emphasizes that one can speak of anxiety equivalents only if the symptoms occur in isolation (without anxiety). Frequently, however, one sees obsessional neuroses with anxiety symptoms or anxiety equivalents. From the standpoint of therapy, the decisive factor is that pure anxiety disappears when the actual, harmful, sexual situation is remedied, whereas this is not the case with mixed anxiety.

Sadger then discusses the various sources of anxiety (chemical, i.e., sexual-toxic, etc.). The anxiety of the hysteric and also that of the obsessional neurotic is fear of losing love(i.e., the love of the parents).

Children who have been exposed to sexual acts in the dark are afraid of darkness.

The overhearing of sexual intercourse, mentioned by Stekel, which evokes anxiety in the child causes him to believe that the parents are fighting, but the child has not yet decided with whom he will side in the struggle.

FREUD first stresses that anxiety is the central problem in all neuroses.

To begin with, Stekel must be reproached with looseness in his use of terminology. In the essay on the anxiety neurosis, he (Freud) is not concerned with *anxiety* equivalents but rather with equivalents of the anxiety *attack*.[7] Instead of the anxiety attack, there appear attacks in which there are only traces of anxiety. Anxiety is replaced by one or several symptoms which otherwise appear only in conjunction with anxiety. This misunderstanding on Stekel's part explains many of the objections to his cases and to his characterization of the symptoms as anxiety equivalents. Everything neurotic is an equivalent of anxiety: for all symptoms come from the libido and libido can be converted into anxiety.[8]

The real question is only why some people instead of an anxiety attack have somatic symptoms which they themselves do not recognize as anxiety and which deceive the physician as well.

---

[7] In the paper on "The Justification for Detaching from Neurasthenia a Particular Syndrome: The Anxiety-Neurosis" (1894), Freud says: "There are consequently *rudimentary anxiety-attacks* and *equivalents of an anxiety-attack* (all probably having the same meaning), showing a manifold and hitherto little appreciated variety of forms" (*C.P.*, 1:81; Freud's italics).

[8] This was the then-current theoretical conception of anxiety. Later (1926) this theory was changed.

As a matter of principle, Freud rejects the extensions Stekel has made. He would designate as anxiety neurosis only those cases in which the mechanism is not psychic. If the mechanism is psychic, then these cases belong to the hysterias.

Two types of hysteria can be differentiated:

(1) those in which the repressed libido manifests itself as a physical symptom (conversion hysteria); and

(2) those in which the repressed libido appears as anxiety connected with all kinds of things (anxiety hysteria).

Stekel's cases are anxiety hysterias: the anxiety neurosis is, as it were, the somatic substructure of hysteria. In hysteria, a detour through the psychic sphere is taken. Anxiety neurosis itself shows only a few typical clinical pictures. The variability is psychological.

We are frequently misled by terminology. Compulsion is everywhere.[9] The term compulsion neurosis has nothing whatever to do with this. The same is true of anxiety: it, too, is ubiquitous.

The typical equivalents of anxiety manifest themselves through those organs which are most involved in intercourse (respiratory organs, etc.), but which do not, just on this account, have to be inferior (Adler).

In his theoretical conclusions, Stekel solders together Freud's findings and a theory of Fliess's (anxiety is the sexual excitation of the opposite sex), which results in his entirely inadequate definition: anxiety is the sexual excitement coming from the unconscious. This is an abuse of language.

Case 3 is a pure hysteria.

Case 1 is not, as Adler thinks, an obsessional idea; the symptom can be characterized only as a hysterical delusional idea of hypochondriacal origin.

Sadger overestimates the importance of sexual trauma; the child's fear of the dark, that is, children's neurotic anxiety, is a primary one.

---

[9] Compulsion comes from the unconscious, that is, from the id. Freud expresses this thought in more detail later on. The same is true of his thoughts about anxiety. See "The 'Uncanny'" (1919). *S.E.*, 17:217-252; and *Inhibitions, Symptoms and Anxiety* (1926). *S.E.*, 20:75-175.

It is the yearning for the loved person (see *Theory of Sexuality*, n. 23).[10] Here lies the root of both neurotic and physiological anxiety.

What Deutsch has described in his case frequently occurs in abstinent women. The fact that many women are ruined by abstinence has much bearing on the problem of women's emancipation: a sculptress loses her skill when confronted with the task of modeling the male body; a girl whom her teacher embraces whenever she successfully accomplishes a task, cannot achieve anything any more.

STEKEL, in conclusion, refers to his recently published paper and stresses that cases of pure anxiety neurosis do not exist.[11]

[10] *Three Essays on the Theory of Sexuality* (1905). The footnote to which Freud refers is the following: "For this explanation of the origin of infantile anxiety I have to thank a three-year-old boy whom I once heard calling out of a dark room: 'Auntie, speak to me! I'm frightened because it's so dark.' His aunt answered him: 'What good would that do? You can't see me.' 'That doesn't matter,' replied the child, 'if anyone speaks, it gets light.' Thus what he was afraid of was not the dark, but the absence of someone he loved; and he could feel sure of being soothed as soon as he had evidence of that person's presence" (*S.E.*, 7:224).

[11] Stekel probably refers to his paper: "Nervöse Angstzustände und ihre Behandlung" ["Nervous Anxiety States and Their Treatment"]. *Med. Klin.*, 3:1039-1040; 1064-1067, 1907. This was published in book form, with a preface by Freud, in 1908.

26

SCIENTIFIC MEETING on October 16, 1907

Present: Freud, Adler, [A.] Deutsch, Hitschmann, Schwerdtner, Sadger, Steiner, Stekel, Wittels, Federn, Rank.

Upon unanimous vote of all present, Dr. Hans Abels[1] is accepted as a member.

[A.] Deutsch and Stekel pay their membership dues.

PRESENTATION

On Functional Impotence

SPEAKER: DR. STEINER

STEINER introduces his paper by stating that it is intended for laymen. It is concerned with that kind of impotence which, according to our present knowledge, lacks any organic basis. It is a symptom of a general neurosis, and in most cases the most important one. The anamneses show masturbation, frustrated sexual excitement, or a combination of both. This alone, however, does not provide an adequate

---

[1] Dr. Abels, pediatrician and friend of Dr. Federn, left the Society after a few meetings.

212

explanation. Since these factors occur very frequently, there must be other, additional factors.

There must be a certain predisposition to this illness. Accordingly, Steiner distinguishes:

1. Innate impotence
2. Acquired impotence
   a) in childhood
   b) in later years.

ad 1. In the first case there is a hereditary inferiority (mostly of a syphilitic nature) manifesting itself in the total behavior: little vivacity in childhood, feminine traits, shyness; enuresis of long duration; clumsiness in youth; prolonged puberty; masturbation. These individuals attempt intercourse late and under coercion; then again revert to masturbation with all of its accompaniments (nocturnal emission, etc.). Before marriage, or after unsuccessful marital coition, they seek a physician.

ad 2a. The group interests us most. Almost all of these patients grew up without a sister, or, at least, had no sister of approximately the same age. Therefore, in later life, they were never able to establish an adequate relationship to a woman. Intercourse alone is never enough for them; they exhaust themselves in frustrated forms of excitement.

ad 2b. This form may be caused by various circumstances: by external influences, by fear of infection, by misunderstood ethics, by a lack of opportunity, by fear of impregnation, etc.

The diagnosis of all of these states is very simple: missing or insufficient erections, especially in contact with a woman; ejaculatio praecox.

The prognosis is determined by the etiology. Steiner mentions two cases which are in psychotherapy.

One concerns a thirty-eight-year-old man, who never had sexual intercourse. In his treatment, repressed love for the mother became apparent.

Sometimes, impotence is only relative; for instance, a man who is impotent with his young wife, whereas he is quite potent with his cook (who is a very energetic woman).

Lastly, local treatment should be mentioned.

DISCUSSION

SADGER: *ad* 1. This is perhaps the case of the true homosexuals. *ad* 2. In this group one is dealing mostly with compulsion neurosis (as in the case of the man with the cook). From his own experience, he can assert that all of the Polish Jews whom he had occasion to see in Gräfenberg[2] were onanists and compulsive neurotics and three quarters of them were impotent. Psychic impotence is a symptom of compulsion neurosis.

SCHWERDTNER mentions a case which, he thinks, is typical: the excitation was too strong for this man and therefore he had no erection. Perhaps the cerebrum exerts an inhibitory influence on the center for erection.

[A.] DEUTSCH mentions a case of impotence caused by the fear of impregnation.

WITTELS asserts that group 1 cannot be completely impotent on a functional basis, since inferiority of the total personality would of necessity include inferiority of the sexual organs.

Relative impotence (not satisfying the woman) can be overcome through practice or through protracted intercourse. Satisfying the woman is a psychic comfort.

He mentions a remark made by Reimann:[3] that man is pathological who claims to be incapable of having intercourse without psychic involvement (for example, with a prostitute).

Man must be in love, else he cannot perform intercourse.

Sisters do not help when there is a neurotic disposition: the individual in question becomes as a result of his incestuous feelings either neurotic or impotent. Alcohol is a good remedy for psychic impotence.

RANK misses an elucidation of the cases in which impotence occurs only in relation to certain sex objects. Being in love is not a sufficient explanation; for the roots of being in love itself lie much deeper: namely, in the rejection of sexuality [*sic*]. The latter is frequently a cause of impotence, as is disgust of prostitution.

2 A spa in Austrian Silesia where Sadger practiced.
3 Emil Reimann, professor of forensic psychiatry at the University of Vienna.

FEDERN reproaches the speaker for unjustifiably having confused functional with psychic impotence. Those cases in which there are local causes must be excluded since they are not of psychological origin. Frequently, their cause lies merely in muscular deficiencies.

Federn doubts that the absence of a sister is a sufficient cause of impotence and mentions cases which are meant to refute Steiner's statement.

He would be inclined to call the third type "presenile impotence."

HITSCHMANN relates the case of a physician who was so disgusted by his first visit to a prostitute that this recollection hampered him during later intercourse. His impotence set in at a time when he could have had relationships with a number of women. He was in love with his mother's housekeeper, and later had a successful relationship with her.

It is well known that one can become impotent when one approaches a woman in too great excitement or with too deep respect (Schnitzler's *Reigen*[4] and a poem by Goethe).

He misses any mention of the psychic impotence of women. It is easy to understand that, in many cases, absence of the psychic prelude (waiting until the need demands fulfillment) causes psychic impotence.

In the case of the homosexual, one cannot speak of psychic impotence because he is potent with boys.

Not having a sister must certainly exert a powerful influence on the entire development of a man.

FREUD, replying to some of the objections, first emphasizes that the speaker intended only to give a first orientation for the general practitioner.

Hitschmann's objection concerning homosexuals, for instance, is not valid since this disposition becomes apparent only later in life.

There must always be a whole series of causes, and several preconditions must always coincide. The factor of not having a sister actually does seem to be influential. We find an analogy in those persons with homosexual tendencies whose inclinations are reinforced when the balance in their object choice is upset by the loss of one parent. (This is true of men as well as of women.)

[4] Arthur Schnitzler (1862-1931), a great Austrian playwright and poet had deep psychological insight.

From the psychological point of view, we must of course set up a classification which differs from Steiner's. The chief factor [in psychic impotence] is that we are dealing with individuals whose sexual activity cannot dispense with the psychic component; whose fantasy life [*Vorstellungsleben*] predominates; or, more generally, individuals whose sexual activity is of the feminine type. All of us civilized people have some tendencies to psychic impotence.[5]

As far as the *mechanism* is concerned, one can postulate three possibilities:

1. When there are strong (unconscious) inhibitory (counter) ideas opposing sexual activity.

Foremost: homosexuality, being in love, and the like.[6]

2. When the libido is not available because it is bound to unconscious (repressed) ideas. This is the mechanism typical of all psychic paralyses. A hysterical woman, for example, cannot speak when unconsciously the idea arises in her that she would like to be kissed.

3. When there is excessive excitement; behind this lies the contrast between imagination and perception. When one has anticipated something with great joy, it is very difficult to divert interest from imagination to reality.[7]

The frequently great disappointments in the wedding night are a case in point.

In groups 2 and 3 there is actually a single mechanism which is based on fixation and on the hampered mobility of the libido.

Goethe's poem: fixation to the absent beloved one.

To Sadger: compulsive neurotics are as a rule not impotent, but usually have a "normal" sex life. However, for them, this sex life is not normal because suppressed sadism is the most frequent cause of obsessional ideas.

All neurotic symptoms in women are basically impairments of their capacity to love. Hence they really should have all their symptoms in

[5] See Freud: "Civilized Sexual Morality and Modern Nervous Illness" (1908). *S.E.*, 9:177-204.

[6] Freud seems to refer to those cases in which sensuous love and tender love are split.

[7] ". . . *das Interesse auf den anderen Weg zu ziehen, das von der Wirklichkeit abgelenkt wurde.*" Literally: ". . . to divert interest, which has been distracted from reality, to another path."

the genitals. However, the erotogenic zones are responsible for the great variety of symptoms which are essentially nothing but sexual impotencies displaced onto another sphere. Psychic impotence is, therefore, the basic symptom of all neurotics.[8]

ADLER points out that organic conditions have their share in *all* cases, including those of psychic impotence; in all such cases they can be demonstrated either in pure form or by a detour via psychic life. In many cases it is the organ which creates or selects the psychic [experience].

He has not encountered the sister motive in his material. Nevertheless, it probably plays a role.

Psychic impotence frequently results from intercourse with women one does not really love.

STEINER, referring to Freud, concludes that civilized man is always to some extent impotent. At the bottom of many an impotence there is an excess of libido: the potency is normal, but the libido is too great.

[8] See Freud: "Contributions to the Psychology of Love" (1910, 1912, 1918). *S.E.*, 11:163-208.

27

SCIENTIFIC MEETING *on October 23, 1907*

Present: Freud, Abel, Adler, Federn, Hitschmann, Rank, Reitler, Sadger, Schwerdtner, Steiner, Stekel.

Adler, Federn, Hitschmann, Reitler, and Sadger pay their membership dues.

Stekel borrows *Archiv* No. 24 (Friedmann, *Münchner Allgemeine*).[1]

Reitler borrows Minutes 2 (returned, October 30).

PRESENTATION

Sleep

SPEAKER: DR. SCHWERDTNER

In all the literature there is no satisfactory definition of sleep. Opinions on this subject still differ widely. The speaker discusses briefly several (physiological) theories concerning sleep, of which the most commonly recognized one maintains that sleep sets in as a result of the accumulation of fatigue-producing matter. According to this theory, sleep is the result of the exhaustion of nervous energy, etc.

---

[1] The meaning of this could not be established.

The speaker then briefly summarizes his criticism of all these theories, showing the weakness of the thesis quoted above and demonstrating this with examples from everyday life.

Unbiased observation shows that sleep serves the purpose of integrating[2] new impressions and ideas received during the day. Sleeping means: to perform supplementary work of apperception. The brain desires to be alone; therefore, any disturbance deprives sleep of its refreshing quality. Through its capacity to put things in order, sleep purifies memory ("to sleep on a matter" in popular language). [In sleep] the average man becomes an ingenious artist.

During sleep, ideas and images behave without restraint [ungeniert]; this is the state which has been symbolized as the Witch's Sabbath. Sleep is one of the most important means of individual psychotherapy; art is the second one (Rank). All in all, artistic creation is analogous to the state of sleep, particularly in so far as consciousness is almost completely obscured. The difference is that the artist has a guiding idea which dominates his consciousness with great energy. The "artist's trance," therefore, is only a more mature, clearer, but basically identical state. Hence, in sleeping one does much the same thing as, for example, in creating a poem.

The speaker himself has always slept without dreaming, but during the day he has felt the urge to compose poems. If he did not yield to this drive, he would be unable to sleep.

The speaker compares the two states at length and cites numerous analogies between them (which are also confirmed in Soren Kierkegaard[3]). Actually, the artist should have no need to sleep. Purely intuitive, creative work not only does not fatigue, it refreshes. Thus, sleep is not a pause for the restoration of spent nervous energy, but rather a shutting off of the senses so that repressed material can be worked up [aufarbeiten].

Finally, the speaker discusses the *effect of soporific drugs* from the standpoint of his theory.

Only that person becomes a morphine addict who requires the morphine psychologically. Morphine acts as a soporific drug simply

---

[2] The original has *"Einordnung,"* which, literally, means "classifying," ordering.
[3] Danish philosopher (1813-1855).

because, by paralyzing perception, it enables one to ward off sensory stimuli even though there may actually be light, noise, etc.

In conclusion, the speaker sets forth the following principles:

Sleep is that state in which the brain receives no stimuli from the external world and in which therefore psychic crystallization can proceed without interruption.

Sleep is absolutely necessary for the preservation of optimum psychic functioning (this is why only animals of a higher order sleep: hounds and zoo animals dream).

The duration of sleep is unlimited. The more time is allotted to normal sleep, the better is the function of memory.

Sleep and hypnosis are identical.

DISCUSSION

ABELS feels he does not criticize the speaker's psychological views merely by supporting the physiological principle that the purpose of sleep is the restitution of spent energies. He then tries to refute some of the speaker's objections to the physiological theories.

Dreamless sleep, he says, can also be brought about by great physical exhaustion.

SADGER cannot express a conclusive opinion but only contribute some thoughts and ideas. A reconciliation of the two theories is not quite so impossible as it might appear. There is only one restitution for psychic functioning and that is sleep, which is then an eminently psychic process.

Last summer, there was an article by Lindau[4] in the *Neue Freie Presse*[5] in which he describes the composition of his first drama: he worked without interruption for thirty-six hours and did not feel tired, hungry, or thirsty. Then he slept for eight hours.

It is known that the mentally ill do not require sleep. Poets (Goethe, for instance) have a great need for sleep during the period of their best production.

The speaker failed to mention the effect which the satisfaction or nonsatisfaction of the sexual instinct has on sleep.

[4] Paul Lindau (1839-1919), German writer.
[5] *Neue Freie Presse*, Vienna daily newspaper, comparable to the New York *Times*.

Concerning the problem of dreamless sleep, one has to take into account that we may, perhaps, dream without becoming conscious of it.

STEINER considers restoration of body heat used up during the day to be the purpose of sleep and adduces several examples in support of his assertion.

REITLER could not gather anything new from the paper, because the connections between sleep and the unconscious are after all the content of the *Interpretation of Dreams*.

He concurs in the explanation of morphine addiction.

In HITSCHMANN's opinion, this discussion of sleep is too personal. The sleep of children and of animals and of quietly living (healthy) human beings must also be taken into consideration, and so must racial differences and other factors. It is not admissible to explain sleep only in terms of the repressed and neurotic (and in the process, more-over, omitting the sexual element) and to assume that one would become hysterical if one did not sleep. The "sleeping on a thing" in popular language is, after all, not something real on which one can base one's theories, but merely a superstition.

RANK suspects that sleep may fulfill all of the individual and main purposes that have been mentioned plus some others of which we still have no knowledge. With this assumption, the comparison with art is also modified in the sense that art too serves not only the one purpose mentioned, although this may be its most important one, but also other purposes which are of lesser interest to us at the moment.

In any case, it is of great psychological interest that the speaker, who suffers from abnormal states of sleep (in the broadest sense: he said that perhaps no one has slept as much as he has) has advanced a theory of sleep.

ADLER stresses that Schwerdtner is attempting to show what goes on in us during sleep. It is a different problem to ask: What is sleep? The speaker has mistakenly identified the nature of sleep with sleep itself.

His work should nevertheless be appreciated as an advance over what has been reported heretofore. His views concerning assimilation of ideas (during sleep) cannot be refuted. The teleological theories, however, are least important.

221

He suggests that each one communicate his personal experiences relating to his own sleep.

Many people fall asleep immediately (seems to be hereditary); others require much time, etc. This may well be connected with the nature of sleep.

It is not true that only the more highly developed creatures sleep; sleep is a phenomenon appearing already in the cell.

FREUD emphasizes that the speaker has provided much stimulation. However, one should refrain from definitions when psychic phenomena are concerned.

One should start with the biological genesis of sleep. First of all, sleep is connected with the alternation of light and darkness (celestial bodies, etc.). Then, individually, the infant's sleep should be considered: sleep is his natural condition, from which he is roused only by his bodily needs. As soon as these are satisfied he falls alseep again. In this way the infant continues his fetal state.[6]

Gradually, when the child learns to use darkness for sleeping, these two conditions are fused. Fatigue apparently plays no part in the infant's sleep. Later there appear certain secondary factors, in view of which the teleological standpoint cannot be rejected so categorically. At a later point in this sequence, there appear those functions which the speaker considers to be the purpose of sleep: the protection from the outside world. This point of view has considerable value and should be supported.

Flournoy,[7] in a short essay, classified sleep among the defense

[6] These are thoughts which Freud developed further. They finally led to the statement that at birth an instinct to sleep is "born"—a drive to return to the womb. See Freud: *An Outline of Psychoanalysis* (1938). New York: Norton, 1949, p. 48.

[7] Theodore Flournoy (1854-1920), Swiss psychologist, professor of psychology at the University of Geneva, famous as the author of books on mysticism and religion. Freud confuses here, however, Flournoy with the Swiss psychologist Édouard Claparède (1873-1940). Both edited together the *Archives de Psychologie*. The quotation to which Freud refers appeared in Claparède's paper: "Esquisse d'une théorie biologique du sommeil" ["Outline of a Biological Theory of Sleep"] published in the fourth volume of the *Archives,* 1905: "Le sommeil est une fonction de défense, un instinct qui a pour but, en frappant l'animal d'inertie, de l'empêcher de parvenir au stade d'épuisement: ce n'est pas parce que nous sommes intoxiqués, ou épuisés, que nous dormons, mais nous dormons pour ne pas l'être." ["Sleep is a defensive function, whose purpose is, by striking the animal with inertia, to prevent it from reaching a stage of complete exhaustion: we sleep, not because we are intoxicated or exhausted, but in order not to become so."]

mechanisms, which would fully correspond with the speaker's point of view. Thus a reversal takes place: whereas initially the infant is roused from his sleep by the world, later, he is made sleepy by the world.

In the dream theory, too, one can find a bridge to the speaker's viewpoint. We are familiar with the important part played by recent material and with the fact that behind this recent material the past is hidden. This recent material is exactly what is worked over during sleep,[8] a process which Schwerdtner incorrectly ascribes to the unconscious (it occurs simply in the psychic sphere). In this way, sleep is used for the protection of the psyche, so that it can perform [*erledigen*] its tasks.

Two points regarding the problem of sleep have so far become accessible to us:

We have gained some knowledge of the psychic conditions during the state of sleep from the interpretation of dreams: the state of sleep is characterized by a weakening of the cathexes (of the psychic censorship).[9]

Falling asleep, however, is an entirely separate problem. Flournoy[10] describes it as a voluntary act, as an autosuggestion, which is in accord with the theory of [sleep as] a defense against the external world.

Freud would not advocate the current physiological theories because they are limited and vague. The influence of fatigue products though cannot be altogether rejected; but this is the theory of drowsiness, not of sleep. The possibility also exists that the body utilizes sleep[11] products as a signal for falling asleep.

It is quite correct that only that person becomes a morphine addict who has to balance a psychic defect with morphine.

One mechanism which might explain the state of sleep is the circumstance that the later cathexes in psychic life are more labile. This circumstance is perhaps utilized in such a way that only the secondary

[8] In other words, during sleep, the recent material, having been connected with the unconscious, is worked over in the preconscious.
[9] I.e., the resistances of the ego are reduced.
[10] This should also read: Claparède.
[11] Freud probably meant fatigue products.

ego (in Meynert's sense[12]) sleeps. In fact, many pathological states (in addition to the senium) bring about the disappearance of numerous later cathexes and thus disclose, as it were, the primary ego.

The question of whether there is dreamless sleep is irrelevant. To dream means to become conscious of a dream content. If, however, one understands by dreaming the unconscious work, from which a dream need not result, then the question of whether we dream every night must be answered in the affirmative. We have dream thoughts every night, but not dream content.[13]

FEDERN would like to divide the paper into that which the speaker wrote in the intoxication of a "sleep-gourmand" and that which he wrote as a soberly thinking medical man. Schwerdtner deserves credit for having emphasized that the true purpose of sleep is achieved only in dreamless sleep. (Heiterethey,[14] this healthy child of nature, does not dream.) Schwerdtner's theory that ideas are assimilated during sleep is only a hypothesis; we also organize ideas during the waking state. Ideas are not worked up and combined with each other during sleep; but they rather fall apart. (That is to say, no work is performed.)

To sleep means many things: certainly it involves also physiological processes, although he does not wish to defend the physiological theories.

Dreamless sleep does exist; this can be deduced from the lack of a sense of time in dreams.

A patient, after the withdrawal of morphine, suffered from insomnia for twenty-nine days (the insomnia was finally cured by coercive suggestion). Consequently, there must also be some compensation [Ausgleich] of excitations in the waking state.

In conclusion, SCHWERDTNER responds to the individual objections: physical fatigue cannot play such an important part, because, if it did, it would always produce sleep and this is not the case. Excessive fatigue often prevents one from falling asleep (Abels). In the case of Lindau, toxic effects were also operative. The sexual instinct belongs

---

[12] Theodor Meynert (1833-1892), professor of psychiatry at the University of Vienna; a teacher of Freud's.

[13] This statement would seem to refute the present-day theories of the invisible "blank" dreams.

[14] Main character of Otto Ludwig's novel of the same name.

to those stimuli which have to be avoided and for this reason was not mentioned separately (Sadger). Assimilation of ideas in a state of rest proceeds in a way totally different from that of the waking state. In the process of assimilation ideas must "fall apart" (Federn).

In conclusion, he mentions that he has endeavored to shed a little light on what the physiologists have overlooked.

28

SCIENTIFIC MEETING on October 30, 1907

Present: All members except Häutler.
Hollerung pays the membership dues.
[A.] Deutsch borrows Minutes 3 (returned December 11, 1907).

PRESENTATION

Beginning of a Case History

SPEAKER: PROF. FREUD

SCIENTIFIC MEETING on November 6, 1907

Present: Freud, Abels, Adler, Federn, Graf, Häutler, Hitschmann, Hollerung, Rank, Reitler, Sadger, Schwerdtner, Stekel, Steiner, Wittels.
Häutler announces a paper on Hellpach's[1] pamphlet *Geistige Epidemien* [*Mental Epidemics*].
Federn returns last year's Minutes 1-5 and borrows 6, 7, 9, 10, 11.

[1] Wilhelm Hellpach (1877-1955), German psychologist and politician.

PRESENTATION

Beginning of a Case History[2]

SPEAKER: PROF. FREUD

This is a very instructive case of an obsessional neurosis (obsessional thinking), the case of a young man of twenty-nine years (a lawyer). He dates his illness from 1903, but it actually began in his childhood.

He is beset by fears that something may happen to two persons whom he loves very much. (This vagueness of expression, this concealment of the content, is characteristic of obsessional neurosis.)

These two persons are the patient's father and a lady whom he admires very much.

He has abstained from sexual intercourse for years; masturbation played a very minor role; first intercourse at twenty-six years of age.

A detailed presentation of the first few sessions of the analysis is given next.

The technique of analysis has changed to the extent that the psychoanalyst no longer seeks to elicit material in which he is interested, but permits the patient to follow his natural and spontaneous trains of thought.[3]

---

[2] The two evenings of October 30, and November 6, on which Freud gave his paper, are recorded together. Paul Federn published this protocol (in a somewhat modified form) together with his annotations in the *Samiksa, Indian Journal for Psychoanalysis*, 1:305-311, 1947 [also in *Yb.*, 4:14-20, 1948]. We have included Paul Federn's annotations, which appear here as footnotes in brackets with the initials *P.F.*

Freud presented this case history at the first Psychoanalytic Congress in Salzburg in 1908. It then appeared in 1909 in the *Jahrbuch für psychoanalytische und psychopathologische Forschungen*, 1:357-421, as "Bemerkungen über einen Fall von Zwangsneurose" ["Notes upon a Case of Obsessional Neurosis." *S.E.*, 10:153-320]. This case became famous as "The Rat Man." Since the publication of the paper was imminent when these minutes were taken, it was not reported in detail. Obviously, Rank decided to summarize Freud's paper very briefly and to combine both evenings into one protocol.

[3] [This remark is of historical interest as it was made in 1907.—*P.F.*].

Here, for the first time, we have a report of an analysis which was carried out with the help of *free associations*. Freud writes about this change in psychoanalytic technique in his *Autobiographical Study* (1925): "I am obliged now to turn to the alterations which gradually took place in the technique of the analytic method. . . . It [the overcoming of resistances] . . . gave place to another method which was in one sense its opposite. Instead of urging the patient to say something upon some particular subject, I now asked him to abandon himself to a process of *free association* . . ." (*S.E.*, 10:40).

In "A Short Account of Psychoanalysis" (1924) [*S.E.*, 19:195], Freud reports that he hit upon the idea of replacing hypnosis by the method of free association.

-44-

IVter Vortragabend
am 30. Oktober 1907.
Anwesend: alle bis auf Häutler. —

Hollerung erlegt den Mitgliedsbeitrag.
Deutsch entlehnt Prot. VI. (§ 15ᵗ 11. XII. 07)

Vortrag: Prof. Freud: Beginn einer Krankengeschichte.

Vierter und fünfter Vortragabend

am 30. Okt. u. 6. November 1907.

Prof. Freud:

Beginn einer Krankengeschichte.

1

Es handle sich um einen sehr lehrreichen Fall von Zwangsneurose (Zwangshandlungen), der einen 23jährigen jungen Mann
(Dr. jur.) betrifft. Sein Leiden datiert seit 1903, eigentlich aber
schon seit seiner Kindheit.

Er hat Befürchtungen, daß zwei Personen, die er sehr liebe, etwas
geschehe (diese Unbestimmtheit des Ausdrucks, das Verlangen des Inhalts,
charakterisiere die Zwangsneurose).

Diese zwei Personen seien der Vater und eine Dame, die er sehr
verehrt.

Er habe Jahre hindurch abstinent gelebt, die Onanie habe eine
sehr geringe Rolle gespielt. Erster Koitus mit 26 Jahren. —

Er faßt nun die ausführliche Mitteilung der Analyse an den
ersten paar Sitzungen. —

Die Technik der Analyse habe sich insofern verändert
als der Psychoanalytiker jetzt nicht mehr das macht, was ihn
interessiert, sondern dem Pat. die natürliche Abwicklung
seiner Gedanken gestattet.

Es handelt sich in diesem Falle, in groben Zügen dargestellt,
um den Kampf des Pat. zwischen seinem Zug zum Manne hin und
dem zum Weibe (der Zug zum Mann ist stärker).

Er hat verdrängte Todeswünsche gegen seinen Vater (Zwangsvorstellungen sind eigentlich Zwangswünsche).

Besonders deutlich tritt in diesem Fall hervor, was man in keinem Fall von Zwangsneurose vermisst:

dass es sich um unterdrückte böse, aggressive, feindselige grausame Gefühle (um sadistische und Mordgelüste) handelt. Diese grausame Komponente könne man mit Recht als männlich bezeichnen — Sie sei aber auch bei Frauen dieselbe. Es ergäbe sich also aus dem Verhältnis der Sexualität zu den Neurosen eine theoret. Folgerung: So sei unmöglich, dass das Maskierte beim Mann einen anderen Grundcharakter habe als beim Weib. Die Neurose entstehe immer auf Kosten verdrängter aktiver Triebe. —

The basic conflict in this case lies, roughly speaking, in the patient's struggle between his drive toward man and that toward woman (his drive toward man is stronger).

He has repressed death wishes against his father (obsessional ideas actually are obsessional wishes).

This case shows with special clarity something that is never lacking in a case of obsessional neurosis:

that it concerns repressed, bad, aggressive, hostile, and cruel feelings (sadistic and murderous wishes).[4] This cruel component can justifiably be called "masculine"; yet it is equally present in women. Hence, the relationship of sexuality to neurosis yields a theoretical conclusion: the unconscious in man cannot possibly be basically different from that in woman.[5] Neurosis always develops at the expense of active drives which are repressed.[6]

DISCUSSION

STEKEL emphasizes that the patient's trust is the most essential factor in treatment. The analyst must guard against routinizing his technique; not all cases follow the pattern of the case presented. The individual features must be taken into consideration. Stekel, in his analyses, waits with [the process of] uncovering the deepest connections until he has full power over the patient.

In the case presented he believes that the patient as a child probably saw his father as a rival in relation to the governess (and not, as Rank said,[7] in relation to the mother).

[4] We find here the first indication of Freud's later formulation that, as far as the participation of the instincts is concerned, anality and sadism are the basis of the obsessional neurosis. This thought was not yet expressed in "Obsessions and Phobias; Their Psychical Mechanisms and Their Aetiology" (1895). C.P., 1:128-137.

[5] [This remark was directed against a general concept of Rank's, namely that the unconscious in man is his femininity and the unconscious in woman is her masculinity. —P.F.]

[6] [In later years Freud changed this point of view, recognizing that repressed masochistic tendencies also play an important part in neurosis. Yet, since one source of masochism is always sadism turned into its opposite, another femininity, and a third one a biological connection between pain and sexuality, the change of opinion is only a partial one.—P.F.]

[7] Apparently Rank had spoken first, without recording his remarks separately. See below.

SADGER raises the question whether homosexual reasons were not mainly responsible for the patient's compulsion to mail his small debt.

Replying to Stekel's remark that some patients insist on being hypnotized, Sadger states that this wish is intimately connected with their homosexual and masochistic character.[8]

HITSCHMANN points out that miserliness plays a prominent role in the patient's compulsion to mail his small debts. It has not been demonstrated that the patient is a homosexual. His obsessional neurosis might also have developed in the following way: apart from the experiences which all children have, he may have developed a mechanism of obsessional thinking already in his early years; these two factors operating in conjunction have produced the neurosis.

SCHWERDTNER raises two questions:

1. Why is it that in some cases sadistic drives are unsuccessfully repressed, while in others they are sublimated?

2. Why do we desire to have only unified feelings (not, for instance, affection and aversion side by side) toward very near and dear persons?[9]

RANK (contradicting Stekel) reiterates his opinion that all factors clearly point to the patient's love for his mother, even though there has not yet been any direct reference to this in the analytic material. In this case, the struggle between [the drive toward] man and [that toward] woman is condensed into a struggle between love for the father and love for the mother. The complication by the homosexual factor is found in all such cases of "incest." The homosexual inclinations (and only these are involved) are proven not only by the unequivocal indications in the analytic material but also by the way in which the patient, in his fantasies, identifies his father with the beloved lady. He has them both tortured at the anus. He uses the woman as he would use a man.

---

[8] Nearly all patients want to be hypnotized. Sadger seems to have sensed intuitively that the desire for a hypnotic cure is based on a passive and masochistic attitude.

[9] Important questions which to this day have not been answered satisfactorily.

FEDERN asks whether we have the right to call cruelty a specifically male quality.[10]

One should not give weight to the *single* trauma, but rather say that every sexual trauma implies a chronic trauma.[11]

GRAF also wishes to know why repression is successful in one person and unsuccessful in another.

ADLER doubts that psychoanalysis can be taught or learned.

In many cases quite a few things must be left unexplained; it is important to take only some of the enemy's positions because their surrender guarantees victory; the enemy need not be slain to the last man.[12]

On the other hand, we must not withhold important connections once the patient has found them. The rules Stekel is laying down are "psycho-diplomacy."

As for the present case, Adler is sure that organic conditions will be found. He thinks it is a case of very strong autoerotism which has not yet been replaced by heterosexuality. Miserliness is also derived from autoerotic drives (anal zone). There is more than one way in psychoanalysis.[13]

[10] Federn here raises a question which also has remained unanswered to this day: namely, what is to be considered a male and what a female trait. See Paul Federn: "Beiträge zur Analyse des Sadismus und Masochismus. I. Die Quellen des männlichen Sadismus" ["Contributions to the Analysis of Sadism and Masochism. I. The Sources of Male Sadism"]. *Z.*, 1:29-49, 1913. "II. Die libidinösen Quellen des Masochismus" ["The Libidinous Sources of Masochism"]. *Z.*, 2:105-130, 1914.

See also Freud: *Three Essays on the Theory of Sexuality* (1905). *S.E.*, 7:125-245; "Some Psychological Consequences of the Anatomical Distinction between the Sexes" (1925). *C.P.*, 5:186-197; "'A Child Is Being Beaten': Contribution to the Study of the Origin of Sexual Perversions" (1919). *S.E.*, 17:175-204; "Female Sexuality" (1931). *C.P.*, 5:252-272; *An Outline of Psychoanalysis* (1938). New York: Norton, 1949; Herman Nunberg: *Problems of Bisexuality As Reflected in Circumcision* (1947). New York: International Universities Press, 1961.

[11] Federn, in the transcript published by him, reworded this sentence in the following way: "He thinks, furthermore, that the single event is not traumatic because of its immediate importance but because every single event creates a chronic impairment and that these impairments accumulate to create a lasting trauma."

[12] [At the time this was said, in 1907, the terminology of war and fight did not present itself as readily to the mind as nowadays. These remarks therefore bear special individual-psychological earmarks.—*P.F.*]

[13] It is not only in the perpetual emphasis on the organic basis of each and every symptom that Adler's future deviation announces itself but also, as in the last remark, in the tendency to find his own way as far as technique is concerned, a tendency which at that time was probably still unknown to him.

STEINER states that other children too have similar experiences. Hatred for the parents originates in punishments (for wetting and soiling). We must assume a certain disposition, an inferiority (but not in Adler's sense).

The woman, too, is cruel, therefore this drive cannot be considered a specifically male quality.[14]

The neurotic man has feminine characteristics.

PROF. FREUD answers the speakers in the order in which they have spoken:

He agrees with Adler's criticism of Stekel. In Stekel's case, the patient's story that the father had beaten the children and then had them urinate in front of him has the mark of a fantasy.[15] We have to ask ourselves—in the case of a neurosis—where is the unconscious, the repressed, if the patient remembers this alleged experience so clearly.

Supplement to the analysis: Since the patient had death wishes against his father already before his eighth year, it was natural to inquire whether at that time or earlier someone in the family had died. And, indeed, when the patient was three and a half or four years old, his sister had died.

His earliest childhood memories are:

1. That his sick sister was put to bed.
2. That he went to his father to find out what was happening.
3. That his mother cried and his father leaned over her.

This sister was three or four years older than he. It was through her that he had noticed the sex difference for the first time when he was about three years old.

Hitschmann's explanation of the obsessional neurosis represents a

---

[14] [This remark is a forerunner of the opinion that cruelty as well as destruction belong to a separate drive, which is not different in men and women. Later on Freud developed this theory into a duality of drives: Eros and Thanatos.—*P.F.*]

[15] [At that time Freud knew already that mere fantasies also act in a pathogenic way, although not to the same extent as actual traumata. For this reason Freud sometimes used witnesses and diaries in order to ascertain whether the analytical material he found consisted in fantasies of the patient or in actual experiences. When he finally found that fantasies which could not possibly have been experienced determined the neurosis of the patient, in general as well as in single symptoms, he concluded that there must be some typical inherited fantasies present in everybody, which are later transformed into memories of assumed actual experiences.—*P.F.*]

purely personal standpoint; the actual conditions are far more complicated. It is true that miserliness plays an important role in the patient's life, but it is not a primary characteristic; formerly the patient was very generous and extravagant.

The question raised by Schwerdtner and Graf is to some extent due to their unjustified disappointment in the achievements of psychoanalysis. For we have no right to assume that we will discover the difference between the sick and the normal, because there is no such difference, at least not in quality.[16]

In the neurotic, precocious activity is followed by periods of the opposite, of repression.

In general, the human being cannot tolerate contrasting ideas and feelings in juxtaposition; it is this striving for unification that we call character.[17] But the affects involved are so intense only in relation to persons close to us (Schwerdtner).

Hatred for the father as strong as in this case can arise only if the father has disturbed the child in his sexuality.

Rank will probably prove to be right in his assumption that incestuous wishes for the mother play a role, though the relationship is complicated by the presence of four sisters (two older and two younger than the patient).

Federn's remark was just to the point, namely, that the patient already at such an early age clearly showed heterosexual inclinations and that his later homosexuality is in sharp contrast with these. The analyses of three overt homosexual men who would have been liable to legal prosecution regularly revealed a very early relationship to a woman which was later suppressed.[18] Conversely, all ladies' men and lady-killers were, in early childhood, more inclined toward homosexuality.

Which drives are to be classified as male and which as female is a

[16] Freud always maintained that there is no qualitative difference between the healthy and the sick. There are, however, quantitative differences in the distribution of energy which we cannot yet measure.

[17] Today we would express this thought by saying, "Contrasting ideas and feelings in juxtaposition cannot be tolerated by the ego." Nunberg has pursued this idea in his "The Synthetic Function of the Ego" (1930). *Practice and Theory of Psychoanalysis.* New York: International Universities Press, 1961.

[18] The same conditions come to light in almost all analyses of homosexuals.

matter of agreement. In no case is it permissible to classify someone as homosexual or heterosexual according to his object.[19]

In reply to Adler, Freud says that there should not be any doubt that the psychoanalytic method can be learned. It will be possible to learn it once the arbitrariness of individual psychoanalysts is curbed by tested rules.[20]

For therapeutic purposes a partial solution is sufficient in some cases, but this by no means delimits the theoretical possibilities. In other cases, however, it is necessary for therapeutic reasons to carry the analysis through to the end.[21]

To Steiner: The experiences must not be underestimated as compared with constitutional factors.

Neurotics turn activity into passivity, so that a neurotic man could in fact be called feminine.[22]

[19] [With this remark Freud stresses the importance of subject homosexuality and rejects object homosexuality. Later on he adopted, as far as I know, Ferenczi's opinion, namely, that both kinds of homosexuality exist. Even so, however, Freud stuck to the opinion that the quality of the drive is the important factor, while the choice of object is dependent on childhood experiences, resistances, and shiftings. —P.F.].

[20] This opinion led to the later foundation of psychoanalytic institutes.

[21] [On various occasions Freud rebuked the idea of the short analysis. He once said that analysis has renounced to cure, "cito, tuto et jucunde." Yet, for practical reasons, he accepted it, especially when there was one main symptom of which the patient needed to be cured, as for instance in many cases of psychic impotence.—P.F.]

[22] Each of Freud's answers to the discussants was taken up in his later work, elaborated, and reformulated.

29

SCIENTIFIC MEETING on *November 13, 1907*

Present: Freud, [A.] Deutsch, Federn, Hitschmann, Rank, Sadger, Schwerdtner, Stekel, Wittels.

COMMUNICATIONS

Prof. Freud informs the members of Dr. Abels's resignation.

PRESENTATION

Venereal Disease[1]

SPEAKER: DR. WITTELS

DISCUSSION

HITSCHMANN first wants to uncover the personal roots [of the paper]. Three factors thwart Wittles's sexuality: impregnation; the chastity of female medical students; and syphilis. That is why he fights these things.

Syphilis presents the greatest dangers.

[1] Wittels's paper is not recorded in the protocol and does not seem to have been published anywhere.

Men of genius (Nietzsche and others) become syphilitic because of their "sexual imprudence." If there has been a case of syphilis in a family, its members tend to adopt an abnormally chaste attitude which has a stunting effect on the psychic development of the progeny.

Ultimately, hysteria and neurasthenia should be called venereal diseases.[2]

Hitschmann advocates the establishment of public agencies for the distribution of contraceptives to lessen the danger of impregnation.

STEKEL suggests that in the phrase, "fear that a neurasthenic generation is growing up," the word "neurasthenic" should be replaced by the word "hysterical," because neurasthenia is very rare in comparison to hysteria. In addition, he advises Wittels to tone down his initial, terrifying description of syphilis out of consideration for impressionable readers.

Stekel thinks that excessive parental affection and tenderness are mainly responsible for the connection between syphilis and neurosis.

FREUD: Concerning the connection between syphilis and the Reformation, Freud remarks that the Catholic Church was at the brink of dissolution at the time of the Renaissance; it was saved by two factors: syphilis and Luther. Panizza,[3] in his drama *The Council of Love*, clearly expresses the thought that the appearance of syphilis strengthened the Catholic Church. In correction of Wittels's statement, he maintains that it was not immediately but *only some time after its appearance* that syphilis was treated as something despicable that should be hidden from others.

From a psychological point of view it is very doubtful that pleasure is not a positive feeling in itself but only a release from unpleasure. Pleasure is a very specific psychological process. It is true, however, that the greater the tension has been, the greater the pleasure; but tension is not always unpleasant.

The damaging effect of masturbation is due mainly to a short circuit: the shortcut between desire and fulfillment. As a consequence, the individual stops exerting himself and the external world loses its im-

[2] Hitschmann apparently refers to a remark of Freud's that syphilis is frequently found in the ancestors of hysterical patients.
[3] Oskar Panizza (1853-1921), German writer and dramatist.

portance for him. Another damaging result of masturbation lies in the consumption of energy used up in the internal struggle.[4]

Gonorrhea may also be considered to have a positive aspect: through the sterilization of women, it makes normal sex life possible for a number of men.

SADGER stresses that fear of infection is not the main reason for masturbating. What about the masturbation of the small child? He raises the question whether bashfulness may not be a kind of fore-pleasure; it increases the man's pleasure and thereby one's [the woman's?] own. Unmarried mothers are held in contempt because of men's craving for a virgin.

FEDERN remarks that comparing Wittels's first essay with today's paper one can clearly recognize Freud's pedagogical influence. The beginning of the paper should be toned down. He cannot share Wittels's pessimistic view in regard to pleasure. The fighting of animals does not serve to arouse displeasure. Robust people are very well capable of abstaining from sexual activity without suffering damaging consequences. He does not think that *children* should be given the enlightenment Wittels proposes, but teenage boys should.

RANK thinks that the masochistic character of the whole Christian movement, particularly in its beginning, should have been stressed. The relationship between artistic productivity and sexual intercourse is not as simple and banal as Wittels described it (if he does not have intercourse, he composes poems). Schwerdtner also envisaged this relationship as far too simple when he some time ago asserted that the man (artist) who dreams (creates) in the course of the day has a dreamless sleep. This notion is far too rationalistic and mathematical. Also in discussing the causes of masturbation, Wittels overrates the external factors (timidity, inaccessibility of the object) at the expense of the more significant, internal ones. He would not recommend the enlightenment of children since sexual ignorance or half-knowledge is one of the most important motives for a child to learn.

(FEDERN considers this opinion to be an erroneous interpretation of Freud's views.)

---

[4] See the discussion of masturbation in Volume II of these Minutes.

SCHWERDTNER first praises Wittels's enchanting, brilliant style, which makes one forget the cause itself Wittels is advocating.

Enlightenment is most certainly to be recommended, but in a way entirely different from that for which, or against which, Rank and Federn argue. The type of enlightenment they imagine, i.e., a tearing down of a barrier, as it were, should not be needed at all; rather enlightenment should come about gradually.[5]

Artistic creation is directly dependent upon sexual life. The pleasure of asceticism has been described by Kierkegaard.

WITTELS, in his concluding remarks, denounces the psychologist's arrogance shown by some of the gentlemen (Hitschmann, Stekel), who consistently overlook the facts and are interested only in theoretical-psychological aspects.

It is not possible to make people understand the connection between sexuality and a poet's creativity in any way except the one he has chosen. Protection from venereal disease is more important than the child's drive to learn.

He is going to moderate the beginning of his paper.

FREUD mentions that impotence plays a certain role in the demand that a woman be a virgin: a man wants a woman who cannot make comparisons about his potency.[6]

---

[5] It is striking how quickly these men draw practical conclusions from knowledge they have just acquired and have barely digested and how eager they are to apply it to everyday life. The problem of the enlightenment of children is not yet solved.

[6] See Freud's "The Taboo of Virginity (Contribution to the Psychology of Love III)" (1918), *S.E.*, 11:191-208. This paper was first read as a communication to the Vienna Society in 1917.

30

SCIENTIFIC MEETING on November 20, 1907

Present: Freud, Adler, Federn, Hitschmann, Sadger, Schwerdtner, Stekel, Wittels, Rank.

Sadger borrows *Archiv* No. 25.

PRESENTATION

Analysis of a Case of Anxiety Hysteria

SPEAKER: DR. STEKEL

This analysis is going to be published in detail.[1]

The patient is a cantor who suffers from an occupational neurosis. Under certain conditions (which subsequently turned out to be strictly determined), he is unable to continue his prayer but must stop at certain points and omit certain passages. At these times, he has anxiety attacks.

He is dissatisfied with his occupation: it is characteristic of those whose neurosis is connected with their occupation that they attempt an escape from this occupation.[2]

---

[1] It was published as Chapter 22 ("An Occupational Neurosis") in Stekel's book *Nervöse Angstzustände und ihre Behandlung*. Vienna: Urban & Schwarzenberg, 1908. [*Conditions of Nervous Anxiety and Their Treatment*. London: Kegan Paul, 1922.]

[2] It is most interesting to note how early the meaning of occupational neurosis was understood.

Another characteristic of all anxiety neuroses is the wish for the death of the spouse; this wish enormously increases the guilt feelings of such persons.

The patient has tried to help himself by inducing pleasant thoughts while he was performing his duties. He would picture to himself scenes of undressing and of sexual acts with women.

The analysis disclosed that this man's "attacks" were intimately connected with his masturbatory activities and that the passages at which he had to stop were related to his feelings of guilt.

DISCUSSION

HITSCHMANN remarks that the consistency of Stekel's material convinced him almost completely.

SADGER thinks that the wish for the death of the spouse is rooted in homosexuality. Homosexuality altogether plays a far greater part in the causation of neurosis than is generally believed.

FREUD joins in the praise of Stekel as an analyst; Stekel really knows [how to present] the essential relationships of a case [*Stekel verstehe das Elementarmachen*]. His view of the occupational neuroses is irreproachable. Man transfers his sexual fantasies onto his occupation (*Gradiva*).[3] He regularly utilizes a sexual component in his profession (*la bête humaine*). As long as this component does not exceed certain limits, it acts as a promoting factor. However, if the sexual component does exceed these limits, its promoting quality turns into an inhibiting factor; that is to say, sexual repression is then transferred onto the profession.

The occupational neurosis of actors is most interesting because it significantly illuminates the conditions of being an actor. If the actor's identification [with the character] goes too far (so that it impinges on recollections related to the actor's actual ego), then it becomes disturbing, inhibiting. A disturbance of this kind, occasioned by her own complex, produced a memory loss in the actress Kathi Frank. When she was playing Maria Stuart, she could not go on with her speech

[3] See Freud's "Delusions and Dreams in Jensen's 'Gradiva'" (1907). *S.E.*, 9:3-93.

at the place where she should have said: "I am better than my reputation."[4]

Listening to the account of such an analysis, one is struck by the monotony of all these matters. The same conditions almost invariably produce the same psychic material.

Criticisms: The dreams have not been accurately interpreted: In the content of the first dream, Stekel has overlooked the sadistic factor which also explains the inhibition at the Deborah passage. This dream has not been fully interpreted by Stekel, but its meaning can be guessed: it contains accusations against the two persons who are the cause of the patient's misfortune—against his grandfather and against his wife. These two have driven him to masturbation. He masturbates because he is dissatisfied with his profession (into which his grandfather led him) and because he is dissatisfied with his wife. Such a rage is found in all these unconscious sadists; it goes back to a prohibition of masturbation issued in childhood. This is the typical castration complex (which also finds expression in the fairy tale of Little Tom Thumb and the Man-Eater).[5]

The dream about Mrs. König [Queen] is a disguised mother dream; the "place of birth" mentioned in it is his mother's vagina. Suppressed rage regularly leads to anxiety.[6]

[4] Actors and other performing artists are, in addition, frequently disturbed by the unsuccessful repression of excessive exhibitionistic tendencies.

[5] Since Rank did not record the account of the analysis itself and summarized the rest of the paper but very briefly, it is not possible to understand the details of the discussion.

The first dream, as recorded in Stekel's published paper, reads: " 'My grandfather, who had been dead a long time—I saw him and talked to him about various matters. What these were, I do not know. I believe about "toilet" ["water closet"]. My wife also was there. Then I dreamed that on weekdays I carried out a more prolonged function, which I should never have done, and I was anxious.' As a supplement he adds: 'My grandfather was fixing something in the toilet [Pissoir]. He wanted to repair something. There were four beaks [Schnabel] in the toilet, and it was on those that he wanted to fix something.' "

The second dream reads: "I wanted to rent an apartment from a Mrs. König [Queen]. But I could not get it. It was promised to me for later. The place is not that of my present residence but my place of birth."

[6] With this sentence Freud already expresses the tenet that suppressed [repressed] rage—that is, hate and aggression—is one of the factors which evoke anxiety. Obviously, he intended to make the point that it is not only repressed libido which causes anxiety. But many years passed before he was ready to present a new formulation of his theory of anxiety in Inhibitions, Symptoms and Anxiety (S.E. 20), which was first published in German in 1926. It was a long latency period, indeed!

To Sadger: the homosexual component only seems to be in the foreground. It lies on a deeper level, and therefore is closer to autoerotism than is heterosexuality. However, the difference in object is of no account for the entire mechanism.

RANK raises the question about the connection between the choice of a profession and neurosis. We are accustomed to consider the choice of a profession as a psychologically determined act which has precisely the aim of abreacting sexuality (consider the artists who after all protect themselves from a neurosis). Therefore, we must conclude that a neurosis develops only when a person is forced into a profession. The answer to this is that persons with an occupational neurosis do not like their profession; indeed their gain [from the neurosis] lies in the fact that they rid themselves of their occupation (Freud). Moreover, it is incorrect to say that they abreact their sexuality. One should rather say that they keep it at a distance [avoid it].

ADLER thinks that, apart from Stekel's acceptable interpretations, there simply is not enough material to explain the patient's essential characteristics. The repression uncovered here is a superficial, recent one; this insight into minor connections of the recent past might be sufficient for the patient's cure. Until a short time before his treatment, the man had indulged in an abnormal type of sexual intercourse, which by itself could very well produce an anxiety neurosis. Stekel has accomplished almost as much by means of discussing sexual hygiene as he has by his fragmentary analysis. With an anxiety neurosis, too, one can succeed in carrying out a psychoanalysis which contains exactly the same components.

WITTELS finds Stekel's presentation most stimulating, though some things are too smooth to be evident. The dream analyses will not convince the layman. This patient, who had a girl in every port, is nevertheless actually the opposite of a Don Juan. The masculine Don Juan works only with his brain; the feminine Don Juan satisfies himself on his own person and for this purpose utilizes a man. The end of the Don Juan is never masturbation but homosexuality.

SCHWERDTNER remarks that forgetting the name in the last dream could also mean that the patient wished to have become another person.

STEKEL is aware of the fact that he has presented an incomplete analysis; the entire treatment lasted six weeks; the case was fully elucidated only later.

PROF. FREUD then recounts a few things from his practice and from the literature.

The obsessional neurotic, whom we already know from his analysis,[7] has developed a peculiar technique for effective prayers. In order to prevent their being disturbed or nullified by his obsessional contradictions, he makes the prayers as brief as possible (often only one word, the first one), and then he isolates them (to prevent the next thought from attaching itself to them); later, he used only the initial letters of each prayer and formed a short (magic) word out of them. This formula, which he uses when he starts to masturbate, is *Glej(i) samen*. *Gl*, he said, was derived from the first word of a prayer: *Glückliche* (= *beglücke*) [Happy ones (= to make happy)]; *e* is derived from the word *alle* [all]; j(i), from *jetzt* and *immer* [now and forever]; *amen* is the end formula. He had forgotten the origin of the *e* and the *s*. From this we can guess that the name of the lady whom he admires and whose name he had not mentioned up to this point is Gisela. The prayers form an anagram of his beloved's name: Gisela.

S-amen [s-emen] means simply that he masturbates with the mental image of his beloved; he wants to unite his semen with his beloved.[8]

The dream of a chemist is also worth mentioning here, because it shows again that the sexual complex lies behind the professional complex.

The problem of the relationship between a poet's creations and his personal life was raised in connection with the *Gradiva* but has remained unsolved. At the time, the poet himself answered that he did not know how he came to write the *Gradiva*. Now Jung has called attention to two earlier short novels by Jensen, "The Red Umbrella" and "A Gothic Mansion" published under the comprehensive title *Übermächte* [Powers Beyond Us]. They show many similarities, even

---

[7] See Minutes 28.

[8] In *Inhibitions, Symptoms and Anxiety* (1926), *S.E.*, 20:77-175, Freud has described isolation as a form of defense mechanisms characteristic of obsessional neurosis. This example shows that the obsessional neurotic isolates not only thoughts, recollections, experiences, and words, but also single letters which he then *condenses*.

in small details, to the *Gradiva*. They are the first preliminary stages toward a solution of the *Gradiva* problem. On this basis one can with certainty determine the experience which compelled the poet to attempt in three different forms a solution of this, for him so significant, impression.[9] It would be interesting if the poet should have been, as he alleges, entirely unaware of it.

[9] A similar process takes place in the dreamer who attempts to solve one problem in several successive dreams of a single night.

31

SCIENTIFIC MEETING on November 27, 1907

Present: Freud, Adler, Federn, Graf, Hitschmann, Rank, Sadger, Steiner, Stekel, Wittels.

Prof. Freud mentions a short paper by Dr. Abraham[1] in Berlin, W. Schöneberger Ufer 22.

Sadger returns No. 25.

PRESENTATION

Two Cases of Anxiety Hysteria

SPEAKER: DR. STEKEL

Both cases will be published in detail:

The first case[2] is that of a typesetter, twenty-four years of age, who wishes to be freed from his manifold nervous complaints by means of

---

[1] This is the first time that Karl Abraham's name appears in the Minutes. The essay referred to is either: "On the Significance of Sexual Trauma in Childhood for the Symptomatology of Dementia Praecox" (1907). *Clinical Papers and Essays on Psychoanalysis,* 2:13-20. New York: Basic Books, 1955; or "The Experiencing of Sexual Traumas As a Form of Sexual Activity" (1907). *Selected Papers on Psycho-Analysis.* London: Hogarth Press, 1927, pp. 47-63. Both were originally published in the *Zb.*

[2] See Chapter XXIII in Stekel's book, *Nervöse Angstzustände und ihre Behandlung,* 1908.

hypnosis. He is an onanist who masturbates mostly with sadistic fantasies (beating little boys on the nude buttocks). He himself traces his sadistic inclinations back to his father's habit of beating him and his two sisters on the buttocks and then forcing them to urinate in front of him.

He is attracted to his sister. His dreams are simple, as the dreams of sadists and obsessional neurotics generally are, for the obsessional idea is simply continued. This case is also a contribution to the psychology of corporal punishment of children: here, the father's sadistic tendencies appear without any ethical disguise.

The second case[3] concerns a famous concert singer who suddenly lost her voice. Believing that she was suffering from an organic disease (cancer of the throat—her father had died of cancer of the rectum), she consulted a physician. This was a case of occupational neurosis. She had definite psychic motives for losing her voice. These were closely connected with the further exercise of her profession. The moment at which her voice failed for the first time was also significant and strictly determined psychologically. After several weeks of psychoanalytic treatment, she has fully regained her voice.

DISCUSSION

PROF. FREUD first expresses his appreciation of Stekel's psychoanalytic skills. Then he adds a few critical observations. It is perhaps quite expedient to devise for oneself, as Stekel has done here, an abbreviated psychoanalysis applicable to very mild cases.[4]

Concerning the scene with his father, which the first patient remembered from his fifth year, Freud says that this "memory" bears the stamp of a fantasy. It probably developed when one of the children wet himself after one of the beatings.

The patient's "business-anxiety" (fear of entering a place of busi-

---

[3] An occupational neurosis in a singer, mentioned in Chapter XXV of Stekel's book (*loc. cit.*).

[4] Freud did not object to a psychoanalytically oriented form of brief psychotherapy if applied only to light cases. See Freud's paper presented at the Congress in Budapest in September, 1918 and published under the title "Wege der psychoanalytischen Therapie" in 1919. ["Lines of Advance in Psycho-analytic Therapy." *S.E.*, 17:157-168.]

ness, a store, etc.), as all such anxieties, is connected with the former erotic pleasure gained while doing his "big and small business."

In the second case, exception must be taken to the technique which is by no means classical and cannot be recommended. Associations as well as free thoughts yield much chaff.[5] It just does not happen that at the very beginning of treatment nothing comes to the patient's mind (so that one is forced to apply the association technique [Jung]) if one encourages him first to tell his story. The first ideas which come to the patient's mind in this connection always refer to his relation to the physician [in the analytic situation].

It is quite correct to consider the horse a symbol for intercourse (the large penis); however, the essential factor is the rhythm felt and heard while one is riding.

The dream in which white blossoms are being torn off means: I have lost my innocence through masturbation (tearing off: typical[6]).

The explanation of the symptom, the motives for being ill, have been recognized and presented correctly. But Stekel has not clearly demonstrated the mechanism: it is the identification with her rival in love (Oda). The mechanism is a combination of self-punishment and revenge. In the scene with Oda, she has the impulse: you must jump at her throat; but her tendency for self-punishment causes her voice to fail. She suppresses her thirst for revenge on her rival, but in its place acquires a symptom herself. Her love for the father is clear. As a child, she intruded as the third between father and mother; now comes Oda and intrudes in her love affair as the third. She cannot carry out her revenge against her rival because she sees her own image in Oda (like Hamlet, who cannot carry out his vengeance for the same reason). Now she feels herself as the mother (compare her statement that she always feels like a mother to men). Through Oda, the dancer, the memory of her mother is aroused. Her mother had beautiful legs, and she too behaves, in the course of her neurosis, like a dancer (identification). Oda found her voice ugly, and since then she has gotten this ugly voice. One might conjecture that her mother also had an ugly voice.

[5] This refers to associations provoked by stimulus words (Jung). See Minutes 21, footnote 7.

[6] Tearing off, "sich einen abreissen," is the Viennese equivalent for "jerking off."

This patient's prominent features are:

(1) the anal character (frequently combined with sadomasochistic tendencies);
(2) the sadistic traits;
(3) the homosexual traits.

Thus she brings an already-restricted libido into her relationships with men.

One might further deduce that she had childhood memories referring to flatus. These anal voices may have aroused her father's displeasure, and her present lack of a voice would then be the corresponding wish fulfillment.

Analyses yield a small additional profit: we learn from them what is really going on in the world; we receive a genuine picture of the world. The analyses are cultural-historical documents of tremendous importance.[7]

FEDERN states that this case, as that of the cantor, are both cases of missed professions. A girl who is as intent as is this patient on preserving her propriety just cannot work as an artist.

The simplest hysteria of men, impotence, corresponds to anesthesia in women. Sexual anesthesia is connected with premature masturbation.

(PROF. FREUD here raises the theoretical question of whether, in such persons, the genital zone is stunted so prematurely, the genital rejection comes about so early, because the other perversions are so strong, or whether, conversely, the perversions can become so strong because genital rejection sets in at such an early point.)

FEDERN: The patient's fantasy that she has lived once before as a young man immediately characterizes her as a Lesbian. On the basis of a thoroughly investigated case, it can be assumed that Lesbians have had a repulsive penis-experience in childhood. (STEKEL asserts that

[7] In his *Interpretation of Dreams* (1900) where Freud sharply formulated the oedipus complex for the first time, he referred to a Greek tragedy more than two thousand years old, a tragedy which was itself the result of a long, historic development. The oedipus complex is indeed a precipitate of this development, but it is not dead; it is still alive today, although unconscious. It seems as if Freud, even at the time of this protocol (1907) had already in mind the connection between phylogenetic and ontogenetic psychological development. *Totem and Taboo* was published much later (1912-1913).

such an experience is typical of anxiety hysterics. In three hysterical patients he found stunted nipples.)

WITTELS suspects that the patient lied to Stekel. Many of her communications impress him as fantasies.

ADLER first refers to Prof. Freud's communication concerning Dr. Abraham's views on trauma. He states that his experiences have been the opposite: nonneurotic individuals who have kept secret their sexual traumata. A classification on the basis of telling or keeping something secret is superficial. Concerning the number of traumata, one must not overrate the trauma: the constitution finds the sexual trauma.[8]

From the first case, one gains the impression that sadism is inherited, and hence all psychic qualities or mental processes.

In the anal character, one can also demonstrate that certain psychic characteristics were present in the forebears. This is true of all inferior organs. In the second case, in addition, the enuretic character is quite prominent. The inferiority of the mammae, which was also present in the mother (the patient has underdeveloped breasts and was not nursed by her mother), is connected with the entire psychic development of the individual. Children's dislike of their mother, in many cases, goes back to the fact that she did not nurse them.[9]

SADGER cannot confirm the statement that the dreams of obsessional neurotics are simple. Behind the patient's love for the musician P. is the homosexual love: she calls him mother; in her relationship with him she can play the part of the man. Her fear of entering rooms where women are gathered also indicates a homosexual tendency (revulsion, respectively).

GRAF feels that his objections to Stekel's method are refuted by Stekel's success. He knows of many cases of singers who did not pursue their career for a few years when they were satisfied with married life, but who later returned to the stage. He knows also that great singers live in abstinence when on tour.

The artistic production of children begins with the first repression.

[8] See Freud's remarks on infantile fantasies in *A General Introduction to Psychoanalysis* (1916-1917). New York: Garden City Publ., 1923.

[9] This is one of the arbitrary statements which we find in these protocols, coming not only from Adler but also from others. However, Adler is the most consistent offender.

252

HITSCHMANN states emphatically that the good result is no proof of the correctness of the analysis. In a satirical manner he expresses doubts about all of the claims made. The shorter and simpler the matter appears to be, the more it raises suspicions.

Reassurance by a physician might perhaps have had the same beneficial effect as Stekel's influence [*Beeinflussung*].

STEKEL wants to contrast the neurosis of the teacher who rejects whatever is new with the neurosis of the pupil for which he himself has so frequently been reproached. He uses the association experiment as a means of overcoming pauses.[10]

The success is due only to the resolution of the repressions and it could not have been achieved without psychoanalysis (to Hitschmann).

---

[10] Refers to *Studies in Word-Association, Experiments in the Diagnosis of Psychopathological Conditions* (1906), ed. C. G. Jung. New York: Moffet, Yard, 1919. See Minutes 1. At that time, the association experiment was frequently applied, much as other methods are used today, partly because the therapist did not sufficiently master the psychoanalytic technique and partly in order to help in rationalizing the resistances.

32

SCIENTIFIC MEETING on December 4, 1907

Present: Freud, Federn, Graf, Hitschmann, Rank, Sadger, Schwerdtner, Steiner, Stekel, Wittels.

COMMUNICATIONS

Prof. Freud reports Jung's suggestion that in the Spring a congress of all "followers" be held (perhaps in Salzburg).
Federn returns Minutes 6-9 (not 8).

PRESENTATION

Konrad F. Meyer

SPEAKER: DR. SADGER

The paper is to appear soon in the Löwenfeld collection; therefore, no detailed summary is given here.[1] Only a few main points will be mentioned. Two factors decisively influenced the poet's development:

---

[1] *Konrad Ferdinand Meyer. Eine pathographisch-psychologische Studie* [*Konrad Ferdinand Meyer. A Pathographic-Psychological Study*]. In *Grenzfragen des Nerven- und Seelenlebens*, Heft 59. Wiesbaden: Bergmann, 1908.
Konrad Ferdinand Meyer (1825-1898), famous Swiss poet and novelist.

heredity and erotism. Actually, he suffered throughout his life from unrequited love for his mother. It was only after his mother's death and after he had, at the same time, gained financial independence, that his talent as a writer could unfold.

DISCUSSION

GRAF remarks that he had no particular liking for Meyer and has never given much thought to him. In Stauffer-Bern's portrait[2] [of Meyer] the joyous characteristics were always more striking to him than the pathological ones. From a psychological study of a poet one can expect to learn something of the connection between the poet's personality and his work. Sadger has not paid enough attention to this essential point.

The core of Meyer's production is found in his immersion in past centuries during his last psychosis.

Sadger construes too many hereditary symptoms. Graf would rather describe as an intense inner life what Sadger calls "aversion to association." Besides, Sadger has been quite careless in supporting his hypotheses and theses. Graf seriously doubts that a hysteria would develop in a man of sixty-three years, just as he doubts that it was only his mother's death which made Meyer a poet. A psychological study of poets should also enable one to discover the typical characteristics of artists who come to produce only very late in life.

SCHWERDTNER stresses that Sadger has merely presented a detailed biography of the poet, whereas a survey of his works would, perhaps even without a detailed biography, have given better insight into the poet's nature. Not all of Sadger's assertions have been proven; there are some striking contradictions; and one does not need "heredity" to explain all of the phenomena.

STEKEL is horrified and fears that this work will harm our cause. Sadger has a formula with which he wants to explain the psychology of all writers [literally: "poetic souls"]; but the matter is not that simple. This is surface psychology. He protests against the claims of hereditary deficiency. The term "aversion to associations" is non-

2 Karl Stauffer-Bern (1857-1891), famous Swiss etcher and painter.

sense: these individuals have a big complex with which they are constantly preoccupied. The anthropophobia points to masturbation. For
this reason, Meyer never felt at ease at home. There is a relationship
between the late onset of his creativity and the late awakening of his
potency which may be inferred from his marriage at a relatively late
age (at fifty). The illness in his advanced age (with diminishing
potency) was most likely an anxiety neurosis. As far as Meyer's first
"psychosis" is concerned, one may surmise an attempt at suicide. The
relationship to his mother should have been indicated just once and
discretely, not emphasized in such an obtrusive manner. One should
study his works thoroughly and demonstrate their connections with his
life. It would have been far more fruitful than Sadger's investigations
to compare the old and new editions of his poems, paying special attention to what the poet omitted from the later edition. (These are the
things which are essential for the psychologist.) Finally he appeals to
Sadger's conscience not to publish his essay in its present form.

RANK remarks that this circle is familiar with the "family psychology" of poets (their relationship to parents and siblings) and that we
are justified in presupposing it where there is no evidence to the
contrary; however, to the general public Sadger should present his
arguments with more evidence and in a more convincing manner. His
own general experience would confirm a few of Sadger's less important
points: Meyer's "writing for his sister" is a general characteristic of
poets. Every poet writes primarily (that is, unconsciously) for himself,
but always has in mind (that is, consciously) one or several beloved
persons.

FEDERN is indignant. Sadger has not said a single word about the
poet's sexual development, because one just does not know anything
about it: therefore, one cannot write a pathography. Meyer must have
had significant sexual experiences. A neurotic person has recognized
from Meyer's work the incestuous relationship to his sister. Meyer was
probably an onanist and was ashamed of this before his mother.

STEINER declares that Meyer interests him only as a patient.
Hereditary tainting is in fact present in this case. The description of
his youth is typical of an onanist; he seems also to have been impotent
for psychological reasons. Being of a rather passive nature, he probably

did not make too much of an impression on women. Altogether he looks like a neurotic in his early as well as in his later life.

WITTELS first takes exception to the personal outbursts of rage and indignation on the part of Stekel and Federn. He considers these entirely out of place. The connection between sexual potency and creative writing is not as simple as Stekel imagines it to be. The concept of "aversion to associations" is quite clear and the objections raised are merely quibbles about words.

PROF. FREUD would first like to advise moderation. At the very least, Sadger's industry is to be commended, though it unfortunately is all too often expended on sterile topics. On the whole, his [Freud's] own judgment is not too far removed from those expressed here. This is not the correct way to write pathographies; Graf has come closer to suggesting the correct way which must proceed from the works. Sadger has a rigidly established way of working. That is, he uses a two-sided scheme: hereditary tainting and modern erotic psychology. [All of] life is then viewed in the light of this scheme.

Sadger's investigation has not clarified anything for him. The enigma of this personality remains unsolved. But there is altogether no need to write such pathographies. The theories can only be harmed and not one iota is gained for the understanding of the subject.

If one already knows a great deal about psychic mechanisms, then the pathological component can be investigated as a residual phenomenon. Moreover, Meyer is not a well-chosen example of the "aversion to associations": he had a solid relationship to the range of ideas of the Renaissance.

A part of his development in his youth has been correctly interpreted: his failure as a young man is rooted in his defiance of his mother.

In attempting to construct Meyer's character, one sees clearly the anal traits, e.g., his stubbornness (his love of cleanliness—as a child he would scream, "clean me!"—is an overcompensation). Moreover, he married an immensely rich girl and later was sentenced to a large fine for tax evasion. This side of his personality, however, cannot be grasped from his works. He shows a deep understanding of psychological processes. His poem, *At the Gates of Heaven*, for instance, discloses the entire secret of obsessional neurosis. His love for his sister clearly betrays itself in his emotional life, especially in the short novel, *Die Richterin* [*The Woman Judge*] which deals with the clearing away [*Wegputzung*] of the danger of incest (at the end of the novel the protagonists turn out not to have been siblings.)

HITSCHMANN finds several illogical propositions in the paper. There is no need always to look for such far-fetched explanations of everything. The urge to travel, for example, does not have to be pathological. It is known that the Swiss travel a great deal.

It would be worth while to investigate what effect it has on a child if the mother who raises him is a widow; whether such sons do not tend to remain bachelors.

Not every relationship of a child is erotic; there are other components too.

There is much that seems to indicate masturbation; the bad breath, as a kind of delusion of being noticed, is typical of it. It is almost a rule that people waver before embarking on writing as a profession. Besides, it may well be that Meyer had been writing before his first publication, but destroyed many of these works.

Material advantages are also regularly renounced (the care which Meyer's mother gives to the imbecile); it is as in novels in which the characters also always live on air.

SADGER, in his concluding words, stresses that he had hoped to learn more than he actually has. He expected to receive information and instruction, but he takes home nothing but some invectives. After rejecting the personal insults, against which, he says, there is no logical argument, he deals with the objections to the material itself and clarifies his point of view. It is not possible accurately to deduce a poet's real experiences from his works because there is nothing to distinguish the real from the illusory; one does not know where truth ends and poetic imagination begins. Therefore, the approach from a poet's work is unreliable.

The concept of hereditary tainting was applied mainly to excessive phenomena.[3]

---

[3] Criticism was frequently severe, not only of Sadger but of everyone in the circle. Subsequently, Sadger was subjected to even sharper criticism. He made himself disliked although his merits in respect to psychoanalysis are considerable.

33

SCIENTIFIC MEETING on December 11, 1907

Present: Freud, Adler, [A.] Deutsch, Federn, Graf, Hitschmann, Hollerung, Rank, Sadger, Schwerdtner, Steiner, Stekel, Wittels.
[A.] Deutsch returns Minutes 3.
Sadger borrows Minutes 22 (returned on January 1, 1908).

PRESENTATION

Methodology of the Psychology of Poets[1]

SPEAKER: DR. GRAF

Last week's debate has been the stimulus for this evening's discussion. Sadger's paper met with such definite and almost unanimous rejection that it seemed desirable to discuss once the method of [studying] the psychology of poets. It seemed to me that the shortcomings of his paper were not at the periphery but at the very core. The entire basis of Sadger's reflections was contestable.

To what purpose does one study the psychology of poets? Is it not

[1] The manuscript of this paper is attached to the original protocol. Since we are publishing here a copy of an unpublished work, we have tried to contact Mr. Graf in order to obtain his permission but have received no reply. However, we are convinced that he would not have refused permission if our request had reached him.

possible to define certain limits of the method? A clarification of these questions seemed desirable to me; therefore, I have suggested this discussion.

You know that it has become fashionable to pursue the psychology of the artist. Recent investigations have furnished some handy tools for this purpose. Lombroso[2] has pointed to the pathological roots of creative writing even though he has done so in a distorted and amateurish manner. The French school of psychologists has coined some fashionable concepts, such as *dégenéré supérieur*, which can be applied to some artists. Thus one has begun to compose analyses of poets on the basis of pathological experiences.

Prof. Freud has made new psychological discoveries, has thrown light on the road to the unconscious, and thus has mightily furthered the understanding of the psychology of the poet. His fundamental views, however, are not those of a neuropathologist but rather those of one who knows the human soul. This means that he knows various groupings of elements of the unconscious and of the conscious; he has shown that conscious and unconscious are superimposed on each other in various positions;[3] he has further shown that psychic illness is nothing but a variant of so-called mental health. He is a psychologist and has erected a unified psychological structure. What Prof. Freud learned from the ill has enabled him to understand the healthy. Just as perversions are merely split-off parts of the normal sex instinct,[4] of which they are the components, so mental illnesses are a dissociation of the psychic elements of a healthy person.

Lombroso looks at poets in the same way as he looks at a particularly interesting type of criminal. The French psychologists see in the poet only a neurotic. Professor Freud is interested in the human soul, the psychic organism. The first two therefore may write "pathographies"; Prof. Freud writes psychological analyses, and everyone who has an analytic interest in poets must decide whether he wants to write a case history or a psychoanalytic portrayal. But he must not, as

[2] Cesare Lombroso: *Genius and Insanity* (1887), *The Man of Genius* (German, 1888; English, 1891), and *New Studies on Genius* (German, 1902).

[3] Graf probably meant to say that the system *Cs.* is superimposed on the system *Pcs.*, and the latter on the system *Ucs.* This conception led to the characterization of psychoanalytic psychology as a "depth psychology."

[4] At that time the structure of perversions was still thought to be that simple.

Sadger has done, constantly confound these two methods with each other.

I shall now speak only of the psychoanalytic method and its application to artists. Allow me to make a preliminary comment:

I have found that many who avail themselves of this technique are under the illusion that mere knowledge of the technique will permit them to probe deeper into a poet's mind than other biographers can— an illusion which betrays itself also in the nice, but easily misunderstood, words of our friend Kahane who differentiates between "depth psychologists" and "surface psychologists." I should like to remark, though, that a depth psychologist too may be superficial and a surface psychologist may be deep. Such works as Herman Grimm's[5] *Michelangelo,* or Dilthey's[6] *Experience and Literature* are brilliant biographies, psychological studies, even though their authors have not used Freud's technique; and a mediocre mind working with Freud's technique will certainly achieve less profound results. Someone may have a deep philosophical mind even if he treats his topics with the dialectics of medieval philosophy; in comparison, someone else may appear to be quite flat even though he is well versed in all of the modern philosophical ideas. The decisive factor, no doubt, is the mental capacity with which a task is approached. Freud's technique by itself does not make a person clever or profound. Its value is that it provides one who knows the psyche with a new and very fine, but also a very fragile, tool for exploring the unconscious. However, it cannot carry forward one who is a psychological botcher.

Thus, I believe that not everyone is fit to pursue the psychology of artists—that is to say, the psychology of the most complex, the most sensitive souls, and whoever undertakes such a task must first ask himself whether he is fit for it; that is, whether he himself knows how thoughts, images, emerge from the unconscious and are transformed into conscious material. In short, he alone shall approach the artist who is himself artistically inclined.

This is the alpha of the psychology of artists.

The next question to be answered is: What shall be the point of departure for my reflections? The artist? His work?

5 Herman Grimm (1828-1901), German historian of art and literature.
6 Wilhelm Dilthey (1833-1911), German philosopher.

It seems simpler to proceed from the artist. Many artists have talked and written about themselves. Their contemporaries have preserved their impressions, conversations, etc. Shouldn't this be enough for learning something about the artist? Contemporary accounts are certainly valuable; yet they are always subjectively tinged, i.e., falsified. In their autobiographies, however, the artists speak always with posterity in mind; they touch up matters; and if one of them, like Rousseau, promises that he will tell everything about himself, including even all his worst vices, then he is the most insincere of all.

One more remark: all artistic creation is rooted in the repressed. But the repressed will offer resistances when the autobiographer is about to relate his most important experiences. Precisely the most significant questions therefore will remain unanswered. The artist overcomes his psychic inhibitions only by creating, and whoever wishes to know the poet must seek him out in his works. The surface psychologist once rhymed, "Wer den Dichter will verstehen, muss in Dichters Lande gehen" ["A poet's soul to understand, one must enter poet's land"].

The more a poet tells about himself, the more he has most likely to conceal. How little we would know of poets if we did not know their works! The tragic poets of Greece, on the other hand, are familiar poetic personalities [*dichterische Persönlichkeiten*] to us and yet we know almost nothing of their lives. Shakespeare is protected from receiving a psychopathographic treatment by the fact that only a few of his signatures and documents exist. Psychoanalytically, however, a great deal can be said about him. We possess four volumes of his works. Is this really too little with which to get to know him when psychoanalysts can draw important, reliable conclusions about a human being from a brief utterance, the motion of a hand, even from an unbuttoned fly? In good conscience, I would advise the musician who cannot discern Mozart's psychological portrait in a Mozart symphony to let music alone since he is either deaf to music or deaf to the language of the soul. Whoever feels like an artist will agree with me.

We must, then, turn to the work.

But how shall we proceed? I myself have found the following expedient helpful for my personal use. I proceed from those motifs which I call typical ones; that is, those poetic motifs which recur in the artist's works.

The figure of Hamlet, for example, is a typical figure in Shakespeare. It is encountered again as Richard II, Henry IV, and as the melancholy Jacques.[7] It is the same figure, and some things which cannot be understood in Hamlet have become clear to me through the other dramas.

Or: the son's hatred of the father is a driving theme in the *Räuber*.[8] But it is also present in *Cabale und Liebe*.[9] In *Don Carlos*, this theme receives a new, meaningful motivation (hatred of the father because he has robbed the son of the mother). Later it is transformed into hatred of the oppressor, the tyrant (*Wilhelm Tell*).

In Goethe's work, the typical figure is a weak man who abandons his beloved and is then overcome by remorse (Weislingen, Clavigo, Faust).

Raphael's pictures and the works of Michelangelo show typical themes.

Richard Wagner's Dutchman, Wotan, and Amfortas are one figure. In the *Dutchman*, Senta leaves her *betrothed* to follow the Dutchman; in the *Walküre*, in *Tristan*, the wife leaves the *husband* in order to follow the lover, a kindred being. It is only here that this motif is completely elucidated.

The desperate man, torn by discord, redeemed by the love of a woman, is a dominant motif in all of Wagner's works.

The central themes of the poet's creations betray the innermost mechanisms of the poet's mind. Here we are in the center of the unconscious. It is especially interesting to observe how these typical themes are veiled in the works, how they are treated from ever-new angles. I have already mentioned this before. It is similar to what occurs in myths. You know Schiller's *Turandot*. The suitors who woo Turandot must solve riddles, otherwise they are put to death. This is a theme of world literature, found not only among the Greeks but also in oriental peoples. Here the theme has another variation: the suitors need not solve riddles, they must be victorious over him [the father] in races and other [contests]. A certain mythmaker has used the

---

[7] *As You Like It.*
[8] In Schiller's work, *The Robbers.*
[9] Schiller's *Intrigue and Love.*

original form of this legend: the father is in love with his daughter, or he has an affair with her; in order to keep his rivals from her he imposes deadly tasks upon them. This is the original theme, which in *Turandot* has already been mitigated by a more humane era. It is, as you all can see, a universal human theme. Even today (enamored) fathers try to keep their daughters for themselves by treating their suitors harshly.

It is also important to compare kindred personalities among the poets and artists, to establish *types of artists*. Richard Wagner and Euripides, Beethoven and Michelangelo, Raphael and Mozart are kindred, identical personalities. What may not be transparent in one becomes clear in the other. The mystery of Beethoven's copybooks became intelligible to me only when I learned about Michelangelo's method of working.

The creative process of all artists discloses kindred features, and the ultimate goal of the analyses of artists, it seems to me, is finally to reach a "theory of artistic creation."

No doubt, the analyses of artists who show pathological traits (in the usual sense of the word) will also yield valuable contributions. But we must be quite clear about the fact that the greatest artists—by virtue of their mysterious productive power, their mighty vital spirits which animate all their creations—appear to be healthy, for illness is inhibition of the productive force, depression of the vital spirits [*Lebensgefühle*].

These, then, are the normal cases which should be analyzed first; all others are variants. The second-rate geniuses who show pathological traits produce little or after long intervals. Their creative process is changed, is destroyed, is inhibited by the illness. The purely medical analysis, the pathography, contributes little toward the understanding of the poet's creative process because it is concerned only with these inhibitions, and not with the positive creative forces. It is not sufficient to focus only on these psychic changes; one must also, with an artist's sensitivity, pursue the creative forces.

If it was the alpha of my discourse that one must be artistically endowed to compose analyses of artists, then the omega of my discourse is the same. I do not know whether one will correctly analyze a neurotic dumbbell if one has a purely clinical point of view; but the highly complicated, sensitive organism of the poet can be understood only by one who is artistically endowed in the first place. Prof. Freud's technique alone cannot unravel the mysteries of creative writing unless it is used with Prof. Freud's artistic sensitivity.

DISCUSSION

ADLER finds several stimulating and valuable ideas in Graf's discourse. However, he does not think that, for the time being, any rules can be set up for the study of the psychology of artists. Other suggestions, which would be just as important, could easily be added. For instance, a poet's early work should be studied with special care; in connection, of course, with his later work. This technique leads to the discovery of certain fundamental conditions of the constitution, of the development of the character Anlage.

It would perhaps be advisable to disregard any artistic qualifications and, using only the Freudian technique, to make a skeletal sketch depicting the psychic currents in poets.

SCHWERDTNER agrees with Graf's arguments. Pathographies can be written about only a very few poets; psychoanalyses about most. The letters of artists must be counted as part of their works.

PROF. FREUD has, already at the last meeting, emphasized that he agrees with Graf in principle. He now wishes to enlarge on this from one particular angle.

Every poet who shows abnormal tendencies can be the object of a pathography. But the pathography cannot show anything new. Psychoanalysis, on the other hand, provides information about the creative process. Psychoanalysis deserves to rank above pathography.

There exist only a few clues and presuppositions for the approach to such analyses of poets:

The relationship between the artistic creation and the poet's life.

Proposition 1 (from the paper "Creative Writers and Day-dreaming"[10]): *creative writing* generally partakes of the same mechanism

[10] "Der Dichter und das Phantasieren" was first presented on December 6, 1907 and subsequently published in *Neue Revue*, 1 (10):716-724, 1908 [English: *S.E.*, 9:141-153].

as the daydream: the "dominant motifs" (Graf) are the desires which are dominant throughout the poet's life (Freud).

He can now add

Proposition 2: *the principle of the transposition of elements*, which is of special significance for the analysis of myths and legends. The relationship between the contents of the conscious and of the unconscious: the elements are the same, but the order is changed in many ways.

Proposition 3: the definition of the types in Graf's sense.

Proposition 4: special emphasis on the early works of the poet as Adler has suggested.

With these resources one can attempt to draw conclusions about the process of artistic creation from the works.

Graf's thesis that creative writing emanates from the repressed is contestable. He confuses "unconscious" with "repressed," which certainly are not identical.[11]

The *Gradiva* is a beautiful example of typical themes. The two short novels by Jensen, to which Jung has called attention (*The Red Umbrella* and *In the Gothic Mansion*), deal with close relatives who are loved: a cousin and a half-sister. The basis of the whole matter, then, is Jensen's relationship to a little playmate, perhaps a sister. The circumstances may have been such that the writer received a powerful impression which left in its wake an unfulfilled wish (perhaps the loss of this companion). The sight of the embossed figure which reminded him of his sister then suddenly reawakened this wish. He reacted to this experience in a variety of ways. The three short novels could be replaced by three formulas:

The first can be translated as: "I can no longer love anyone since I have lost her" (might perhaps refer to a cooling off in his marriage).

The second: "Even if she had remained alive, I still would have had to lose her; by giving her to another man as his wife." Here he furnishes proof that they are not siblings.

The third: "I shall see her again"—in the sense of consoling himself. Belief in resurrection.

This companion (whom he may have elevated in his fantasy to a

---

[11] Freud distinguishes two kinds of unconscious: the primary unconscious which was never conscious, and that which became unconscious through repression.

266

sister because he had no sister in reality; or who may really have been his sister) was, most likely, a sickly child. This illness—possibly a deformity of the feet—may have been blurred by a glorification in fantasy. The embossed figure then showed him that this defect could also be reinterpreted as a positive quality.

That solution may perhaps be too simple; but still, in a more complicated form, it may be true. The person in question might be his own child, etc.

Shakespeare is a good subject for the psychological method, the more so since Brandes[12] has paved the way. In *Hamlet* the connections with the poet's personal life are manifest. This work is his reaction to the deaths of his father and his son.

The period of his embitterment raises a suspicion of venereal infection (*Timon of Athens*). *Macbeth* gives proof of what a poet can do with a drama written for a special occasion.

WITTELS is opposed to this method of writing biographies of poets. For the temptation would be too great to use the unwritten dictionary of unconscious meanings, which one has in one's mind. It is more fruitful to apply Freudian teachings to life itself, to make people understand the sexual need. At the present time, the psychologies of poets are of no advantage either for Freud's teachings or for the public in general.

SADGER argues against the method proposed by Graf. He himself writes pathographies purely out of medical interest, not for the purpose of throwing light on the process of artistic creation, which, by the way, remains unexplained even by psychoanalytic interpretation. Graf's method is nothing but the age-old method of the literary historians who compare life and work, augmented by the key which Freud has put in our hand. At the last meeting, he already discussed how difficult and daring it is to infer a poet's life [circumstances] from his works.

The puzzling problem of how the poet's unconscious suddenly becomes preconscious is not solved by Graf's method either.

After arguing against the principle of the thesis, Sadger raises

[12] Georg Brandes (1824-1927), famous Danish historian of literature, wrote a widely known study, *William Shakespeare*, in 1897.

some objections to individual assertions which Graf has advanced; for example, that second-rate writers show pathological traits more frequently than first-rate writers; as counterevidence, he mentions Kleist, Grillparzer, and others.

He arrives at the conclusion that the purely psychoanalytic method does not succeed either in shedding more light on the problems involved.

FEDERN would like to mention a suggestion in relation to the first proposition advanced by the Professor: the fact that the artistic daydreams retain far more the characteristics of a game gives the artist an advantage over the daydreamer. The theme of ambition and the theme of playing could perhaps be subsumed in a higher category: namely, the craving for power and domination. The poet can represent his characters in whatever way he wishes. What Graf calls "increased vital energies" is a higher form of the capacity to let the unconscious do psychic work. The unconscious works correctly (never incorrectly) on a higher level of correspondence to the external world [*Aussenweltentsprechung*].[13] The poet is ahead of general development and is by no means a phenomenon of degeneration.

The poet is never, as Sadger believes, inhibited by the laws of artistic creation: they are never an inhibition but an analogue of his artistic capacities.

HITSCHMANN comments that one should first search for the specific characteristics of each individual great poet. Then one should investigate why a creative individual chooses to express himself just in this particular artistic form. (GRAF declares that this question is answered by the theory of the erotogenic zones.) Brandes shows that at certain times in Shakespeare['s life] there (periodically) appear similar figures in his work, an observation which is worthy of attention.

RANK first points out that Graf has sharply defined the standpoint of all of us who are studying the psychic life of poets on the basis of Prof. Freud's method. Individual personal divergences have been voiced by several members.

For the time being, we are not at all interested in the poet's experi-

---

[13] This is one of the almost unintelligible passages, probably because Rank condensed Federn's remarks too much.

ences (his external life) but only in the way these experiences are worked over [and absorbed] (in his inner life).

PROF. FREUD disapproves of Sadger's bringing into the discussion the much larger, more comprehensive problem of the relationship between conscious and unconscious. This is a problem which theory alone can solve.

GRAF directs his concluding remarks primarily to Sadger, the only one who offered serious criticism. First, he defends the literary historians, who bring us the "day's residue," as it were. Sadger's question as to how one can explain the poet's psyche from his works, which are distorted, is settled by the answer that science is not meant to explain anything but rather to give descriptions which leave no gaps.

34

SCIENTIFIC MEETING *on December 18, 1907*

Present: Freud, Adler, Graf, Federn, Hitschmann, Hollerung, Sadger, Schwerdtner, Steiner, Stekel, Wittels, Reitler, Rank.
Dr. Abraham from Berlin as a guest.

COMMUNICATIONS

Dr. Wittels proposes Dr. Rudolf Urbantschitsch as a new member.

Federn, Graf, Hitschmann, Hollerung, Sadger, Schwerdtner, Steiner, Stekel, Wittels, Bass (through Federn) give 2 *Kronen* each as a New Year's gift for the maid.

Graf and Bass (through Federn) pay their contribution for the first semester.

Adler, Häutler pay 2 *Kronen* as New Year's contribution.

DISCUSSION ON SEXUAL TRAUMATA AND
SEXUAL ENLIGHTENMENT

HITSCHMANN first stresses that, according to Freud's present view, sexual trauma, because of its frequent occurrence, is no longer considered to be of such paramount importance in the etiology of neuroses as we previously thought. The need for sexual enlightenment is generally acknowledged, with the reservation that it should be given without infringing on the sense of modesty. Actually, enlightenment should be given in three stages of life:

1. When children begin to ask about their origin—between eight and ten years of age.[1]

2. Somewhat later in a more specific way.

3. In puberty (at about sixteen to seventeen years) on the dangers of and the protective measures during sexual intercourse.

Such enlightenment, however, cannot provide protection against the childhood traumata: besides, it is hardly possible to convey the full meaning (for example, of the perversions).

Moreover, one must also take into account that, for example, an overly severe injunction against masturbation may have just as injurious an effect as a trauma, that it may act as an inverted trauma, as it were. The anesthesia of women may be connected with this.

FEDERN, too, stresses that enlightenment cannot provide protection against the first childhood traumata. The trauma is the condition of and at the same time the reason for the first enlightenment. The normal child, having suffered a trauma, investigates and soon calms down; the child who is predisposed to neurosis withdraws and hides himself. The precondition for the severe effect of a trauma is continuous psychic isolation. Horror may perhaps be the soil in which a neurosis grows. In particular, horror of the erect penis is a factor in neuroses connected with intercourse.

SADGER speaks of the ignorance of most parents. They themselves are in need of enlightenment and are therefore incapable of enlightening their children. Lies about sexual matters undermine parental authority and love for the parents. Hatred for parents frequently stems from untruthful sexual enlightenment in early years.

The most significant and most severe traumata are inflicted on the infant by excessive demonstration of affection. Moreover, the nurse cannot avoid setting in motion some sexual excitement. If sexuality has once been awakened, for instance, through a trauma, then the fantasies following in its wake are of great importance.

[1] Today we know that children start at a much earlier age to ask where babies come from.

271

GRAF asks why infantile traumata can result in severe neurosis in one individual, whereas they have no effect on another. Also, to what extent can enlightenment succeed in diminishing or preventing the harmful consequences? Complete sexual enlightenment may perhaps be more dangerous than the "natural" enlightenment which, as a rule, occurs gradually.

REITLER, contradicting Hitschmann, states that crass, crude traumata do lead to neurosis. He has overlooked the fantasies which Sadger stressed later. It is problematic whether enlightenment itself does not act as a trauma. In any case, one has to begin with it long before puberty.

WITTELS remarks that the essential factor is to be found not in the trauma but in the constitution. Of the latter, however, we know nothing. A normal child does not worry about sexual experiences. One should leave a child alone and fuss about him as little as possible.

Enlightenment received from contemporaries is much more useful; for parents are incapable of speaking so bluntly.

DR. ABRAHAM takes a skeptical stand in regard to the opinion that traumata could be avoided through enlightenment. It does not help children who are so inclined, and others do not suffer such traumata. First of all, enlightenment must be given to parents who would otherwise inflict sexual traumata on their children.

The main concern is to begin with enlightenment as early as possible. He doubts that enlightenment given in the framework of the school is useful. The mother's caresses are necessary for the child.

PROF. FREUD formulates the basic questions of today's discussion: whether it is possible to gain from enlightenment a kind of protective inoculation against traumata.

The position of traumata in the etiology of neuroses: the symptoms stem from fantasies which are patterned after experiences of gratification. Sexual traumata take first place among such gratifying experiences.[2] Since on the one hand it was not very likely that these traumata had actually occurred, and since on the other hand they were found

---

[2] Freud expresses here an idea which he later formulated more clearly in the case of the Wolf Man. See "From the History of an Infantile Neurosis" (1918). *S.E.*, 17:3-122.

to be similar in all individuals, one was forced to conclude that they were of no importance in the etiology of neuroses.[3] In this sense, Abraham's essay[4] is an advance. He shows that children themselves seek out their traumata. If traumata are of no significance as an etiological factor, they nevertheless determine the form of the neurosis if a neurosis ensues. They determine the form of the neurosis because they provide the child with the old fantasies of gratification. (Under certain circumstances the trauma may, for some children, assume even etiological significance.)

To Sadger we have to reply that the stimulations of the infant do not belong with the traumata.

The factor of repression has considerable bearing on the whole set of questions. The child's reaction, his sexual activity or his neurosis, is dependent upon repression.

When abstinence from sexual intercourse is demanded over a long period of time, then the infantile sexual traumata acquire importance. Since the effects of infantile traumata appear only in later life (in puberty), they can be counteracted effectively by enlightenment. A social reform allowing a certain amount of sexual freedom would be the best way to render sexual traumata harmless.[5]

The trauma inflicted by prohibition (Hitschmann) is the most significant of all because it furthers the factor of repression. Children should see the facts of sexual life treated in the same way as all other matters. Precocity is so harmful because the child is so helpless in the face of strong sexual excitement; he does not possess the intellectual means of mastering this feeling. Education deflects the intellectual capacities entirely away from the sexual theme; consequently, the trauma makes insurmountable intellectual demands. The child, therefore, must repress this excitement. It is very likely that enlightenment could countermand the effect of such traumata. The enlightenment, however, must not be given in an objective [detached] way, but the

[3] Later, Freud gave a somewhat different formulation of the significance of trauma in the development of neurosis: there is a complementary relationship between the etiological factors; that is, the stronger the trauma, the less need for a strong constitutional predisposition, and vice versa.

[4] See Minutes 31, footnote 1.

[5] Freud has nowhere stated precisely what he understood by "a certain amount of sexual freedom."

child must feel a certain—appropriate—degree of sexual excitement which one must not shun.

In spite of all precautions, however, one will succeed only in limiting the severity of neurosis, not in avoiding it altogether; for there are a number of individuals who, for constitutional reasons, react in different ways. Enlightenment can no doubt accomplish something, but it is no panacea.

ADLER emphasizes that he is more inclined to agree with those who are against the systematic enlightenment of children. Enlightenment impedes the child's independent striving for making contact with the external world; the child's inquisitiveness, his craving for knowledge is stifled. The infantile traumata are of significance only in connection with the inferiority of organs. The traumata are not only sought out, but they result necessarily from the clash of the individual with the civilization into which he is born. The experiencing of traumata is often inherent in the character.

STEINER is surprised that so far no one has mentioned the usefulness of sexual traumata. Life provides us with no other enlightenment but that gained through traumata. Traumata do not really harm us. People have been stricken with an "enlightenment neurosis." The best enlightenment is that which occurs automatically as it does in rural areas.

STEKEL remarks that we do not know what a sexual trauma is: under certain circumstances an experience becomes a trauma; under others, it does not. Constitution has no bearing on this. The milieu is more important than constitution. The child inherits sexuality. He denies that it is possible to prepare a child psychologically for a trauma. Matters must be left to chance. One must not, however, instill in the child's mind concepts of sin and the like.

RANK tries to summarize the topic aphoristically: traumata are natural enlightenment. The enlightenment which is being demanded (the artificial one) is not to be recommended for many reasons: in the first place, the psychology of parents (or of other persons giving enlightenment) has to be taken into account; then the question arises what kind of people one would raise in this way, and it is most doubtful whether a comparison would turn out to be in favor of the "enlightened ones"; we suspect that enlightenment would destroy a superior endowment ("of a genius" as we understand this term). This new race of men would, moreover, be less vital and far more sober. This, however, is not meant to deny enlightenment any value. One should certainly be somewhat more cautious than one has been so far, and one should by all means try not to harm children; thereby they will benefit most.[6]

---

[6] The problem of the sexual enlightenment of children has not been solved to this day. Far more experiences have to be collected and scrutinized before a definitive answer can be given to this question.

35

SCIENTIFIC MEETING on *January 8, 1908*

Present: Federn, Heller, Hitschmann, Rank, Reitler, Sadger, Schwerdtner, Steiner, Stekel, Wittels, Prof. Freud.

COMMUNICATIONS

[A.] Deutsch and Heller pay 2 *Kronen* as a New Year's contribution. Hitschmann returns *Archiv* 21; Sadger, Minutes 8 and 22.

Dr. Rudolf Urbantschitsch accepted as a member upon unanimous vote of those present.

PRESENTATION

At the Border of Psychosis

SPEAKER: DR. STEKEL

STEKEL presents two cases of psychosis which are to be published in his book on anxiety hysteria.[1] In these cases, he has succeeded in seeing the reverse side of psychosis. The underlying factor is a love

---

[1] They appeared as Chapter 24 in *Nervöse Angstzustände und ihre Behandlung.* See Minutes 30 and 31.

motif linked with severe psychic conflicts which sets the whole illness in motion.

DISCUSSION

HITSCHMANN remarks that Stekel's discourse is a compilation of several papers which he has given before. At first, the psychic conflict was in the foreground everywhere; later again, everything was exquisitely sexual. The question arises whether there are not states which could primarily call forth a depressed mood. In Stekel's cases, the ensuing depression is out of proportion to the experiences. No probing analysis was carried out but rather a kind of suggestive therapy.

SADGER denies that any psychoanalytic elucidation has been given. Stekel has achieved his success with the benefit of his knowledge of the family relationships, which he acquired during the many years he was their family physician, and with the help of information about the patients which he obtained from other people. To solve such cases, something bearing some resemblance to psychoanalysis should be used. He has gained no new knowledge from the discourse—neither diagnostically nor therapeutically. Surely, much can be traced back to childhood: in her psychosis, the patient merely carries out what she did not dare to do earlier (for instance, beating her mother).

Something very specific probably caused the typical symptoms of melancholia (impoverishment, etc.), as Hitschmann already indicated in his reference to the monotony of the psychotic picture.

RANK doubts that the psychic conflicts which were uncovered are sufficient to cause the outbreak of a psychosis, as Stekel seems to think. The effect of interpretations given in the form described by Stekel is likewise questionable. To say a thing directly to a patient's face cannot really have a profound effect.

FEDERN replies to Rank that psychic conflicts of such gravity do indeed suffice to make a person neurotic. The effect of direct interpretation is evident in the [patient's] crying to which Stekel referred. The crying must be considered a powerful abreaction. The typical complaint, "I am a poor woman," etc., is transferred from the psychic onto the material sphere; poor woman equals unhappy woman.

The neuroses developing in individuals after they have, to the point of exhaustion, nursed a sick person are not always caused by a death wish and the defense against it, as Stekel believes. We do not yet know to what extent affects have a toxic effect (hounded animals taste better).

It is of value to demonstrate, as Stekel has done, that some people react to such intense affects with a psychosis.

WITTELS is inclined to link the typical symptoms of fear of impoverishment—particularly frequent in female melancholics—with the peculiar role which possessions [*Eigentum*] play in the sexual life of women. It seems that a wish is hidden behind this symptom. Such women, when they were still well, may have understood that the restriction of their sexuality had to do with property. In the psychosis this is expressed by an opposite wish.

SCHWERDTNER believes that Stekel, who as family physician could gain such insight into these cases, has made a valuable contribution since we know so little about psychoses. He, too, in contrast to Rank, must emphasize the significance of psychic conflicts. He feels that they may be important in all psychoses. The brain, weakened by toxins, and hence less capable of resistance even in the face of normal affects, no longer has the power of resistance necessary for equilibrium.

PROF. FREUD, after a few tangential remarks, first calls attention to the fact that the morbid phenomena in Stekel's cases are proportionate to the patients' life experiences.

One must contradict the assertion that the neuroses which follow after the nursing of a patient (nursing-neuroses) always involve a repressed death wish. In many cases, another solution is found: especially in those cases where a daughter nurses her father (as in the case published in the *Studies*[2]) the problem centers on the temptation to see the patient nude (scoptophilia). When a brother has been nursed by his sister, the mourning of his death is often mingled with a feeling of regret: what a pity that the beautiful penis is buried with him. In accord with this tendency, there exists an ancient custom among Japanese, where the widow keeps the embalmed penis of her husband.

Stekel should be defended against the reproach that he has dis-

[2] Breuer and Freud: *Studies on Hysteria* (1895). *S.E.*, 2.

278

regarded the organic (somatic) factor. We just leave this factor aside in our discussions when we are investigating psychological factors. Stekel wanted to show the psychological background of the psychosis. Of course, this alone does not produce the psychosis.

Hitschmann's reference to the uniform [*einheitliche*][3] picture of the psychoses and its specific causes can be dispensed with by a comparison with the neuroses, which are likewise poor in variety of manifestations but rich in psychic motivations.

Stekel was right to examine first the individual's attitude toward real conditions. Then there still remains the great realm of fantasy, and finally the entire pathological factor.

Fear of impoverishment is a highly complicated symptom: at the core of melancholia, there is a lack of freely disposable libido. In this sense, the patients are right when they characterize themselves as poor; that is, poor in libido.

The classical description of all melancholics shows that they are indifferent to everything, that they can no longer care for anyone.[4] Similar explanations can be found for other stereotypes.

He wants to suggest to Stekel that he should not include these cases which are exquisite psychoses in the book on anxiety hysteria.

Stekel should be reproached on two accounts: his presentation was incorrect, and he has jumbled everything together. In this respect one must agree with Hitschmann's criticism and his demands for precise information about the certainty of the solution found.

The objection that no analysis was carried out in these cases raises the question of the technique of dealing wth psychoses. The technique practiced until now cannot be applied here. We cannot learn anything from the psychoses; we can only apply what we have learned and what we know from our experience. We should endeavor to collect enough experience so that, when we have been told about a patient, we are able to have a clear notion of his complexes and experiences. In the

---

[3] This is probably an error. Freud refers to the same remarks which Sadger mentioned before: *"einförmig"* ["monotonous, uniform"].

[4] Later, Freud ascribed a broader base to the pathological conflict in melancholia. He saw the source of the inhibition, the feeling of guilt, and the ego impoverishment in a detachment of the libido from the ambivalently loved object and in an identification with it. See the discussion of suicide in Minutes 104 (Vol. II) and "Mourning and Melancholia" (1917). *S.E.*, 14.

psychoses, we have to confront the patient with this directly after a while.[5]

It is also necessary—and Stekel neglected to do so—to investigate the psychic mechanism. In the first case, Stekel has not taken into account at all that repression is the necessary precondition of compulsion. When studying the life circumstances of the psychotic, one must emphasize the equivalence, even pre-eminence of fantasy.[6] It appears certain that in both cases, the psychosis was connected with the flare-up of libido before the menopause.[7]

STEKEL, in conclusion, says that he is horrified at the lack of understanding which he has encountered tonight. It is not his fault that he could not discover more about this case. He also must refute Rank's doubts.

[5] These are important hints for the technique applicable in the treatment of psychoses. In one of the following meetings, Freud becomes more explicit.

[6] Already at that time Freud had some idea of the fact that in the psychoses the id overpowers the ego.

[7] This sentence too was confirmed by later observations to the effect that there is an immense increase of libido immediately before the onset of acute illness (see Freud, "Psycho-analytic Notes on an Autobiographical Account of a Case of Paranoia (Dementia Paranoides)" [The Schreber Case] (1911). *S.E.*, 12:3-82; and Nunberg, "The Course of the Libidinal Conflict in a Case of Schizophrenia" (1921). *Practice and Theory of Psychoanalysis.* New York: International Universities Press, 2nd ed., 1961.

36

SCIENTIFIC MEETING *on January 15, 1908*

Present: Freud, Adler (at about 11 o'clock), Federn, Graf, Häutler, Heller, Hitschmann, Rank, Reitler, Sadger, Schwerdtner, Steiner, Stekel, Urbantschitsch, Wittels.

PRESENTATION

My Developmental Years Until Marriage

SPEAKER: DR. URBANTSCHITSCH

With the help of notes from his diary, the speaker describes his sexual development up to the time of his marriage.

DISCUSSION

STEKEL first thanks the speaker for his frank discussions. He considers them especially valuable because they freely offer us what we must extract from neurotics with great effort. Furthermore, the arguments confirm his own views concerning the harmlessness of masturbation. It is only the *struggle against* masturbation and the delusional ideas connected with it which are injurious. The sense of guilt over masturbation is at the core of most neuroses. The speaker has recovered through masturbation.

His account also demonstrates how far repression can go. The speaker has repressed his sexual knowledge, as young neurotic women often do; hence his long-lasting ignorance of sexual matters.

The speaker was from the beginning of a highly erotic nature. This erotism was probably awakened by his mother's tempestuous affection. Because he was such an intensive thumb sucker, he was later inclined to fellatio.

HÄUTLER stresses that it is characteristic of the speaker that he can, with such ease, abandon some sources of his pleasure (i.e., exchange them for others). This capacity actually is proof of his health and indicates a great latent energy.

As a solution to the first scene which he remembers—that with the governess and his father who wanted to take him to his mother—Häutler suspects that the speaker was jealous of the father.

The speaker has taken little notice of the cultural aspect of homosexuality. It would be of particular interest to study the effect of the erotic drives on artistic activity. It could also be worth while to know whether his religious phase had arisen from want, need, depression, or had proceeded from exuberance.

PROF. FREUD says that the speaker's desire to learn something new about himself in return for his gift can be fulfilled only to a small extent. He can set him right on one point on which his memory deceives him: his mother was hysterical.[1]

One may assume that the speaker was one of those children who loved father and mother equally; this influence is obvious in his later life. From the beginning there is a rather equal cathexis of the male and the female sex object.

Without an analysis, it is impossible to elucidate the childhood memories; for these memories are incorrectly focused by the individual himself.

One point can be elucidated: one may assume that with the onset of puberty as described by Urbantschitsch (in his eleventh year),

[1] Dr. Urbantschitsch came from a prominent, well-known, aristocratic Viennese family (See Minutes 4, footnote 2).

the sensuality, setting in anew, cathects the same paths which it had taken previously. Its first goal now is exhibitionism in front of women, and only later in front of men. This is a repetition of undressing in front of mother and governess in early childhood. Every subsequent strong homosexual impulse is preceded by a period of very intense affection for a woman. Generally valid: if an individual shows an abnormal propensity for one sex, we find behind it an earlier and forcefully overcome tendency to the opposite sex.

In the speaker's first period of sexual development, one can recognize some repression concerning love for a woman. His account clearly demonstrates what harm may ensue from lack of sexual enlightenment.

It should also be mentioned that in aristocratic circles young people are allowed much greater freedom in their sexual activity. In this way, one avoids many occasions for repression. Contrary to Stekel's opinion, Freud is by no means convinced of the harmlessness of masturbation.

The speaker's fantasy, from his seventeenth year—to get a child from his [male] friend—is clearly a feminine trait. This demonstrates to what extent a man is capable of sensing what a woman feels, and vice versa. A number of hysterical symptoms (especially in men) cannot be understood without taking this factor into account; the bisexuality of hysterical symptoms is of great significance.[2]

HITSCHMANN emphasizes that it is of great interest to know what has become of a man with such a history.

The speaker's history is completely devoid of preoccupation with "philosophical problems"—an absence which is striking; nothing becomes a problem to him. This may account for his lack of interest in theoretical issues. It is also noteworthy that the abundance of sexual traumata has had no neurotic consequences.

The detrimental effect of masturbation refers in this case only to the somatic sphere. Masturbation was always performed by others; consequently absence of an external object plays hardly any role in this case.

This history shows again that the early development of an Aryan differs from that of a Jew.

He married his first romantic love, and not his first sexual love.

[2] See Freud: "Some General Remarks on Hysterical Attacks" (1909). *S.E.*, 9:227-234.

SCHWERDTNER remarks that it is most interesting to hear for once the clinical history of a healthy individual.

The temporary predominance of the homosexual component may perhaps have been merely an accidental phenomenon, called forth by the frequent company of young men.

HELLER stresses the harmfulness of masturbation which he has observed in his own developmental years. Whenever the speaker inserted the remark, "This has been asexual," he [Heller] could recognize a strong erotic inclination. It seems strange that for such a long time the speaker felt no need to seek enlightenment.

SADGER was struck by the uninhibited practice of all sexual perversions. The childhood theft of chocolate has a sexual source (chocolate often has the meaning of feces).

His piety developed out of homosexual love for a priest.

It is a question whether the speaker is really quite as healthy as has been asserted.

The different development of Semites is connected with their overvaluation of family life.

GRAF thinks that it would be desirable to supplement this paper in some respects; for instance, by a psychoanalytic treatment of this life history.

On the basis of this history, one would have to assume that the speaker is severely hysterical. The amount of repression, the flight from women, and other matters indicate this.

(HELLER interjects the remark that repression has *succeeded* here.)

PROF. FREUD confirms this and adds: in this case, repression encounters no obstacles; there are no traumata, and therefore he *must* remain healthy. The demands of theory are here fulfilled in a classical manner.[3]

FEDERN describes the case of a male voyeur who, throughout his life, felt pleasure only when women were undressing in front of him; the reason was a fixation to his mother.

Today we have seen a classical example of the way in which an individual with all kinds of strong sexual Anlagen becomes, of necessity,

[3] This means repression has been successful, and therefore no neurosis develops.

a normal being—because two conditions of abnormality are not present: he had a strong sense of shame which was sufficient to cause him to repress for so long. Furthermore, through other activities, he mastered his sexual drives which could have become harmful. All along, Sadger spoke of perversions: these are not perversions but developmental inhibitions.

STEINER calls attention to heredity, that is, to the good family background of the speaker. His feminine character shows everywhere in his pleasure in passive pursuits. His sexual activity is normal, adapted to his character.

RANK expresses his admiration for the speaker's frank and instructive confessions. The long-lasting and persistent sexual ignorance is remarkable. However, in contrast to Stekel, he would view this ignorance not as a repression of what was once perceived, but as a not-wanting-to-receive what was offered, that is, as a warding-off (a kind of negative hallucination).

URBANTSCHITSCH objects to the reference to his "homosexuality" and perversions. In his opinion, as long as one is still sexually immature, it is all the same whether one is sexually active with a man or with a woman.

Sucking did not lead him to fellatio, since he was passive in this.

He has always loved his mother more than his father.

He is alternatingly sadist and masochist. He has a kind of psychic sadism.

37

SCIENTIFIC MEETING *on January 22, 1908*

Present: Freud, Adler, Bass, Federn, Graf, Hitschmann, Hollerung, Rank, Sadger, Steiner, Urbantschitsch, Wittels.

COMMUNICATIONS

Adler requests a week's postponement of his paper, "A Contribution to the Problem of Paranoia," which was to be given today.

GENERAL DISCUSSION

A general discussion on various topics fills the evening.

DR. WITTELS reads a pamphlet on Viennese psychiatrists, entitled, *The Normal Psychiatrist*. PROF. FREUD summarizes the result of this discussion by asking the author to refrain from publishing it in its present form, at least for the time being.[1]

HITSCHMANN gives a short report on a case of coitus interruptus and its consequences in a woman.

[1] Apparently Wittels did not publish this article.

PROF. FREUD, referring to his lectures on the Beginning of a Case History,[2] relates two instructive solutions of symptoms from the further course of the treatment of this compulsive neurotic. He adds a few general remarks on obsessional neurosis:

In obsessional neurosis displacement occurs in a different way from that in hysteria: it is a displacement toward generalization.[3] Whereas in hysteria one must ask: "When was this real?" in an obsessional neurosis one must ask: "When was this specific?"

In the obsessional neurotic, excessive tenderness is combined with hate; these two currents within him must find release either simultaneously or alternately.[4]

The first of the two solutions [of the symptoms] concerned the meaning of the pince-nez [*Zwicker*] in the whole story. It followed from the word displacement: *Zwicker-Kneifer*[5] (reproach that he has bolted [*ausgekniffen*], he is a *Kneifer*).

The second solution, hinging on the key word "Dick," referred to the connection between his desire not to be stout [*dick*] and his jealousy of his rival whose name was "Dick."

---

[2] Compare Minutes 28.

[3] It is due to this particular disguising technique that the clinical picture of an obsessional neurosis is, at first, so confusing.

[4] The excessive tenderness overcompensates for the hate, which again contributes to the confusion of the clinical picture.

[5] *Zwicker* has a double meaning: pince-nez (eyeglasses) and pincher; to pinch [*kneifen*] has also the meaning of evading or running away from something.

38

SCIENTIFIC MEETING on *January 29, 1908*

Present: Freud, Adler, Federn, Hitschmann, Rank, Reitler, Sadger, Steiner, Stekel, Wittels.

COMMUNICATIONS

Prof. Freud reports on the plans for the first Congress to be held in Salzburg.

Dr. Wittels proposes Dr. Albert Joachim, Director of a mental institution in Rekawinkel,[1] as a member.

Urbantschitsch, Schwerdtner, Heller ask to be excused.

Wittels borrows *Archiv* 14. Stekel returns No. 24.

PRESENTATION

A Contribution to the Problem of Paranoia

SPEAKER: DR. ADLER

ADLER uses as his starting point a short analysis which was not carried out continuously and which was broken off too soon. He raises several issues for discussion.

[1] Rekawinkel is a village near Vienna.

Setting aside Jung's work on dementia praecox[2] and Freud's well-known arguments, he discusses the significance of trauma in connection with Bleuler's work on affectivity and paranoia.[3]

It is important, first of all, to pursue that manifestation which expresses itself in the character Anlage. Another task is that of investigating the way in which repression makes itself felt in paranoia and how it is undone during the attack [Anfall] (the entire paranoia is actually one continuous attack).[4]

He then gives a résumé of the course of repression in obsessional neurosis, hysteria, and paranoia, laying special stress on the intimate relationship between repression and fear (anxiety):

The attack in *obsessional neurosis* is an occasional one and is precipitated by a particular event. On that occasion the repressed character Anlage breaks through and expresses itself either in the attack or in fear or both. The obsessional neurotic manages the attack within himself, as it were.

In *hysteria*, repression manifests itself in essentially a similar way. Here, too, in the attack we are confronted with the expression of a repressed drive (character Anlage) or else with the expression of repression linked with fear. The hysteric discharges his attack onto the outside world.

In *paranoia*, the repression of the character Anlage goes extremely far. The character Anlage manifests itself mostly in the form of its opposite, or it manifests itself—and this is characteristic of paranoia—in a highly sublimated form (politician, artist).

The lifting [Aufhebung] of repression may be preceded for some time by fear.

In obsessional neurosis, the greatest amount of fear is present.

In hysteria, the attack replaces fear.

In paranoia, repression is lifted so completely that the paranoiac is spared fear. The paranoiac expresses his delusional ideas without any particular fear. This circumstance is of great significance for the understanding of paranoia. The paranoiac succeeds in having his

2 See Minutes 12.
3 Eugen Bleuler, *Affectivity, Suggestibility, Paranoia* (1906). Utica, N.Y.: State Hospitals Press, 1912.
4 It is impossible to understand what Adler wanted to say.

drives (character Anlage) break through by changing his environment. (FREUD: he projects his unconscious impulses outward.[5]) This explains his delusional ideas as well as the illusions (which play a prominent role in paranoia) and hallucinations. (Adler here does not examine the question raised by many authors of whether the hallucinations or the delusional ideas are the primary factor.)

He then discusses the sexual root of paranoia, that is, the unconscious sexual impulses which are connected with other primary character Anlagen of the individual. He is inclined to believe that the difference between the three neuroses is dependent upon the interaction of the various character dispositions, the sexual Anlage included, and on their fusions.[6]

Having presented these theoretical formulations, he proceeds with the case history.

The patient (thirty-two years of age) came to him complaining that somebody has had someone spying on him.

From his history: a few months earlier, he had left his father's business after the latter had accused him of theft. He describes his father as a contentious, quarrelsome man who had become so obnoxious to the patient's mother that she left him.

Shortly before that, a friend had snatched away from him a woman with whom he had a platonic relationship.

He could not say who is having him spied upon, but he suspects that it is the mistress of his sixty-six-year-old father.

He began to masturbate rather late (only at the age of twenty-two) and then had intercourse with prostitutes which disgusted him. He was able to perform coitus only when the prostitute was dressed; otherwise he feared that he would be nauseated. At times, intercourse was unsuccessful—ejaculatio praecox; he has had no sexual intercourse for months now.

Later, he blamed everything on the Social-Democratic representative [in the Austrian Parliament], Pernerstorfer, the literary editor of the

[5] This correction by Freud is a very important one: the paranoiac projects.

[6] It is necessary to point out that Adler confuses character disposition with instinctual disposition. The difficulty in understanding Adler seems to result from his inadequate grasp of the concept of repression and from his confusing the repressed with the repressing agent. The neurosis does not develop as a consequence of repression. It develops if the repressed threatens to break through. The repressed is not the character disposition but the instinct—the id. Character traits belong to the ego.

Arbeiter Zeitung. According to the patient, he misuses the patient's writings and has someone spy on him; he is the sole source of the patient's misfortunes.

Adler drew the patient's attention to the fact that he, a freethinker, behaved like a believer, who also attributes everything that happens to him to a single being.

Adler then briefly mentions the analyses of the patient's dreams. The first dream, a wet dream (a prostitute takes his penis in her hand and he ejaculates), led to the recovery of a childhood memory. At a party which he attended when he was seven years old, a man fussed with his trousers near his penis. In both instances one important element is in the foreground: touching the genitals with the hand.

The last session brought out a dream which dealt with exhibitionistic desires; looking at a nude female body ("the autumnal mood" in the dream points to an older person). He also sees a troup of soldiers with French caps: to become a soldier is associated with the wish for a freer sexual life.

Adler will refrain from any attempt to bring this scanty material into accord with the problems stated at the beginning, and will briefly touch only on the most important problem.

In paranoia, it is primarily the exhibitionistic drive which has been suppressed. The delusional ideas of the paranoiac (particularly the delusion of being noticed but also the ideas of persecution and megalomania) can be traced back to exhibitionistic impulses. Paranoia, in its consolidation, requires the exhibitionistic drive as its mainstay. The ideas of persecution go back to repressed exhibitionism.[7]* The patient rids himself of the repression and sets his instinct free by way of a new interpretation of the outside world.** In his delusional ideas he is the object which can be seen by everybody. In the delusions of being heard and of hearing, similar matters are involved. From this it follows that in paranoia we are dealing with a psychic superstructure of the organs of seeing and hearing,*** of the "inferiority" of these two

---

[7] In the original protocol, insertions are penciled in at the places which we have marked with asterisks. The following are the insertions:

* which is being released

** in which he brings to the fore mainly what is of interest to exhibitionism.

*** which has become defective.

This protocol is the only one which shows Adler's name (and address) on the first page; it was probably sent to him for correction.

organs. He has often observed in paranoiacs: occasional blinking, high degree of myopia, and unequal refraction in the two eyes.

The emphasis on exhibitionism in paranoia does not imply any negation of the importance of the other components of the sexual instinct, particularly that of sadism.

DISCUSSION

HITSCHMANN considers the topic too difficult and too remote, especially the theoretical part, to enter into a detailed discussion on the spur of the moment.

As far as the case itself is concerned, he misses those traits which he has learned to consider characteristic of paranoia. Nowhere does the patient go beyond neurasthenic delusions of being noticed. There is no delusional system in this case.

Furthermore, information from the patient's relatives is lacking. For an insane person can be judged only by what the people around him say about him.[8]

SADGER raises the point that ideas of reference, persecution mania, and megalomania are also encountered in the analyses of hysterics and in normal people. This is, for example, true of Goethe (in *Dichtung und Wahrheit*) in whom the first ideas of reference appear with the first sexual experiences. Furthermore, after a fight with his playmates, he insisted on eavesdropping when they were whispering and learned that he was believed not to be the son of his father. He then thought that he was the child of a prince.[9]

The only thing, then, which is characteristic of paranoia is the fixation and incorrigibility of the delusional idea. Adler has failed to give any explanation of these factors.

It is doubtful whether a recent trauma plays such an important role as Bleuler, and, following him, Adler seem to think. It is not true that

[8] This is a valid remark, for the schizophrenic is, indeed, highly narcissistic, and hence it is very difficult to influence him. Therefore one has to endeavor to learn as much as possible from his environment, as one does in the treatment of children. In this way, as well as through long and careful observation, one can sometimes establish contact with the patient at some point and even form a relationship with him. The modern therapy of schizophrenia attempts to make use of these conditions.

[9] Here we find the idea of the "family romance" which Freud elaborated in 1909 in Rank's book *The Myth of the Birth of a Hero*. Compare footnote 10, Minutes 3.

the paranoiac is spared fear; paranoiacs commit the most hideous crimes which they would not do if they had no fear.

In dementia paranoides, the affect is missing as Adler has described.

Also, Adler has failed to elucidate the circumstance that the patient can have intercourse with prostitutes only if they are dressed.

It is striking that the father accused the patient of theft, and that the patient in turn accuses the editor of the same offense: perhaps a homosexual transference from the father has taken place.

His predilection for small children and his fear of them are probably connected with his relationship with younger sisters.

The prostitute who in the dream holds his penis in her hand most likely takes the place of the mother in an infantile scene. He probably wanted to take his father's place with his mother. The usual ideas of grandeur generally go back to the father.

The theoretical arguments are not substantiated by what has been presented. The delusional ideas need not have an exhibitionistic basis; and the assumption of a psychic superstructure for the organs of seeing and hearing is not justified.

RANK first comments on the statement that the paranoiac is more interested and active in artistic endeavors [than in other fields]. He thinks this would apply rather to those with a hysteric disposition; for, quite apart from other, deeper causes, the paranoiac soon loses the capacity to fulfill the aesthetic demands.

The identification of Pernerstorfer with the patient's father is quite evident, and the patient was so greatly impressed by the explanation concerning the belief in God because this identification goes much further (God = father, etc.). The relationship to his mother is also indicated.

If paranoia, a continuous attack, is rooted mainly in exhibitionism, then the hysterical (temporary) attack is, after all, also nothing but showing oneself, exhibiting oneself.

It is noteworthy that there are so many "normal" traits in this as well as in other case histories.

FEDERN apologizes for his fragmentary remarks by referring to his scanty knowledge of paranoia. The various criticisms raised in the discussion are misdirected, since Adler intended merely to indicate a general train of thought. Paranoia is a particularly egocentric illness and everyone with an excess of self-consciousness has an exhibitionistic past.

Adler's remarks concerning the relationship between exhibitionism and paranoia are very plausible. The paranoiac's insufficiency of intelligence would seem to be in accord with Adler's superstructure theory since the external world is indeed absorbed through the eye and the ear.

PROF. FREUD regrets that he must restrain himself in regard to discussing the most important point, the problem of the choice of neurosis, since he has come close to the solution of this problem and does not want to anticipate a later communication by giving either too extensive or too incomplete indications.

In order to obviate any misunderstandings, it seems useful to speak of "anxiety" (which has no object) rather than of "fear" (which always has an object). Adler probably meant anxiety.

The question whether hallucinations or delusional ideas are primary becomes irrelevant with the introduction of the unconscious. The authors [writing about this topic] took into account only that which first enters consciousness, whereas each emerges from the whole process without any relation to the other; at one time, hallucinations appear first; at another, the delusional ideas.

One is just as little the cause of the other as the dream, for instance, is the cause of a psychosis. The dream is, of course, merely a manifestation of the whole process.

Adler has contributed something new in two points:

1. the observation that the paranoiac does not develop anxiety, which is in fact an important characteristic of paranoia. But this is characteristic only of pure, chronic paranoia. Adler must, however, be contradicted in one detail: the most intense anxiety states are not found in the obsessional neurosis, where the anxiety is to a great extent psychically bound; the greatest anxiety is found in hysteria.

The second metapsychological characteristic of paranoia is the mechanism of projection: the paranoiac "throws" his internal transformations outward. In this way first the illusions and then the memory distortions come about, as Adler has seen correctly.

Concerning the clinical history, the case can be interpreted in terms of a detachment of the homosexual affect from the father and its transference onto Pernerstorfer (Sadger).[10] The old "family romance," which is the core of all neuroses, expresses itself also in this case (the patient's suspicion that his father's mistress has someone spying on him, etc.).

2. The second important discovery is that ideas of reference are traced back to the scoptophilic instinct. In general, however, it is not feasible to explain the special character of neuroses by derivation from individual instincts.

In support of Adler's contention, Freud can cite his analysis of a paranoid patient whose ideas of reference were fed by exhibitionistic childhood memories. However, Adler seems to go too far when he connects also delusions of persecution and megalomania with exhibitionism. These forms merely appear in paranoia but they are not created by paranoia.[11]

In confirmation of the assertion that superstructures of the organ of seeing are involved here, he can mention the abnormal eye movement [Augenmimik] which he has observed in paranoiacs; however, he is inclined to consider them a manifestation of the secondarily changed innervation. (ADLER: Why just the eyes?)

One might also venture the suggestion that this patient might have had Napoleonic fantasies (the soldiers with French berets, revolution, the column, etc.).

Paranoia can be studied very well in nonmorbid cases. The reformer, as long as he is alone, is considered a paranoiac (lately Richard Wagner). The fact that he has followers protects an individual against being declared ill. Thus, the founding of the Christian religion, for example, is a paranoia of twelve men (the vision of resurrection, etc.). Had the religion not found so many adherents, it would certainly have been judged a morbid fantasy of a few men.[12]

[10] It was only later, in 1911, that Freud formulated the homosexual basis of paranoia in his "Psycho-analytic Notes on an Autobiographical Account of a Case of Paranoia (Dementia Paranoides)." S.E., 12:3-82.

[11] Certainly, ideas of reference, megalomania, and persecution mania have different roots. The ideas of reference are a reaction to exhibitionism; megalomania is a reaction to the detachment of the libido from a love object and the absorption of this libido by the ego; persecution mania appears as a reaction to homosexuality.

[12] See Freud's "Obsessive Actions and Religious Practices" (1907). S.E., 9:115-127.

The recent trauma is indeed important (contradicting Sadger's remark); in this case it was the father's accusation.

STEKEL says that he has come with great expectations but goes away disappointed. In presenting his papers, Adler has the shortcoming of proceeding from abstractions which one cannot grasp at once. For this reason, Stekel cannot enter into a discussion of the theoretical theses.

Adler has taken a wrong course in the analysis: he has overlooked an intimate connection. The paranoiac's delusion represents a wish fulfillment; the paranoiac escapes into illness. Therefore, he has no anxiety. His ideas are to be understood symbolically.

Spy equals penis: he sees himself surrounded by penises and of this he need not be afraid. The soldiers (raised bayonet) mean the same.

Autumn in the dream represents the relationship to his mother; the incest ideas connected with her are evident.

The neurotic has two ways by which he can come closer to the mother:

(1) if he is not his father's son;

(2) if his mother is a harlot whom everyone (thus he too) can have.

A special liking for children is a special liking for the genitals.

Two powerful currents can be observed in the patient: the affection for his mother and the homosexual inclination toward the father. The whole delusion consists of the fact that the unconscious desire to have so many penises around him breaks through (homosexual component).

Neurotics are either very pious or atheistic. Rebellion against God and Emperor is rebellion against the father, which shows how deeply rooted in personal experience are political attitudes.

Rousseau, a paranoiac, was markedly masochistic in his youth. This circumstance is typical of persecution mania.

WITTELS confirms from his own experience that paranoiacs show no anxiety even when faced with the most horrifying things. A woman patient, for example, said with utmost calm that he would stab her with a dagger. The unconscious thought underlying this is, of course, scarcely apt to arouse anxiety in the patient. Another patient, on the other hand, reported with strong affect that everywhere people called after her "whore." (FREUD: There is affect here because there is no distortion.)

Exhibitionism is present in all psychoses. Hospitalized patients masturbate in front of their physicians.

The fact that Adler's patient acknowledged the displacement from the father speaks against the diagnosis of paranoia, for a paranoid patient does not accept corrections.

HITSCHMANN adds that defects of the eye and ear lead to great distrust (deaf people, for example, are very suspicious). Such matters, however, should be confirmed by thorough statistical studies.

Early in paranoia, the factor of disappointment plays an important role: disappointed ambition (as repressed character Anlage) in the man, disappointment in sexuality in the woman.

ADLER, in his concluding remarks, first replies to Wittels by saying that paranoiacs do make corrections in the beginning and also at the end. One can speak of incorrigibility only if one excludes psychoanalytic considerations; and this also raises the question of the curability of paranoia. In his opinion, the answer does not have to be a negative one.

It is self-evident that exhibitionism is present in all neuroses and psychoses; what else should break through but the primary Anlagen?

He then refutes briefly Stekel's remarks and thanks Federn for sharing his viewpoint. Some of the interpretations suggested are correct, many of them are probable; but some have no foundation whatsoever.

Finally, he briefly summarizes his aims in giving this paper:

(1) to demonstrate the significance of exhibitionism and of the psychic superstructure of eye and ear in paranoia;

(2) to show the type of repression which the paranoiac performs in the preparanoid period and how this repression is lifted during the illness. That this requires a recent precipitating event cannot be denied.[13]

[13] It is only natural that the opinions on paranoia, a problem of which little was known at that time, were divergent. Nevertheless, these men had a vague idea of the hidden meaning of the schizophrenias and of their mechanisms. They divined much which has subsequently in part been confirmed, and in part been more precisely formulated. (See pertinent writings of Freud, Jung, Karl Landauer, Nunberg, M. Katan, and others.)

39

SCIENTIFIC MEETING, *on February 5, 1908*

Present: Freud, Adler, Bass, [A.] Deutsch, Federn, Graf, Heller, Hitschmann, Hollerung, Rank, Reitler, Sadger, Steiner, Stekel, Wittels, Urbantschitsch.

COMMUNICATIONS

Adler and Federn make motions and proposals concerning the reorganization of the meetings.
Archives borrowed: Wittels, No. 14; [A.] Deutsch, No. 30; Hitschmann, No. 24.
Urbantschitsch announces a report [no title given].
Federn announces: "Sexual Consciousness of Guilt."

[AGENDA]

1. *Motions Concerning Reorganization of the Meetings*

   DRS. ADLER AND FEDERN

2. *An Introductory Report on Sexual Anesthesia*

   DR. HITSCHMANN

MOTIONS CONCERNING REORGANIZATION OF THE MEETINGS

ADLER makes several proposals and motions for the reorganization of the Society meetings.

1. Abolition of the urn and, with it, the annulment of the obligation to speak: instead, a system of voluntary participation in the discussion.[1]

2. Papers should be read only every fortnight. The intermediary meetings should be devoted to a continuation of the discussion of the latest paper and to the communication of book reviews and reports. This proposal should facilitate a more thorough preparation and elaboration of the papers as well as a serious, entirely objective discussion. The discussion should be conducted in the following way: the speaker himself, or one of his colleagues, or the Professor should summarize for discussion the topic's most important problems.

3. When the names of new candidates for admission are proposed, balloting should be secret, and a majority of votes should be decisive.

FEDERN makes an additional motion:

4. The abolition of "intellectual communism." No idea may be used without the authorization of its author. Otherwise one would feel inhibited in freely discussing [one's views]. In addition, those who contribute something new could edit the protocol.[2]

These proposals are now open to debate.

STEKEL, after rejecting Federn's personal arguments, discusses the individual proposals.

ad 1. He agrees.

ad 2. He doubts whether interest in the discussion will remain active after a lapse of eight days. One should not make specific rules on this point. He believes that book reviews and reports are valuable.

---

[1] Until that time the members were under the obligation to speak. The "urn" contained slips of paper with the members' names and the persons whose names were drawn at random had to speak. Federn, commenting on this rule in later years, said that it was meant to keep a few members from monopolizing the discussion; it was also intended as an important measure of self-discipline. It did not have the desired result as many members preferred to leave the meetings early rather than to participate in the discussion.

[2] This measure was meant to reduce friction among the members who had accused each other of stealing ideas, of plagiarizing, etc.

ad 3. He approves of secret balloting. However, a simple majority should not decide, instead three negative votes should suffice for refusing admission.

HITSCHMANN

ad 1. He agrees, though choosing from the urn has a psychological attraction.

ad 2. He proposes the selection of co-speakers or reporters. Perhaps those who have prepared themselves should always speak first. There should be no more of these hasty departures after the paper [and before the discussion]. The discussion should be postponed only when it is necessary, but not regularly.

ad 3. He is in favor of reports and of secret balloting.

ad 4. Only a tactful procedure can regulate this matter.

SADGER

ad 1. He agrees. This would automatically do away with the early departure after the paper.

ad 2. He is against postponing discussions. If a sufficient number of reports or book reviews has been announced, then a whole evening should be devoted to them.

ad 3. No one should be proposed for membership who is not known to two or three of the members.

ad 4. Every paper which has not been explicitly declared available for everybody's use is to be considered protected.

5. He proposes the following motion: Personal invectives and attacks should immediately be suppressed by the Chairman who shall be given the authority to do so.[3]

WITTELS defends Stekel against the personal attacks which have been going too far. He himself is incapable of writing anything without using the Professor's ideas; he does not always give the source.

FEDERN seconds Motion 5, since he feels guilty in this respect.— The discussion of important topics should be carried over. Some older books could be included in the reviews. He had not meant to offend Stekel.

ad 3. He is in favor of the secret ballot and a two-third majority.

[3] Arguments, quarrels, dissensions became increasingly frequent until Adler, and later Stekel, resigned. "Henceforth we can work peacefully and undisturbed," Freud said when I [H.N.] met him for the first time immediately after Stekel's resignation.

[A.] DEUTSCH proposes another motion:

6. To facilitate better preparation two papers should always be announced simultaneously.

ad 3. Those proposed for membership should be invited on a designated day of each month, so that one can get acquainted with them.

BASS

ad 2. He is very much in favor of introducing book reviews.

ad 3. The sponsoring member should give the names of candidates for admission only to the Professor who then shall make their names known. One or two of the members should report on the person proposed for membership.

REITLER agrees with the proposals, except for 5, which he opposes.

SADGER replies:

ad 3. He does not consider such information sufficient for judging a person's character.

HELLER agrees with the last point. The sponsor should vouch for his candidate.

ad 4. This cannot be regulated by resolutions; it is a matter of personal tact. Moreover, such a resolution would restrict literary activities.

WITTELS moves to close the debate. Motion carried. The gentlemen who had announced their intention to speak are given leave to do so.

GRAF: These proposals to reorganize stem from a feeling of uneasiness. We no longer are the type of gathering we once were. Although we are still guests of the Professor, we are about to become an organization. Therefore, he suggests the following motion:

7. To move the meetings from the Professor's apartment to another place.

PROF. FREUD

ad 5. He is opposed. He finds it painful to reprimand anyone. If the situation is such that the gentlemen cannot stand each other, that no one expresses his true scientific opinion, etc., then he cannot help but close down [shop]. He has hoped—and is still hoping—that a

301

deeper psychological understanding would overcome the difficulties in personal contacts. He would make use of the authority offered to him in Motion 5 only when some people were disturbing the speaker by their conversation.

He hopes for a certain degree of seriousness and candor, and thanks the two sponsors of the motions for their frank approach to these painful topics.

8. Lastly, he moves that a committee be elected to work out the first three proposals which concern, after all, purely technical matters, and to have this committee summarize the proposals in a practical form and submit them at the next meeting.

However, the discussion concerning "intellectual communism" should be continued now, and therefore the closure of the debate should be repealed.

His own viewpoint on this question is exactly the same as it has always been. In his opinion, nothing essential is to be changed here. He completely shares Heller's views. Besides, each person might himself state how he wants his ideas dealt with. He personally waives all rights to any of his own remarks. [They are available for general use.][4]

Motion 8 is carried and a committee of five members is appointed: Adler, Federn, Graf, Hitschmann, and Wittels.

DEBATE ON "INTELLECTUAL COMMUNISM"

STEKEL feels that the protection of intellectual property is justified, though many of these ideas "are in the air." He himself has considered it his duty to spread the Professor's ideas; if in so doing he has occasionally slipped, he says a *pater peccavi*; it will not happen again; he will give up this type of journalism, and will try to avoid giving rise to friction.

After Federn has withdrawn his Motion 4, ADLER turns to this point and discusses it in detail. It was not the intention of his proposal to place every detail under supervision but rather to obviate restraint in the discussion. However, it was also his intention to prevent the "communism" in regard to the problems raised here and to their

---

[4] This is characteristic of Freud's true magnanimity.

solutions. This applies, of course, only to important topics which someone has chosen to work on.

URBANTSCHITSCH wants strict rules to be applied to new admissions. As far as "intellectual communism" is concerned, only personal tact can decide.

Adler's motion, on the abolition of "intellectual communism," as amended by Steiner, is then put to vote:
"Every intellectual property set forth in this circle may be used as long as it has not explicitly been claimed by the author as his property."
Carried unanimously.[5]
End of business meeting. Point 2 of the agenda:

PRESENTATION

On Sexual Anesthesia

SPEAKER: HITSCHMANN

In view of the fact that psychic impotence in the male has recently been discussed in this group,[6] the speaker will disregard anesthesia in the male and concentrate on anesthesia in the female.

One encounters different viewpoints already in regard to *definition:* some call anesthesia only the complete absence of any sexual sensation, of the libido, which cannot be restored to the individual. These cases are differentiated from those who have sexual feelings but no sensation during intercourse. Hitschmann will not make such distinctions.

Apparently there really are cases of anesthesia, which are frequently combined with aplasia of the genitals, and with stigmata of severe degeneration. Sexual anesthesia (complete lack of sensual pleasure during intercourse) occurs quite frequently (according to some statistics, it affects one third of all German women). These individuals, however, know sensual pleasure from other sources. This state, in view of its high incidence, is a physiological one. It is often corrected in the course of married life.

---

[5] Disputes on questions of priority took up much time and energy in this circle.
[6] Compare Minutes 26.

Aside from the first, the temporary form, there is

(2) an occasional form that involves psychic matters; the problem here is the type of man whom a woman needs.

In the third, the relative form, the fault lies with the man. She cannot achieve discharge with one man, whereas another man can satisfy her.

The speaker presents as evidence two cases from his experience and then refers briefly to the consequences of sexual anesthesia. Total anesthesia has no direct consequences.

Chrobak[7] has found complete anesthesia only in patients with inferior organs.

Increased sterility is one of the consequences (according to Kisch,[8] 38 per cent of all anesthetic women are sterile).

Partial anesthesia is said even to cause illnesses.

Another result is sexual neurasthenia, which occurs frequently in those who do experience sexual excitement but find no gratification; these individuals may also acquire anxiety neuroses (Freud).

Concerning the *psychological* picture of the anesthetic individuals, the truly anesthetic women have psychic abnormalities.

Others display strikingly altruistic behavior already as young girls. When they give themselves to a man, they do this only for his sake: they sacrifice themselves, as it were. They entertain numerous platonic friendships, and are always surrounded by a circle of friends, etc. (Rahel Varnhagen[9] may have belonged to this type.)

Other anesthetic women are driven to adultery when they find no satisfaction with their husbands. However, one can also readily understand that a woman who is anesthetic during intercourse turns to other types of sexual relationship.

The speaker then discusses the relationship between hysteria and

[7] Rudolf Chrobak (1834-1910) was the famous gynecologist at the University of Vienna whom Freud mentions in his "On the History of the Psychoanalytic Movement" (1914). *S.E.*, 14:3-66.

[8] E. Heinrich Kisch: *Das Geschlechtsleben des Weibes in physiologischer, pathologischer, und hygienischer Beziehung* [*The Sexual Life of Woman in Its Physiologic, Pathologic, and Hygienic Aspects*]. Vienna: Urban & Schwarzenberg, 1904; 2nd revised edition, 1907.

[9] Rahel Varnhagen (1771-1833) was the wife of a German statesman and writer. She became famous in her own right through her letters and on account of the influence she exerted on famous men of her time.

anesthesia. The latter is a psychically acquired state. Unsuccessful repression of sexual experiences is probably also *the cause of anesthesia* (as it is of hysteria). In addition to anatomical matters (by the way, anesthesia is as little connected with the ovaries as male libido is with the testicles), one must take into consideration other causative factors: "constitutional weakness of the genital zone" (Freud), and excessive masturbation of the clitoris (Freud: *Theory of Sexuality*). This leads to the assumption of a latency period during which, normally, every girl is probably anesthetic. Not local, but psychic factors are involved here, and among them the trauma of prohibition may also play a role. Prolonged love for the parents can also result in anesthesia (Freud), and so can a protracted period of engagement. Another factor is a preponderance of homosexual inclinations.

In regard to *prophylaxis and therapy*, sexual enlightenment is of great importance. Furthermore, that the man entering marriage is fully potent and that he proceeds gently and carefully. Absolute virginity is not the ideal condition.

The actual remedy consists in subjecting the clitoris to a certain amount of friction; then the woman should be helped to obtain gratification from other zones.

In certain cases, psychological treatment may be undertaken.

One might also mention that some primitive people try to excite the woman by means of stimulants (stimulating rings).

The report closes with the description of another case.

Summary of the main points for discussion:

1. Definition
2. Psychic picture
3. Consequences (in part, organic: sterility, etc.; then nervous: anxiety hysteria, etc.)
4. Causes
5. Prophylaxis and Therapy
6. Case material
7. Male anesthesia
8. Distinction between anesthesia which is due to purely organic causes and psychic anesthesia.

40

SCIENTIFIC MEETING on *February 12, 1908*

Present: Freud, Adler, Bass, [A.] Deutsch, Federn, Graf, Heller, Hitschmann, Rank, Reitler, Sadger, Schwerdtner, Steiner, Urbantschitsch, Wittels.
Dr. Joachim is admitted [as a member].

AGENDA
1. *Discussion on Sexual Anesthesia*
2. *Resolution Concerning the Organization of the Meetings*

DISCUSSION ON SEXUAL ANESTHESIA

ADLER first emphasizes that it is very difficult to talk about anesthesia without the benefit of sufficient experience gained from analyses. He himself has conducted only one such analysis; however, the patient did not come to him because of her anesthesia, but because of hysterical pains in the region of the liver. The analysis disclosed a vehement aversion to her husband. She was not anesthetic with her lover.

There are many women who are anesthetic but who have no suppressions and repressions worth mentioning. One might say they are anesthetic by conscious choice. Quite consciously they resist the man and his caresses. We are reminded of the popular belief, according to which anesthetic women do not love their husbands.

Great skepticism is in order concerning the second group mentioned by Hitschmann: those women who apparently love their husbands. Many women do not even know whether they do or do not love their husbands. (He has often seen that in the analysis of men.) These are probably the cases that can easily be seduced to adultery, in spite of love for the husband.

He does not know anything about the repressed material and therefore is not in a position to confirm Hitschmann's views, which he shares.

It would be of interest to investigate experiences of rape. Many anesthetic women, because of a sadistic impulse which was awakened at one time, remain anesthetic throughout their lives; however, as sometimes happens, these sadistic impulses may exhaust themselves if they have no nourishment, or if they are uprooted. (He mentions such a case.)

Psychoanalytic treatment of anesthesia is very successful if it is dealing with cases of this type or if the problem is intercourse with other men. But it can scarcely succeed if the fault lies with the man. This applies also to the men who are psychically impotent with their wives.

Women are only just beginning to lead their own independent lives, apart from their family, and to develop their characters; these tendencies may constitute a certain barrier to complete merging in intercourse. This circumstance may be the reason for the particularly high incidence of anesthesia in our time.[1]

[A.] DEUTSCH presents two cases; however, he cannot say anything conclusive about them. The first case is that of a woman who was anesthetic with her second husband.

The second case was that of a happily married woman who was temporarily anesthetic. After each menstrual period she was anesthetic for about two weeks. It was not possible to establish with certainty whether this was due to a fear of becoming pregnant, since she was

[1] Adler may rightly be considered the first pupil of Freud to attempt a correlation of psychoanalysis and the social sciences.

aware of the heightened chance of conceiving immediately after menstruating.

URBANTSCHITSCH regrets that he missed Hitschmann's report. In his opinion, a genuine anesthesia can occur only in the presence of abnormal physical changes. In that case it is permanent. All the others are only temporary. These occur when there is aversion. He cites the case of a prostitute who had sensations [was *"esthetic"*] only with her lover. A diversion of thoughts can also cause anesthesia (the case of a woman whose worries about the evening dress she wore while having intercourse made her anesthetic on this single occasion). It is well known that the fear of [having] children as well as the feeling of shame can cause anesthesia. Anesthesia after menstruation may be due to the dependence of pleasurable feelings on the moisture of the vagina.

FEDERN presents several cases from his rather extensive experience.

Certain cases of temporary anesthesia (for example, after menstruation) are connected with the periodicity of all life. This is a physiological problem which does not belong here.

From the Freudian standpoint, anesthesia is a central problem (similar to anxiety):

If a woman has reasons to turn away from sexuality, it may normally lead her to becoming an "old maid"; at the other end of this series, there is the entirely successful repression (the woman who is anesthetic "by conscious choice"—Adler). In between there is an immense number of intermediate stages: the conversions, all degrees of hysteria.

There is a second parallel series: as a result of the repression of the sexual instinct, all kinds of perversions appear.

Anesthesia in men is more unequivocal. In women, the individual lot plays a greater part. Such anesthesias caused by accidental factors or by fateful experiences can be cured by changing the external life conditions. The main cause of this "fate anesthesia" is the man's inability to satisfy the woman.

In regard to the rest of the cases, he concurs with Hitschmann's and Adler's arguments.

Strongly sadistic or Lesbian impulses can also cause anesthesia.

308

Parallelism between men and women: there are men who are sexually impotent, i.e., they have no ejaculation or orgasm; there are others who perform normal coition but are anesthetic. Correspondingly, there must be women who have sensations [are *"esthetic"*] but no orgasm, and others who have intercourse but feel nothing.

Supplement to Federn's case reports: a case where the man's penis was simply too short. Two women, who subsequently became permanently anesthetic, had been raped by the *beloved* man (one of them during her married life). Two sisters who were both permanently anesthetic.

SADGER doubts that there is such a state as absolute congenital anesthesia. One could easily find reasons for doubt in a number of historically famous persons, who are said to have been absolutely anesthetic: e.g., Newton, Kant, Leonardo, Goethe's sister. In most of them, early sexual repressions can be demonstrated. The only question is: how did these repressions come about? Perhaps a decreased sensitivity of the sexual sphere must be assumed. In the case of men, attention should be directed to certain professions: mathematicians, natural scientists, artists.

Acquired anesthesia may be general or partial; here again two groups can be distinguished: those who are anesthetic only in intercourse (most women can be aroused to sexual enjoyment by certain stimulations) and those who are anesthetic only with a certain person.

He then mentions several cases from his analytic practice: one woman rejected coitus probably because of a discharge stemming from infantile masturbation; then, three sisters who were anesthetic with men whom they loved.

In summary, he must emphasize: as long as a sufficient number of such cases has not been analyzed, the problem cannot be solved. There is no absolute anesthesia, but only a relative one; it can be partial, that is, only for intercourse, or, finally, only in relation to *one* particular individual.

FREUD says he has only a few short remarks to contribute to Hitschmann's careful and complete report.

Anesthesia is a symptom which occurs so frequently that one is bound to find a great variety of etiological causes. The problem merely cuts across the area of the neuroses; it is not identical with it. Not all anesthetic individuals are neurotic. For the time being, however, the final word cannot be said.[2]

Anesthesia in women should be regarded as essentially a product of civilization (otherwise it occurs infrequently), as a result of educational influences: due to the man[3] (inadequate sex objects) or directly as a consequence of education. A large number of anesthetic women have been brought up too well as young girls. The repression of sexuality has achieved not only its purpose, but far more than was intended. Anesthesia subsides in the course of years.

Another point of view refers to unfaithfulness. If one concedes sexual gratification to the woman, one must not exaggerate the demands for marital fidelity. Another way to avoid neurosis and to submit to the demands of civilization is character distortion [*Verderbung des Charakters*, literally, ruining, spoiling, one's character]. All oddities and queerness of people are substitutes for a neurosis. There are three ways among which a choice can be made: that of neurosis, that of transgressing the rules (infidelity, etc.), or that of virtue and queerness.[4] A large number of people choose this third path. Charming and attractive women acquire and sustain these qualities only in sexual freedom.

The psychic behavior of the anesthetic women: those who love their husbands and are anesthetic for other (physical) reasons are extremely demanding and needful [of proofs of love]; they constantly expect gallant acts and attentions, whereas the woman who is physically satisfied does not make such claims.

One should also distinguish degrees of anesthesia. Many are not anesthetic but do have certain sensations, which can be intensified. Complete anesthesia probably occurs very rarely. Some women do not know themselves whether or not they are anesthetic.[5]

[2] It seems that Freud had a biological factor in mind. See also footnote 5 below.

[3] Obviously, Rank went too far in condensing the discussion at this place. Therefore it is difficult to see what Freud really meant.

[4] In other words: the sexual demands can be dealt with either by unsuccessful sexual repression, that is, by neurosis; or by rebellion against the social rules (infidelity) ; or by feelings of guilt and character changes.

[5] Later Freud seems to have thought that women initially reject sexual intercourse as such. See: "The Taboo of Virginity (Contributions to the Psychology of Love III)" (1918). *S.E.*, 11:191-208.

Since anesthesia can be understood to mean only the absence of pleasurable sensations, the question arises whether a woman can feel sensual pleasure without discharge or have discharge without sensual pleasure.

Women with many lovers are anesthetic individuals who over and over again are in search of the man who can satisfy them.

Accidental influences should not be underrated: for instance, we know of no case of sexual anesthesia in female rulers.

Remarks about a case: three sisters, of whom one was a great hysteric, the other entirely healthy but a harlot [*Haderlump*], the third absolutely anesthetic.

Lastly, he would like to suggest that educational programs introduce a topic of instruction which flourished in Antiquity: the founding of an academy of love where the *ars amandi* would be taught.

BASS places particular emphasis on the important social etiology, which Adler had touched upon: anesthesia is an illness of the *bourgeoisie*, of the class whose choice of a husband is not directed by natural selection but by *social* and *economic* factors, where the girls are directly trained for repression and where virginity and—at least theoretically—monogamy are a strict requirement. The more liberal sexual customs of the peasant population result in a considerably lower percentage of anesthetic individuals.

The periodicity (Federn, [A.] Deutsch) of man and woman ought to coincide in the most favorable way possible.

Cases of patients with serious organic defects, surgical intervention, etc. (Urbantschitsch), do not belong here.

Force used in the wedding night and psychosexual traumata in particular (violation of sexual feelings, etc.) play a significant role.

Therapy should first of all be directed to the social aspect.

Case reports: five cases; a girl who later on became anesthetic did not use an opportunity to have intercourse; in a second case, the girl's overhearing of intercourse followed by continuous excessive masturbation led to anesthesia later in her married life. In another case, coitus interruptus had caused serious illness in both spouses, whereupon the woman, in order to prevent conception, anesthesized herself artificially and subsequently became genuinely anesthetic. Another woman loved

311

not her own child but his playmate. Love for the latter's father may have been behind it.

All these patients, with the exception of one, have children.

STEINER first introduces some general points of view: he draws a parallel between anesthesia and functional impotence in men and then applies his classification of the latter to anesthesia in women. According to this classification, there exists also a congenital and total anesthesia.

A physiological anesthesia is often found in recently married young women.

Anesthetic women frequently develop other [*sic!*] talents, especially musical ones. (RANK mentions Robert Schumann's wife[6] in this connection.)

The man who is sexually gratified, is the one who is most chaste.

Case reports: a case in which a sexual attack in childhood played a significant role; the case of a girl who warded off even the slightest physical contact with and advances by any man. (SADGER: Hysteria!)

The type of anesthesia which is acquired as a consequence of later influences will be most accessible to therapy, whereas anesthesia stemming from congenital factors will have the most unfavorable prognosis.

Many anesthesias which have been acquired later in life or are partial can be removed through normal stimulation.

REITLER wants to add only a few remarks to the very exhaustive discussion. He does not think that psychic impotence in men can be equated with anesthesia [in women]. One should focus more on bisexuality and on the analogous organs (penis equals clitoris). Total anesthesia is very rare; it is based on aplasia.

It is difficult to know whether women can have a discharge without sexual sensations. Men certainly can (with typical masturbation). Normal discharge is probably always accompanied by pleasurable sensations. Male anesthesia is frequently found in masturbators, who in intercourse miss the stronger excitation of masturbation.

As an illustration of anesthesia in licentious women, he reports a

[6] This example is completely inappropriate since the pianist Clara Schumann was a famous child prodigy.

case of anesthesia combined with aplasia of the clitoris; this woman demanded the most excessive sexual performances of her husband. The counterpart to this [type of case] is that where the man's penis is too short or [the man suffers from] ejaculatio praecox.

He mentions another case of a woman who had sensations [was *"esthetic"*] only when a man's penis was flaccid, a condition which stemmed from an infantile experience (attempt at intercourse with a younger brother).

HITSCHMANN, in his concluding words, stresses only that *stuprum* or brutality in the wedding night were mentioned comparatively frequently in the discussion.

As a therapeutic measure, physicians often recommend intercourse a tergo or in a lateral position, or intercourse with the woman on top.

Referring to Professor Freud's remark on the "queerness" of people, Hitschmann is sure that a great part of the nervous unrest of our times is attributable to the lack of sexual gratification (prohibition of having children).

According to Adler's contention that anesthetic women have difficulties in giving birth, it appears likely that anomalies (inferiorities) are involved (to which ADLER remarks that such anomalies can easily be found in the patients' families or in the patients themselves).

MEMORANDUM

The committee consisting of Drs. Adler, Hitschmann, Wittels, Federn, and Graf (the two last-named gentlemen did not show up), which was appointed at the meeting on February 5, 1908 for the purpose of formulating suggestions regarding changes in the proceedings discussed at that meeting, submits the following resolutions to the vote of all the members:

1. The urn [ballot box] is to be abolished; the obligation to speak is no longer in force; discussion takes place as is customary in other scientific organizations; that is, everyone speaks whenever and as often as he asks to be recognized; the chairman may speak at any time; the reporter is entitled to make concluding remarks, though he may renounce this prerogative.

313

Reasons: Unquestionably, several members—rather than staying away altogether—used to leave the meetings in a hurry immediately after the presentation of the paper, because they dreaded the obligation to speak. This is detrimental to the dignity and the work of the Society. Furthermore, the obligation to speak may easily tempt those who have nothing better to say to indulge in personal invectives. On the other hand, those who have something to say gain time for more detailed discussions and possibly for speaking several times.

II. Some evenings should be devoted specifically to reviews of books and articles. To this end, one should select a member who every Wednesday before the lecture will list, simply by authors and titles, the recent pertinent literature (books and periodicals). By relative majority, the membership chooses from this list the topics which it deems important enough for extensive review. Reviewers will volunteer on each occasion. The review evenings take place, on the one hand, according to the amount of literature accumulated, and, on the other, according to the number of papers announced; however, in principle, they should take place once a month.

At these meetings case material shall also be presented. It is superfluous to *justify* the need for such review evenings. The procedure indicated seemed to be most expedient. One of the gentlemen is selected to make the short weekly communications. Before each meeting, if possible, he should be advised of any new literature which may have escaped his notice. As a rule, he should list only authors and titles, and for this purpose should regularly look through a large medical journal, preferably the *Münchner medizinische Wochenschrift,* for references to the literature. Occasionally he may be in a position to indicate in a few words the contents of the papers. In the event that no one volunteers for a desired review, one will just have to forego it. Coercion shall not be exercised.

III. A paper must be announced at least two weeks before the date of delivery; members will then have at least a fortnight to prepare reports pertaining to the same topic. To help in the execution of this resolution as well as in continuously rounding out the program, the

314

secretary is to have an adviser who, in addition, shall organize the review evenings.

Reasons: It is the aim of this resolution to facilitate a more thorough preparation of speaker and discussants. In each year there are about twenty-five to thirty evenings available of which six or eight will be used for reviews; some papers together with their discussion require two or more evenings; there are now twenty members, each of whom should, in the opinion of this committee, give at least one paper a year; in view of these facts the yearly program can easily be filled. In regard to each member presenting a paper once a year, no special resolution was formulated because it was felt that the moral obligation as such carries sufficient weight.

IV. Whoever misses the meetings without excuse four times in succession is considered to have resigned.

The *reason* for this motion lies in the dignity of the Society and in its way of functioning.

V. New members shall be accepted according to the rules observed until now.

Reason: Having thoroughly considered all of the suggestions submitted, the committee has returned to the old procedure because it seems to be the simplest and least expensive one. Mistakes like those referred to in last week's discussion have so far done no harm to the Society; besides, no voting rules can completely obviate them. For several reasons the committee does not think it advisable to introduce, at the present moment, more stringent requirements for admission; particularly in view of the fact that this assembly is something in between a group invited by Professor Freud and a society; therefore, whoever is acceptable to the Professor must also be acceptable to the others. This motion of the committee is opposed by a separate proposal of Dr. Adler's which he himself will plead. He suggests monthly meetings in some other locality (perhaps a small auditorium at the University), to which all those who apply should be admitted if they have been approved by a two-third majority. From this group some could be selected for membership in the more intimate Wednesday circle by the voting procedure practiced until now.

In addition to these proposals, the committee expresses the following opinions of the assembly: a change of locale is, for historical reasons, not desirable. The place as well as the character of the meetings has become so dear to all the members, that they desire to make as few changes as possible.

It is impossible entirely to check through rules and regulations the "ill humor in the empire" which has lately arisen; however, it is to be hoped that the good intention alone will suffice to stifle all frictions in the future.[7]

With this in mind, the committee recommends that the five motions proposed be accepted without discussion and that all members of the Society be informed of this memorandum in writing.

CONCERNING THE ORGANIZATION OF THE MEETINGS

ad I: HITSCHMANN makes a minority motion to *retain* the "urn" [ballot box] but to do away with the obligation to speak; everyone whose name is drawn may refuse to speak. If a co-speaker has been announced, he speaks before other names have been drawn from the box.

After Wittels has spoken in favor of the abolishment of the urn and Heller for its retention, *Hitschmann's motion is carried.*

ad II: Upon Professor Freud's suggestion a three-member committee (Freud, Adler, Hitschmann) is chosen to work out the practical implementation of this motion. The reviews of the literature should be assigned to *one definite* person. In accordance with a modification by Freud, these reports shall be given once a month.

ad III: Dr. Hitschmann is chosen to supervise the arrangements of lectures ("The Whip").

ad IV: This motion is carried with a mitigating amendment by Prof. Freud: a member who has stayed away four times without an excuse will be asked whether he wishes to resign.

ad V: Motion carried.

[7] We do not know the cause of the "ill humor in the empire" ["*Reichsverdrossenheit*"] referred to in this resolution.

Adler's minority motion evokes a lively discussion. At the end, Adler withdraws his motion and recommends the acceptance of a proposal by Prof. Freud: the formation of a larger group shall take place entirely independently from the Wednesday circle and shall in no way affect the latter's composition or its method of working. Motion carried.

317

41

SCIENTIFIC MEETING on February 19, 1908

Present: Freud, Adler, Bass, [A.] Deutsch, Federn, Hitschmann, Hollerung, Rank, Reitler, Steiner, Sadger, Stekel, Wittels, Urbantschitsch, Joachim.
Stekel borrows *Archiv* No. 30.

PRESENTATION

The Nature of the Symbol[1]

SPEAKER: DR. JOACHIM

DISCUSSION

ADLER comments that the speaker considered the problem from a point of view to which we are not accustomed. He subordinates the other phenomena to the element of symbolism. As far as the origin of the symbol is concerned, Adler sides entirely with the speaker who has proceeded from the sensations and earliest activity of the organs, as he himself has done; he, too, has traced the prominent phenomena of psychic life back to the organs. Increased symbolic activity will be found with inferior organs, which are striving for a certain degree of perfection.[2]

[1] We know nothing of the contents of this paper.

[2] Scherner and others had long before asserted that organ sensations produce psychic symbols. (See Freud: Introduction to *The Interpretation of Dreams.*) It is interesting to pursue Adler's endeavor to reduce all of psychology to a single pattern.

The supposed "deception by the environment," which the speaker relates from his own experiences, may be based, as it is in similar cases, on intensified distrust, which also plays an important role in paranoia. In this instance, too, we must go back to the organ from which these phenomena arise: the eye. The hesitant speech of paranoiacs is likewise connected with this distrust. The "formulae" of paranoiacs are symbols in the Freudian sense; another meaning is hidden behind them.

Joachim's ideas about *déjà vu* can probably be confirmed (the feeling during a dream of having had the same dream before is a similar case). These are people who have a heightened presentiment, who have already thought through situations before encountering them. From here one can easily see a path leading to telepathy.

The "intensification of longing" is far more complicated. In such cases manifestations of repression may be involved.

The discourse on rhythm, etc., is, in Adler's opinion, a bit of literary extravagance.

He summarizes: he feels very much in accord with the arguments which approached, in a different way, processes demanding our attention every day.

FEDERN confines himself to criticism. On the whole, he denies that the paper offers anything significantly new and constructive in spite of a number of profound observations and the great amount of work invested. It was a mere repetition, in different words, of Freud's teaching. In the course of this, the term "symbol" has been arbitrarily expanded in its conceptual meaning. Symbol has been confounded with means of expression.

Symbolism comes into being only with language, and it is brought about by the impossibility of adequately reproducing the details of the outside world. Moreover, the multiple meaning of language determines the possibility of symbol formation.

The speaker's second mistake is that he always relates symbols to personality contents [*Persönlichkeitsinhalt*]. A great number of symbols refer to the interrelationship of two elements in the external world.

It is not feasible to connect paranoia exclusively with impotence.

He must contradict the speaker's remarks on rhythm: all of this is an expression of inner rhythm.

BASS adds, as a supplement, the meaning of the symbol as a wish. As a wish fulfillment, the symbol establishes harmony between the world of intellect and the world of affects, of feelings. Therefore he shares Federn's opinion that the formation of a symbol is possible only when the individual becomes aware of a certain discrepancy between thoughts and feelings, i.e., when he begins to repress. It is the symbol's task to release repressed material, to replace it by something of a harmless nature.

He then points to the role which symbols play in the life of [common] people; how in legends, myths, and sagas, the strong desires of common men[3] are symbolically fulfilled.

Another symbol-creating factor is the wish to communicate with the external world beyond what language can consciously convey. The symbol represents the bridge which spans the impossibility of exhaustively expressing the entire thought content in words. One could set up an equation: word is to thought as consciousness is to unconsciousness. Hence, the symbol is the better chosen the more contact it establishes between the unconscious of its creator and the unconscious of the recipient.

PROFESSOR FREUD says that it would have been more instructive to proceed from the individual case and in this way to arrive at a general formulation. It is an omission of the paper that it neglected to deal with the symbol which is a precipitate of historical development and plays an important role.

The symbolic meaning of numbers is of astral origin.

The childhood memory of Joachim's and the corresponding one related by Wittels, which refer to the deception by the external world (Kant's discovery of the thing-in-itself), can be analyzed in the following way as can all such judgments based on endopsychic perceptions:

(1) to reduce the general to the specific (obsessional neurosis);

(2) then this specific meaning is to be understood in a sexual sense.

When these rules are applied the phenomenon proves to be the

[3] The original has *Volksseele*, the soul of common men, the people's psyche.

child's reaction to the fable of the stork.—The sudden turning around is a technique which seems designed, as it were, for snatching a glimpse of a sexual occurrence.

The *déjà vu* in dreams indicates that the dreamer has experienced such a feeling in his waking life. (A region in the dream, where one has been once before, means the mother's genitals.) The explanation of *déjà vu* is contained in the second edition of the *Psychopathology of Everyday Life;* one has actually had this experience before, but in fantasy.

Adler's application of his theory to this case is very forced. Besides, our interest is focused on the way [in which something comes about, develops], not on the final goal.

The paranoiacs' hesitancy in speech is caused by the circumstance that, being in the process of reconstituting their entire ego, they recast their memories and transform the external world, because they are changing themselves.[4] Consequently they must also change their language; the paranoiac searches for words (his hesitating), because he behaves like a creator.[5] The core of paranoia is the detachment of the libido from the objects (a reverse course is taken by the collector who directs his surplus libido onto the inanimate object: love of things).

SADGER: Symbol formation is most pronounced in childhood, especially in that of future neurotics. Healthy people retain their unconscious symbolism in dreams. Conscious symbolism occurs only in hysteria and quite extensively in the obsessional neurosis. The symbol is chosen because sexual matters are objectionable, although, on the other hand, it offers an opportunity to indulge in sexual matters.

STEKEL, disregarding the abstract part of the paper, turns to its practical side: his own experiences do not confirm the assertion that the capacity to form symbols is diminished in melancholia. On the contrary, he can cite cases of melancholia where a symbolic idea dominated the picture. The same is true in paranoia.

---

[4] This idea already indicates the later formulation that a considerable part of the symptomatology of schizophrenia is an attempt to reconstruct the external world.

[5] See Freud's analysis of the Schreber case, "Psycho-analytic Notes on an Autobiographical Account of a Case of Paranoia (Dementia Paranoides)" (1911). *S.E.*, 12:3-82; also Nunberg "The Course of the Libidinal Conflict in a Case of Schizophrenia" (1921) and "The Synthetic Function of the Ego" (1931). *Practice and Theory of Psychoanalysis.* New York: International Universities Press, 1961.

In an earlier paper he had already made an attempt to explain the *déjà vu:* we experience a process unconsciously; if it suddenly becomes conscious to us at a later date, the unconsciously perceived image impresses us as something we have experienced before.

WITTELS, being the last discussant, tries to define the positions which the various members have taken toward the speaker; he finds that on the whole metaphysical considerations have predominantly been undervalued; in his opinion, Joachim's explanation is a felicitous continuation of the systems of Kant and Schopenhauer, and this method is the most sublime which human mental activity has produced.

JOACHIM, in his concluding remarks, first protests against Wittel's overestimation of him.

To Adler: Distrust is a symptom which is a result and not a cause. The same applies to the faculty of foreseeing [things].

To Federn: Language itself is full of symbolism and could not be formed if the technique of symbolism were not already developed.

Replying to Stekel, he stresses the different ways of understanding the concept of melancholia.

The problem concerning the relationship between symbol and language depends entirely on what is understood by symbol.

ADLER remarks that we owe the speaker more acknowledgment than Wittels gave him. Entirely in accordance with modern thinking, he has based his work on emotions; hence his achievement is not to be placed in the developmental line of metaphysics but in that of Avenarius and Mach.[6]

Adler then emphasizes once more that symbolism is connected with the inferior organ, which explains especially the type of symbol. In

[6] Richard Heinrich Ludwig Avenarius (1843-1896), German philosopher, professor of philosophy in Zurich. He was one of the chief proponents of the school of positivism. He tried to gain a natural concept of the world from the standpoint of "pure experience." Therefore he called his doctrine "empiriocriticism." All metaphysics is to be excluded; reality is to be comprehended as it is, still untouched by the contrast between somatic and psychic which developed only through "introjection." Avenarius aims particularly at describing the pervasive relationship of dependence between the individual and the world surrounding him. Biological and physiological points of view are in the foreground.

Ernst Mach (1838-1916), physicist and philosopher, professor of philosophy at the University of Vienna. According to Mach, it is the task of philosophy to unify the individual branches of knowledge; all insight is based solely on experience; he rejects any kind of metaphysics.

the same way, the question of how symbolism is connected with language is solved: someone who had difficulties in his language development will certainly look upon the symbolism of language as the only possible one.[7]

HITSCHMANN reports, according to the proposals of the committee, on the technical arrangement of the evenings devoted to reviews.

A number of German, and some French and English periodicals on nervous and mental diseases will be checked regularly, as well as psychological magazines and the *Zeitschrift für Sexualwissenschaft*.

Furthermore, it is planned to cultivate also related fields: the pedagogic, urologic-gynecologic, sociologic, philosophic, the field of *belles-lettres* with special attention to biographies and pathographies.

In addition, there will be reviews of books which will be suggested by all and then selected for reviews. Articles found in the periodicals can be reported by every one without special approval.

Case material should also be presented on these review evenings.

The *Archives* will be supplemented by a library, to be purchased with the help of a book fund.

The central committee for literature consists of the following gentlemen: Prof. Freud, Drs. Adler and Hitschmann.

There now follows the assignment of periodicals which should be perused, according to the various disciplines:

urologic-gynecologic literature	Steiner
pedagogic "	Adler
sociologic "	Adler, Bass
philosophic-psychologic "	Hitschmann, Joachim, Häutler
belles–lettres (biographies, etc.)	[A.] Deutsch, Sadger, Reitler, (Bach), Heller
scientific literature on sex	Urbantschitsch
French " " "	Stekel
English " " "	Federn

---

[7] Freud maintained that the problem of symbols is not a psychoanalytic problem. Psychoanalysis makes use of symbols for the interpretation of certain unconscious psychological processes.

42

SCIENTIFIC MEETING on *February 26, 1908*

Present: Freud, Adler, [A.] Deutsch, Federn, Heller, Rank, Steiner, Sadger, Schwerdtner, Stekel, Urbantschitsch, Joachim.

[A.] Deutsch returns *Archiv* No. 30.[1]

Hitschmann excused; announces through Federn a paper on "Neurasthenia As an Illness of the Blood Glands."

PRESENTATION

On the Significance of the Psychogalvanic Reflex[2]

SPEAKER: DR. URBANTSCHITSCH

The core of the topic which will be discussed and substantiated is contained in the following assertion:

1. If a human body is connected to a galvanic current equipped with a galvanometer, psychic processes within the subject can be inferred from the oscillations of the galvanometer.

---

[1] This is obviously an error. Stekel had borrowed *Archiv* No. 30. Minor mistakes like this occur frequently. As far as possible, we have investigated all the contradictions in the original and were able to clear up most of them (compare the Introduction).

[2] The manuscript of this paper is included in the original protocol. It is handwritten.

Féré[3] was the first person who investigated the influence of psychic processes on changes of electrical resistance. In 1904 the engineer E. K. Müller set up experiments on the changes of the body's conduction-resistance to galvanic current; through him Veraguth became acquainted with this phenomenon; he, in turn, called Jung's attention to it.[4] Jung then reported it to Binswanger.

At the present stage of our knowledge, the literature on this topic opens up perspectives in three different directions:

(1) the electrobiological;

(2) the neurological and neuroanatomical (in the strict meaning of the terms);

(3) the experimental-psychological one, which is of special importance for us.

I shall not spend much time on the first two fields because, despite an abundance of descriptive literature, the ridiculously thin eggshell of the problem has not yet been cracked.

1. *The Electrobiological Phenomena*

Two major unanswered questions dominate this field. The experimental subject is connected to a galvanic current; the current flows placidly through the body. Suddenly the galvanometer's needle jumps up; the subject has just thought of a past love; and gradually the needle falls, while he is thinking of his wife to whom he has been married for years.

What was it that actually caused the galvanic current to be intensified, while the real conveyor of the galvanic current, the galvanic element, remained constant? Are we dealing with changes of resistance in the human body or with variations in the electromotor force?

Although some authors (Semmel[5] and Fürstenau, 1905) have voiced the opinion that muscular contractions and the ensuing contact-

---

[3] Charles Samson Féré (1852-1907), assistant professor of neurology in Zurich.

[4] *Diagnostische Assoziationsstudien*, edited by C. G. Jung. Leipzig: Ambrosius Barth, 1906. In addition to the fundamental work by Jung and Bleuler, this series contained the following publications: L. Binswanger: "Über das Verhalten des psychogalvanischen Phänomens beim Assoziationsexperiment" ["The Reaction of the Psychogalvanic Phenomenon in the Association Experiment"]; and H. Nunberg: "Über körperliche Begleiterscheinungen assoziativer Vorgänge" ["Physical Phenomena Accompanying Associative Processes"]. These papers refer extensively to Féré's and Veraguth's work and to Jung-Peterson: "Psycho-physical Investigations with the Galvanometer and Pneumograph in Normal and Insane Individuals." *Brain*, 30, 1907.

[5] Cited incorrectly in the original. It should read: Sommer.

changes at the electrodes produce the change of the current, the majority is nevertheless inclined to assume, or at least does not contradict the opinion, that the oscillations of current are caused by the more or less intensified activity of the cutaneous glands.

While I venture to foresee a much greater problem here, I miss on the other hand in the entire pertinent literature any experiments with drugs producing perspiration or restricting secretion, such as Pilacarpine or Atropin—experiments which indeed could disprove or substantiate these assertions.

Involuntary changes of contact of hand or foot with the electrodes when affects arise were also mentioned as a cause of the oscillation of current; although such contact-changes could themselves be regarded as an unconscious expression of affect, my own experience gives me confidence to discount this influence. I myself have observed this phenomenon years ago in the so-called four-cell bath, where the extremities do indeed not come into contact with the electrodes, and where water is the sole stable conductor. I cannot quite understand why this unambiguous and so very practical apparatus has never been used for these investigations.

For the rest, the palms and the soles were found to be the only body areas which produce the psychogalvanic phenomenon. So much for point 1.

2. *Specifically Neurologic Considerations*

In this field the psychogalvanic reflex is of value, because it is first of all a means for the objective registration of sensory disorders. An individual's sensibility for exogenic stimuli may be disturbed either in the direction toward anesthesia or toward hyperesthesia. If such an individual is connected with the current and the respective body areas are then stimulated, the stimulus curve is absent or considerably reduced if the stimulus touches anesthetic body parts, while the stimulus curve rises if hyperesthetic body parts are touched. I will quote here two examples from Veraguth's writings:

"1. Traumatic paralysis of the lower arm plexus. The little finger is anesthetic for the faradic current. The patient is connected to the galvanometer circuit; faradic currents are applied alternatingly to the anesthetic little finger and the normally sensitive index finger of the same hand. If the latter is stimulated, the galvanometer oscillates; if

326

the anesthetic finger is stimulated, the galvanometer registers no change.

"2. Neuralgia in the area of the trigeminus. While the patient is in the circuit, finger pressure is applied alternatingly to the Valeixian points of the affected side of the face and to the corresponding points of the normal side of the face. Pressure on the painful spot provokes galvanometric deflections of 12 to 15 millimeters on the scale, whereas the same pressure on the corresponding healthy spots provokes deflections of 2 to 3 millimeters."

Because of its practical implications, we may stress that the psychogalvanic reflex provides us with an objective tool for checking the statements of accident victims concerning pain and anesthesias. In this connection it is also of interest that the stimulation of hysterically anesthetic zones leads to the same galvanometric oscillations as the stimulation of normal body areas. This finding is not insignificant for the theory of hysterical anesthesia as well as of hysteria in general.

I shall now turn to:

3. *The Field of Experimental Psychology*

Veraguth, Jung, and Binswanger are deeply engaged in this work.

Unfortunately, it is not possible for me to discuss separately the achievements of the individual men, since in working through the literature coming from them I find that the experiments are too closely connected and interdependent.

In any case, Veraguth deserves to be named as the true originator of this entire line of thought; and in this context I consider the originator not the often accidental discoverer of facts but only the first person who consciously evaluated them. (Otherwise Vigoroux [1879] and Féré [1888] would have to be mentioned in the first place.)

Veraguth named his promising offspring "psychogalvanic phenomenon."

a. The subjects of the experiments were physicians, male and female students, male and female nurses, patients (mentally sound ones and patients with dementia praecox [Jung], also hysterics).

b. The apparatus used in the experiments is a Bunsen element of 1.5 volt tension; the electrodes consist of thin brass plates on which the hands are placed; a sensitive Deprez-d'Arsonval mirror galvanometer is in the electric circuit; the galvanometer's oscillations are quickly brought back to the point of rest by means of a "shunt."

A scale with a lamp fastened on top of it stands at a distance of about one meter from the galvanometer; the lamp throws a vertical ray of light onto the galvanometer mirror. This ray of light is reflected by the mirror onto a celluloid scale which is divided in millimeters. The oscillations of the mirror and thereby the oscillations in the strength of the current are measured by the movements of the light ray.

If associations of the experimental subjects are recorded, the light ray moves more or less far on the scale with almost every reaction; it stops for a moment at the highest point and then returns to the point of departure—galvanic amplitude.

c. The stimuli originally applied to the subjects were initially tactile, acoustic, and optical ones, and manifested themselves by means of a stimulation curve if the stimulus was accompanied by an affect (even if this affect was only that of attention). If the subject is engaged in reading something uninteresting, the rest curve results; the latter changes into the stimulation curve when the reading matter arouses the subject's interest. Indifferent reading material, adding relatively simple numbers, purely intellectual mental activity, even feelings of low intensity produce no deflection of the galvanometer—thus a rest curve.

The influence of anticipation, on the other hand, becomes clearly evident in the so-called anticipation oscillation.

d. In preparation for the association experiment, the subject receives the following instruction: "We shall call out words to you, and you must, without deliberation, answer with a word, whatever comes to your mind; for instance, I call out to you the word 'garden,' and at that moment you recall, let us say, a bowling alley; then you must immediately say this word clearly."

e. In our example, "garden" would be the stimulus word, "bowling alley" the reaction word, and the time elapsed between the pronouncement of the stimulus word and the reaction word is called reaction time. The greatest distance traveled by the light ray on the scale in a positive direction is considered the amplitude. As soon as the positive oscillation recedes again, that is, becomes negative, starting and end points of the distance are noted down. The reaction time is measured by means of a 1/5 second watch; when the stimulus word and the reaction word are pronounced the reaction time is fixed by pressing a button on the watch, and this reaction time is then noted down in the curve. On the average, about one hundred associations can be graphically represented in this way in thirty to forty minutes.

f. As soon as one experiment is finished, the experiment is immediately reproduced; that is, the subject is asked to repeat his first reaction word to each stimulus word. In those instances in which the subject does not recall the reaction word or in which he now has to think for a long time we are confronted (mostly) with a disturbance caused by an emotionally toned ideational complex.

g. It happens not infrequently that before a new stimulus word is called out, the negative oscillation which had already set in is once more reversed into a positive one or that the galvanometer needle does not return at all; this is the result of a persevering feeling or a newly arising one; however, the new curve is always figured from the culminating point of the preceding one. Therefore it is most important to distinguish carefully the absolute height of the galvanometric amplitude from the relative height of each individual reaction experiment; we shall see what significant conclusions result from this distinction.

h. For each reaction we then have the following categories:

Stimulus word	*Amplitude* absolute in cm.	Reaction word
Time in 1/5 sec.	*Amplitude* for the individual reaction in mm.	Reproduction

Example: Stimulus word: Head
  abs. amplitude: 14 cm.
  Reaction word: Hand
  Time: 9
  rel. amplitude: 15 mm.
  Reproduction: normal

The reproduction experiment is followed by the analysis.

1. The speed of the experiment depends upon the negative oscillation following the positive one—if a negative one sets in at all; in short, until the oscillation comes to a standstill.

The time which elapses between the appearance of the psychic process and its galvanic manifestation—precisely speaking, between the time the stimulus word is pronounced and the oscillation of the current appears—represents the latency period (it varies between 1.5 to 5 seconds).

As mentioned before, certain body movements influence the galvanometric amplitude: for instance, movements of the arms, increased pressure on the electrodes, etc. However, these factors need not be overrated.

Concerning the influence of respiration on the phenomenon, Prof. Peterson and Jung report in a joint paper that in spite of numerous experiments they have not yet been able to achieve conclusive results. Still, they found that the affective, mounting galvanometric curve is accompanied by fewer but deeper inspirations. Respiratory and galvanometric curves yield for the most part contradictory results. Unusual amplitudes of the galvanometric curve correspond rather frequently to even respiratory curves and vice versa. But abundance of excitations, anticipatory attention, nervous tension result in changes of the pneumographic curve in so far as the inspirations are initially reduced. "Nevertheless," says Jung, "one must not forget that respiration is a tool of consciousness, that, unlike the galvanometric curve, it is subject to voluntary control." Very deep inspirations can affect the strength of the current. Also laughing, coughing, sighing; the latter, however, mainly on account of the emotional tone inherent in it.

That sighing without accompanying emotions does not affect the strength of the current follows from the experiments made by Jung and Peterson, who had their subjects take many deep breaths in succession. In one of their cases, the excessively great amplitudes with deep inspirations were caused by the fact that the latter revived the subject's fear of being tubercular.

A systematic repetition of the same stimulus demonstrates that the psychogalvanic phenomenon is influenced not by the perception of the stimulus as such but by the emotional tone connected with it. If through frequent repetition the emotional tone of a sensation, for instance, of a pin prick, can be reduced, then there is no longer an oscillation of the current. What has been said about sensations also applies to ideas; this has been demonstrated in the work of Veraguth, in the repetition experiments by Jung and Peterson, as well as in Binswanger's work.

I believe I have now introduced you to the most essential points of these experiences. To facilitate the discussion and further elucidation, I will illustrate an association experiment by means of a curve which I have copied roughly. [This curve is attached to the manuscript, see pp. 332-333].

Now I still want to add a few very brief examples concerning a patient with traumatic hysteria. They are taken from Veraguth, who writes:

"Most neurotics show anomalies in the realm of affectivity; they do not suffer so much from an abnormal intensity of affects as from their abnormal course. Until now we did not possess an objective method for registering these psychic processes. I should like to support with the following examples the assumption that the psychogalvanic reflex may to a certain degree fill this gap.

"In the course of his painful experiences on account of a liability suit, a traumatic neurotic had suffered much injustice at the hands of his superior A. and the director B. On August 1, 1905 he was particularly badly off; on that day he was frightened by violent nose bleeding; during his worst period, Drs. X and Y took care of him. In the course of the winter semester 1906/07 I subjected this patient six times to the same association experiment; while he was in the circuit, I called out to him at definite intervals, among a hundred indifferent words which were identical each time, the always identical stimulus words: 'Superior A., Director B., August 1, Nose bleeding, Dr. X. and Dr. Y.' The effect was such that throughout the half-year the emotionally toned words were in each experiment followed by large galvanic amplitudes; whereas the hundred other indifferent words produced no amplitudes or considerably smaller ones—in any case, none which would remain constant in the experiments.

"As a counterpart, I will sketch here the experiment with a healthy architect which I started one day after he had experienced a profes-

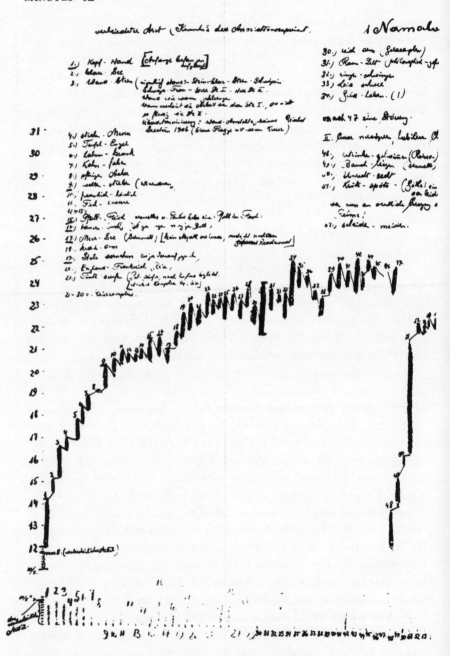

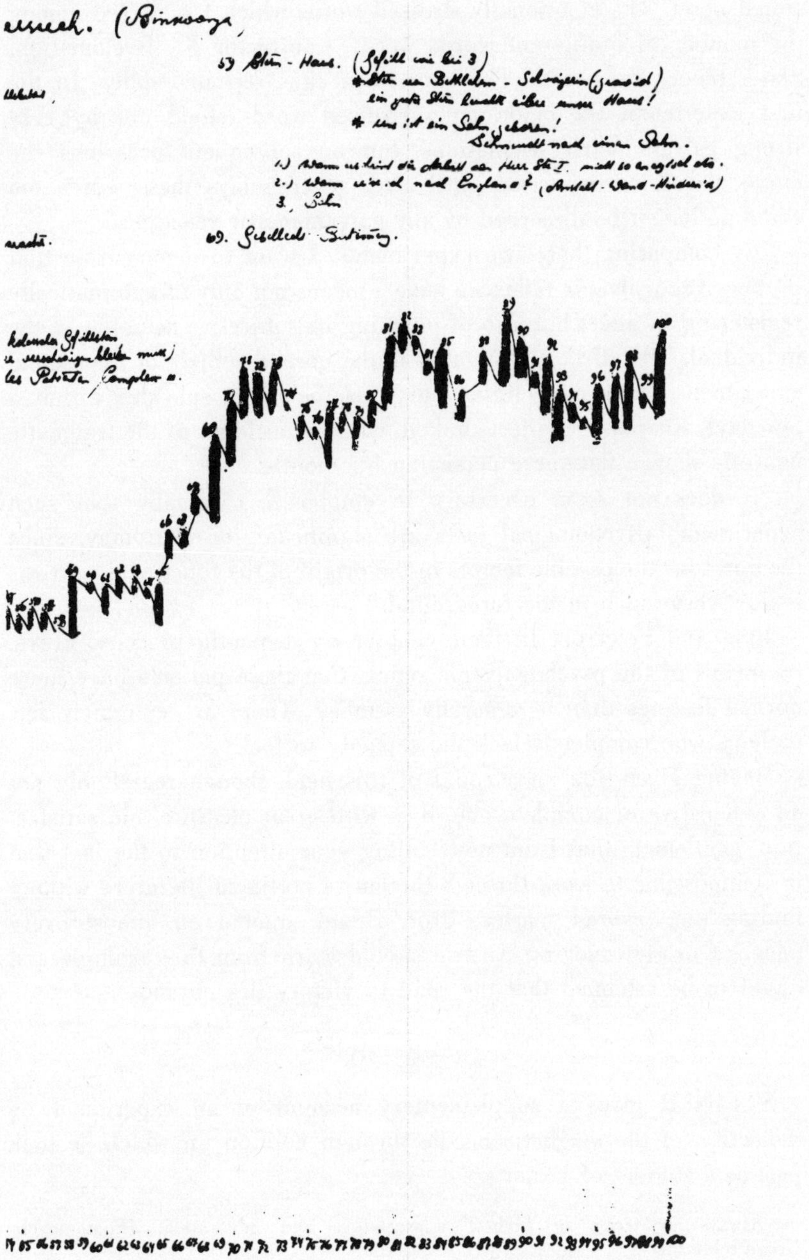

sional upset. The emotionally stressed words which I scattered among the number of indifferent words were: 'Contractor X., Reclamation, Slate, Floor, Furniture.' The experiment was repeated daily. In the first experiment the emotionally stressed words stood out by very strong galvanometric oscillations, but on subsequent occasions the curve elevations decreased until after several days these words too could no longer be discerned by any galvanometric reactions.

"By comparing these two experiments, I want to demonstrate that in the psychogalvanic reflex we have a means not only of automatically registering an affect but also of pursuing its subjective actuality in the individual. The affect investigated in the normal subject of the second experiment shows a declining curve as the affect subsides within a few days, whereas the affects linked with the accident of the traumatic neurotic show a flat curve persisting for months.

"It does not seem necessary to emphasize especially that such experimental-psychological facts are significant for neurology, since the quest for the psychic factors in the origin of the functional neurosis is now very much in the foreground."

Jung and Peterson, in their chapter on dementia praecox, prove, by means of the psychogalvanic reflex, that these patients have more normal feelings than is generally assumed. There are extremely few patients who completely lack the capacity to feel.

Having given you an account of this field, though regrettably not an exhaustive or complete one, it is with great pleasure and satisfaction, gentlemen, that I am now calling your attention to the fact that it is impossible to work through the entire pertinent literature without finding our revered master, Prof. Freud, quoted on almost every page.* Our slow-moving Austria should learn from this example and ought to be ashamed that the road to victory lies abroad!

DISCUSSION

STEINER gives a supplementary account of an experiment on deflection of the magnetic needle through volition, in which he took part as a student of Exner's.[6]

* Always in terms of highest appreciation and admiration. [Footnote by Urbantschitsch.]

[6] Sigmund Exner (1846-1926), noted physiologist.

STEKEL first stresses that he is not partial to experimental psychology; not much can be gained there. But he would exclude this galvanometric reflex from his criticism, because it seems to be useful for proving whether an individual is malingering, and in studying traumatic neurosis. The question remains whether this method is not also open to error.

Concerning the associations, he himself has already abandoned the method of calling out stimulus words to his patients.

He concludes by thanking the speaker for his brief and precise presentation.

PROF. FREUD joins in this praise for the speaker.

His own attitude toward the association experiment is an ambiguous one: on the one hand, it is most valuable since it has brought us Jung, who with this experiment has in turn drawn the attention of wider circles to psychoanalysis. On the other hand, it is a coarse method, to which psychoanalysis is far superior: when the diagnostic association experiment will have fulfilled its role as a means of instruction, it probably will no longer be of value.[7]

It is gratifying that Stekel's innovation (to call out stimulus words in the analysis) has proven a failure. When in the course of an analysis something becomes unintelligible or there is a standstill, the [psychoanalytic] technique no longer searches for the complexes but deals with the resistances.[8] The separate single words which may come to a patient's mind are frequently much distorted and difficult to explain (several single words with the same initial letter in succession means: dictionary).

In perseveration, we are dealing with substitute words or with words resulting from condensation. We need only remember that for children too a word has several meanings, a fact which becomes very apparent in the language disintegration of dementia praecox (Jung).[9]

The association method is not suitable to find anything new; it has

[7] Prophetic words indeed.
[8] This remark shows that as early as 1908 analytic technique focused primarily on the resistances.
[9] The substitution and condensation of words in the dream and in schizophrenia thus go back, by way of regression to the primary process of the unconscious id, to the infantile formation of words and may perhaps give us an inkling of the development of language.

merely confirmed what psychoanalysis has discovered. It is a useful expedient only in those cases which are inaccessible to psychoanalysis: the demented. The mere demonstration that demented patients have some normal feelings is an important result of this method.[10]

Anticipating the evening devoted to reviews, he must refer to a bit of literature already tonight. The paper of a certain Mr. von der Pforten[11] was recently reviewed in the *Frankfurter Zeitung*. He claims that the effect of high-voltage electric currents can be considerably modified by the individual's attitude of attention. This fact is significant inasmuch as it throws light on the psychogenesis of traumatic neurosis, which he [Freud] would not venture to explain in purely psychological terms. The illness may perhaps arise because the person concerned is not expecting the trauma; if he fears it, then its effect is probably mitigated; but if it takes him by surprise, so that he has no time to adjust himself to it psychologically, the traumatic neurosis appears.[12]

SADGER, with regard to this point, presents clinical material proving the opposite.

STEKEL also doubts that this ingeniously thought-out theory is correct.

JOACHIM raises the question whether in some cases the effect might not be an indirect one; that is, the affects call forth muscular tension and only thereby the psychic reaction becomes manifest; even in this case, however, the experiment would not lose in value. With a certain amount of sustained, focused attention, some degree of muscular tension is unavoidable.

ADLER says that the experiment involving deflection of the magnetic needle originated with Dubois-Reymond[13] and was later divested

---

[10] The best evaluation of the association experiment!

[11] Otto, Freiherr von der Pforten, German chemist and author of "Elektrizität und das Problem der Aufmerksamkeit" ["Electricity and the Problem of Attention"], *Naturwissenschaftliche Wochenschrift*, Vol. 23, 1908.

[12] This thought was subsequently further pursued in the attempt to understand the traumatic neurosis, and found full confirmation in those wounded soldiers of World War I who were in a state of shock. See Freud: *Beyond the Pleasure Principle* (1920). *S.E.*, 18:3-64; and *Inhibitions, Symptoms and Anxiety* (1926). *S.E.*, 20:77-174.

[13] Emil Dubois-Reymond (1818-1896), famous German physiologist.

of its miraculous character: it could be explained by thermoelectric currents which appear as a consequence of raised pressure.

He does not venture to examine the experiments described here in respect to their relations to the modern theory of electricity; one probably has to agree with Joachim's opinion that one is dealing here with remotely derived [indirect] reactions. Freud has just characterized in very appropriate words the significance of the psychogalvanic reflex.

Concerning the traumatic neurosis, he does not think that matters are as simple as Freud described them; these individuals are probably predisposed. From psychoanalyses one can see that such individuals were already anxiety prone before [the onset of traumatic neurosis]. In his opinion, there is always a certain anxiety readiness.

FEDERN asks the speaker for information on various technical details. It is an important observation that a hysteric patient reacts with a normal reflex to [the stimulation of] an anesthetic area. One should investigate whether the repressed complexes of neurotics react like conscious complexes.

In reference to speech disturbances and the disintegration of language, Federn remarks that aphasia leaves deep-rooted disturbances in its wake.

In the traumatic neurosis, it seems that it is not so much anxiety as expectation and courage which play a role.

The experiments are valuable inasmuch as they make the physician independent of the patient, and thus may at times help in establishing the true state of affairs.

43

SCIENTIFIC MEETING on March 4, 1908

Present: Freud, Adler, [A.] Deutsch, Federn, Graf, Heller, Hitsch-
mann, Rank, Reitler, Sadger, Steiner, Schwerdtner, Stekel, Joachim,
Wittels.
Bass and Urbantschitsch excused.
Reviews and case reports.

Brief Reviews of Literature and Case Reports
by All Present

BRIEF REVIEWS OF LITERATURE

ADLER: In connection with Friedländer's review,[1] Adler mentions
the report of a convention in Frankfurt-on-the-Main where Friedländer
said the same thing as in his review, but where Auerbach who knows
something of our views took a stand against Aschaffenburg[2] in
particular.

From the *Folia Neurobiologica* he mentions a paper by Orszanski,
professor in Kharkov, on "The Genesis and Nature of Hysteria" (given
at the International Congress [for Psychiatry and Neurology] in

---

[1] Probably A. Friedländer, an opponent of Freud.
[2] Gustav Aschaffenburg, professor of psychiatry in Cologne, edited a monthly on
criminology, wrote several papers on criminal psychology; adversary of Freud.

Amsterdam, 1907); he looks for the root of hysteria in developmental anomalies of the sexual organs.

An abstract of the work of an English psychiatrist has come to Adler's attention. This man classifies the neuroses in a peculiar manner, calling one of them avarice neurosis.

Lastly he mentions Bumke's report on Mitmann [sic].[3]

Books: Paul Albrecht: *Fritz Reuters Krankheit* [*Fritz Reuter's Illness*] (Halle: Marhold, 1907).[4]

L. von Szöllössy: *Mann und Weib. Zwei grundlegende Naturprinzipien. Eine sexualphilosophische Untersuchung.* [*Man and Woman. Two Fundamental Principles of Nature. A Sexual-Philosophical Investigation*]. Würzburg, 1908.

Ziehen: *Das Gedächtnis* [*Memory*].[5]

Max Kassowitz: *Welt, Leben, Seele. Ein System der Naturphilosophie in gemeinfasslicher Darstellung* [*World, Life, Soul. A System of Natural Philosophy in Popular Presentation*] (Excerpts from general biology). Vienna, 1908.

Zeitschrift für angewandte Psychologie: der Menschenkenner [*Journal of Applied Psychology: The One Who Knows Men*] Wiegand, Leipzig.[6]

RANK reads a passage from a letter which Schiller wrote to Körner on December 1, 1788. This passage strikingly characterizes the nature and meaning of free association in the Freudian sense.[7]

---

[3] Ostwald Bumke, German psychiatrist, later professor at various German universities, was one of the most vicious opponents of Freud. The report referred to is probably a review of A. Muthmann's *Psychiatrisch-theologische Grenzfragen* [*Psychiatric-theological Border Problems*] (Halle: Marhold, 1907) or of *Zur Psychologie und Therapie neurotischer Symptome. Eine Studie auf Grund der Neurosenlehre Freuds* [*On the Psychology and Therapy of Neurotic Symptoms. A Study Based on Freud's Theory of the Neuroses*] (Halle: Marhold, 1907). A. Muthmann was an early follower of Freud.

[4] Fritz Reuter (1810-1874), famous poet and humorist who wrote in the Low German dialect.

[5] Theodor Ziehen (1862-?), German philosopher, psychologist, and psychiatrist. *Memory* was an address delivered in celebration of the anniversary of the foundation of the Kaiser Wilhelm Academy of Military Medicine, in Berlin, on December 2, 1908.

[6] *Der Menschenkenner: Monatsschrift für praktische Psychologie* [. . . *Monthly Journal of Practical Psychology*], ed. F. Dunstrey and Magdalene Thumm-Kintzel; Vol. I, April, 1908-March, 1909; later suspended.

[7] It is probably the passage about which Rank spoke at the Congress in Salzburg. See E. Jones, *The Life and Work of Sigmund Freud*, 2:42. New York: Basic Books, 1955.

Books: Hoche: *Moderne Analyse psychischer Erscheinungen* [*Modern Analysis of Psychic Phenomena*].[8]

HITSCHMANN: In connection with this review, Hitschmann refers to Nietzsche's deep psychological insight in *Zur Genealogie der Moral* [*On the Genealogy of Morality*] (Section 3 of the Ascetic Ideal) and proposes it for review and discussion.

In the *Zeitschrift für die gesamte Strafrechtswissenschaft* [*Journal for the Entire Discipline of Criminal Law*] (Vol. 27, p. 601, 1907), there is an essay on "The Fundamentals of Diagnosing True Psychological Facts," in which Karl Heilbronner expresses doubts about Jung's experiments.

An essay by M. Rosenfeld on "Psychische Störungen bei der vasomotorischen Neurose" ["Psychic Disorders in Vasomotor Neurosis"][9] should be mentioned.

Books: [Willy] Hellpach: *Geistige Epidemien* [*Mental Epidemics*] [Frankfurt: Rütten & Löning, 1907].

Ehrenfels: *Sexual-Ethik* [*Sex Ethics*].[10]

Stoll: *Das Geschlechtsleben in der Völkerpsychologie* [*Sexual Life in Ethnopsychology*] [*Leipzig*, 1890].[11]

STEKEL first mentions a novel, *Edele Prangen*, by Otto Gysae,[12] in which the conflict caused by incestuous thoughts about the sister is solved by marrying a cousin.

From Emil Lucka's book, *Die Phantasie* [*Fantasy*],[13] he reads several passages from the chapter on fundamentals of characterology.

Lastly he refers to Adler's interpretation of "Zwei Träume einer Prostituierten" ["Two Dreams of a Prostitute"] in the *Zeitschrift für Sexualwissenschaft* [*Journal for the Study of Sex*], No. 2, 1908.

Among books dealing with the psychology of genius, he mentions: one by the psychiatrist Sommer from Giessen; furthermore, *Die*

---

[8] Alfred Erich Hoche (1865-1943), psychiatrist, opponent of Freud. This paper was read at the Congress of German Natural Scientists and Physicians in Dresden on November 16, 1905, published in Jena, 1907.

[9] *Zentralblatt für Nervenheilkunde und Psychiatrie*, Vol. 31, 1908.

[10] Christian Freiherr von Ehrenfels (1859-1932), Austrian professor of philosophy at the University of Prague.

[11] Otto Stoll, professor of ethnopsychology in Zürich.

[12] Otto Gysae (1877-1947), German author.

[13] Emil Lucka (1877-1941), Austrian writer and philosopher.

Entwicklungsgeschichte des Talentes und Genies [*The Developmental History of Talent and Genius*], by Reibmayr, a sociological study, which Stekel offers to review.

FEDERN mentions two favorable reviews of Freud's books by [Havelock] Ellis in *Brain;* further, a paper in the same journal by Johns who claims that the relapse of mental patients depends upon social conditions.

A work by Boltan deserves to be mentioned. It deals with the relations of progressive paralysis postluetica to senile dementia: according to Boltan, only those are afflicted with paralysis who would become demented if they were not infected.

[A.] DEUTSCH briefly reviews Heinrich Mann's *Herzogin von Assy* [1903] and Ginzkey's novel, *Jakobus und die Frauen* [*Jacobus and Women*] [1908].[14] He recounts an anecdote about Wagner to demonstrate how close love comes to art in the state of ecstasy.

HELLER proposes Gerhart Hauptmann's drama *Kaiser Karls Geisel* [*The Hostage of Emperor Charles*, 1908] for review.

PROF. FREUD briefly mentions [Ludwig] Löwenfeld's book: *Homosexualität und Strafgesetz* [*Homosexuality and Penal Law*] which deserves an extensive report. In this book Löwenfeld forthrightly presents Freud's views on homosexuality. (Bloch's attack in the second number of *Zeitschrift für Sexualwissenschaft.*)

CASE REPORTS

RANK attempts to prove that inferiority of Schiller's eyes (myopia, blinking, inflammation, heredity) was one of the roots of his Tell figure by referring to the myth of the blind archer and to some characteristic passages in the Wilhelm Tell drama. This leads to a long discussion.

STEKEL feels that the continuous recourse to the doctrine of inferiority has by now become painful. The myth of the blind archer [*Schütze*] by no means proves its correctness; for one does not know whether the archer was blind from birth or became blind later on, nor does one know the cause of his blindness. It seems to him more to the

14 Franz Karl Ginzkey, Austrian author of numerous short historical sketches.

point to interpret the blind archer as the God Amor; the shot is a love-shot which can be performed even by a blind man. The little one (Tell's boy) symbolizes the genital; and the apple, too, is a well-known sexual symbol.

HITSCHMANN finds Rank's explanation paradoxical and forced, and inferiority dragged in by the hair.

ADLER can explain the opposition to the doctrine of inferiority only by assuming that it has not been understood: of course, erecting a superstructure[15] is not the driving motive of Schiller's drama. However, in his opinion, there cannot exist a dramatist who would not have an inferior visual apparatus: he creates a scene in his mind and has to visualize it as it will later really be performed in the theater. The figures of ghosts (Shakespeare) constitute a minor transition to neurosis.

GRAF states that he does not know Adler's book; but one must guard against the application of the theory where it does not belong. Even a very understanding person will listen to Rank's argumentation with a sense of disbelief. The Tell myth is intimately related to the Odysseus myth. Behind Odysseus there originally was Apollo, the sun god who returns at the time of the winter solstice.

One may perhaps admit some traces of "inferiority of the eye" in the Melchthal scene.

In contrast to Adler, he states that he cannot imagine a poet without perfectly organized eyes; the poet thinks with his eyes. The greatest poets possess a very sensitive visual organ. It is more likely that second-rate poets, the introverts (for instance, Novalis[16]) might have weak vision.

FEDERN also objects to Rank's explanation. It might very well be that the choice of the shot is connected with inferiority, but the proofs are not conclusive.

PROF. FREUD emphasizes that from the standpoint of comparative mythology on which Rank's interpretation is based, a number of

[15] The original has "*Das Hineinlegen des Überbaues bei Schiller* . . ." The meaning of this sentence is obscure. Lit.: "Inserting, putting in, a superstructure in Schiller . . ."

[16] Novalis (1772-1801), famous representative of the romantic school of German poets.

342

objections can be dismissed. Comparative mythology is concerned only with the theme and does not at all consider the transpositions. Rank's interpretation is a particularly beautiful mythological confirmation of Adler's principle and secure as are few interpretations. The myth of the archer is ancient and is connected with the stellar constellation of Sagittarius. The psychological meaning may be considered of equal importance as this astral meaning. It is only Stekel's method which is objectionable.

FEDERN reports on the resolution of a single severe symptom in a hysteria: abdominal pain was relieved when the patient recalled that as a boy he had swallowed his own semen in a period of excessive masturbation, because he had heard the loss of semen was injurious to the whole organism.

STEINER recounts two cases of impotence. The first patient, a thirty-four-year-old man, suddenly became impotent for unknown reasons. The advice to have intercourse with the lady whom he was courting cured his impotence and his rejection of sexuality.

The second case is that of a man who has been having an affair for ten years; he has intercourse once in two weeks; he is tired of this affair and would like to take up a relationship with a young girl.— States of anxiety.—Another patient suggested the idea to him that agoraphobia might be connected with the feeling of too small a penis in too large a hole.

In all of the cases the patients had either no sisters or there was an age difference of ten years.

WITTELS, in confirmation of a previous assertion that hysterics are dangerous, now relates two incidents which recently occurred in real life. A dog bit off the nose of an actress as she tried to kiss him.— Then the affair of Colonel von Goeben who took Frau von Schöne-beck's hysterical trifling seriously. Both cases show that the coincidence of a life guided by fantasies with actual circumstances has sad results.

(RANK remarks that the case of Goeben looks very much like a case of love for the mother: adoration of the wanton woman as if she were a saint; killing her husband in order to conquer her.[17])

[17] Lack of more details in this protocol makes these reports utterly unsatisfactory.

HITSCHMANN speaks about the case of a girl who suffered from heart palpitations. A platonic admirer had thrown himself upon her while she was lying on a couch; he must have hurt her in the region of her heart, she says. This man played a significant role in her childhood.

She had to give up playing the piano because of pains in her hand; she then has the association that this is the hand which this man had once grasped in a rough manner twenty-five years ago.

HELLER reports an observation made on his boy as a small contribution to infantile sexuality. From time to time the boy wakes up in fear at night, talks about various things, and finally says that he did not play with his penis. He has given up this habit months ago.

STEKEL relates a case, where the first words of a dream contained almost the entire solution. The patient dreams he has the vague feeling of somehow participating in the murder of Frau von Biedermann. Associations: *Lucrezia* by Musäus.[18] Lucrezia Borgia who indulged in incestuous relations with father and brother. His father is a "Biedermann" [*bieder Mann* = honest man]. Then he associates Grimm's fairy tale "Fitcher's Bird" (which is almost identical with "Bluebeard") where the magician looks for a virgin who will obey the prohibition (to enter a certain room, which entails all kinds of consequences). The two older sisters transgress the prohibition and are slaughtered (deflowered), the third finds a way of evading it: she transgresses without being found out (she masturbates). Here the patient has the feeling that he murdered, i.e., deflowered, his sister when he was still a boy.

The second case is a counterpart to the one communicated by Federn. A patient with dog dreams, beating dogs, etc. He has no pleasure with women; at present he has an affair, but is relatively impotent. As a child, he owned a dog who masturbated and licked him. Today his wish for this [type of gratification] is unconscious. The beating stems from his original impression of his parents' intercourse as a fight. (FREUD: The sadistic conception of intercourse.)

PROF. FREUD remarks that the first part of the interpretation of the myth [fairy tale] is probably correct. Later on, however, the fairy

18 Johann Karl August Musäus (1735-1787), German author.

tale may refer to masturbation just as well as to yielding; he may be searching for a girl who did *not* masturbate.

A contribution to the problem of *telepathy*, which Adler promised to explain rationally. A man who foresees important events, especially deaths: he is, of course, an obsessional neurotic.

1. A prophetic vision. He has an affair with a seamstress; in the process of helping her draft a reply to an advertisement, he asks her what she demands as her daily wages; she says, 1.60; and he suggests she raise that to 2 *Kronen*, which is done. She is to begin her work on a certain day somewhere near Vienna, since her employer has agreed to pay the wages, and has invited her to come. While reading this letter of invitation the patient says he clearly had the vision of the number 1.20. On the day on which the girl was supposed to begin work, she surprises him in Vienna and tells him that upon her arrival the woman had offered her 1.20 *Kronen*, which she refused to accept. He rejects the surmise that his memory was deceiving him and that he probably had the vision of 1.60. Later on the girl agrees to work out there and the entire story proves to have been a lie; she had not been there at all on that day. Thus what he had prophetically foreseen, was not true at all.

(ADLER remarks that such occurrences usually turn out to be a swindle. The girl had probably counted on the man's telepathic tendencies.)

PROF. FREUD: The man had not told her anything about his vision; subsequently it turned out that he had the vision of 1.60, not 1.20 which was the minimum wages.

2. About the same patient. One morning he sees an old gentleman in a trolley car and, erroneously taking him for the father of a lady whom he knows, he addresses him and asks about her health. Two days later his mother asks him whether he has already been told about this lady's illness, to which he replies in the negative. The same day he learns from a friend that this lady had been buried that morning. He figures out that she must have died at about the time when he talked to the old gentleman whom he believed to be her father. The patient himself gave the following explanation: he never reads the paper thoroughly but only glances through it and always in the eve-

ning. On the day before he spoke to the gentleman he probably fleetingly glanced at the announcement of her death (her surname was printed in bold-face type) and perceived it unconsciously.

Another case concerns an elderly lady who occasionally expresses a childish fear for her twenty-year-old son. When he sits on the toilet for a long time—and that is an inherited family habit—the mother comes to the door and anxiously knocks to convince herself of his well-being. The older brother of this young man had learned from his father the circumstances surrounding the boy's birth. When the mother was pregnant with him she had made every possible effort to prevent the birth of this child, to kill him. At that time, she simply wanted to have a miscarriage [*abortieren*] and today she fears that her son could die on the toilet [*Abort*].

This younger son whose whole life is spent in altruistic feelings and actions has a peculiar history, as does his older brother who is an egotist. His excessive kindness is designed to atone for something. At the age of five he had made a contract with the devil in whose name he carried out many naughty pranks (he set dogs on people, etc.); later he atoned for them compulsively. In the prehistory of his present kindness, sadism occupies a large place.

The older brother, on the other hand, had fantasies of benevolence and charitableness in his boyhood (at the age of ten, eleven), while these altruistic interests are alien to him today. In the fantasy kingdom over which he ruled, there were public eating-houses where everyone who came had to be fed. Today he is completely callous in such matters. These impulses probably abate because of their premature appearance, as do the heterosexual impulses in the homosexual.[19]

---

[19] This means that prematurely emerging impulses—that is, impulses which are too strong for the ego to master—are repressed with the help of reaction formations (conversion into the opposite). Many homosexuals have had, in very early childhood, an intense heterosexual attachment. Later, in his article on "The Disposition to Obsessional Neurosis: A Contribution to the Problem of Choice of Neurosis" (1913), *S.E.*, 12: 313-326, Freud said that one factor determining the choice of neurosis was the discrepancy of ego and instinct development.

44

SCIENTIFIC MEETING on *March 11, 1908*

Present: Freud, Adler, Bass, [A.] Deutsch, Graf, Hitschmann, Joachim, Rank, Sadger, Stekel, Urbantschitsch, Wittels.

Reitler, Federn, Steiner send their excuses.

Adler's motion to create a library fund is carried; a committee is formed to work out the details.

Stekel and Bass pay their dues.

PRESENTATION

The Natural Position of Women

SPEAKER: DR. WITTELS

Starting with the problem of menstruation, which subsumes the problem of femininity, the speaker discusses the meaning of the menstrual period among primitive peoples, in myths and popular beliefs (according to Plinius,[1] rings become filmed at the time of the period; a ploughshare over which a menstruating woman steps becomes blunt, etc.); the understanding that animals (especially birds and dogs)

---

[1] Caius Plinius Secundus, the elder (23-79 A.D.), Roman polyhistorian.

have for this phenomenon (according to Brehm,[2] canaries prefer humans of the opposite sex). He then briefly discusses the scientific theories about the menstrual period. Pflüger's theory,[3] that the ovum matures every month, has been disproved experimentally; at present, menstruation is explained in terms of inner secretion: woman rids herself of poisonous substances once a month. Adherents of the theory of bisexuality deny the significance of menstruation; they assert that not only woman but also man has a period and that this is not the only period which occurs in organic life. Woman herself despises menstruation, feels mortified by it, and keeps it secret. Women should not discard the belt of the Charites.[4]

The speaker then discusses his topic from the genealogical-biological-Darwinian point of view and outlines the developmental history of mankind whose origin has been placed in the glacial period. For many reasons this cannot be correct.

Man differs from the animal primarily in two points: his sexual instincts, particularly those of the male, are not subject to periodicity (the rutting time of animals); the sex instinct of animals exclusively serves the purpose of propagation, whereas in man it has the additional purpose of gaining pleasure. This mode of gaining pleasure requires, in addition to a certain amount of intelligence, also particularly favorable external circumstances (paradise) which were present only in the tertiary period.

Some other important characteristics of the process of becoming human are connected with love life: e.g., man's erect posture which may owe its origin merely to a primitive exhibitionistic act, namely, the display of sexual readiness. The problem of nudity, which has so far not been solved, may perhaps also be explained in terms of the high intensity of sexual feelings in the period man began to evolve; man may have divested himself of his hairy fur in order to be able to embrace more ardently. The evolution of mankind would thus be partly to the credit of the female—a passive achievement, to be sure, for she needed to do no more than be a female. Soon, however, fer-

[2] Alfred Brehm (1829-1884), famous German naturalist, editor of the Zoography, *Brehms Tierleben*.
[3] Eduard Pflüger (1829-1910), German physiologist.
[4] In later Greek mythology, the Goddesses of loveliness, grace, and charm.

tility became an impediment since it caused loss of time from the enjoyment of love. A part of woman's libido was sublimated by diverting it into motherhood; hence woman's libido diminished in comparison with man's. A scarcity [Not] of females set in, which may have been the first need [Not] man came to experience (as woman may have been the first possession man valued). Thus man too was forced to sublimate a part of his sexuality if he wanted to gain any pleasure from it at all; thus, he invented sublimated sexuality: erotism (song, dance, music). Spoken language probably originated in song and may perhaps have served the purpose of conveying love to woman more emphatically than music can. The origin of perversions should also be placed in this primeval period; they developed in order to restrict the great fecundity.

Woman may also have been the cause of primordial religion: she was venerable, originally occupied a regal position, and she feels happy in this role even today. For woman, in contrast to eternally changing man, is the most conservative creation.

The glacial period put an end to this magnificent natural state. The hard struggle to preserve their existence reduced the value of love for the few surviving humans. Man's misery taught him to believe also in evil gods now. He invented fire and axe and thus became approximately what primitive peoples are today. Woman was forced to become a worker, and since in this role she could not accomplish much, she was despised and regarded as the essence of evil, just as in religion the gods who are initially adulated are later regarded as inimical forces. Neither chastity nor fidelity were demanded of woman; her inner freedom was left to her. But having thus lost her status as the beloved one, she regained it as mother. Man invented life in hordes. Love among comrades may have been patterned after mother love. Woman was the object of adoration only until property was invented. Wanting to leave his possessions to his own progeny, man locked woman in the cage of monogamy. Man needs children for himself; he himself, as it were, gives birth to children (man's childbed) [couvade]. But woman now had to abandon her position as mother when the child obtained a father. However, woman often transgressed the rules of this new civilization; now she no longer needs to be beautiful, but chaste; it is no longer sufficient that she give pleasure, she must also be faithful; she now must adorn herself. The result of this state of affairs is our accursed present-day culture in which women bemoan the fact that they did not come into the world as men; they try to become men (feminist movement). People do not appreciate the perversity and senselessness of these strivings; nor do the women themselves.

DISCUSSION

BASS does not consider valid the statement that woman's sexual value is lessened in times of need. On the contrary, we can observe today that just those strata of the population whose life is hardest are the ones who indulge most in sexual pleasure, because sexual pleasure must make up for all the other pleasures of life.

SADGER, in doubt whether the paper was meant to be taken seriously, points out a number of errors resulting from the assumption that the golden age is based on sexuality. Prof. Karsch has demonstrated the existence of perversions in undomesticated animals.[5]

[A.] DEUTSCH believes there is some support for the hypothesis concerning nudity.—Hypertrichosis is found in women whose sex organs show an anomaly.

STEKEL characterizes the paper as a poetic fantasy. Wittels is inclined to transpose his personal experiences into earlier periods (historical novels). Stekel then criticizes a few details. According to Darwin, the existence of hairiness as well as lack of hair can be proven. Since nowadays hairiness is preferred, a period of hairiness had to be brought about, according to the principle of natural selection.

URBANTSCHITSCH comments that the paper is a hypothesis, but an ingenious one. There are several points worth pursuing.

According to Bölsche,[6] clothes are the cause of nudity.

HITSCHMANN first pursues the psychological sources of this paper. The speaker seems to be fighting a series of obstacles which he

[5] Ferdinand Karsch: *Päderastie und Tribadie bei den Tieren. Auf Grund der Literatur Zusammengestellt.* Leipzig: M. Spohr, 1900. [*Pederasty and Tribadia in Animals. Compiled from the Literature.*] Reprint from *Jahrbuch für sexuelle Zwischenstufen.*

[6] Wilhelm Bölsche (1861-1939), German writer, author of many popular books on the natural sciences, an ardent Darwinist.

350

resents as impeding his sexual life; he fights: pregnancy, women who have become inaccessible because they are educated, then syphilis; and now he vividly describes the otherwise insignificant phenomenon of menses. One can characterize all that only as the fantasies of a youthful reactionary. He has almost completely neglected the most important factor, the economic one. The single passage where he deals with the economic condition of girls indicates merely that he wishes to get married.

Otherwise, he has said some nice things. The gestation period is an important principle which plays a significant role. It is difficult to explain a coexistence of polygamy and scarcity of women. It is quite improbable that woman first served as a goddess; rather, she participated in the creation of the idea of God.

PROF. FREUD first expressed his pleasure in listening to the paper which amused and stimulated him. Of course, it is a fantasy; but the lines which we are accustomed to pursue in science are extended here in the right direction. A few points really deserve to be taken out of the realm of fantasy, e.g., the idea that the evolution of mankind must have taken place in a period of abundance in which libido was unhampered; also that man began to practice perversions at that time.

The essential distinction between man and animal is correctly characterized as the contrast between the permanence of human libido and the periodicity of animal libido. The details of the process of human evolution are under the influence of sexuality to a much greater extent than is generally believed; the economic factors are overrated as far as their potential significance is concerned.

Bass's objection can be met by calling attention to the fact that the speaker talks about the esteem of woman, about erotism which has been stunted under these conditions. In an essay on woman's bondage, John Stuart Mill has overlooked the fact that a woman cannot earn a living and raise children at the same time.[7] Women as a group profit nothing by the modern feminist movement; at best a few individuals profit.

[7] John Stuart Mill (1806-1873), an outstanding figure among the English philosophers and economists. Freud refers in this passage to Mill's work, *Subjection of Women*, which Freud translated for Theodor Gompertz's edition of Mill's works (1880). See E. Jones: *The Life and Work of Sigmund Freud*, 1:56. New York: Basic Books, 1953.

ADLER remarks that there may be some stimulating thoughts in Wittels's paper, but one would have to make a determined search for them. Wittels should have been more concerned with the present and perhaps also with the future; instead, being a reactionary, he has turned to the most distant past in order to look for shortcomings there. The essential differences between Adler's own viewpoint and that of the speaker and the Professor is the following: whereas it is generally assumed that the framework of present relationships between men and women is constant, Socialists assume that the framework of the family is already shaky today and will increasingly become so in the future. Woman will not allow motherhood to prevent her from taking up a profession; motherhood may either remain an obstacle for some, or else it will lose its hardship.

Concerning the erect gait, the formation of the foot is a sign of degeneracy: legs are degenerated arms. Perhaps, exhibitionism may have come as a later addition.

The discussion of matriarchy was too meager. Through the right of inheritance, patriarchy displaced matriarchy. In his studies Karl Marx shows how, under the sway of ownership, everything becomes property. Woman also becomes a possession and this is the root of her fate. Therefore, first of all, the attitude that a woman is a possession must be given up.[8]

[8] It is interesting to note how Adler's attention was attracted by the social and political aspects of the problem, whereas Freud thought of it in psychological and anthropological terms. Adler refers here to the Marxist doctrine that the modes of production predominant in a society at any given time determine its political, social, and cultural conditions. Thus, in a capitalistic society, according to Marx, woman, too, becomes a private possession. At that time marriages for reasons of money were quite common among the bourgeoisie, and the nobility utilized marriage for political and economic purposes as a matter of course—circumstances which certainly gave support to Marx's theory. Rank seems to have condensed Adler's discussion to a point where it becomes almost unintelligible. Adler must have said approximately the following: "Just as, under the sway of private ownership, everything becomes private property, so does woman. First she is the father's possession; then the husband's. That determines her fate. Therefore, first of all, the idea of owning a woman must be abandoned."

Marx's ideas on this subject were generally misunderstood to imply that Marxists favored the socialization of women. These views were much discussed among the educated of Vienna in those days, and the members of the Wednesday circle were, of course, familiar with them. We may mention at this point that Freud was a close friend of the Eckstein family, of whom E. Jones in his biography of Freud mentions only Emma. The two families spent their summer vacations together for many years. Fritz Eckstein, an important philosopher, was a friend of Anton Bruckner and Hugo

Lastly, Adler reads the story "Adam and Eve," from the *Fairy Tales of the Present*, by Carl Ewald.[9]

JOACHIM confines himself to a few critical remarks. In judging the paper, one has made the error of taking a single link out of a chain. That legs develop as a consequence of degeneration would indeed be a result and not a cause; and the same is true of the right of inheritance.

HITSCHMANN adds the title of another book, *Man as a Quadruped*, by Ernst Klotz.[10]

Anterior intercourse has created conditions unfavorable for the stimulation of the clitoris; he asks whether this might not be of significance in anesthesia.

PROF. FREUD mentions an essay by Schroeder, "The Erotogenesis of Religion,"[11] in the *Zeitschrift für Religionspsychologie*. In this essay, the genitalia are said to have been the first gods, and religious feeling is derived from the ecstasies of intercourse.

WITTELS first replies to Adler. He quotes a dictum of Paracelsus on the fundamental difference between man and woman. The differentiation of the sexes becomes increasingly greater, the higher one goes in the animal scale. Menstruation is the most important difference between man and woman.

One cannot be a Freudian and a Social Democrat at the same time; this is the source of Adler's contradictions. The foot is degenerated only in relation to the hand; but not otherwise.

Wolf as well as of Freud. In later years he was one of the men with whom Freud used to play cards. Gustav Eckstein and Therese Schlesinger, a younger sister, member of Parliament, were already at that time distinguished leaders of the Social-Democratic party. Thus Freud was as familiar as Adler with the socialistic ideas of his time, although Freud, as Jones correctly states, never belonged to a political party.

[9] Carl Ewald (1856-1908), Danish writer known for his animal stories dealing with evolutionary history.

[10] Ernst Klotz, painter, gave his book the subtitle, *Eine anatomische Entdeckung samt neuer Erklärung der bisher falsch gesehenen menschlichen Fortpflanzungsorgane* [*An Anatomic Discovery and a New Explanation of the Human Reproductive Organs which Heretofore Were Misinterpreted*]. Leipzig: Wiegand, 1908.

[11] Theodor Schroeder published in 1907 a paper, "The Erotogenesis of Religion" in *Alienist and Neurologist*, 28:330, 1907, which appeared in German in *Zeitschrift für Religionspsychologie*, Vol. I, No. 11, March, 1908.

Exhibitionism with the erect gait: the penis of higher[12] mammals is hidden; exhibition which becomes increasingly evident plays an important role in the biology of higher mammals. Bölsche's explanation of hairlessness must be termed a failure. According to Exner, the growth of hair around the mons veneris serves to lessen friction.[13]

[12] Wittels's argumentation indicates that "higher" must be an error of the recorder; it should be "lower."

[13] In spite of sharp and even personally painful criticism, one was lenient at that time. Freud enjoyed Wittels because he had a wealth of ideas, even though his ideas often came closer to fantasy than to scientific thinking.

45

SCIENTIFIC MEETING on *April 1, 1908*

Present: Freud, Adler, Federn, Graf, Heller, Hitschmann, Hollerung, Sadger, Steiner, Stekel, Rank.

Sadger, Steiner, Adler pay membership dues.

Sadger borrows *Archiv* No. 34.

Bass, [A.] Deutsch, Wittels, Reitler excuse themselves.

Adler proposes the creation of a library fund and the foundation of a library for the Society.[1]

READING AND DISCUSSION

Nietzsche: "On the Ascetic Ideal"
(Section 3 of *Genealogy of Morality*)[2]

DR. HITSCHMANN, before reading the passage, says a few introductory words: as Moebius did with psychology, so we could adopt the hopelessness of all philosophy as a theme of discussion, taking the relativity of all philosophy as our point of departure. A philosophi-

---

[1] This sentence is crossed out in the original manuscript. However, in his biography of Freud (*loc. cit.*), Jones relates that a library was started at about this time.

[2] The Complete Works of Friedrich Nietzsche. The first complete and authorized English translation (18 vols. [1909-1913]), edited by Oscar Levy. *Genealogy of Morals*, translated by Horace B. Samuel. New York, 1923.

cal system is a product of an inner urge, not very different from artistic creations.

Actually, Nietzsche cannot be called a philosopher; he is a moralist, though one distinguished by unusual sagacity.

The most important facts of his life are not known. According to Moebius, his mother was hereditarily tainted. The fact that he was constantly surrounded by women strongly influenced his development. From his sister's report of his boyhood it becomes evident that already as a boy of thirteen he posed the principal questions—the origin and development of morality—which later dominated his life, and that he wrote an article on the origin of evil.

In Nietzsche's case, as in that of Winckelmann[3] and many others, love for philology, a special predilection for antiquity (art), and a powerful inclination for friendship (inversion) cooperate.

There is a striking contrast between his behavior in daily life and the main theme of his writings:[4] while in real life he was always sad and gloomy, his works overflow with joyfulness ("joyful science"), Dionysian jubilation, and dance. In contrast to his portrait, which leads us to believe that he was a fine, delicate, and compassionate person (which he is said to have been), in his writings he praises and defends cruelty and vengeance ("the blond beast"). The *Genealogy of Morality* is also dedicated to the defense of these instincts. He wrote this voluminous pamphlet in twenty days, that is, with pathologically accelerated speed.

Hitschmann then reviews very briefly the contents of the first two sections of *Genealogy of Morality:* "Good and Evil," "Good and Bad," and "Guilt, Bad Conscience, and Related Subjects," before he begins to read aloud the third part: "What Is the Meaning of Ascetic Ideals?" (Sections 5 to 9 incl.).

Then Hitschmann briefly discusses what he has read. It is interesting to note that Nietzsche discovers the crucial factor in the psychology of others, while he does not succeed in recognizing in himself that his own ideals correspond to his unfulfilled wishes. In criticizing and psychologically interpreting the ascetic ideal, in advocating that one

[3] Johann Joachim Winckelmann (1717-1768), famous German archeologist.
[4] Our patients frequently display a similar contrast between their actual and fantasy life.

should live ruthlessly according to one's own desires, he repudiates his own life circumstances which were forced upon him. Nietzsche's life can be called ascetic; his tendency toward asceticism and sexual abstinence is connected with his admiration for Schopenhauer (we do not know of any [sexual] relationship with a woman except for occasional visits to prostitutes). When he came to recognize that he had cheated life as well as himself, he rejected the ascetic ideal. Thus a philosopher's subjective views may be determined by his personal characteristics and experiences; this is beautifully illustrated in this work.

From our point of view, his paralysis with its complications is not only not the most interesting factor but on the contrary an interference, because without it the purely psychic processes would be more clearly evident.

Finally, we should raise the general question: What is it that causes a man to *remain* a philosopher?

DISCUSSION

STEINER only wishes to express his doubt whether the ascetic ideal is really a philosopher's necessary optimum.

SADGER emphasizes that the born philosopher is, by vocation, an obsessional neurotic; if punishment is more important to him, he becomes a jurist; if speculation, he becomes a philosopher. Schopenhauer is known to have been an obsessional neurotic. As far as Nietzsche is concerned, this topic cannot yet be discussed since the most important data have not yet been published. His mother was not hereditarily tainted, only some relatives, but Nietzsche himself is a model of hereditary stigmata. There is also much hysteria in him; the epileptoid states without loss of consciousness, which he himself reports from his childhood, were probably hysterical symptoms. His relationship with his family is of great importance: his "master morality" ["*Herrenmoral*"] may be associated with the fact that he was the only man [*Herr*] in his family. When he reached the age at which his father died, he feared he would die of the same illness; this identification with the father may have taken place on a homosexual basis.

357

ADLER first stresses that among all great philosophers who have left something for posterity, Nietzsche is closest to our way of thinking. Adler once tried to establish a direct line from Schopenhauer, through Marx and Mach, to Freud. At that time he omitted Nietzsche. There exist arguments against ascribing [the preoccupation with] philosophy to a single neurosis: the philosopher is much too complex, and the technique of philosophizing is essentially related to something totally different. However, it is possible to localize a philosophical system; that is, to specify the point at which the philosopher's mechanism of thinking sets in. Hegel,[5] for instance, begins where repression is involved, where thesis changes into antithesis. In Nietzsche's work, one finds almost on every page observations reminiscent of those we make in therapy, when the patient has come rather a long way and is capable of analyzing the undercurrents in his mind. Thus it was given to him to discover in all the manifold expressions of culture just that primal drive which has undergone a transformation in civilization, and which is then, in the mind of the philosopher, condensed as the ascetic ideal. Adler has always been struck by the fact that in paretics a number of cultural ideals are nonexistent; their previously unconscious instincts (which were not repressed) have gained a certain measure of freedom—a circumstance which accounts for the crass mood swings of paretics. Due to organic changes, paretics cannot transform processes originating in the instincts into their opposites.

GRAF first expresses his appreciation of Hitschmann's remark that that man is a philosopher who continues to think and to speculate beyond the time of his puberty. Nietzsche is not a good example if one wishes to establish the conditions for becoming a philosopher; he is not a philosopher in the same sense as Plato, Aristotle, and others. His works, written under the influence of French moralists, are a self-cure. From his weak nature he came to his strong ideals. His personality is not entirely that of a philosopher; his development does not follow a straight line as does that of many other thinkers and explorers; nor is there a sudden shift in the midst of life (as, for instance, in Wagner). His is a thrice-broken line: first, he abandons

[5] Georg Wilhelm Friedrich Hegel (1770-1831), one of the most important German philosophers.

philology when he becomes a Wagnerian and a Schopenhauerian; at this point, something must have broken through, which perhaps is a consequence of the repudiation and repression of sex following in the wake of his infection.

Nietzsche's later philosophy is rooted in his struggle against his illness by means of self-analysis.

FEDERN states that Nietzsche has come so close to our views that we can ask only, "Where has he not come close?" He intuitively knew a number of Freud's discoveries; he was the first to discover the significance of abreaction, of repression, of flight into illness, of the instincts—the normal sexual ones as well as the sadistic instincts. His philosophy is formed in direct contrast to his own existence. According to a reliable source, Nietzsche had at certain periods of his life homosexual relations and acquired syphilis in a homosexual brothel in Genoa.

The entire problem evolved from his childhood conflict. Although Nietzsche discovered the conditions of mankind's childhood, he never recognized the conditions of his own childhood. The problem of Nietzsche cannot be approached psychoanalytically.

The analysis of two philosophers (patients) disclosed that the tendency to strive for an understanding of the world, apart from the ego, appeared at an early time and became stronger with the repression of sexual drives.

It is worth mentioning that Otto Weininger[6] also had to struggle with the suppression of sadism (ideas of lustful murder); his book shows him to be a highly ethical individual.

PROF. FREUD first emphasizes his own peculiar relationship to philosophy: its abstract nature is so unpleasant to him, that he has renounced the study of philosophy. He does not know Nietzsche's work; occasional attempts at reading it were smothered by an excess of interest. In spite of the similarities which many people have pointed out, he can give the assurance that Nietzsche's ideas have had no

[6] Otto Weininger (1880-1903), Viennese writer, who committed suicide. His book *Geschlecht und Charakter* [*Sex and Character*] played an important part in the conflict between Freud and Wilhelm Fliess. Fliess accused Freud of having "betrayed" his ideas of bisexuality to Weininger. Ernst Kris discusses this affair in detail in his Introduction to *Origins of Psychoanalysis*. New York: Basic Books, 1954, p. 41.

influence whatsoever on his own work. To demonstrate how complex, and at times peculiar, the origin of new ideas can be, he recounts, on this occasion, how his idea of the sexual etiology of the neuroses developed: three great physicians, Breuer, Charcot, and Chrobak, had expressed this idea in his presence. Yet he recalled this fact only later when, faced with the [general] repudiation of this concept, he attempted to justify himself.[7]

Nietzsche failed to recognize infantilism as well as the mechanism of displacement.

Hitschmann has judiciously raised some interesting problems: (1) the question concerning the psychology of Nietzsche, the man; (2) what factors in the psychosexual constitution turn a man into a philosopher? (3) the question concerning the subjective determination of the seemingly so objective philosophical systems.

He wants to add just a few remarks: the sister reminds one of those patients who prepare themselves [for each analytic session] to prevent the possibility of anything becoming known spontaneously (uncensored).

That Nietzsche raised questions about the origin of evil already as a boy of thirteen is in keeping with the fact that other great thinkers and discoverers also established their life tasks at about that age: at eleven years of age, the discoverer of hieroglyphics set himself the task which he solved some twenty-five years later.

SADGER: Ostwald.[8] He names some chemists and physicists [who established their life task at an early age].

GRAF names Schliemann,[9] whose life interest began when he was seven years old.

ADLER names Mayer[10] who (at the age of eight) raised the question of the conservation of energy.

[7] Freud mentions this in "On the History of the Psychoanalytic Movement" (1914). *S.E.*, 14:3-66; see p. 13.

[8] Wilhelm Ostwald (1853-1932), German chemist, author of biographical sketches of scientists.

[9] Heinrich Schliemann (1822-1890), German archeologist. First a successful businessman, he retired and fulfilled his childhod dream of finding Homer's Troy.

[10] Julius Robert Mayer (1814-1878), German physician and physicist.

FREUD: Some day one should investigate how infantile impressions influence great achievements, and not only how they influence later illness.

Adler's ideas concerning paretics have an analogue in the case of Maupassant.[11]

RANK: Reading Nietzsche one gains the impression that the sadistic instinct (masochistic) and its suppression play the chief role in Nietzsche's life. In view of this suppression we can understand his delicacy, politeness, and mildness (as in the obsessional neurotic), but on the other hand also his glorification of cruelty and thirst for revenge. His thoughts on the origin of evil are vindications directed against his self-reproaches (Kant also wrote on the basic evil). The emphasis on the oral zone (the serpent in Zarathustra's mouth and the toad dreams) corresponds to his sadism. His relationship to Wagner becomes clearer when one knows of his love for Cosima.[12]

That he explored not the external world, as did other philosophers, but himself is a manifestation of a development which reversed the original transfer from within onto the external world.

STEKEL is inclined to see a kind of confession in Nietzsche's mentioning Lupulin and camphor. The philosophic drive stems from sexual curiosity; the sexual enigma becomes the enigma of the world (displacement).

[11] Guy de Maupassant (1850-1893), great French novelist, master of the short story.
[12] Wagner's wife.

46

SCIENTIFIC MEETING on *April 8, 1908*

Present: Freud, Adler, Bach, [A.] Deutsch, Federn, Graf, Heller, Hitschmann, Hollerung, Joachim, Sadger, Steiner, Stekel, Wittels, Rank.

Motion concerning library carried: monthly contribution for the time being between 1 to 2 *Kronen;* semi-annual accounting; the committee decides on the acquisition of books suggested. Contact with the *Wiener klinische Rundschau* about review copies. Proposed subscription to journals:

Sexualwissenschaft [*Sexual Science*]
Sexualprobleme [*Sexual Problems*]
Literarisches Zentralblatt [*Central Journal for Literature*]
Politisch–Anthropologische Revue [*Politico-Anthropological Revue*]
Archiv für Rassenbiologie [*Archive of Racial Biology*]

Reviews and Case Reports by All Members Present

REVIEWS

FEDERN reports on his scant selection from English journals: a purely casuistic paper (twenty cases of hysteria) in *Brain;* then a paper by D——[?], who views anxiety psychoses as illnesses of the involutional period; lastly a report from the *Société de Neurologie de*

Paris on cases of hysteria where hysteria is not diagnosed according to stigmata; the symptoms, so this report says, can be removed by means of persuasion.[1]

STEKEL found a long paper on epilepsy in the Brussels *Journal Médical,* where various forms of aura are described. The term "epilepsy" is often misused. Frequently such cases are hysterias—as, for instance, the case of Dostoyevsky. (SADGER mentions in this connection Edgar Allan Poe.) With this view in mind, one should pay more attention to the aura epileptica. The *Archives de psychologie* contains a paper on the interpretation of several dreams by the Swiss A. Maeder,[2] throwing light on the etymologic and ethnologic meaning of certain symbols (snake, house, etc.).

E. Claparède, in a paper on hysteria, published elsewhere, professes Freud's point of view (defense).[3]

Among books, he mentions Strindberg's *Confession of a Fool,* in which Strindberg describes his masturbatory boyhood history and the psychic conflicts resulting from it. His mother is said to have suffered from hysterical attacks. He saw in every woman some part of his mother. He hated his stepmother; but behind this hatred, one distinctly senses his suppressed desire. Four years ago Strindberg suddenly succumbed to anxiety attacks and delusions of persecution: he considered himself a sinner, wanted to do penance, etc.

[A.] DEUTSCH quotes two passages from Gustav Wied's tale, *From Childhood Days:*[4]

Advice to fathers and mothers: He found it wrong, even positively injurious, that boys were often left in the care of maid servants; they undressed and dressed the children, washed and bathed them, and put them to bed. In this tale he wants to relate what he

[1] The representative of "persuasion therapy" was Paul Dubois, professor of psychology in Berne.

[2] Alphonse Maeder: "Essai d'interprétation de quelques rêves" ["An Attempt to Interpret Some Dreams"]. *Archives de psychologie,* 6:354-375, 1907. A gifted young psychiatrist and psychoanalyst, Maeder viewed dreams as prophesies; soon he left psychoanalysis.

[3] Edouard Claparède (1873-1940), professor of psychology in Geneva. He did not stay with psychoanalysis as it developed further. The paper referred to is "Quelques mots sur la définition de l'hystérie" ["Some Remarks on the Definition of Hysteria"]. *Archives de psychologie,* 7:169, 1908.

[4] Gustav Wied (1858-1914), Danish writer.

himself has experienced: A nursemaid, a god-fearing, friendly, and faithful old servant, was one evening sitting beside his bed and taught him to say the psalms and to pray the pater noster. His hands were folded on top of his blanket, and he and the maid were singing and praying loudly and clearly, but her hands were under the blanket, caressing his body until Gunnar, trembling and feverish, threw his arms around her neck and bit her cheek . . . .

This he wanted to tell as a warning and to convey what evil had been done to him by others—and to so many! This one and that one had confided to him similar stories from their childhood. And all of them are still suffering to a greater or lesser degree from the consequences of the lascivious caresses received from dissipated housemaids, teachers, and elderly aunts.

Dream

And he stood in the garden of his parents' manor, an open blade in his hand. In front of him, leaning against a tree, was his father. He too was armed with a sharp knife, but between them, like a symbol of peace, was his mother. And Gunnar raised his knife and wounded his father all around, also on arms and hands; but whenever the old one tried to rush upon him, his mother moved her body between them, as a protective barrier. Suddenly she sank to her knees exhausted, and cried for mercy and mercy. But father and son thrust their knives into each other's arms, breast, neck, and hands. And Gunnar saw blood flowing from his wounds. He lost his knife, wanted to cry out for help, imploringly stretched out his arms, and sank to the ground. And there he lay for a time, unconscious, his eyes closed. And then, suddenly, he felt his body permeated by a still, comforting, painless peace. It must have been his mother who was kneeling beside him and who placed her soft hands on the wounds which his father had inflicted upon him. And gratefully he put his arms around her neck and offered her his lips for a kiss. But then he saw two sparkling steel-gray eyes burning under raven-black hair. A blood-red mouth sucked his. A body, soft and supple and gentle, nestled to him. And while he bent trembling in lust as if in an embrace, he heard Bruse's voice close to his ear whispering: "My glorious little boy, this is how I want you. . . ." [Found among the Minutes of April 8, 1908.]

STEINER reports on an essay by Knochenhauer in the *Zeitschrift für Bekämpfung der Geschlechtskrankheiten:* "Familienleben und Prostitution bei aussereuropäischen Völkern" ["Family Life and Prostitution in Non-European Peoples"], the gist of which is that the savages are really better people than we are.

HITSCHMANN calls attention to several reviews by Näcke[5] in the *Archiv für Kriminal-Anthropologie:* on "Sexuelle Perversitäten bei Tieren" ["Sexual Perversities in Animals"] (none beside masturbation), on "Erotische Tätowierung" ["Erotic Tattooing"]; further, a review of Krauss's *Anthropophyteia.*[6]

Everywhere in the literature one encounters reviews of [*Psychopathology of*] *Everyday Life* and of Jung's *Dementia Praecox.* Ziehen's *Monatsschrift*[7] contains Jung's report given at the Congress in Amsterdam. Then a paper on sexual contrast dreams,[8] in which Näcke reaches the conclusion that very decent individuals can have indecent dreams. Even normal people may have homosexual dreams.

Books

[Georg] Lomer: *Liebe und Psychose* [*Love and Psychosis*]. [Wiesbaden, 1907.]

[Siegfried] Weinberg: *Über den Einfluss der Geschlechtsfunktion auf die weibliche Kriminalität* [*On the Influence of the Sex Function on Female Criminality*]. [Halle, 1907.]

BACH discovered a paper by Fliess on the proportion of male and female births[9] in a recent issue of *Morgen* [April 6, 1908].

WITTELS reports on Nietzsche's recently published letters about his sister in which he speaks about her in a very derogatory way. In

---

[5] Paul Näcke, German psychiatrist. "Sexual Perversities in Animals" appeared in *Sexualbiologie*, ed. Robert Müller. Berlin, 1907; "Erotic Tattooing" is a paper by Lüdecke which appeared in *Anthropophyteia.* "Exhibitionism and Superstition" was published in F. S. Krauss: *Das Geschlechtsleben in Glauben, Sitte, und Brauch der Japaner* [*Sexual Life in Religion, Morals and Customs of the Japanese*], Leipzig, 1907. Näcke did not review Krauss's *Anthropophyteia*, but he reviewed Freud's *Psychopathology of Everyday Life* (in *Archiv für Kriminal-Anthropologie und Kriminalistik*, 29:303-304, 1908) and Jung's *Dementia Praecox.*

[6] Friedrich S. Krauss (1859-?), German folklorist and ethnologist, was the editor of *Anthropophyteia, Jahrbücher für folkloristische Erhebungen und Forschungen zur Entwicklungsgeschichte der geschlechtlichen Moral* [*Anthropophyteia, Yearbooks of Folkloristic Investigations and Research into the Developmental History of Sexual Morality*]. See Freud's letter (June 26, 1910) to Krauss, *G.W.*, 8:224-225.

[7] Ziehen's *Monatsschrift für Psychiatrie und Neurologie*, 28(4):310, 1908. The title of Jung's paper was "Die Freudsche Hysterietheorie" ["Freud's Theory of Hysteria"].

[8] The full title of the essay was: "Kontrastträume und speziell sexuelle Kontrastträume" ["Contrast Dreams and Sexual Contrast Dreams in Particular"]. *Gross Arch.*, 24:1-19, 1907.

[9] The paper was entitled "Knabenüberschuss" ["Surplus of Boys"].

the *Berliner Tageblatt* Wittels himself has made an attempt, on the basis of Freud's teachings, to vindicate Nietzsche's sister: she may be lying, not consciously, but because of infantile factors. He sees an analogy to Nietzsche's relationship to his sister in Schopenhauer's hostility toward his mother, which is reflected in his philosophy about women.

RANK reads aloud Nietzsche's letters just mentioned. The sister's behavior is undoubtedly motivated by her jealousy of Lou, the brother's loved one.[10]

Books

Monographien über die seelische Entwicklung des Kindes, No. 1 [*Monographs on the Psychic Development of the Child*], edited by Clara and William Stern.

Dr. M. Hirsch: *Die Kindersprache: eine psychologische und sprach-theoretische Untersuchung* [*The Language of the Child: An Investigation from the Point of View of Psychology and of the Theory of Language*]. [Leipzig, 1907.]

Max Verworn: *Zur Psychologie der primitiven Kunst* [*Contribution to the Psychology of Primitive Art*]. [Lecture, Jena, 1908.]

[Bernhard] Stern: *Geschichte der öffentlichen Sittlichkeit in Russland* [*History of Public Morality in Russia*]. [Berlin, 1907.]

Dr. [Heinrich] Stadelmann: *Die Stellung der Psychopathologie zur Kunst. Ein Versuch* [*Psychopathology and Art. An Attempt*]. [München, 1908.]

[Otto zur] Strassen: *Die neuere Tierpsychologie* [*Modern Animal Psychology*]. [Lecture, Leipzig, 1908.]

[Cesare] Lombroso: *Neue Verbrecherstudien* [*New Studies of Criminals*]. [Halle, 1907.]

[Willy] Hellpach: *Prostitution und Prostituierte* [*Prostitution and Prostitutes*]. (Berlin, 1905, 1907.]

[Jules] Lachelier: *Psychologie und Metaphysik.* [*Die Grundlage der Induktion*] [*Psychology and Metaphysics. The Basis of Induction*]. [Leipzig, 1908; Paris, 1907.]

---

[10] Lou Andreas-Salomé (1861-1937) was among the early followers of Freud. See the Introduction to this volume. See also Freud: "Lou Andreas-Salomé" (Obituary) (1937). *G.W.*, 16:270.

Franz Chyle: *Der Selbstmord* [*als Spekulation des modernen Verbrechertums*] [*Suicide as a Speculation of Present-day Criminals*]. [Vienna, 1908.]

[Erich] Wulffen: *Psychologie des Verbrechers.* [*Ein Handbuch für Juristen, Ärtzte, Pädagogen und Gebildete aller Stände*] [*Psychology of the Criminal. A Handbook for Jurists, Physicians, Pedagogues and the Educated of All Classes*]. [Gross Lichterfelde Ost, 1908.]

[Franz Ludwig von] Neugebauer: *Hermaphroditismus beim Menschen* [*Hermaphrodism in Man*]. [Leipzig, 1908.]

Paul Kronthal: *Nerven und Seele* [*Nerves and Soul*]. [Jena, 1908.]

Sarah Bernhardt: *Mein Doppelleben, Memoiren* [*My Dual Life, Memoirs*]. [Leipzig, 1908; Paris, 1907.]

[Max] Höfler: *Die volksmedizinische Organotherapie und ihr Verhältnis zum Kultopfer* [*Organotherapy in Popular Medicine and Its Relationship to Religious Sacrifice*]. [Stuttgart, 1908.]

[Herman] Swoboda: *Die Motive des Duells* [*The Motives of Duelling*], *Österr. Rundschau.*

HELLER mentions [Rudolf] Kassner's dialogue between two horses [in his "Die beiden Schwätzer"] ["The Two Gossips"], *Österr. Rundschau.*

PROF. FREUD reports on a reply by Jung and Bleuler[11] to a critique by Ernst Meyer, in which he accuses them of having revived the notion of the purely psychic causation of neuroses, an assumption which had been disposed of long ago. This reproach is not entirely unjustified because they stopped halfway, and Bleuler in particular does not go along with the sexual etiology; its acknowledgment would have spared him this reproach.

In the last number of the *Archiv für Psychiatrie und Nervenkrankheiten* Robert Tomson published a paper which does not show any progress;[12] his authority is Oswald Bumke.

Alphonse Maeder, in the *Archives de psychologie*, published new

---

[11] Bleuler und Jung: "Komplexe und Krankheitsursache bei Dementia Praecox" ["Complexes and Cause of Illness in Dementia Praecox"]. *Zentralblatt für Nervenheilkunde und Psychiatrie*, 31:220-276, 1908.

[12] "Zur Klinik und Ätiologie der Zwangserscheinungen; über Zwangshalluzinationen und über die Beziehungen der Zwangsvorstellungen zur Hysterie" [On Clinical and Etiological Considerations of Obsessional Symptoms; on Compulsive Hallucinations and on the Relationship of Obsessional Ideas and Hysteria.].

"Contributions to the Psychopathology of Everyday Life," which reveals his familiarity and skill in these matters.

FEDERN suggests, in order to avoid the confusion in terminology, to rename the neuroses and to call them instinctual and affective diseases.[13]

CASE REPORTS

FEDERN relates his observation of a case of relative psychic impotence; the meaning of the patient's enuresis nocturna (never diurna) was established historically; the enuresis persisted until his fourteenth year and was replaced by the first act of masturbation. This man has morning erections in the course of which he urinates with an erect penis. This may be a continuation of the enuresis, or it may have been one of its conditioning factors.

A second case concerns a severe anxiety neurosis; the patient was unable to use a certain trolley line (the O line). After intercourse became possible, this symptom disappeared. O, as a symbol of the vagina, represented to him the shame over his sexual failures.

ADLER cautions against exaggerations in interpreting symbols. He himself has rarely found knives used as penis symbols. The revolver likewise does not always seem to symbolize the penis as our preconceived notions would lead us to expect. In one of his cases the revolver was used as a symbol of the anus; many of the revolver's characteristics tally with this.

To this FREUD remarks that the most common symbols are occasionally used in a different way (individually adapted symbols); moreover, the most unlikely things can on occasion be employed as symbols. The meaning of the revolver as a symbol for the anus is noteworthy and very plausible (shooting-shitting; function). However, it may be a secondary transference.

JOACHIM, having read Adler's book,[14] contributes, from his own family, an example of segmental organ inferiority; it concerns a peculiar affliction of the left leg in several members of his family.

[13] The diversified interests of this group are really admirable, and so is the time and energy they devoted to the discussion of books and articles.
[14] *Studie über Minderwertigkeit von Organen*. Vienna: Urban & Schwarzenberg, 1907. *Study of Organ Inferiority and Its Psychical Compensation*. New York: Nerv. & Ment. Dis. Publ., 1917.

GRAF reports an example of the determination in name giving. His son's name is Herbert, his daughter's Hanna. As a student he was infatuated with a cousin named Hedwig; the initials of both his children's names are H, the letter which as a student he wrote everywhere, taking pride in the especially beautiful way in which he wrote it. (He had also considered naming his son: Harry and Hans.)

Then he recounts two telepathic events which concern himself. On a certain day after his marriage he thought with great intensity of his old sweetheart, his cousin, and several times believed that he had seen her in the street. Later his mother told him that on that day his cousin from Trieste had actually been in Vienna. The second event occurred in relation to his present wife; one day while they were still engaged he suddenly broke off with her, and for four weeks they did not hear from each other. At the end of this period while he was at a gay party he was suddenly overcome by longing for his wife and he wrote her. The following day he received a letter from her; their letters had crossed. (HITSCHMANN explains this by saying that individuals who attract each other have a similar rhythm.)

RANK relates that Bruckner[15] spent most of his life abstaining from women and masturbating instead; at forty years of age he fell ill with a compulsion to count; because of a disease of the ear which made him hard of hearing he was subjected to electrotherapy.

STEINER mentions the case of a man who had an anxiety neurosis and diabetes. His wife's vagina was too wide; having followed the advice to take a younger woman, he lost both anxiety and sugar. A second case is that of an impotent man, whose failure in intercourse was accompanied by severe headaches. There were marked sadistic tendencies in childhood. When he was told that this headaches were the punishment for the pains he had inflicted upon women, his symptom disappeared.

Furthermore, he wants to call attention to the eczemas which suddenly appear in springtime in people who have little sexual activity ("eruptions"). Then he gives a detailed description of his first attempt to psychoanalyze a young hysterical girl; this case confirmed

15 Anton Bruckner (1824-1896), Austrian composer.

in the most convincing manner all that he had learned theoretically. She is dominated essentially by the idea of losing her virginity.

HITSCHMANN tells of a young pianist who wears his hair long; already as a boy he would cry when his hair was cut.

The two older girls of a family, where the father is neurasthenic, the mother a cured hysteric, suffer from facial pains; the youngest son has atrophied genitals.

Two nudity dreams: one that of a painter who claims he has this dream only when he uncovers himself; now this dream has recurred a day before the opening of his exhibit (stage fright). The second case concerns a beautiful woman who dreams on the day preceding her first performance in a concert hall that she is standing nude on the stage and the audience demands a song which she does not know. She then actually sang badly.

Two people who show sadistic traits in everyday life (beat women while flattering them) and are voracious eaters. One should consider the problem whether there is a connection between the oral center and sadism.

A personal experience: he attended a concert where he talked to a girl with whom he was acquainted. When he left before the end, he had the feeling that he had been impolite to her. Dream: he walks on the street with the same girl; his schoolmate, Zimmermann, walks in front of them and produces flatus. The girl asks him whether he had not contributed to this production. He then awoke with the need for breaking wind.

STEKEL, referring to Steiner's remark, stresses that sugar occurs not infrequently with anxiety. Intoxication of the sex organs in anxiety neurosis.

PROF. FREUD reports on the solution of the rat idea in the obsessional neurotic;[16] it means:

1. Guess (numbers). He admits that he does not distinguish between *Ratten* [rats] and *raten* [to guess].

2. The identification with his father, who also was in the army and contracted a gambling debt there; a friend loaned his father money

[16] See Minutes 28, the analysis of the Rat Man.

to settle this debt; his father probably never paid this debt since he was a *"Spielratte"* ("gambling rat").

3. A very special type of *"Ratten": Heiraten* [getting married].

A few hints concerning the most important characteristics for an understanding of hysterical attacks which can be regarded as a representation of a fantasied sexual situation.

1. In representing the situation the female patient plays both the male and the female part (published).

2. Innervations are transformed into their opposites, a process which greatly resembles dream distortion; for example: the patient's hands are crossed on her back—the opposite of embracing. The arc during a major hysteric seizure: the body is curved outward, the legs are pressed together—the opposite of the position during intercourse where the body is curved inward and the legs are spread apart.

3. Reversal of sequence (also known from the *Interpretation of Dreams*). For example, first a spasmodic attack with the usual swallowing, foaming, the typical motions, etc., which represents intercourse; then she begins to utter tender words; finally she sits down quietly and may read something. Reversing the sequence, we get an attempt at seduction which ends in intercourse.

ad 1. This is analogous to dream condensation.

ad 2 and 3. These are analogous to dream distortion.

The complication that in her later seizures the patient displays epileptic trends can simply be explained as due to medical suggestion: she has been questioned about these symptoms. Thus these are manifestations of resistance expressing distrust of the physician who, she feels, does not understand her anyway.

47

SCIENTIFIC MEETING on *April 15, 1908*

Present: Freud, Adler, (Bass), Hitschmann, Hollerung, Joachim, Rank, Sadger, Schwerdtner, Steiner, Stekel, Wittels.

DISCUSSION OF DR. HIRSCHFELD'S PROPOSAL TO COLLABORATE IN DRAWING UP A QUESTIONNAIRE

PROF. FREUD reports that Dr. Magnus Hirschfeld proposed the joint drawing up of questionnaires for the purpose of exploring the sex instinct. He himself accepts this proposal and now submits it to the Society to consider whether they wish to participate. It is to be discussed whether the proposal should be accepted and, if it is, how it should be executed.

STEKEL is opposed to an association with Hirschfeld; for personal as well as objective reasons.

SADGER agrees in principle to the proposal. Hirschfeld should use the questionnaires in his name, and we shall function as silent collaborators.

ADLER is in favor; one might learn more by this means than seems likely at the moment. He sees no objection to it.

HITSCHMANN likewise is of the opinion that Hirschfeld's advances should not be rejected. The value of the questionnaires cannot be doubted.

STEINER favors the suggestion; and so does RANK, who makes the additional proposal that the questionnaire be sent out in several languages.

WITTELS is prejudiced against Berlin.

PROF. FREUD points out that in addition to Hirschfeld's points of interest, we could take into account the infantile, etiologic, and organic factors; the questionnaire would provide us with a good idea of what remains in the memory of the normal individual. We must not molest everybody with sending the form; it should be sent only to those who are willing to fill out the questionnaire.

The motion to participate in this project is then carried by a majority vote. The society which, on this occasion, is to appear before the public for the first time, is named: *Psychoanalytic Society* (by majority vote).[1] Concerning the questions and the chief points of view, Prof. Freud proposes that the next meeting be devoted to the definitive formulation of these questions; every member is asked to prepare questions, formulations, and points of view; these individual questionnaires will then be discussed. Motion carried.

DR. HITSCHMANN assumes the special responsibility of drawing up a questionnaire on the basis of Hirschfeld's model form.

The chief foci of interest would be:
1. Family relations;
2. Development of sexuality in childhood; and
3. after puberty.

One might include such questions as:
Ad 1. About parents and siblings: age, position
among siblings.
Early deaths.
Methods of rearing.
Persons bringing up the child.

---

[1] It was on April 15, 1908 that the group around Freud, in connection with Hirschfeld's questionnaire, introduced itself to the public as the "Psychoanalytic Society."

Ad 2. When does your recollection start?
First recollection?
When does your recollection become continuous?
What bad habits or childhood defects did you or your siblings have?
Importance should be attached to:
talent for imitation
fantasy life
sleep, etc.

48

SCIENTIFIC MEETING *on April 22, 1908*

Present: Freud, Adler, Bach, Brecher, [A.] Deutsch, Federn, Frey, Graf, [Rank, Joachim, Sadger, Reitler, Heller].

DISCUSSION OF HIRSCHFELD'S QUESTIONNAIRE

HITSCHMANN submits a provisional questionnaire, briefly giving the reasons for its composition: it deals with statistics concerning the sex life of healthy and ill people. Part of the questionnaire must be filled out by the physician, because one cannot dispense with the physical aspects of the sexual status. In this respect, special attention should be paid to developmental anomalies. Apart from that, one might learn all sorts of things, for instance, about sexual physiognomics. Anyone who answers the questions must sharply distinguish between what he has experienced and what he has learned by hearsay.

Hitschmann reads his questionnaire which is then discussed.

FEDERN suggests that different forms be worked out for men and women. Questions: length of the membrum; whether brought up in sexual freedom or in puritanism; first coition: whether accompanied by pleasure, feelings of guilt.

BRECHER: At what age the differentiation between sublimated love and primitive sexuality took place. The same question in regard to sexuality and propagation.—Prostitution and venereal diseases.—Mode of nutrition (bottle—alcohol, coffee).—Psychic manifestations: precociousness, curiosity.—Whether the child was considered good or naughty.

SADGER: Erections in puberty.—Temper tantrums.—Observation of adults in sexual intercourse.

REITLER: Behavior when confronted with deaths; when [was] fear of death [experienced].—Urge to ask questions.

HELLER: Cruelty to animals.

RANK: Anomalies of sense organs; teeth.—Artistic activities.—Fantasy life.—Favorite sports.

JOACHIM: Urge to collect things.—Special food preferences.—Impotence.

PROF. FREUD is of the opinion that in the general questionnaire homosexuality should be mentioned only casually; those who prove to be homosexual could then be sent a second questionnaire.

He will work out the questionnaire himself making use of the suggestions received.

QUESTIONNAIRE PREPARED BY HITSCHMANN[1]

* Distinguish between what has been experienced and what one has been told.*

I. *Physical status* (to be filled out by the physician)	Sexual physiognomy; Sex organs, especially developmental anomalies (possibly including the anus, etc.)
II. *Ancestry* (Hereditary disposition)	(a) Grandparents: professions, city or country; sexual anomalies; number of progeny; neuroses, psychoses, etc.

[1] Written by hand with ink. Words marked with asterisks at beginning and end were inserted in pencil.

376

(b) Parents: data pertaining to their sex life (what inherited? inferior organs?)

Marriage: At what age? for love? harmonious? Family life, *cheerful?* early deaths, affectionate with each other? Profession, Characteristics. Neuroses? etc.

III. *Self-observation in Early Childhood* (Infantility)

(a) First recollection

(b) When does continuous recollection begin

(c) First sexual experiences, curiosity—satisfaction, enlightenment, seductions. *Infantile sexual theories.*

Parents: Caresses. Preferred father or mother? Why? ("Family romance"). Dislike, jealous of one parent? "Taken into bed." Spanking. *Watched* Sexual-erotic feelings in connection with the child's love for his parents?

Persons rearing the child: *Wet nurse?* Methods used in training? *Sleeping together*

Siblings: Age, sequence, sex. Special preference? Hatred? Their abnormalities; childhood habits, peculiarities. *Sexual frankness.*

Playmates:

(d) Bad habits in childhood (thumb sucking, anal erotism, etc.), *rubbing buttocks,* enuresis, masturbation (where), *Nail biting, pavor, rubbing buttocks*[2]

Perversion. Inversion. Fetish.[3] *Exhibitionism*

[2] "Rubbing buttocks" [*wetzen*] is crossed out here and appears above "anal erotism."

[3] Crossed out in original.

377

Childhood: Pavor nocturnus, Childhood anxieties and the like, nail biting (sleeping alone, falling asleep)
Religious feelings
Friendships with schoolmates, love for teachers.

III [*sic*]. *Later childhood:* Incest self-reproach? Incest repression? *Accessibilty to training.* Shame. Disgust.

Peculiarities: Eating, *precocious* kissing? talent for imitation, wit, *masochism,* sadism, peeping, lying, etc.

I. Childhood Pavor nocturnus. Infantile anxieties and similar things. Nail biting.

Sleeping alone. Falling asleep. *Religiosity.*

Friendships in school, love for teachers.

IV. *Puberty:* Becoming aware of it. Affects called forth thereby. First emission. In females, first local sensations, first menses.

Masturbation (mutual?); how often, how, where? What fantasies? Compulsive?

Threats, admonitions, prohibitions. (Degree of severity, asceticism.)

Daydreams, mental masturbation. Dreams *(typical).* Pubertal anxiety, struggle with oneself, abstinence possible? Consequences? Sublimation (arts, religiosity, confession).

School—Sex. Mental work—sex. Friendship

Aversion to sex. Enlightenment. Depression. (Suicide). Moralist. Philosopher. Interests.

First kisses. Seduction. Disgust. Lack of feelings of love, frigidity, anesthesia.

First coition, *(feelings of guilt?)* Subsequent coitions. Satisfaction?

Contrectation. Detumescence.[4] Prostitution. *Sports:*
Use of preservatives.

Degree and extent of sexual knowledge at that time.
Do they just lack money to find satisfaction? Syphilophobia. Infections.

Love relationships (similar to parents'?). Sexual compulsion? Emissions. Frustrated excitation.

Genital-nasal reflex. Urogenic reflex. Anal reflexes.

Inversion (compare Hirschfeld's questionnaire)

Neuroses?

V. *Present Adult State*	Wedding night. Defloration. Anesthesia.
(married life, children)	Malthusianism.[5] Potency, Marital life.
	Perversions. Details. Abstinence pos-
	sible? Consequences.

Place――――――――― Date――――――

QUESTIONNAIRE NO. ――[6]

In the interest of scientific research and the better understanding
of persons with abnormal inclinations, we ask you to take the time
and trouble to answer the following questions as accurately and truth-
fully as possible. You can count on *absolute discretion.*

[4] "Contrectation" and "detumescence" are concepts which were introduced by Moll
but never gained general acceptance. By "contrectation drive" he understood a kind
of supplement to the sexual instinct, specifically the drive to touch and embrace the
sex partner. He attributed to this also the development of the sexual instinct into a
psychic and mental factor. "Detumescence drive" designates, roughly, the drive for the
relaxation of genital excitement through physical contact.

[5] Malthusianism, in this context, means control of propagation. Malthus was an
English clergyman who wrote on population policy. His "An Essay on the Principle
of Population or a View of Its Past and Present Effects on Human Happiness" (1803)
exercised a great influence on the thinking about these problems.

[6] This is the questionnaire worked out by Dr. Magnus Hirschfeld, forty years
before Kinsey began his comprehensive statistical studies of human sex life.

The questionnaire consists of several printed sheets. The text appears in the left-
hand column; the right-hand column is left blank. On the questionnaire attached to
these Minutes, several notes in pencil appear in the right-hand column, probably by
Hitschmann (judging by the handwriting). We do not reproduce these notes.

Name, residence, sex, present age, race, profession, married or single?

Anyone who is reluctant to sign the answered questionnaire with his full name may mark the questionnaire with a number and simultaneously send us this number together with his address in a separate envelope. We call your special attention to the fact that keeping the information secret falls under the medical privileged communications. We request that questions that can be answered briefly be answered in the margin, the others on a special sheet. *The addition of a photograph would be most welcome.*

A. HEREDITY

1. As far as you know, have any cases of homosexual love or similar tendencies occurred in your parents, grandparents, or any of their relatives?

2. Have any of them suffered from nervous or mental disorders, such as convulsions, hysteria, debility, melancholia, or from moral defects, from alcoholism, syphilis, hernia, goiter, or defective physical development, etc., or some noteworthy peculiarities?

3. Did any suicide occur among your relatives and, if so, for what reasons?

4. What caused your parents' death? If they are still alive, are they healthy?

5. Were the parents or grandparents blood relations?

6. What was the age difference between father and mother? At what ages did they get married? How old were your parents when you were born? Did your parents live together happily or not? Did your parents get married for love or for external reasons? (Continuation of an old family, financial interests, etc.)

7. Do you rather resemble your father or your mother?

8a. Are there any sexually peculiar persons among your siblings or your first cousins?

b. Are there any male members of the family who have a feminine appearance or female members who look masculine (if this is the case with relatives other than siblings, indicate whether they are relatives on the mother's or father's side)?

9. Did your mother intensely wish for a child of the opposite sex

(to which you do not belong)? Are you the oldest or youngest child or are you in the middle? How many sisters and brothers do you have? What is the sequence and age of your siblings (for instance, brother, brother, sister, I, brother)?—If any of them are homosexuals or bisexual, list them in sequence.

B. Childhood

10. Did you learn to walk and talk at the appropriate time? How was the first and second teething?

11. Did you suffer from any cerebral inflammation, head injuries, headaches, convulsions, chorea? Were you cross-eyed? Did you have enuresis, or dental abnormalities? Were you anxious and easily frightened?

12. Did you bite your nails or pick your nose? Was there a tendency toward lying, to vagrancy, disobedience, stealing, an inclination to cry easily? Was there masturbation? Accompanied by what fantasies? When did you start it? What brought you to it?

13. Did you prefer to play with little boys or girls? Did you prefer boyish games, like soldiers, hobby horses, throwing snowballs, fighting, etc., or did you prefer girlish games, like playing with dolls, cooking, crocheting, and knitting? Were remarks made such as: "She is a real boy" or "He is like a little girl"? Did you notice that you were different from other children? Did you look very much like a girl, or like a boy respectively, before puberty?

14. What kind of education did you get? Were you brought up together with many others in boarding schools, convents, military schools, or were you brought up at home by your parents or relatives? What was life like in the institutions? Did sexual seductions occur? In what way? Through contemporaries or through younger or older individuals, and of what sex were they?

15. What were your intellectual capacities? What subjects interested you most in school?

16. Were there passionate friendships in school (with or without sexual acts) or unusually strong veneration of adult persons? Of whom?

17. When and how did the first sexual impulses arise?

381

18. When did sexual maturity set in? When and how did your voice mature, a beard develop, the breasts? Did you notice (if you are male) a swelling of the breasts with the onset of puberty (sexual maturity)?

C. Present State

I. Physical Characteristics and Conditions

19. What are the characteristics of your figure, especially what is the width of your hips?

20. Are the lines of your body more angular or round, thin or fat?

21. Are the upper arms and thighs more flat or rounded?

22. Are hand and foot small or large, the hand rather soft or strong?

23. Is the flesh softly turgescent or firm and hard?

24. Are the muscles strong or poorly developed?

25. Is there a preference for strong muscular activity, a tendency to move energetically and fast, or to move quietly with a rolling gait; do you like to go on walking tours, to dance, and the like? Did you like calisthenics? Were you interested in gymnastic games, sports, swimming?

26. Are your steps short, slow, tripping, skipping, lurching, or firm, long, fast, solemn; is there an unconscious turning of shoulders or hips while walking or is the body held quiet, straight or bent forward?

27. Do you know how to whistle?

28. Is the color of your skin (of the face as well as the body) rather white, delicate, clean, or dark and unclean?

29. Is the skin of your body rough or smooth?

30a. Are the breasts full, round, fleshy, or flat, thin? Are the nipples and aureola especially large?

b. Are there any external malformations of the genitalia, for instance (in the man), phimosis (tight foreskin), hypospadia (abnormal opening of the urethra), cryptorchism (undescended testicles), varicocele, split testicles, and the like; or (in the woman) hypertrophic clitoris (particularly large), vagina too narrow, labia hanging down low?

382

31. Is your hair thick? Are breast and body very hairy? What is the color of your hair, how do you wear it, parted, straight, curled or unarranged?

32. Is there a downy beard, weak or strong growth of beard?

33. Do you easily blush or turn pale?

34. Is your sensitivity to pain great or insignificant?

35. Are your ears large, projecting, or small, pretty?

36. Is your gaze steady or restless, very soft, tender, or does it show any other peculiarities?

37. Is the expression of your face more masculine or feminine? (Photograph requested.)

38. What is the structure of your larynx? Does the Adam's apple protrude a little, much, or not at all?

39. Is your voice high or deep, loud or low, simple or affected?

40. Is there a marked tendency to speaking or singing in a falsetto or bass voice?

41. Are there any disorders of the nervous system such as vertigo, migraine, insomnia, trembling, left-handedness, excessive lassitude, or the like?

II. Mental Characteristics and Capacities

42. Is your disposition gentle or stern, more feminine or masculine?

43. Are you very susceptible to joy and pain? Do you cry easily (sentimental)? Is there a tendency to morbid fits of laughing and crying? Are you capable of feeling great enthusiasm or are you easily depressed?

44. Is the desire for a family, the desire to have a child of your own not at all, weakly, or strongly developed? Would you be capable of having normal intercourse, just for the sake of getting a child of your own? Would you not shun the hardship of a delivery in order to have a child?

45. Are you religious? In need of love, affection? Are you amiable, good-natured, self-sacrificing, a philanthropist? Do you have a tendency to longing, homesickness, to excitability, vehemence, rage?

46. Is there a great longing, ambition, are you given to exaggerating your personality, susceptibility to admiration and applause, a tendency to attract attention?

383

47. Do you have a propensity for gossip and garrulity, for excessive distrust, malice? Are you inclined toward superstitiousness and enthusiastic belief in miracles?

48. Do you have a desire for adventures, a tendency to eccentricity, to tramping about, to wastefulness, to collecting; to improper, provocative behavior; to indecency? Is order important to you or are you careless in this respect?

49. Do you have an even and tranquil temperament, or are you dependent on whims and moods? Are you resentful and implacable or rather inclined to be forgiving and magnanimous?

50. Do you have a strong or weak will; are you constant or inconstant, fearful or courageous?

51. Are you more inclined to good or plain living; to mental and physical work or to comfort? What are your drinking and smoking habits? Can you stand a good deal of alcoholic beverages or only a little?

52. Is your intellectual education superficial or deep? How is your memory, attention, fantasy?

53. Are your mental gifts more in the direction of productivity and creating new things or more reproductive and entering into another's feelings, more examining and judging or more receptive (that is, productive or reproductive, critical or receptive).

54. Is there a greater aptitude for mathematics and abstract problems or is there a more literary, artistic gift; a talent for music, painting; a predilection for the plastic arts, for instance, Greek statues?

55. Would you like to become an actor?

56. Which mythical and historical persons (also of contemporary history) are you most interested in? Who are your ideals?

57. Do you have a liking or a dislike for female occupations, such as cooking, cleaning, needlework, or for male occupations such as sports, hunting, shooting, fighting? What subjects are of special interest to you (for instance, politics, fashions, theater, horses, flowers, etc.)? Do you read and study a great deal? What kind of reading matter do you prefer (scientific works, poems, light literature, etc.)?

58. What profession attracts you?

59. Does clothing occupy an important place in your thoughts? Do you prefer simple or conspicuous clothing, tight or loose garments,

high collars or a free neck? Do you have an outspoken predilection for or aversion to jewelry?

60. Do you feel the urge to wear clothes of the opposite sex? Do you have a great liking for accessories of the opposite sex, such as earrings, bracelets, long stockings, fans, perfumes, powder, cosmetics; or masculine caps, collars, boots, trousers? Have you a predilection for a particular color?

61. Are you generally popular or unpopular? Do you like social intercourse or do you prefer to be by yourself?

62. Do you have special achievements or merits to your credit?

63. How does your handwriting look? Is it large, firm, definite, or small, thin, delicate? (Samples of your handwriting would be very welcome.)

III. Sex Instinct

64. At what age did definite sexual feelings appear?

65a. Was the sexual drive directed to men or women?

b. Was it the same before, during, and after maturity, or did it change?

66. Is the sexual drive directed to both sexes in the same degree or is the degree different; if so, in what way?

67. Is intercourse possible for you with persons of one sex exclusively or is it possible also with persons of the other sex? If it is possible with individuals of your own sex as well as with those of the other, is it necessary for you to imagine a person of your own sex while having intercourse with an individual of the opposite sex? Is there indifference, disgust, or hate vis-à-vis one sex or aversion to the normal act? Were attempts made at intercourse with a subsequent feeling of lassitude, exhaustion, and dissatisfaction?

68. Did your dreams of love refer to individuals of the same or of the opposite sex?

69. On the stage, in the circus, in museums, did women or men interest you more?

70. Are you very free in your asexual relations with persons of the opposite sex? Do you feel more shame facing women or men?

71. Is your love directed to persons younger or older than yourself, or to those of your own age, or does the age make no difference to you? What, approximately, are the upper and lower age limits of

the persons who attract you? Did you notice any change in the direction of your instincts before, during, and after puberty, or has it always remained the same? If your love extends to an individual of your own sex, kindly indicate whether it refers to persons whose exterior as well as character come close to the opposite sex—that is to say, to youthful men or women with masculine characteristics—or whether it refers to persons who represent the outspoken type of their sex, thus to strong, genuinely masculine, or delicate, genuinely feminine types.

72. Were you more attracted by cultured or common, gentle or crude, delicate or forceful persons? Do you have a preference for certain professions, such as artists, actors, prostitutes, especially people in uniform, in particular soldiers? Do you love persons whom you can educate (in the broadest sense of the word)? Do you have marked pedagogical inclinations?

On what impressions is the attraction based which certain individuals have for you of the sex attractive to you?

a. Are they visual perceptions, thus beauty (1) of the face, (2) of the body?

b. Auditory perceptions, that is, does the voice of the person who excites you have a special attraction for you?

c. Tactile perceptions? Is, for instance, the musculature of the man, which is hard and taut to the touch, or the soft, luscious skin of the woman particularly attractive to you?

d. Olfactory perceptions? Are you excited by the odor of perspiration in certain individuals? Is the odor of certain places of the body (which ones) of particular importance?

e. Or do you believe that attraction to be a purely or predominantly psychic one, based on qualities of character, will, intellect, etc.?

73. Did you have friendships, unions of long duration, like a marriage, or relationships that were short-lived and fleeting (here the addition of your sexual history, possibly written on separate sheets, would be desirable). Were there episodes of strong jealousy?

74. In what manner was sexual intercourse performed? Was the type of desire more masculine and active or more feminine and pas-

sive? Did you wish to have been born a man or a woman? Which type of activity is normal in your own feeling?

75. How strong and how controllable is your sex instinct? Do you consider it unconquerable for a long duration? How far were the urges suppressed, how far did you give in to them, or how far were they replaced by self-gratification? What type of sexual intercourse gave you the feeling of strength and well-being?

76. For a permanent, close friendship, do you absolutely require sexual intercourse, or is the joy in physical beauty and in mental and moral excellencies enough for such unions?

77. Was there ever a liking for immature, sexually immature individuals? If so, have you gratified this inclination?

78. Did you ever notice in yourself an inclination to other sexual abnormalities, such as inflicting pain (sadism); suffering pain (masochism); a passion for certain objects, such as boots of a special kind, handkerchiefs, or for parts of the body, such as hands, feet, braids, liver-spots (fetishism). Is there an urge to show the genital parts (exhibitionism) or the like? Have you ever become sexually excited by animals?

Have you ever satisfied these deviant instincts?

79. Did you marry? For what reasons? What kind of married life did you have? Did you have children? Do you love them? Have you noticed certain sexual predispositions in them (homosexual, for instance)?

80. When and on what occasion did you discover your own nature?

81. Can you state a cause of the deviation of your feelings from the norm? Do you believe them to be congenital or acquired, perhaps through a seduction or a definite experience, as, for instance, illness of your wife, disgust, or other matters. Furthermore, what are the impressions—according to the same subheadings (a) to (e) of question 72—which have a repulsive effect on you in the sex which does not attract you?

82. Have you fought strongly against your disposition? By what means, and what was the result? Did you submit to hypnosis, with what success? Did you feel very unhappy? Were you tired of life, did you try to commit suicide?

83. Did you have conflicts (vexation) with your family, the author-

ities, difficulties with blackmailers or such of any other kind? Did your drive cause you to feel in conflict with religious or social views inculcated in you?

84. What do you yourself think of your sexual state?

85. Would you desire to have your sexual nature changed, if it were possible, or are you satisfied with your present sexual disposition?

86. Are most of your acquaintances people with normal sexual inclinations or homosexual ones? Where do you feel more at ease? Do you enjoy social intercourse with ladies? By what indications do you recognize homosexuals?

87. How many homosexuals do you know at your place of residence and how many do you know altogether? What is your estimate of the number of homosexuals; for what reasons?

88. Do you think that in a country where homosexual activities are punishable by law, such activities occur less frequently? Have you observed more homosexually inclined individuals in certain peoples, races, classes than in others? Or are such individuals equally distributed among all of them?

89. Have you formed an opinion on the natural purpose of homosexual feelings, and what is it?

90. Other remarks.

Send replies to:

Dr. M. Hirschfeld, Charlottenburg,
Berlinerstrasse 104.

Note: If at all feasible, it is recommended that you present yourself to a competent physician for physical examination (larynx, measurement of the pelvis, feminine and masculine contours, possible signs of degeneration, etc.).

49

THE CONGRESS IN SALZBURG[1]
on April 27, 1908

PROGRAM

OF THE

CONVENTION IN SALZBURG

April 26-27, 1908

April 26: Arrival in Salzburg in the evening.
Informal meeting in the Hotel Bristol
Rooms are reserved in the Hotel Bristol for the gentlemen
who have given notice of their participation.

April 27: 8 A.M.: Session (The place will be announced on the
evening of the 26)

Papers

1. Prof. Dr. S. Freud—Vienna: Case Presentation
2. Dr. E. Jones—London: Rationalization in Everyday Life
3. Dr. Sadger—Vienna: Contribution to the Etiology of Psycho-
pathia Sexualis

[1] This is a printed program, inserted in the Minutes.

4. Dr. Morton Prince—Boston: Experiments Showing Psychogalvanic Reactions from the Subconsciousness in a Case of Multiple Personality[2]*

    Dr. Riklin—Zurich-Rheinau: On Some Problems of the Interpretation of Myths

5. Dr. Abraham—Berlin: Psychosexual Differences Between Dementia Praecox and Hysteria
6. Dr. Stekel—Vienna: On Anxiety Hysteria
7. Dr. Adler—Vienna: Sadism in Life and in Neurosis
8. Dr. Jung—Zurich: On Dementia Praecox

Each speaker has half an hour at his disposal. Discussion will take place in the evening.

1 P.M.: Luncheon in the Hotel Bristol

Afternoon: In good weather, the participants will take a walk together.*

In the evening: Convention in the Hotel Bristol
1. Discussion of the Papers*
2. Dr. Stein—Budapest: How Can the Libido Released by Analysis Be Guided into Therapeutically Propitious Paths?*
3. Dr. Ferenczi—Budapest: What Practical Hints for Child Education Follow from the Freudian Experiences?
4. Administrative Problems

LIST OF PERSONS PRESENT

Name	Place of Residence	Address
Dr. Karl Abraham	Berlin	W. Schöneberger Ufer 22
Dr. Alfred Adler	Vienna	II. Czerningasse 7
Dr. [?] Arend	Munich	Mannhardtstrasse 3, part. [ground floor]
Dr. [? ?]	Munich	Glückstrasse 3
Dr. D. J. Bach	Vienna	VII. Wimbergergasse 7
Dr. H. B. Bertschinger	Schaffhausen	Breitenau
Prof. Dr. Bleuler	Zurich	Burghölzli

[2] The lines marked with an asterisk have been crossed out in the original.

390

Name	Place of Residence	Address
Dr. Guido Brecher	Gastein-Meran	
Dr. A. A. Brill	New York	Hospital, Central Islip
Ed. Claparède	Geneva	11, Champel
M. Eitingon	Zurich	Dolderstrasse 78
Dr. Paul Federn	Vienna	I. Riemergasse 1
Dr. S. Ferenczi	Budapest	VII. Elisabethring 54
Prof. Dr. Sigm. Freud	Vienna	IX. Berggasse 19
Dr. Otto & Mrs. Gross	at pres. Munich	Mandelstrasse 1d
Dr. Eduard Hitschmann	Vienna	I. Gonzagagasse 16
Dr. Edwin Hollerung	Vienna	IV. Favoritenstrasse 70
Dr. Ludwig Jekels	Bistrai near Bielitz (Austria)	
Doz. Dr. C. G. Jung	Zurich	Burghölzli
Dr. Ernest Jones	London	13 Hartey [Harley] Street, W.
stud. med. Paul Klemperer	Vienna	I. Tuchlauben 7
Prof. Dr. Leopold Königstein	Vienna	I. Biberstrasse 11
Dr. Hans Königstein	Vienna	I. Biberstrasse 11
Dr. A. Löwenfeld	Munich	
Dr. A. Ludwig	Munich	Franz Josefstrasse 13
Otto Rank	Vienna	IX. Simondenkgasse 8
Dr. Rudolf Reitler	Baden near Vienna	Franzenstrasse 17
Dr. Franz Riklin	Rheinau-Zurich	
Dr. J. Sadger	Vienna	IX. Liechtenstein-strasse 15
Dr. Hugo Schwerdtner	Vienna	I. Weihburggasse 4
Dr. A. Stegmann	Dresden	Moscniskystrasse 18
Dr. F. Stein	Budapest	IV. Semmelweiss-gasse 11
Dr. Maxim. Steiner	Vienna	I. Rotenturmstrasse 19
Dr. Wilh. Stekel	Vienna	II. Kastellezgasse 2
Dr. Warda	Blankenburg (Thüringen)	
Dr. Fritz Wittels	Vienna	I. Graben 13
Prof. Ehrismann (Mrs.)	Zurich	

391

50

SCIENTIFIC MEETING on *May 6, 1908*

Present: Freud, Adler, Bass, [A.] Deutsch, Federn, Brecher, Graf, Hitschmann, Reitler, Rank, Sadger, Steiner, Stekel, Wittels. Dr. Jones from London and Dr. Brill from New York as guests.

PRESENTATION

Some Remarks on the Genesis of Psychic Impotence

SPEAKER: DR. STEKEL

Referring to Steiner's classification, Stekel first discusses impotence appearing at a later age. Impotence appears for unconscious reasons. A man has the notion that he is impotent and this idea then causes him to be impotent. As a consequence of abstinence an anxiety neurosis sets in; the released anxiety attaches itself to the idea. The entire process is a perpetual interplay between instinct and inhibition; in such cases, the physician can perform miracles.

Then Stekel talks about impotence which reaches way back into childhood [*sic!*]. He himself has never seen congenital impotence. All of these people have erections when they are not with a woman. These cases are a mixture of anxiety hysteria and obsessional neurosis.

In all such cases analysis reveals that the first sexual aggression has been followed by an action that caused this recollection to be permanently associated with unpleasure. To prove his thesis Stekel presents a few cases.

In all cases of psychic impotence there is a marked homosexual component which is derived from the violent repression of early incestuous ideas. These individuals take flight from incest into homosexuality; in relation to women, they frequently have a brotherly or filial feeling.

One frequently finds that a compromise with the incestuous wish has been reached by means of marriage to a distant relative.

Finally Stekel summarizes the most important points of his paper by reading the four theses from his book (p. 200).[1]

DISCUSSION

REITLER finds Stekel's conclusions too general. In many cases of impotence the homosexual component is present. In the paper which he read at Salzburg, Sadger disregarded the three groups of homosexuals which Freud distinguishes in his *Theory of Sexuality*.

HITSCHMANN refers to his report on anesthesia in women[2] where he, too, was able to cite homosexual dreams. For the rest, Stekel has gone much too far in his conclusions; the four theses cannot be based on just a few cases. His analyses are neither exact nor thorough.

DR. BRILL of New York asks whether the morning erections are actually as important for the prognosis as Stekel assumes; in his

---

[1] Stekel's book has the title *Nervöse Angstzustände und ihre Behandlung* [*Nervous Anxiety States and Their Treatment*]. Berlin-Vienna: Urban & Schwarzenberg, 1908. Prof. Freud wrote a foreword.
The four theses are:
1. An incestuous idea can be shown in all cases.
2. The feeling of guilt acts as an inhibition. This feeling of guilt is actually remorse about masturbation and bad conscience on account of incestuous fantasies [compare Minutes 39 and 40].
3. The recollection of the first sexual aggression is for various reasons unpleasurable. This is particularly true if the aggression was punished by a whipping.
4. A distinct homosexual component diminishes the energy of the heterosexual drive.
[2] Compare with Minutes 39 and 40.

patients they are caused by excessive drinking on the preceding evening.

(STEKEL believes that the important thing is that erections occur.)

STEINER contests the prognostic importance of morning erections and refers to the fact that patients with prostate disorders have erections which are of no value. Otherwise, all the factors mentioned by Stekel play an important part, even though his classification will not be a lasting one.

WITTELS confirms the correctness of Stekel's four points, judging from one of his cases.

ADLER immediately emphasizes his critical attitude toward Stekel's statements. Stekel has not demonstrated why a repressed recollection leads to a muscular inhibition when intercourse is intended. Stekel could have traced all of the symptoms back to the original instincts. If a man, during intercourse, needs to moan and express pain—also pointing a knife to father and brother; and, furthermore, syphilophobia, which is found in most cases of impotence—then all these factors indicate an accumulation of various impulses in the instinct of aggression and in its transformation. This instinct is destined to have the last word in the problem of psychic impotence. Here also belong the turning of the instinct of aggression against one's own person; the desire to lie underneath; a considerable part of the exhibitionistic component (idea of the small penis; women). Incestuous and homosexual ideas are found in everyone; particularly, however, in all neurotics. They originate in an early intense development of the sex instinct. Unpleasurably toned recollections of the first aggression do not play such an important role, or perhaps are important only for individuals who because of unsatisfied excitation get into a state of aggression.

DR. JONES of London confirms Stekel's conclusions, especially if the first sexual experience results in unpleasure. As the most valuable viewpoint he stresses the importance of psychic influences on physical processes.

BASS, having little experience in this field, can mention only one case of psychic impotence which occurred after many years of married life and was provoked by the intervention of a second woman.

FEDERN is inclined to decide in Stekel's favor regarding the meaning of the full bladder.

In many cases thoughts which were not necessarily unconscious have led to impotence.

He can confirm that the four basic conditions are actually present in the majority of cases. Mutual masturbation may perhaps play an important part. In his cases he found a weak sexual instinct.

BRECHER, on the basis of two cases (which he could not, however, carry through to the end), confirms the occurrence of all the phenomena found in neurosis, and especially that of incestuous thoughts. He again raises Federn's question whether there are not cases of impotence which may be termed normal. (PROF. FREUD: Normal impotence is *not wanting* [to perform intercourse].)

The brother of an impotent man suffered from obsessional neurosis; there were also aggressions against the mother.

PROF. FREUD first reproves Stekel for relapsing to surface psychology; those men who in mature life become impotent on a particular occasion and then remain impotent are impotent the second time and on subsequent occasions not because of fear that the first incapacity will be repeated, but because the same reasons which caused the first impotence continue to operate.

The difficulties encountered in the detailed study of neuroses have been precisely pointed out by Adler:

1. It must not be forgotten that accidental factors meet with constitutional factors (the psychic and organic factors), and that it is very difficult to discriminate between them.

2. In all neuroses, as in normal persons, all of the factors always occur together. The investigation must be aimed at discovering wherein lies the pathological use of these factors.

Weakness of the sexual instinct is a viewpoint to be kept in mind.

3. There is the problem of the choice of neurosis. In psychic impotence, Stekel lays stress on the condition that the first infantile sexual activity has been linked with unpleasure. Could this be proven as an *accidental* cause, the problem of impotence would be solved. His own experiences with psychic impotence tend to favor Stekel's assertion. There are also certain details which tally with it: usually

these are individuals who cannot look at the vagina; seduction by ugly and elderly persons, etc. Nevertheless, Stekel's etiology of psychic impotence seems too narrowly conceived.

As far as the special case is concerned, he agrees with Adler; in general, however, he must contradict him. The neuroses cannot be considered to be dependent upon the instincts, because all instincts are again found in all neuroses. However, he can confirm that psychic impotence originates in an inhibition of the instinct of aggression. Many impotent men were, in their youth, obsessional neurotics with compulsive rituals. He has become accustomed to consider cases of psychic impotence as obsessional neurosis. Psychic impotence is in general the chief symptom of neurosis (analogous: anesthesia in women). What we have to ask ourselves is how it comes about that there are any other symptoms; that is an enigma.

In any case, he cautions against rash, dogmatic publications, and advises that we wait to see whether there may not nevertheless be an additional organic factor involved here.

The problem of the choice of neurosis will have to be discussed at another time and in continuity.[3]

SADGER remarks that the idea of the mother as prostitute is frequently found in those who later have much contact with women who may be termed prostitutes. The severe threats referring to the consequences of masturbation are an additional factor in the causation of psychic impotence. The physical methods are effective because of love for the physician.

STEKEL disagrees with Steiner. The same cases belong in the third category as in the first. Besides, the classification of psychic impotence is a matter of taste. As he has mentioned before, it is a mixture of anxiety hysteria and obsessional neurosis.

[3] The choice of neurosis is an ever-recurring problem.

51

SCIENTIFIC MEETING *on May 13, 1908*

Present: Freud, Adler, Bach, Brecher, Federn, Häutler, Hitschmann, Hollerung, Joachim, Rank, Stekel, Urbantschitsch.
[A.] Deutsch, Sadger, Steiner, Schwerdtner, Wittels excused.

Reviews and Case Reports

REVIEWS

The secretary lists the recently published literature ([information gathered] from *Literarisches Zentralblatt*). Furthermore:

Dr. [Julian] Marcuse: *Die sexuelle Frage und das Christentum* [*The Sexual Problem and Christianity*]. Leipzig: Werner Klinckhardt [1908].

[Max] Meyerfeld: "Byron und seine Schwester" ["Byron and His Sister"]. *Neue Rundschau*, May, 1908.

[Dr. Richard] Bolte: "Assoziationspsychologie und Assoziationsexperiment" ["Association Psychology and Association Experiment"]. *Die Umschau*, XII, 4.

[Dr. Leopold] Lauer: "Nervosität und moderne Kultur" ["Nervousness and Modern Civilization"]. *Die Umschau*, XII, 7.

Walter: "Zur Geschichte der sexuellen Pädagogik" ["Contribution to the History of Sexual Pedagogy"]. *Allgemeine Rundschau*, V, 5, ed. Kausen [Dr. Armin Kausen].

[Hans] Gross: "Mnemotechnik im Unterbewusstsein" ["Memory Mechanisms in the Subconscious"]. *Archiv für Kriminologie*, XXXIX, 1.

[Paul] Näcke: "Beiträge zu den sexuellen Träumen" ["Contributions to Sexual Dreams"]. *Archiv für Kriminologie*, XXIX, 4.

Woltär [Oskar Woltär]: "Über das sogenannte neurasthenische Vorstadium der Psychosen" ["On the So-called Neurasthenic Prodromal States of the Psychoses"]. *Wiener klinische Wochenschrift*, XXI, 4.

STEKEL mentions that there is an interesting chapter on "Logic in Neurasthenia" in Strindberg's latest work [*A Blue Book*].

HITSCHMANN mentions a paper by Dr. B. Risch (Eichberg) in the *Allgemeine Zeitschrift für Psychologie* [*Psychiatrie und psychisch-gerichtliche Medizin*, 1908], "Beitrag zum Verständnis der psychogenen Zustände ["Contribution to the Understanding of Psychogenic States"], which is not far from Freud's views, since the author sees sexual matters as the cause of these phenomena.

Hitschmann furthermore gives a detailed review of a paper (mentioned already on a previous occasion) by the Russian Drobin [B. A. Drobniy]: "Chronische Prostatitis als Ursache der Neurasthenie" ["Chronic Prostatitis as Cause of Neurasthenia"], [St. Petersburg, 1907].

Then he reports on [Theodor] Ziehen's[1] address on memory, an English paper by Pierce on unconscious cerebral activity (Abstract in *Zeitschrift für Psychologie und Physiologie der Sinnesorgane*);[2] then an essay by [Ernst] Neumann (*Arch. ges. Psychol.*) on visceral sensations, dreams, and peculiar dream memories.

He next mentions a paper by Binet[3] about graphology. In reference to a case that was published (*Neurol. . . .*) Hitschmann tries to gain

---

[1] Ziehen, professor of psychiatry in Berlin. See Minutes 46, footnote 7. For some time he was the leading psychiatrist in Germany.

[2] A. H. Pierce: "Should We Still Retain the Expression 'Unconscious Cerebration' to Designate Certain Processes Connected with Mental Life?" *Journal of Philosophy, Psychology and Scientific Methods*, New York, 1906.

[3] See Minutes 10, footnote 8.

some understanding of the psychology of vegetarianism. The case con-cerned a ten-year-old boy who behaved aggressively toward his father; he was a vegetarian and intended to starve himself to death. Hitsch-mann knows three couples who are vegetarians; all three couples are childless. Two of the wives are anesthetic. Aside from the hope that by changing their mode of living they would be blessed with children, the dissatisfaction of these people with their entire situation plays a role: such people want to change their own selves. The symbolism of "flesh" is also of importance here (people who consider themselves lewd).

PROF. FREUD adds as a deeper root the sadistic disposition; this is confirmed by Adler. Prof. Freud relates the earliest recollection of a vegetarian who has not eaten meat since his childhood: His father says to a visitor: "Be careful, he bites."

HITSCHMANN adds at the end that he suspects syphilis in all vegetarians.

BACH reads some passages from [Zur] Diätetik der Seele by Feuchtersleben,[4] in which some of Adler's viewpoints are already hinted at.

CASE REPORTS

URBANTSCHITSCH reports a dream of his, which he was not able to interpret completely and asks several theoretical and practical ques-tions which Prof. Freud answers.

HITSCHMANN reports on a lady who consulted a gynecologist because of the diminution in size of her labia. Shortly afterward she related a dream: she was again in possession of a jewel box which she had owned when she was a young girl.

HOLLERUNG reports on a gradual removal of a symptom in a severely hysteric woman patient suffering from agoraphobia.

ADLER recounts the case of a woman who suffers in springtime from early morning vomiting and ructation. After some interviews it became evident that this was a case of avarice; thus, avarice can sometimes hide behind vomiting.

---

[4] Count von Feuchtersleben (1806-1849), Austrian physician, poet, philosopher.

FEDERN reports a case of psychic impotence in which it could not be demonstrated that the first sexual activity was connected with unpleasure. The first activity consisted of mutual masturbation; the patient had his first emission with a limp penis, which probably is important.

RANK, referring to Adler's case, remarks that some time ago he already had had the opportunity to observe a case showing the connection between avarice and vomiting. He is inclined to postulate such a connection for all excretory functions; he knows cases in which the passing of urine or semen was connected with avarice. He thinks that prostitution should also be mentioned in this connection.

He refers to his book[5] in which he attributes great significance to the sadomasochistic instinct in all of its transformations (including anxiety), gradations (as far as suicide), and artistic expressions. In support of his view he mentions three cases of artists in whom this instinct played an important role.

1. A sculptor with an eminently sadistic disposition, who leads a masochistic love life and gives vent to his sadism in art. All of this probably goes back to sucking at the mother's breast and the concomitant lust of taking possession.

2. A passage from a letter by Wilhelm Busch[6] in which he stresses the lustful component of the sadistic instinct.

3. A death dream of Segantini's[7] and its artistic representation.

ADLER, reacting to Rank's reference to the connection between sadism and anxiety, remarks that he is not aware of having seen that in Rank's book; he wishes to inform himself about this and to rectify the matter if it is actually in the book. He claims [as his discovery] having separated sadism from sexuality and having placed the former above all other instincts.[8]

---

[5] Der Künstler. Ansätze zu einer Sexualpsychologie [The Artist. Beginnings of a Sexual Psychology]. Vienna: Heller, 1907.

[6] Wilhelm Busch (1832-1908), great German humorist.

[7] Giovanni Segantini (1858-1899), Swiss painter of Graubünden. Karl Abraham published an essay about him in 1911 which he termed "a psychoanalytic essay"; in this paper he refers repeatedly to Rank.

[8] We see here an example of the arguments about priority of ideas which almost disrupted the Society.

52

SCIENTIFIC MEETING on May 27, 1908[1]

Present: Freud, Adler, Federn, Häutler, Hitschmann, Hollerung, Rank, Joachim, Steiner, Stekel, Wittels.

REVIEWS AND CASE REPORTS

STEKEL mentions a paper by [A.] Schmiergold and P. Provotelle on "Freuds Abwehrneuropsychosen" in the *Archiv für Psychologie* (1908, No. 7/8).[2] He further mentions Sadger's essay on narcissism in the *Grenzfragen der Medizin und Technik* [*Border Problems of Medicine and Technique*].[3]

He then stresses Heinrich Mann's psychological acuteness and quotes some examples of his deep understanding of unconscious psy-

[1] No protocol was found of the preceding meeting on May 20; however, there is a notice that a meeting was held on that date.

[2] "La méthode psychanalytique et les 'Abwehrneuropsychosen' de Freud." *Journal de Neurologie*, 13, 1908. The paper refers to Freud's "The Defence Neuro-psychoses" (1894). *C.P.*, 1:59-75, and "Further Remarks on the Defence Neuro-psychoses" (1896). *C.P.*, 1:155-182.

[3] This reference probably is to Sadger's "Psychiatrisch-Neurologisches in psychoanalytischer Beleuchtung" ["Neuropsychiatric Matters in the Light of Psychoanalysis"]. *Zentralblatt für das Gesamtgebiet der Medizin und ihre Grenzgebiete*, No. 7/8, 1908.

chic processes. These are taken from the collection of short novels, *Stürmische Morgen* [*Stormy Mornings*].

FEDERN mentions two English papers on the unconscious.

HOLLERUNG reads a passage from a paper by Paul Magnin, published in the *Revue de l'hypnotisme et de psychologie physiologique* (April, 1908, No. 10). It deals with Freud's theories and asserts that they were, in fact, Charcot's mental property.[4]

STEINER speaks about a paper by O., who calls attention to a swelling of the nipples as a newly discovered sign of masturbation in boys.

ADLER maintains that this is an old view which should be met with distrust.

STEKEL points to the antagonism between sexual glands and breast glands.

HITSCHMANN has also noticed these swellings in albuminuria in puberty (connection with masturbation). We should in general continuously follow up the connection between glands and neuroses (Basedow, anxiety neurosis, neurasthenia and prostate); it seems to play an important role.

STEINER reports a case of impotence.

STEKEL speaks of a new form of disguised anxiety; a man suffers from severe depressions, which actually are anxiety: fear of himself (he has intense incestuous ideas).

PROF. FREUD states that this is not a new form; depression is a separate symptom.

ADLER also considers Stekel's assumption to be unjustified. What is involved here is the aggressive instinct which has turned against the subject; its various forms of expression are anxiety, depression, dejected mood, etc., all of which may be found together in some cases.

PROF. FREUD relates some experiences from his practice.

Erythrophobia involves, first of all, a suppressed feeling of shame;

[4] "Aucune des définitions actuelles de l'hystérie n'est légitime" ["None of the Modern Definitions of Hysteria Is Sound"].

such individuals are onanists who were initially ashamed when facing their parents because of their understanding of sexual matters. The blushing occurs frequently in the early years and disappears in the seventeenth or eighteenth year. Erythrophobia in later years occurs in persons who have become afflicted with syphilis and who are now just as ashamed of syphilis [as they were of masturbation]. The second root—aside from the unconscious feeling of shame—is suppressed rage.[5]

ADLER adds that the rage was originally directed against the father, as is to be expected; in the postluetic period it is expressed in the desire to infect the entire world (ideas occurring when at the barber, etc.).

PROF. FREUD remarks that these people have their attacks [of blushing] mostly while in the barber shop.

PROF. FREUD then recounts the dream of a woman suffering from anxiety hysteria; she is unhappily married to a masochistic man whose love dialect she cannot understand. She will have to interrupt the treatment shortly because of the summer vacations, and she dreams of the place where she will spend the summer: it is night; clear moonlight shines on the lake near which she lives; she walks on the shore and throws herself into the water just where the moonlight strikes it.

Interpretation: On the preceding day she had reported some reminiscences of Leipzig where she had spied on a gentleman (*"la lune"*) while walking with a girl friend in a rose garden. Thus the dream must be considered a birth dream, if we take into account the infantile sex theory of giving birth through the anus, and the mechanism of inversion (plunging in instead of pulling out). The patient says: she feels newborn as a result of treatment. She wishes Prof. Freud would come to her during the summer in order to continue the treatment. The dream has, of course, an additional, delicate and deeper meaning (transference).

STEKEL asserts that "moon" almost invariably symbolizes the penis (growing large and small).

---

[5] This remark is very important in that it calls attention to the aggressive component in erythrophobia. This aggression is often converted into persecution ideas; in fact, erythrophobias are frequently disguised paranoias.

FEDERN has come across the moon as a symbol also of increasing and decreasing potency.

WITTELS remarks that, in Arabic fairy tales, the girls are often likened to the moon; this may be connected with the Mohammedans' preference for buxom women.

PROF. FREUD calls attention to the fact that the difference between regular and occasional symbols must be strictly observed.[6]

ADLER, in this context, relates the dream of an avaricious patient. She dreamed that the king and queen had come to stay with her in her apartment and they were living together very intimately (the woman is Hungarian). In this case, the king represents the king of cards [Kartenkönig].

PROF. FREUD then reports a case of love obsession: a man is unable to free himself of a love affair. With the uncovering of the infantile model (the mother) the obsession ceases. A childhood memory of this man: as a small child he bathed together with his mother in the same bathtub. He can still see everything very clearly, every detail of the furnishings, all except his mother's body (displacement).

Then Prof. Freud relates the interpretation of a hysteric attack during which a girl rapidly tore off her apron. All the time before and after the attack her thoughts were preoccupied with the female genitalia. She regards her mother as a rival. It turns out that she had learned from a dictionary the expression *Hottentot apron* (i.e., an enlargement of the small labia). In connection with this interpretation, she used the words: "Offen gestanden . . ." [this has a double meaning in German: "frankly admitted" and "standing open"], which evidently referred to the genitalia of her mother to whom she was superior in that her genitalia were closed. On the other hand, however, there are fears which she harbors in regard to the consequences of masturbation (Hottentot apron). Instead of masturbating she throws

---

[6] Freud calls attention to the fact that there are two types of symbols: those which are generally employed and have generally the same meaning—they are, one might say, timeless; and those which are created by the individual on certain occasions. Freud expounded this in several of his writings, for instance, in *A General Introduction to Psychoanalysis* (1916-1917). New York: Garden City Publ. Co., 1943.

off her apron. The meaning of the attack is the suppressed desire to look and see whether she has been damaged by masturbation. In her fourth year she exhibited herself to her brother.

Finally Prof. Freud reports [fragments] from the analysis of a latent homosexual. This case confirms a statement made by Sadger, and also found in Stekel's book, namely, that homosexuality sets in only after a certain period and that the libido is then transferred from the woman onto the man. This analysis shows in what way such a transposition takes place. The patient has always preferred boys. Initially he loved his mother tenderly. In his presence, his mother used to praise other boys for their physical and mental superiority; this made him furious at them (on the other hand, it also instilled in him a liking for them). In the wake of suppressing his love for his mother, he transformed his rage against the boys to a liking for them; his love, then, is a love born of jealousy and hate, and therefore easily turns into discord,[7] thus betraying its original character.

STEKEL presents the case of an active homosexual, who had incestuous thoughts about his mother. Severe trauma with an older sister, and exhibitionism with a younger sister at the age of six. Then he became religious; concept of sin, repression. He first transferred his love onto his brother, whom he had previously hated as a rival.

PROF. FREUD gives the following formulation of this mechanism of transposition: with the repression of one object an inversion of the affect felt for the other object takes place.[8]

---

[7] Later, Freud described this specific type of homosexuality in his paper: "Some Neurotic Mechanisms in Jealousy, Paranoia and Homosexuality" (1922). *S.E.*, 18:221-232.

[8] See Footnote 7.

53

SCIENTIFIC MEETING on June 3, 1908[1]

Present: Freud, Adler, Bass, [A.] Deutsch, Federn, Graf, Heller, Hitschmann, Hollerung, Rank, Stekel, Wittels, Joachim.

PRESENTATION

Sadism in Life and in Neurosis[2]

SPEAKER: DR. ADLER

DISCUSSION

HITSCHMANN believes that Adler has recognized, quite correctly, that the new psychology has to proceed from the instinctual drives [*Triebe*]. Characters and actions are thus to be defined in terms of the

[1] June 10: Informal social gathering at the "Schutzengel" on the Hohe Warte [a suburb of Vienna]. [Note in original.]

[2] This paper appeared under the title, "Der Aggressionstrieb im Leben und in der Neurose" ["The Aggressive Drive in Life and in Neurosis"], in *Fortschritte der Medizin*, No. 19, 1908.

Karl Abraham in his "Bericht über die österreichische und deutsche psychoanalytische Literatur bis zum Jahre 1909" ["Report on the Austrian and German Psychoanalytic Literature up to the Year 1909"] (*Jb.*, 1:575-594, 1909), summarized the paper as follows:

"Every instinct derives from an organ activity. Inferior organs are distinguished by

instinctual drives. A symptom is no longer considered to be exclusively a product of the mind, but is also derived from the instinct. It is true that Adler's concept of drive is new in that he assigns an instinct to each organ; this, however, would be legitimate only if drive were defined as an activity.[3] In general, Adler's view does not change much of what we had implicitly assumed.

By no means have Adler's assertions been proven. Nor can Hitschmann become reconciled to the idea of transformation of instincts into their opposite. After all, one cannot reduce everything to this single point of view.

HOLLERUNG expresses pleasure that a real beginning has been made with the problem of the instincts. The term "aggressive drive" is a pleonasm: the concept of drive implies aggression, aggression against the outside world.[4] He would suggest that the term "drive" be replaced by the term "reaction." The turning into the opposite is not a second drive but, rather, the incapacity to react to the external world.

In STEKEL'S opinion, Adler's assumptions bring nothing new for practical purposes, nor are they valuable as far as analysis is concerned. Everything is already contained in the Professor's writings. By the term, "defense neurosis," Freud has indicated that all neuroses are based on the defensive drive [sic!]. Freud has also introduced [the concept of] sublimation.

Adler's assertions cannot be proven.

There is no instinct of defecation; this is a reflex, and the rest is incorrect. All in all, it is dangerous to attempt to reduce everything to a single point.

---

an especially strong instinct. The inferior organs play an important role in the development of neurosis.

"Sadism is based on the intertwinement of the aggressive and sexual drives. The instinct of aggression—like every other instinctual drive—may enter consciousness in a pure or in a sublimated form, or else it may be turned into its opposite as a result of the inhibiting effect of another drive, or it may turn against the subject, or it may be displaced onto another goal. The author gives a succinct survey of the manifestations and meaning of these forms of the instinct of aggression in the healthy as well as the neurotic individual."

[3] It is astonishing that Hitschmann makes this qualification; every instinct implies activity.

[4] In so far as the aim of the drive is active.

PROF. FREUD first observes that he fully concurs with the study of organ inferiority. *Adler has rapidly passed through psychology in order to make a connection with medicine.*[5] Today's paper, however, still moves in the realm which borders on both the psychic and the somatic field: the instinctual life [*Triebleben*].

He agrees with most of Adler's points, for a definite reason: what Adler calls aggressive drive is our libido.

Adler must be criticized for confounding two things: (1) he lumps together the aggressive drive and sadism (sadism is a specific form of the aggressive drive which involves inflicting pain).

A drive is that which makes an individual restive (an ungratified need); the instinctual drive contains: a need, the possibility of gaining pleasure, and something active (the libido).[6] The libido, however, cannot be separated from the possibility of a pleasure gain.

On this basis, Adler's conception of anxiety also becomes clear. We conceived of anxiety as a stage of ungratified libido.[7] For Adler, anxiety is a phase in which the transformed aggressive drive is turned against the subject.

To base repression on the drive to look is also a kind of masking. The driving forces of repression (repression is a certain insufficient process of suppression, which concerns only the sexual processes and is determined by the infantile development) are the other powers of civilization among which the sense organs, of course, play a paramount role.[8]

For the rest, Adler's description of the instinctual life contains many valuable and correct remarks and observations. Adler has taken notice only of the instinctual drives in normal psychology; the pathological has escaped his attention. He has made an attempt to explain illness in terms of normal psychology; this was the viewpoint of the *Studies on Hysteria*, a viewpoint to which Hellpach still adheres.

---

[5] Italics by editor. This remark indicates that in spite of his appreciation of Adler, Freud was beginning to have some doubts about Adler's innovations.

[6] Freud always considered libido as an active force.

[7] This is still the early conception of anxiety. It was only later that Freud modified his views of this subject.

[8] The meaning of this passage is not clear. Here, as in many other passages, particularly of Freud's discussions, Rank condensed and abbreviated what was said to such an extent that it has become unintelligible.

FEDERN, in contrast to the Professor, stresses that it is not in accord with Adler's intention to replace "aggressive drive" with "libido." In Adler's view, it is the frustration of various ways of obtaining pleasure that makes the child aggressive.

Rank's "libido" has been something mystic; its great formative and differentiating effect could not be understood. Adler has avoided this term; he has clarified Rank's vague expression and has explained its specific meaning. After briefly comparing the contrasting views of Freud and Adler, Federn characterizes his own position on Adler's views: he thinks that Adler was wrong to abandon so rashly the primary significance of the sexual drives.[9]

It is a fallacy to infer the existence of an inferior organ from the presence of a strong instinctual drive; this confounds relative and absolute inferiority. The turning of the aggressive drive into its opposite is, in his opinion, a great exaggeration.

[A.] DEUTSCH understands by aggression that which is contained in every drive and is its essence; it is an addition to the libido.

ADLER, in his concluding words, deals only with the most important points: it is only natural that there are similarities between his and Freud's views; he himself, in the introduction, spoke of this original source [Mutterboden]. Defense neurosis, by the way, is not the exact point on which he differs from Freud's views.

One must not start with the developmental viewpoint, according to which the organ must necessarily be connected with aggression; the primitive organ activity is not aggressive. There is no organ drive in Rank's work. Adler advocated the conception of libido in the artist before Rank did, in a paper which Rank has correctly quoted; in it, two functions are allotted to each organ: the cultural and the sexual one which has to be suppressed. Later, he has abandoned this view.

Rank's libido is not identical with his aggressive drive. Rank separates the aggressive drive from the libido.

Sadism and masochism are already complex phenomena in which

[9] Federn seems to have been one of the few who at an early time called attention to Adler's tendency to abandon the view of the importance of sexuality for the neurosis.

sexuality and aggression are combined. Aggression need not always be cruel.

He gives an example in reference to repression: a patient says, "I see what is going through another person's mind, but he does not see what is going on in me." That is where repression sets in [*sic!*].

A long debate follows on the identity of or difference between Adler's aggressive drive and our libido.